D0296730

FORGOTTEN VOICES

FORGOTTEN VOICES OF THE SECRET WAR

AN INSIDE HISTORY OF SPECIAL OPERATIONS DURING THE SECOND WORLD WAR

IN ASSOCIATION WITH THE IMPERIAL WAR MUSEUM

RODERICK BAILEY

EBURY
PRESS

3 5 7 9 10 8 6 4 2

Published in 2008 by Ebury Press, an imprint of Ebury Publishing

A Random House Group Company

The Random House Group Limited Reg. No. 954009

Addresses for companies within the Random House Group can be found at
www.randomhouse.co.uk

A CIP catalogue record for this book is available from the British Library

The Random House Group Limited supports The Forest Stewardship Council (FSC), the leading international forest certification organisation. All our titles that are printed on Greenpeace approved FSC certified paper carry the FSC logo. Our paper procurement policy can be found at www.rbooks.co.uk/environment

Printed and bound in Great Britain by Clays Ltd, St Ives PLC

ISBN 9780091918507

To buy books by you[…]w.rbooks.co.uk

Contents

Author's Preface

The Imperial War Museum has long been concerned with preserving the records and memories of men and women with experience of recent war and conflict. *Forgotten Voices of the Secret War* draws on hundreds of hours of interviews in the museum's sound archive that tell of the exploits of the Special Operations Executive, a secret British organisation set up early in the Second World War to encourage subversion and carry out sabotage in enemy-occupied territory.

During its short, six-year existence, SOE helped channel vast amounts of arms and supplies to tens of thousands of resistance workers and guerrillas. It dispatched hundreds of its own agents, men and women, to provide training and encouragement, destroy key installations and harass enemy forces. In Europe, SOE was the principal Allied force engaged in stimulating and supporting resistance movements. By the end of the war, its reach was global and its deeds ranked among some of the most daring and dramatic carried out by Allied forces.

What follows is a narrative history of SOE told through personal testimonies: snapshots of life in SOE and of the cloak-and-dagger work in which agents engaged. With official permission, almost two hundred survivors tell their stories here, speaking freely about their experiences and bringing fresh perspectives to bear on this remarkable organisation. The popular image of SOE may remain dominated by the efforts and sacrifices of its agents in occupied France, but the museum's oral history recordings, hitherto barely tapped, reflect very fully the spread and diversity of SOE's activities and the variety of personnel involved. Interviewees include Britons and foreign nationals; civilians and servicemen; officers and other ranks; instructors who taught agents specialist skills; technicians who developed specialist weapons and equipment; staff at secret headquarters as far apart as London, Cairo and Colombo; aircrew and naval personnel who transported agents and stores into occupied territory; agents who were dispatched to attack specific targets, from vital enemy lines of supply to Germany's atomic bomb plans; agents who were sent out to arm, train and fight alongside groups as different as the French resistance, partisans in Yugoslavia and tribes in the Burmese jungle; and agents who survived brutal treatment after falling into enemy hands. Indeed, this book seeks to underline both the complexities of SOE and the realities of behind-the-lines work, from the terrible risks run to the appalling reprisals on occupied populations which agents' actions could precipitate. There are stories here of treachery and tragedy and of some of SOE's greatest disasters. There are tales, too, of the dilemmas encountered as SOE sought to work with individuals and groups focused as much on civil war and revolution as on fighting the Axis.

Roderick Bailey

Acknowledgements

My first acknowledgement must be to the former members of SOE and related units who have agreed over the years to share their memories with the Imperial War Museum.

I would next like to highlight the contribution made to this book by the Gerry Holdsworth Special Forces Charitable Trust, whose generous support of the museum's SOE collections allowed me to search for and interview a number of the men and women who tell their stories here. I am also grateful to Duncan Stuart and Christopher Woods, former SOE Advisers at the Foreign & Commonwealth Office, for help with my search for potential interviewees.

At the Imperial War Museum, I would like to thank Margaret Brooks, Richard McDonough and John Stopford-Pickering of the Sound Archive, Roderick Suddaby and Amanda Mason of the Department of Documents, Alan Wakefield and Louise Macfarlane of the Photo Archive and Liz Bowers, Publications Manager, and her staff. Thank you to Terry Charman for taking the time and trouble to check, as far as possible, the factual accuracy of the final text. I am indebted, too, to Dr Conrad Wood, who recorded a good many of the interviews quoted in this book. That the Sound Archive has become the extraordinary primary source it is today is due in no small part to him.

Joshua Levine and Lyn Smith gave me valuable advice on how to research and structure an oral history book like this. For help with transcribing interviews, I am grateful to Chris Bailey, Judy Bailey and Jill Merrett. For double-checking and correcting my French, German and Albanian, I would like to thank Alexandra Pesch, Judith Moellers and Gillian Gloyer.

At Ebury, I am grateful to Ken Barlow, my editor, and Jake Lingwood for their patience and enthusiastic support.

Finally, I would like to thank my agent, Gillon Aitken, and Sebastian Faulks.

Introduction by Sebastian Faulks

The story of the Special Operations Executive, the secret army set up by Winston Churchill at the low point of the Second World War to 'set Europe ablaze', is one that, however much you know about it, never loses its power to make you gasp – in admiration, amazement, humour and disbelief. You could argue that in its mixture of cussedness, heroism and amateurishness, SOE epitomised all the most memorable aspects of the British war effort.

Memoirs can be unreliable, often tending to vainglory, reticence or deceit; official accounts can also be defective. All the more reason to value the oral witness collected by the Imperial War Museum, a pungent sample of which has been selected by Roderick Bailey. 'I was invited, aged just over 21,' recalled Julian Amery, 'to start a revolution in Albania against the Italians and given a budget of about £50,000 to get on with it.' That is the authentic SOE tone: 'Don't know what I'm doing, let's start tomorrow.' But later, Amery touches on the contribution made by even the most harum-scarum SOE operations: 'Even if we couldn't help these countries, if we could divert the Germans from what they were doing or planning to do against us, that would be a plus.'

The training was tough and sometimes hilarious: Outward Bound with a touch of Ealing comedy. At its best, as in the intensive month in the Highlands, it was not only good practical preparation, but also gave agents the sort of other-worldly confidence they would need in the field. Childish fear persisted. Robert Ferrier recalled that in order to shame the more timid men into making a trial parachute jump, dispatchers made sure the trainee women jumped first. No *Boy's Own* device was infra dig so far as the boffins of SOE were concerned: booby-trapped rats, exploding cow-pats – anything that might annoy the Germans.

The dangers in Europe were terrible. The agents, if caught, were not treated as regular prisoners of war; they faced torture and death in a concentration camp. It is impossible to recall in tranquillity that one of SOE's bravest women agents was betrayed to such a fate in Paris, not by her own shortcomings but by a French woman jealous of her looks.

One or two survived even concentration camps. Robert Sheppard gave an account of being in Dachau: 'I wanted to keep my dignity as a British officer. I thought, "I won't let them destroy my personality" . . . We were starving, we were dressed like clowns, but we always wanted to keep dignified in front of everybody. It was the last part of our duty in the war . . . I think many of our friends and comrades from the camps of all nations remember this. Difficult sometimes.'

Good agents came in different guises. Here is Robert Wade in Serbia, on seeing the five Yugoslav partisans he was meant to be leading get shot down: 'So I thought, "Well, you can't do it on your own, Wade – return!" My word, it was awful.' By contrast, Benjamin Cowburn revealed an extraordinary level of cool efficiency, shuttling across the border of Occupied and Free France in a hollow compartment beneath the engine of a locomotive. His book *No Cloak No Dagger*, a masterpiece of gritty understatement, is for my money the best of all SOE memoirs.

The French Section of SOE, while it contained many men and women of almost unbelievable courage, was disaster-prone. One of its best organisers, Henri Déricourt, was a double, perhaps treble or even quadruple agent: a bad lot in any case, a man addicted to deceit. The radio protocols were frequently ignored by wireless operators in the field and, less forgivably, by Baker Street – by the people who had invented them. Not all the women were as cool and resilient as Violette Szabo, while many of the men grew bored and depressed by their double lives and took unforgivable risks to find company in public places. In Holland, the entire network was captured by the Germans.

A problem faced by agents in all countries as they tried to organise the nationals into resistance units was that there was not much appetite for guerrilla action, for blowing up trains and factories. The German occupiers were quick to trace local suspects and, if they couldn't, took exemplary reprisals against the innocent civilian population – usually ten or more killed for each German life taken. Not every factory owner producing steel or pneumatic tyres under German rule was keen to open his works to sabotage, and SOE action was actively discouraged by its British sister organisation, SIS (MI6), which regarded them as interfering amateurs whose loud bangs merely drew attention to their, and SIS's, presence.

It was different when there was real fighting going on alongside. SOE spread far beyond its initial European mission. In Burma, the nature of the terrain meant there was less distinction between what the regulars and irregulars were doing. The small Lysander aircraft – in symbolic terms the SOE's Spitfire – was still in operation, though later in the war it was used in Burma as much to lift out Japanese prisoners as to drop in SOE personnel. The valleys were short and tight and the Lysander needed four hundred yards in which to land, measured out by eight bamboo markers at fifty-yard intervals. If the landing area was too short, Maurice Roe recalled, they just squeezed the markers down to forty-yard intervals and trusted the pilot. 'What could you do? These were tight valleys.'

In some ways the war in Burma was more up SOE's street, because the operatives didn't have to spend lonely months of planning and recruitment; they could get stuck in. 'The extent of the damage and mayhem that we created amongst the occupying forces in Burma was really quite something,' said Ron Brierley. 'Maybe the lessons one had learned in Europe were more readily translatable into a country that certainly does lend itself to guerrilla warfare.'

Even here, there could be boring or gloomy moments. Richard Broome said they were driven to making board games with what materials they had. The Chinese in their small battle group managed to improvise a mah jong set, and in return the British made 'Monopoly': 'It was a bit wild to see these Chinese sitting in the middle of the Malayan jungle, buying and selling Piccadilly and Leicester Square.'

SOE was an extraordinary organisation: distrusted at home, betrayed abroad, leaky, rash, frequently – and fatally – in breach of its own basic security rules. And yet . . . You only have to read a dozen of these oral witnesses to see that the quality of the men and women SOE recruited far outshone the failings of the organisation. Here is sacrifice; here is raw, selfless, bloody-minded courage, not always wisely applied, but applied, as the French would say, *à l'outrance*.

And when they were good, they were very, very good. They harried, they disrupted, they fought and, perhaps above all, they inspired. You could ask no better summary of the value of SOE than that volunteered by General Eisenhower, whose assessment in 1945 was that the disruption to German troops caused by SOE-led resistance throughout Occupied Europe 'played a very considerable part in our complete and final victory'.

Sebastian Faulks

1939–41

We were totally amateurish, totally one hundred per cent amateurish, and it couldn't have been otherwise.

By the summer of 1940, Britain was reeling from Germany's lightning conquests of Poland, Denmark, Norway, the Low Countries and France. Invasion from across the Channel was expected daily. Turning the tide seemed impossible and ways of hitting back were few. There was, however, one idea of growing interest to British leaders: the concept of encouraging the occupied peoples of Europe to harass the Axis from within. And in July 1940, days after the fall of France, SOE was formed, with Winston Churchill's famous exhortation to 'set Europe ablaze'.

SOE inherited many of the plans and personnel of two short-lived organisations set up in 1938. One was Military Intelligence (Research), a secret War Office department whose job had been to investigate irregular ways of causing trouble in enemy-occupied countries. Among MI(R)'s officers was Colin Gubbins, a dynamic and visionary Scot in his forties who had written handbooks on guerrilla warfare – he had fought in Ireland – and was to command SOE for the last two years of the war. The second organisation was Section D, a department of the Secret Intelligence Service. Section D had been concerned mostly with action in countries that seemed likely to come under Axis control and attack.

MI(R) sent men to Poland in 1939 to do what they could to hinder the German advance. Others went to Scandinavia to counter German intentions there and try to help the Finns when Stalin, who would stand aloof from the struggle against Hitler until 1941, sent the Red Army to seize Finland. MI(R) even inspired the idea of setting up stay-behind parties to resist a German occupation of Britain. Elsewhere, particularly in the Balkans, as Italian and German threats and influence grew, Section D officers sought also to lay plans for action and boost anti-Axis spirit. When MI(R) and Section D were wound up, SOE pressed on with several of their

schemes until the German juggernaut swept the British out of the Continent altogether in the spring of 1941. Few of these ventures met with success and many served merely to underline the amateurism and inefficiency of these early secret bodies. But they did at least blood a few SOE officers and lay some foundations for later work.

POLAND

Colonel Roly Sword

British military attaché, Warsaw

On the morning of 1 September, I was rung up by the consul in Katowice saying, 'There are firey balls flying in the sky, I think it's started.' He was talking about flares, and the Germans, of course, had invaded. Very shortly after, German bombers came over and bombed us in Warsaw. They didn't bomb the embassy, where I was, but they bombed the outskirts. There was quite a lot of flak flying around and noise and things and we had to liaise all the time with the Polish General Staff as to what we were going to do. And I had arranged with Gubbins, who was the G1 of the military mission, to liaise with the Poles and attach British officers to the Polish Army behind the lines to help them blow up bridges. Unfortunately war broke out first and Gubbins didn't arrive until the third, when England declared war.

Captain Peter Wilkinson

MI(R) officer with British Military Mission, Poland

During the four days that we were in Warsaw, Gubbins and the head of the mission, General Carton de Wiart, were desperately trying to find out from the Poles what they needed from the British, not that the British were in any position to provide it. Almost all the Polish war industries had been in the western territories, which had been bombed and destroyed; consequently, they wanted everything. The situation was so serious that Gubbins decided to send back Captain Tommy Davies, via Lithuania or Latvia or somewhere, to report directly to the War Office, really stating the full horror of the situation which no telegram could possibly convey. Of course one had to keep up a very brave face on both sides: the Poles couldn't admit to their allies the desperation of the situation and nor could we, really, apart from a nod or a wink to intimate that we realised and knew and understood.

Everybody was absolutely overtaken by the rapid advance of the Germans. I, for instance, in the original orders, was down to cover the Western Front,

HU 83162

Polish civilians after an air raid on a Warsaw suburb, September 1939.

no less, as a liaison officer, but in point of fact there was no Western Front left. And so, when the mission withdrew, as it did from Warsaw on 5 or 6 September, I found myself in charge of the baggage.

The traffic was unbelievable, every sort of civilian and military vehicle, Poles on foot, Poles on bicycles, and of course the thing got absolutely snarled up. Gubbins and I went on ahead, in our British uniforms, to try and sort things out. We found that only about three trucks had got stuck in the road and it just wanted a little bit of intelligent coaxing to get the thing straight. And while we were there a Polish officer emerged and Gubbins shouted to me, 'Look out Peter, he's going to shoot!' so I dodged behind a car. He'd drawn his pistol, which he was persuaded to put away; then he said, 'Well, what the hell are you doing here, you British, ordering Poles about? A fat lot of help you've been to us.' And I must say we could hardly deny the fact.

Colonel Roly Sword
British military attaché, Warsaw
Carton de Wiart and a small group, including myself, decided that we'd stay on as long as we could but finally it was decided that the whole of the mission would evacuate Poland into Romania. I was in the leading car and I had to go across a river at Kuty, dividing Poland from Romania, and the Romanian military attaché stopped me on the bridge and recognised me and saluted and said, '*Bonsoir, mon colonel. Comment ça va?*' I said, '*Je ne suis plus un colonel maintenant*' – 'I'm not a colonel any more.' I'd taken off my uniform and cap. He said, 'Oh, I understand.'

We thought we were going to be interned, so I went off to see the checkpoint people. And as they were taking my particulars, they said, 'What are you?' I said, 'Well, the British Embassy.' And they said, 'That's funny. You're the third British Embassy that's passed this morning. Where are all the generals?' I told them we hadn't got any generals. In the meantime we'd dressed up old Carton de Wiart as far as we could in plain clothes and gave him a passport as Mr Carton the author. I was Mr Sword the statistician.

Captain Peter Wilkinson
MI(R) officer with British Military Mission, Poland
Carton de Wiart was all for going in full regimentals. He was a magnificent officer. He'd been in the Guards so everything was impeccable. And when we got to the first sentry on the other side he stood up and addressed him, first in English and then in French, saying there were only three sorts of Romanians: they're either pimps, pederasts or violinists, and bloody few are violinists.

Fortunately the Romanian sentry, thinking this was mutual regard, saluted and we passed through.

Colonel Roly Sword
British military attaché, Warsaw
Next day we made our way to the British Legation in Bucharest, which, of course, was British soil, so we were home and dry.

SCANDINAVIA

Captain Andrew Croft
MI(R) officer, Norway
They wanted me to be in charge of a little War Office mission with a view to getting arms through the then neutral countries of Norway and Sweden into Finland, in support of the Finns, because the Russians had attacked them. Malcolm Munthe was my second-in-command and we had to proceed to Bergen, where a number of ships full of armaments and aircraft arrived, and we managed to get various weapons of war, aircraft and so on, through Norway and Sweden up to Tornio. Before Christmas 1939, when the first ships arrived in Bergen, until 21 January, about eight shiploads of stuff passed through my hands.

We had our problems. We provided vast quantities of ammunition, rifle ammunition, and our rifle is, of course, .303, or the equivalent of 7.7 millimetres, and theirs was the equivalent of the German one, 7.6 millimetres. But the Finns were out to kill and were damned good marksmen and they just filed down the cartridges by .1 of a millimetre or whatever it was. Very effective.

Captain Mervyn Walter
MI(R) officer, Norway
In January 1940 I was sent to Norway with two other British Army officers, Andrew Croft and Malcolm Munthe, to do a reconnaissance of the ports and railways in Norway with a view to assessing their logistic capacity for war. When we arrived in Stockholm we were told by the British military attaché that four British naval officers had been put into prison by the Swedish government because they had been monitoring the supply of special Swedish iron ore to Germany, and that if we were discovered we were on our own and nobody had heard of us.

The method of reconnaissance was straightforward. At that time Britain and France were sending large quantities of war stores to Finland and these stores were mostly coming through the Norwegian ports of Oslo and Bergen and the smaller ports like Trondheim. By going to these ports, to check up on the cargoes coming through, we were able at the same time to do a reconnaissance of the capacity of the harbours, their facilities, their warehouses, their power supply and so on.

We took the railways section by section. In each section we noted down the crossing loops, the watering points, workshops, turntables and also the tunnels and bridges and we recorded on the relevant sheet of the railway timetable, by a series of dots, the facilities and in that way built up a picture of the line. From time to time we returned to Stockholm and tore out these sheets of the railway timetable and they were then sent to London.

Croft and Munthe spoke between them Norwegian, Swedish and I believe some Finnish, and their job was to talk and my job was to keep my big mouth shut and get the technical data which was the purpose of the visit. By seeing me look for this and look for that, they gradually learned, so we all three worked together. During our journeys from time to time we met up with two or three people who seemed to be doing at the stations what we were doing. We came to the conclusion that they were German transportation officers, like myself, doing a reconnaissance of the Norwegian railways.

Captain Andrew Croft
MI(R) officer, Norway
There was a top-secret telegram that Munthe and Croft were to report to a Captain Palmer at the Bristol Hotel in Oslo. There we got our instructions, which were to greet the British Army arriving in Norway. Malcolm Munthe at Stavanger, myself at Bergen and Palmer at Trondheim. I had an easy cover story for being in Bergen: cleaning up after the armistice and peace in Finland; cleaning up the ships that were still unloaded.

Gerry Holdsworth
MI(R) officer, Norway
Malcolm Munthe, Axel Munthe's son, succeeded me in Stavanger. I went to Oslo. And the Germans arrived at Stavanger and Malcolm, assuming it was the English fleet he could see in the gloaming at night, went down to the end of the quay and did 'da da da-da da da' with his torch. Well, I don't suppose it helped particularly. He was very surprised when the chaps came ashore in different tin hats to what he expected. Malcolm was half-Scandinavian, of

course, spoke Norwegian, and he realised that this was no place for him and he took to the hills.

Captain Andrew Croft
MI(R) officer, Norway

The first I realised about the invasion, which I expected of course, was seeing a fish shop with a blackboard. Instead of the price of fish it said, 'German fleet cruising north through the Kattegat.'

That night I slept rather badly and at 3.30, I remember, I heard the dull booming of a gun, so I got up immediately, dressed and went to Tyskebryggen quay which was the inner port where my ships had unloaded their stuff for the Finns earlier on. I saw a Norwegian ship, a fjords steamer, offloading a whole lot of Norwegian troops; no guns, just rifles, horses, hay, straw. I asked them where they were going – one knew the language of course – and they were going up to Voss. No intention of defending the town.

It was then ten to five. German aircraft came over at a height of not much more than a hundred metres dropping leaflets. Immediately thereafter, just below me, about thirty yards away, came a large boat full of Germans. They landed and progressed towards the centre of the town in threes, led by three officers. I remember the middle one carrying a standard or banner. Very lightly equipped all the soldiers were, with the usual grenades stuck into their jackboots.

I then went to my hotel where I saw a German, who had been staying in the hotel, giving orders and instructions. He was one of the spies who had been there and who one knew about. I got to my bedroom, just had time to put on my large, fur-lined overcoat and get my British passport and some money and the only decent shoes I had, not boots, and went out through the back door. I went to a friend of mine and he gave me a map and a compass and a loaf of bread, which I stuffed in one large pocket, and a bit of meat in the other. I went on and had quite a journey: 150 miles in five days.

Ronald Turnbull
Section D officer, Denmark

I was woken up early in the morning by the sound of aircraft. Quite frankly the Danes were not usually out at that time. I looked out of the window and there on the aircraft flying happily overhead was what the Germans called the *Hakenkreuz* – the swastika, the twisted cross. What on earth was happening? Then I realised. Someone phoned me. He was a British journalist for the *Daily Sketch*. 'Turnbull,' he said, 'we're trapped.'

I phoned the Brazilian Legation and checked that Dr Gastão was there. He said, 'Stay there, I'll send a car for you'; and Brazilians, when their Foreign Service puts on a show, they put on a show. He got his chauffeur with a large limousine, the Brazilian flag flying, and got through all the controls, I think the Germans didn't really know what to do, and he picked me up. He didn't take me direct to the legation; he took my things to the legation but he took me up to the Danish Foreign Office, accompanying me as a minister. He did a very good job. Brazilians are very prickly; they won't allow any nonsense even if they haven't got any authority whatever. He took me in and handed me over to the head of one of the sections of the Danish Foreign Office. Very soon, Howard Smith, my own minister, arrived. That was when I saw Dr Munch, the Danish [Foreign] Minister, having obviously been interviewed by Renthe-Fink, the German Minister, and, having received an ultimatum, coming out into the corridor, going into the bathroom and being sick. I heard it quite clearly. He must have been absolutely horrified by the whole thing.

Nothing happened to us. The Danish attitude was, 'All right, we can't do anything about it. But this is force-majeure and you will respect our sovereignty'. That's why they said to the Germans, 'You can't fiddle around with the British Legation or the French Legation. Just let them alone. They are our responsibility. And if they can't stay, we ourselves will take them out through Germany, Holland and Belgium.' We were exceedingly well treated thanks to the Danes.

After about five days and a lot of partying and farewells we got on the train and were taken out. That was the occasion I was asked to look for a Pole called Freund, which is German for 'friend'. We went knocking on doors, knocking at daytime compartments, and I remember saying 'Freund?' and the Germans saying, 'Ah, freund? Ah, ja.' It was all rather ridiculous. It was still the Phoney War. You had the first burst of activity and then everything had settled down to nothing, practically. The legation in The Hague took us all in, our opposite numbers, and I spent the night there with a very nice couple. Then we got on the train back to the UK.

Peter Tennant
Section D and SOE officer, Sweden
George Binney had come over as a representative of Steel Control to buy special steels, ball bearings, machine tools and so forth, from Sweden and Norway. He did the rounds and set up an office. Then the Norwegian invasion started, and there was George, cut off in Sweden, unable to come back even if he'd wanted to, but also unable to ship back supplies. So, as a man of typical

initiative, he decided he'd break the blockade himself. He went to our minister, Victor Mallet, and said, 'What about this?' Mallet said, 'Don't be such an ass. It looks like the war's coming to an end.' That was the time, you know, when people were caving in at home, it was very, very dicey. So George said, 'Well, as far as I'm concerned, the war's never coming to an end until we've beaten them. If they succeed in invading us, we'll have to fight the war from Canada, we shall continue. And I am going to start my ships.'

George got his ships together. They were partly British, partly Norwegian. Then came the question of crews. There were various crews who had come off British cargo ships sunk by the Germans in Narvik and they weren't particularly keen to go on such a dangerous expedition again. George said, 'All right, we'll see who else can come – Norwegians and Swedes,' and he got a mixed crew in the end. They got five ships ready to go, loaded them and put explosive charges on board, so that they could sink them if necessary, and then moved from Gothenburg up to Brofjord, up the coast, to lie in wait and choose an appropriate moment to go. When the right moment came there was a slight snowstorm, George decided to go out and then they got through and were met by the Royal Navy, at a certain point in the North Sea, and escorted to Kirkwall, with a complete load of supplies, which was a wonderful achievement. It was as much as a whole year's supply of steel from Sweden in peacetime. The supplies got down to SKF, the Swedish ball bearing factory in Luton, where they were very welcome indeed. George was knighted for the achievement. He went to a private dubbing at Buckingham Palace and the King asked him to tell him the whole story, which he did. And there the King said, 'You know, there are a lot of remarkable people who I can't decorate or thank in any way because they're really neutrals, but they're taking part in this.'

THE BALKANS

Basil Davidson
Section D and SOE officer, Hungary
I was a journalist. I had joined Section D on the understanding that I would be sent to the Balkans, which was a part of the world I knew something about, especially Yugoslavia, having lived there. They decided to send me to Hungary. I said I'd never been to Hungary – a totally different language – and didn't know anything about it. Of course, to that I got a rather rusty answer that there was a war on and that I should do as I was told.

This was the end of '39, beginning of '40. Italy had not yet come into the war and the Germans had not yet invaded France. So I went by train to northern Italy and from northern Italy into Yugoslavia and across Yugoslavia into Hungary. In Milan I was joined by another Section D operative, a very excellent man called Ian Pirie. He had a lot of big blue sacks which he put in the luggage rack and he said, 'We've got to get those across the frontier and they mustn't be looked at.' Fortunately they weren't looked at because he had diplomatic immunity. Then he revealed to me that they consisted of high explosives.

Our job in Section D was to go to various countries which were not yet under Nazi or Fascist control but which might easily become so, which might be invaded or might be turned into satellites, and Hungary was one of those. It was, in fact, pretty well a satellite, so there was almost nothing to be done there. I was sent to run a legal news agency, supplying news from the Ministry of Information to the local papers, and also to set up a clandestine printing press. And of course I hadn't the foggiest idea of how to do that.

Captain Peter Wilkinson
MI(R) and SOE officer, Hungary and Yugoslavia
Financed by Section D, in February 1940, I set out on a tour of inspection, in great comfort, travelling on the Simplon-Orient Express, which still maintained its standards. I had one nasty moment leaving Italy, at the Italian–Yugoslav frontier, where there was an extremely stroppy Italian control who seized my rather virgin-looking passport and started questioning me on it. Among other things he asked me what its number was. Well of course I didn't even know the number of my proper passport let alone this one that had just been issued to me. To which he replied, 'Well, naturally not, because it's false.' Morale was beginning to sink. However, since I was on my way out of Italy and I had a service visa he didn't feel inclined to make trouble and that was that.

I went first of all to Budapest, which I must say looked absolutely miserable in the February weather with the cold central European wind and flaky snow coming down, and I saw the Section D chaps there. I also saw the military attaché and the ambassador who all agreed that if it could be arranged the best thing to do would be to hire an assistant military attaché who could handle all the subterranean work from the sanctity of the legation.

I came back via Belgrade where I went through the same arrangements. But I had a ridiculous incident because I arrived very late at night at the main station and there was a legation car which took my confidential bag off me

Peter Wilkinson, of MI(R) and SOE.

and from then on I was more or less on my own. I only knew the name of one hotel in Belgrade so I told a taxi driver to take me there. By that time it was about half past twelve or quarter to one and I noticed that the hall porter looked rather disconcerted when I gave him my British passport. However, he gave me a bed and I went to sleep. Well, next morning, I travelled down in the lift with a very nice German woman and two small boys and, since I'd always been brought up to believe war was no excuse for discourtesy, we exchanged 'good mornings'. By the time I got to the breakfast room it was perfectly clear to me that not only was I the only Englishman but indeed I was the only foreigner: the place was absolutely crammed with Germans. Not wishing to make myself conspicuous, I wished my neighbours '*Guten appetit*', shook hands with them, and then hastily ensconced myself behind the largest German newspaper that I could find. They were frankly not in the least interested in me. I think they probably took me for a Swede. In due course I emerged and paid my bill and took a taxi to the British Legation who were not at all pleased at this adventure. Apparently, in order to avoid any unpleasantness, the Yugoslav authorities had arranged that British visitors should be accommodated at The Majestic whereas the other hotel, The Three Kings, was to be reserved entirely for Germans. I pointed out that nobody had told me this and how was I to know.

Nicholas Hammond
MI(R) and SOE officer, Greece and Crete

I had spent most of the year after taking my degree, 1929–30, in south Albania and north-west Greece. I was living in villages and I talked modern Greek fluently by the end of that time and of course I had a unique geographical knowledge of all that area. Subsequently I became a Fellow of Clare College, Cambridge, and a university lecturer and I continued in that until the outbreak of war. I volunteered to serve at once but I was told to wait until my special knowledge could be used. The War Office had circulated to all fellows of colleges a questionnaire to see whether they had any special expertise for the war and I had replied giving my knowledge of this area of south Albania and north-west Greece. But they said I must wait until I was sent for and that didn't happen until May 1940, when we were retreating from Europe, and I was told to go to London.

Once I was interviewed and commissioned I was given some elementary training in sabotage: bits of railway track and things of that sort. Another man with me was John Pendlebury who was another Greek archaeologist, an expert on Crete. And there were two older men who had been respectively a colonel and a major in the police force of King Zog's Albania. They had been dismissed – at one point all the British personnel had been dismissed by Zog. We were all going to be sent to Greece and the idea was that these two and I were to try and organise a revolt in Albania against the Italians, because it was expected that the Italians would come into the war. They weren't at that stage in it. Pendlebury was to go to Crete and begin to organise, what we thought would probably happen, a post-occupation resistance movement.

So off we went, about June, in a flying boat to Athens. When we arrived, the Greek Government, which was neutral, refused admission to the English colonel and major and myself. They suspected we were up to no good, that we were going to cause trouble in Albania and might involve Greece. Pendlebury was accepted as consul, which was his cover, so he established himself in Crete.

Julian Amery
Section D and SOE officer, Yugoslavia

I was, in practice, assistant press attaché in the embassy, or the legation as we called it in those days, in Belgrade. And the assistant naval attaché, with whom I shared a flat, came and asked me if I would do a memorandum on the situation in Italian-occupied Albania. I knew almost nothing about Albania but I rang up the *Times* correspondent and asked him if he could put me in touch with some Albanians the same day. He did and I met the first Albanians I'd ever met and cross-examined them, went back to the office and wrote a report and then went round to our flat where the head of the Balkan section of Section D, later SOE, was having dinner. I gave him this memorandum, which he thought highly significant, because he knew even less about Albania than I did. And within a fortnight I was invited, aged just over twenty-one, to start a revolution in Albania against the Italians and given a budget of about £50,000 to get on with it.

I collected some refugees. The next thing was to run lines of communication into Albania. That meant smuggling agents across the border. This required the help or collusion of the Yugoslav police and frontier authorities, so I had to get in touch with those branches of the Yugoslav Government responsible for this sort of thing. I had to find some advisers and I got a separate but similar organisation started in Greece, to work into Albania from the south. Having established some contact we smuggled in literature, propaganda, some money for tribal chiefs and presently some arms, which went through in carts covered with maize or other crops, smuggled in with the collusion of the Yugoslav authorities.

Alexander Glen
Section D and SOE officer, Yugoslavia
The British Legation in Belgrade was concerned primarily with trying to sustain Yugoslav independence and Yugoslav refusal to enter association with the Axis powers. But there was a very important secondary objective, a long-term one, of the River Danube itself and particularly its significance to German economy both in terms of grain and oil brought upriver from Romania. So the fledgling Section D were active in trying to find ways and means of blocking the Danube. The ways and means considered would have made a pretty good red-nose comedy film today. We purchased a bit of land above the Iron Gates, in the Kazan Gorge, where there was a suitable cave and the idea was to fill this with high explosives and bring down a two thousand foot high precipice. The chances of doing that I should think were about zero.

Basil Davidson
Section D and SOE officer, Hungary
I got £500 through the diplomatic channel in those lovely, big, white, crisp, five-pound notes which we had in those days, and the instructions were to bribe politicians. I sent them back on the grounds that I didn't know any politicians and didn't know in any case how to bribe them. They came back to me of course saying, 'Do what you are told.' I can't say I was able to carry out that instruction.

Alexander Glen
Section D and SOE officer, Yugoslavia
There was spoken of an attempt to have King Boris of Bulgaria killed. It was a bit of a *Boy's Own Paper* effort. I remember there was a chap who used to come along to claim his monthly cheque for this but circumstances were always not propitious. He collected his cheque, several cheques, but I think that bit is best forgotten.

Julian Amery
Section D and SOE officer, Yugoslavia
The situation was so desperate after the fall of France and the prospect of the invasion of Britain was so absolutely onerous that we thought we couldn't leave any stone unturned. And even if we couldn't help these countries, if they could divert the Germans from what they were doing or planning to do against us, that would be a plus.

Basil Davidson
Section D and SOE officer, Hungary
One of the instructions was to find a person or persons who would be able to attach limpet mines to German shipping on the Danube: very sensible idea. Limpet mines are metal mines which have a magnet and you clamp them on beneath the water and they stick until they go off when the detonator is timed to do so. We had collected quite a quantity of high explosive and limpets and other things that we called 'toys' in those days and, for want of a better place to keep them, we kept them in the cellar of the legation. Well, after all, why not? The cellar was very big, the minister didn't drink wine, nobody went there and it was full of cobwebs, and there were our little sacks. Nothing could happen to them: they couldn't be detonated unless they were detonated deliberately.

This went on until early '41 and by early '41 the situation had become quite desperate for us: for the British, for our cause. We had been driven right out of Europe. We had a tiny garrison in Gibraltar. There was nothing else anywhere. We had the Battle of the Atlantic. We had a very great naval shortage. We had everything against us. The Germans were winning every kind of battle there was. And it looked very much as though we had lost the war and there were those who thought they should provide for this contingency. And a senior British diplomat with whom I was concerned had come to the conclusion that the outlook was very gloomy. He caused his staff to search the cellars and they found our sacks and he called me up and said, 'Are these yours?' I shuffled my feet and said, 'Well, they're not mine exactly.' He said, 'Never mind that. I've thrown them in the Danube.' So after all the high explosives which we had brought in which were enough to cause quite a bit of havoc on Danube shipping – and we had mobilised some persons to do this work, Hungarian patriots who were anti-Nazi – we were left with nothing at all.

Alexander Glen
Section D and SOE officer, Yugoslavia
We were a very amateur bunch. I think that's the first observation I must make. Immensely keen. What is gratifying, perhaps, was that the Germans at that time were just about as amateur as we were.

Basil Davidson
Section D and SOE officer, Hungary
We were totally amateurish, totally one hundred per cent amateurish, and it couldn't have been otherwise. You can't suddenly create an effective

HU 55646

A Belgrade street after the first German air raid, April 1941.

organisation with the aims that SOE had, which were to support resistance and promote resistance in countries that might be occupied and, when they were occupied, to keep the links going and to help the people who were resisting. Very difficult things to do. And none of us had the first idea of how to do it. We were all very young, very inexperienced, very amateurish and very ignorant.

Alexander Glen
Section D and SOE officer, Yugoslavia
The German air attack on Yugoslavia started at about six in the morning of 6 April 1941 and continued all day. Belgrade had been declared an open city. Fighter defence was shot out of the skies or shot up on the ground, it was a very heavy bombing by any future standards and we had to spend part of the day trying to move. We had a lot of packing cases of plastic explosives in safe houses in Belgrade so we tried to get as many of these out and into the country. We got most of them away to safer places, including the swimming pool of the house that the later German commandant of Belgrade occupied.

Julian Amery
Section D and SOE officer, Yugoslavia
In the spring of '41, the British were pushed out of the Balkans completely. We brought some of the army back through Crete. Then Crete fell to the Germans and what was left of the SOE organisation – some of them were captured – fell back on the Middle East, on Cairo and Jerusalem, and a number of the Yugoslavs and Greeks we'd been able to get out with us were there too. And there we were, uncertain when the opportunity would come to get back into the Balkans.

The Auxiliary Units

Captain Peter Wilkinson
MI(R) and SOE officer, London
One of the things spawned by MI(R) were the Auxiliary Units, which were supposed to be the nucleus of a guerrilla organisation in Britain in the event of a German invasion.

Captain Andrew Croft
Auxiliary Unit organiser, Essex and Suffolk
Auxiliary Units were the stay-behind people, with underground shelters, which we had to construct, stiff with sticky bombs and grenades, phosphorous grenades as well, Bren guns and Stens and ammunition galore and fully stocked with food of the non-perishable variety. My job was to create fifty such bases in Essex and Suffolk reasonably near the coast. Peter Fleming was in Kent. He was very keen on poisoned arrows.

Captain Peter Wilkinson
MI(R) and SOE officer, London
Finally we had units posted all the way from the north of Scotland down the whole coast to Land's End and even to the Pembroke tip of Wales. We didn't have anybody seriously inland because they were essentially intended as units to interfere with the original perimeter the Germans might make. There was no question, at least when I was there, or when Gubbins was there, of a nationwide guerrilla force, although I confess we had this vaguely at the back of our minds if we were granted time.

Captain Andrew Croft
Auxiliary Unit organiser, Essex and Suffolk
Each patrol, as it was called, was about seven to ten men in size, members of the Home Guard. These men were marvellous. Gamekeepers, smugglers, poachers, all that. Grand people. Tough. A very awful job if the Germans had landed, to stay behind and sabotage their communications, but that was the aim and object and that's what would have happened, I think, by these splendid people I had to train. I think they would have been quite a problem for the Germans to compete with and I think they would have been effective. But of course they couldn't have had a profound effect, just a nuisance effect.

Lieutenant John Marchant
Auxiliary Unit organiser, Hampshire
It's very difficult to say how much trouble we could have caused to the Germans had they invaded, but I think that the Germans had been so good at overrunning people that they could have dealt with little pinpricks like this fairly quickly. The other thing that worried me was that you would have immediately caused immense suffering to the local population. If anything like that had happened in their village, the whole village would probably have gone.

Forging the Weapon

I was told that I should be working outside the international law concerning soldiers and the only thing I could expect if I was caught would be a bullet in the back of the head.

From modest beginnings, SOE reached an estimated peak strength of thirteen thousand, of whom five thousand were agents and the remainder staff. In all, it is thought, SOE would recruit, train and equip more than nine thousand agents. Yet when it came to recruitment, there was no standard method. The organisation was highly secret and its needs were not easily advertised or met. Early recruits were often friends or family of men and women already in the service. In time, as more were needed, quiet inquiries were made among army, air force and naval units inviting applicants for hazardous duties but not letting on much more.

Motives for volunteering were many and various. Backgrounds, too, were diverse. So were the skills that volunteers had to offer and for which SOE was looking. It is a myth that all those who were recruited as agents had to speak a foreign language. As SOE sought to find men willing to work in the Balkans or the Burmese jungle, for instance, few nationals of those places were judged reliable enough to be recruited and only a handful of Britons could be found who had been out there before. Outside France, the Low Countries, Scandinavia, Poland and Central Europe, most agents whom SOE dispatched into enemy territory were young British soldiers who knew nothing of the local languages and had no prior experience of where they were being sent.

SOE had its main headquarters in London's Baker Street. As the war progressed, the organisation grew. More office space had to be found in nearby flats and hotels; outside London, a wealth of premises, many of them grand country houses, were commandeered for training and housing agents, forging documents, developing and producing specialist weapons

and equipment and maintaining radio contact with agents in the field. Where possible, SOE established headquarters and training schools abroad to be closer to the countries in which it was trying to work. Cairo became the principal base for operations into the occupied Balkans, for example, and hundreds of agents bound for southern Europe were instructed at schools in Palestine, while India and Ceylon became centres of planning and training for activity across the Far East.

RECRUITMENT – STAFF

Major Dick Barry
Staff officer, Operations Section, SOE HQ, London
I wasn't recruited, really. It was a perfectly straight military appointment. I was at the Staff College doing the short wartime course at the end of 1940 and as the course was coming to an end you were all handed out your appointments. I was handed a piece of paper which said that I was to be GSO II, Ministry of Economic Warfare, which meant absolutely nothing to me at all or to anybody else present. It was a War Office decision: Gubbins had asked for me and had been allowed a pew for a GSO II and that was it. I did what I was told, which was to report to room something or other in a flat in Berkeley Court, which again meant absolutely nothing, and I marched in and said, 'Here I am,' and was confronted with Gubbins, whom I had known in a small way, and he told me what the form was.

Major Peter Wilkinson
Staff officer, Czech–Polish Section, SOE HQ, London
Gubbins' arrival really put a professional backbone behind SOE. Without him, in my opinion, or someone like him, it would certainly have gone the way of Section D and disappeared in fantastic dreams and fury among the military establishment in Whitehall.

Major Dick Barry
Staff officer, Operations Section, SOE HQ, London
You fought the War Office for staff appointments and eventually you were allowed x number of GSO IIIs or another GSO II or something like that. One would get on to the War Office and say, 'Now look, I want, or I'm authorised to have, so many bodies. Can you wheel some up for interview?' And then one went down to Horse Guards and interviewed them. You didn't reject

anybody, much, because you were jolly lucky to get anybody. Your main problem really was battling for resources. One heard a great deal from Gubbins of the difficulties he encountered when fighting for resources at a higher level.

Captain Jack Beevor
Staff officer, SOE HQ, London
The interviewers were under orders not to disclose the function of SOE or even its name. It had a cover name of ISRB and offices in 64 Baker Street. I was not unique: nobody after his interview really knew what it was all about. You were told, 'This is a new, secret organisation. We won't tell you what its objectives are until you have been cleared with security.' And I very nearly said 'No' because they simply wouldn't tell me anything.

Captain Peter Lee
Staff officer, Security Section, SOE HQ, London
ISRB was the Inter-Services Research Bureau. The idea was that Inter-Services would allow officers of three services, from the security point of view, to go in and out of the place without arousing any comment. Also it was possible for people in civilian clothes, male and female, to go in and out because a research bureau would have civil servants. We also had to have a War Office department cover so we cooked up this name 'MO1 (SP)' which didn't exist and had it put in the War Office telephone directory so that anybody who got hold of it knew that it really did exist. And of course that number was another Whitehall number hooked up directly to Baker Street. 'MO1 (SP)' we thought was terribly clever. We said it stood for 'Mysterious Operations In Secret Places'. We reckoned that the Germans, with their lack of sense of humour, would never be able to unravel that one.

Captain Aonghaìs Fyffe
Staff officer, Security Section, SOE HQ, London
It was pretty busy, the main office, 64. Another place was Michael House, which was next door across the lane. That was the headquarters of Marks & Spencer and the Security, Photographic and Passports Sections were there. Then there was Norgeby House across the street and Montague Mansions as well and eventually Bryanston Square, later on. Plus all the various country sections had their flats.

Vera Atkins
Civilian staff, French Section, SOE HQ, London
It still stands, 64 Baker Street. It was, I suppose, five floors, a medium-sized modern block.

Captain Peter Lee
Staff officer, Security Section, SOE HQ, London
Heavily sandbagged entrance. All very Sherlock Holmes.

Patricia Stewart-Bam
FANY staff, Air Liaison Section, SOE HQ, London
The place was like a beehive or an ant-heap the whole time.

June Darton
Civilian secretary, Finance Section, SOE HQ, London
You went in through a rather dark passage and I went up to the first floor. It was very dreary, frightfully dreary, but there we were, we couldn't argue.

Mildred Schutz
Civilian secretary, SOE HQ, London
There were a lot of corridors with hardboard divisions and doors which did not have anybody's name on. And they would test you, I think, by saying, 'Take these papers to Colonel so-and-so. It's the third door on the left.' And next time they'd say, 'Take it to Colonel so-and-so,' and you had to remember which was his office.

June Darton
Civilian secretary, Finance Section, SOE HQ, London
I worked for John Howard who was Number 1 to Wing Commander Venner, head of all finances, who was terrifying. He used to just march in and say, 'Give me that file!' and you didn't know what it was because you'd never heard of Skefco ball bearings. The very first day I was there he said, 'Can you get that file?' I just fiddled around with the papers and didn't find it, needless to say. And my first day there – I'd never been in an office in my life – I thought that at half-past four it was time to go home. Of course, it wasn't. The worst thing was that one had various typing that you'd chuck in the waste-paper basket, but it had to be all very carefully torn up, you just didn't leave it in the waste-paper basket. It was all a big learning curve.

Elisabeth Small

Civilian secretary, French Section, SOE HQ, London

The first day, they said, 'We would like you to sign the Official Secrets Act.' So I did. Then they said, 'You're going to the French Section, you'll be working for Captain Noble.' Captain Noble was a captain in the British Army. There were also two RAF officers there and a civilian secretary to Buckmaster, who, I was told, was head of section. Captain Noble said 'Good morning' and something else and I thought, 'You're not English,' and it was quite obvious after about half an hour that he was French. One of the RAF officers, taking the mickey out of George Noble, said, 'Well, it's George's first secretary! Hooray!' And I nearly turned round and said, 'It's my first job!' but I thought I should keep quiet for the moment.

George Noble said, 'I'd like you to type this for me, please.' It was all numbers and dates, about a page; there was no sense in it at all. 'I want one copy and I'll ask you to go and get it reprinted and you'll have to ask them to put it on edible paper.' I looked at it and it meant nothing and he said, 'You won't make a mistake will you?' I said, 'I hope not.' He said, 'Somebody's life may depend on it.' So I then typed this page, which was a schedule for a wireless operator, as I was to learn later. Afterwards I went across to Buckmaster's secretary and said, 'Would you mind checking this with me?' Then I asked where I was to take it to be put on edible paper. And that's how we began.

George Noble was very un-French: very quiet, very unemotional. I didn't know very much and he said, 'Now look, we have a filing room in here for the section and you go in there, if I don't need you to type, and take a file. They're all files belonging to agents sent to France. You can pick up what you want and read it and, like that, you will know more about this section than anyone can tell you. The only thing is, this is the section. We keep to ourselves. The less you know about other people's work in the building, the better.'

Odette Brown

FANY secretary, French Section, SOE HQ, London

The greatest requirement in F Section was the knowledge of French. Fortunately I was completely bilingual because I'd had all these years of school in Paris. I also knew the geography of France very well because we had learned all about the departments, the districts and provinces, all their principal towns and secondary towns.

Apart from taking dictation from Major Bourne-Paterson and long briefings to the agents, which had to be typed with several copies with lots of stencils, I did a lot of the letter writing. And there was a group of people on the floor below us who did nothing but forge documents and identity cards and papers for agents going over to France, and, from time to time, so that it shouldn't always be the same kind of handwriting on these things, they would ask me, and people like me, to write in a name or a signature on an identity card.

Gwendoline Lees
FANY signal planner, Grendon Hall signals station, Buckinghamshire
FANYs in uniform were, in the majority, responsible for and working all the wireless sets dealing directly with agents in the field, listening for and receiving their 'skeds' as they were known, their schedules, and sending messages. The FANY organisation, the letters stand for First Aid Nursing Yeomanry, had been founded in 1907 and, during the first war, served with the British Army in France, chiefly as nurses and driving troop transporters. From the end of the war the unit remained intact as a voluntary organisation, helping occasionally with major disasters, particularly in the London area. My sister was already serving in the FANYs. I'd assumed she was having rather a jolly time in Oxfordshire driving troops around, which was what she told the family she was doing.

Captain Peter Lee
Staff officer, Security Section, SOE HQ, London
At one stage my sister was really browned off with the canteen work she was doing in London and I got her an interview at Baker Street. I had to warn all the people that she was coming in, I watched her come into the back of Michael House, where we were, and I had to stay in my office until the girl who was interviewing her rang through and said she'd left the building. She never knew, until after the war, that I'd worked there or that I'd seen her going in and out.

Odette Brown
FANY secretary, French Section, SOE HQ, London
We would say we were in the FANYs and people would say, 'What do you do?' We were not supposed to say that our work was secret, which was far more difficult than if we had been allowed to say so. Lots of people worked in all sorts of things in wartime and if you asked them they used to say, 'Hush-hush,' which meant, 'I can't talk about it.' But we were not supposed to say that we couldn't talk about it, so one of the cover stories was the FANY Equipment

Office. The other one was the Inter-Services Research Bureau. That was a bit easier. The FANY Equipment Office made no sense at all. Why did you work all hours? What could you possibly be doing till midnight at the FANY Equipment Office?

Pamela Niven

FANY staff, Polish Section, Gardener's End holding school, Hertfordshire

A girlfriend and I, actually, when we were in London, went and had tea at the English-Speaking Union and a very nice colonel came up to us and chatted away and he said, 'Do you know, I've met some girls who are doing the most extraordinary thing.' And he told us exactly what we were doing. By the grace of God both Anna and I said, 'Gosh, how exciting.' He said, 'Well, would you like to do something like that?' We said, 'Well, yes, it would be wonderful.' 'What do you do?' 'Nothing like that, of course. I'm just on washing-up.' But we found out afterwards that he was sent to find out what our reactions would be.

Patricia Stewart-Bam

FANY staff, Air Liaison Section, SOE HQ, London

You were very close to the ground, to what it was like. One's friends wouldn't have an idea what it was like to be in an occupied country, but we did, not by experience, but by very near experience. We could read about it, things that were never published at that time, and sometimes people came in and talked to us, people who'd been over there.

Elisabeth Small

Civilian secretary, French Section, SOE HQ, London

One day, after about a couple of weeks, Noble was out, I was busy getting a file and I brought one out and put it by my desk. It was for Operation 'Bombproof', I remember, because that was rather a strange name. It was about a Frenchman, a French Army officer, who'd come to England and been sent back as a wireless operator – the first one to be sent by the French Section. He'd been captured at one stage but had got back to England. This was fascinating stuff. One of the RAF officers was passing by and said, 'You're interested in another file?' and I said, 'Well, yes, sir. This is extremely interesting, because it's the first wireless operator that was sent.' He said, 'Don't you know? You're working for him.' 'George Noble?' 'Yes, that's not his real name, can't have his real name, his family's in France.' And that did throw me.

RECRUITMENT – AGENTS

Robert Boiteux
French refugee, London
I happened to be in London, on holiday from Kenya, when war broke out. I was called up by the French consulate and I thought, 'It's only going to last a few months. Might as well join up.' I was quite happy – a little adventure. I couldn't join the British Army. They wouldn't take anybody over twenty-seven in 1939. I was already over thirty.

After the collapse of the French, June 1940, I got demobbed and came back to England. It took me a long time. I had to walk half the way through Spain; I walked as far as Barcelona. There I was given a ticket to Madrid. Then I walked into Portugal and eventually got to Lisbon. I was put on a boat, had to work my passage as a deckhand, six weeks on the boat, and got back to England.

I didn't know what to do. I didn't particularly want to join the army. I wanted to get back to Africa, where I had a goldmine and had custody of my child, a little girl, ten years old. Couldn't get back. I did have permission to go back but no berths were available. Then one day I was walking down Piccadilly and met an old friend and started talking about the war and this, that and the other. He said, 'What are you doing?' I said 'Well, I've got to do something, I can't get back to Africa.' His exact words were, 'Well, old chap. They're looking for some silly buggers like you to parachute into France. They've asked me but I'm not mad, but you might be interested.' So I went straight to the War Office and a couple of months later I was in SOE.

Raymond Neres
Cambridge University student
I was bilingual in French, my mother being French, and I was recruited when I was still an undergraduate at Cambridge. I was due to be called up, there was a joint recruiting board, and when they interviewed me I said I wanted to join the Secret Service. Nobody batted an eyelid. About three weeks later, when I was still at Cambridge, before the long vac holidays, I received a letter from the War Office asking me to come for an interview.

Lance Corporal Harry Rée
Intelligence Corps NCO and former conscientious objector
I started off as a 'conchie', actually, but just before the fall of France I realised that I didn't think political objection stood up logically. I was fairly far to the Left at the time and I realised that this war was much more than a capitalist

war. I think the concentration camp business and the anti-Jewish business convinced me that I, with the rest of the country, should do everything possible to defeat the whole Nazi thing because of its racial policies. My father was part Jewish; you couldn't live in Manchester in the Twenties without having a lot of Jewish friends.

So I said 'OK, I don't mind where I go' and I was called up into the field artillery in 1940 and trained as an artilleryman in Exeter for about six months. That was an absolute nonsense. You had guns with wooden wheels and there was a wonderful sergeant, who we were terrified of, who called me 'Gonorrhoea': Gunner Rée. 'Come on, Gonorrhoea!' It was so unrealistic, pulling guns on wooden wheels; there was a suggestion that horses were going to be used and so on.

My brother, who had been farming in France and escaped with his family at the last moment in 1940, had been called up and he wrote to me from where he was, which was somewhere in remote Gloucestershire looking after the security of people who were going to be dropped into occupied Europe, and he said, 'If you want an interesting job, using languages and so on, why don't you transfer?' So I requested to go into field security, and, after about six to nine months of training and doing a little port security work in South Wales, I got brought in to the security side of SOE.

Captain Robert Wade
Northamptonshire Yeomanry, Western Desert
I was in the desert and I asked the general what had happened to a friend of mine, a Captain Wiggington, who was at headquarters in charge of transport. He said, 'Oh, he's gone to a place in Cairo. You can look him up there, no doubt.' I went on down to Cairo and I happened to look up Wiggington in Rustem Buildings, which was the SOE headquarters, and when I asked for Wiggington he arrived in the most awful state and said, 'How did you know I was here?' But everybody knew about Rustem Buildings, including all the Arabs and everybody else in Cairo, I think. I said, 'Well, the general told me you were here and I thought I'd look you up,' and we started to talk and other people saw me and said, 'Would you like to join us?'

Major Brian Dillon
Special Air Service, Western Desert
I got the names of one or two SOE people in Cairo and went and knocked on the door of the chap who ran the caique section, 'Skipper' Poole. I said to him, 'Any chance of getting a job with your outfit? I know a bit about boats.'

He said, 'I'm full up at the moment but the Greek section upstairs want somebody. I'll send you up if you like.' That's how it was done in those days. I was interviewed and they said, 'Do you know anything about Lewes bombs?' I said, 'Yes, the SAS used them for blowing up aeroplanes.' 'Well, we have a chap in Greece who has access to German airfields round Athens but he knows very little about explosives. Would you like to go and join him?' I said, 'Well, if you insist.' This was on a Tuesday and by Friday I was in Greece.

Joachim Rønneberg
Norwegian refugee, London
I fled from Norway, as a rather young chap, in a fishing boat. I was the only one on board not being seasick and I decided on my way over, 'I'm going to join the navy, that's the quickest way to get into action. I'll be trained on board and be in it from the first day.' Then I met a friend of mine, in London, and he said, 'Well, you mustn't go in the navy until you've talked to a certain Captain Linge.' Captain Linge was from my home district actually and I was interested to hear what he suggested. He had been a liaison officer to the British expeditionary force in Norway in 1940 and been evacuated to England and then they had decided to form special companies for warfare behind the German lines and he had been given the job on the Norwegian side. It was SOE organising it and I hadn't talked to him many minutes before I forgot everything about the navy.

Adam Benrad
Officer cadet, Polish Army, England
A man came from London. I don't know the identity of the man, we could only surmise that he wasn't a front-line soldier because his battledress looked very new. They were looking especially for young men, rather tough, which I was in those days, and he put the proposition in front of us that there was a possibility of a transfer or a flight to Poland which would involve parachuting. Would we consider the option? Well, everybody had been over here for two or three years, cooped up in this country, there was no talk of any second front at that time, and for obvious reasons we wanted to fight. He told us to think about it, not to take the decision rashly. I said, 'Yes, I will do it.'

Private Paul 'Yogi' Mayer
German Jewish refugee serving in Pioneer Corps
A man arrived in uniform. I'd never seen anybody wearing such an ill-fitting uniform. His name was Hartmann and he worked with us – we were building

a camp near Carmarthen. Then he suddenly said, 'I am looking for people for the commandos.' He was a recruiting person from the special services. I got a bit more friendly with him. He was an arms trader from Hungary. He was already in his fifties and looked like Richard Wagner. Then he said to me, 'Look here, I can't forward your details. You've got family. You've got a little boy.' I said, 'That's the reason I want to do this.' He said, 'But what about the risk?' I said, 'I have had enough of all this pioneering and all that nonsense. I can't stand it any longer. I want to do something.'

Flight Lieutenant Edward Shackleton
RAF intelligence officer, St Eval aerodrome, Cornwall
I remember some SOE people coming to me and saying that if I joined SOE as an air force officer I'd immediately be promoted to squadron leader. I went to my squadron commander and said I'd had this approach from SOE and I remember him saying, 'Don't touch it. They're not the sort of people you want to be mixed up with.'

Lieutenant Duncan Guthrie
Duke of Cornwall's Light Infantry
One day a little note came round saying, 'Anybody interested in joining special operations?' I thought, 'Well, that would be better,' because, really, although I enjoyed the Scillies, I didn't enjoy the officers' mess. I thought it was terrible, actually. It's not my kind of life. There was the regimentalness of it, you know, and they were so childish. Every day, after dinner in the evening, we used to play games in the mess, the sort of games I gave up when I was fourteen. One I remember particularly was where everybody was blindfolded and got a rolled-up newspaper and hit each other, and, of course, whenever the colonel was being hit, we all took our blindfolds off and saw exactly where he was and bashed him because we didn't like him very much. That's not soldiering, that's not beginning to save the prisoners from the concentration camps in Germany and so on. It really seemed so remote from anything that I wanted to do.

Trooper Norman Smith
Northamptonshire Yeomanry
When they started coming round for glider pilots, suicide missions, we had a feeling that the Germans couldn't possibly be as bad as our own unit and everybody volunteered en masse. There was nothing we didn't volunteer for, just to get away from this lot.

Private Alf Holdham
Royal Armoured Corps
A notice came on the unit board for volunteers for special duties. 'Must be radio operators or qualified at least eight words a minute.' I was a radio operator in the tank corps, a gunner-operator, so I applied. We had to have an interview with the CO, who did his best to put us off, saying it was a one-way ticket and all that sort of business, like the commandos, but I still carried on.

Private Glyn Loosmore
Royal Armoured Corps
People could see that the Armoured Corps was in a sad plight. I was in a Churchill tank regiment and we couldn't run the tank for a day without major maintenance and it was quite clear that our armour was no match for the Germans. But I don't think people were getting out to save their own lives, they were just bored stiff with the incessant maintenance that went on in the Armoured Corps, the spit and polish. It's hard to believe how the British Army could grind down people's enthusiasm with this everlasting maintenance. It's often said that there are some people who could be kept in the army all their lives if every week you could give them a new piece of equipment and some kind of case to carry it in. I was probably one of those.

Trooper Eric Child
Fife and Forfar Yeomanry
I thought it was about time I did something. I thought the war was passing me by without my making any definite contribution. All my friends were either flying or going down to the sea in ships and my brother had taken part in the Dieppe Raid. I suppose I was young and foolish.

Signalman Thomas Collins
Royal Corps of Signals
I've always had the feeling that if you don't volunteer you'll never know what you might have missed. Anybody can be a stay-at-home.

Private Gordon Tack
Royal Armoured Corps
I thought this might be a better chance of seeing some action. I still hadn't satisfied my original grudge against the Germans for killing my father.

Captain John Smallwood
Royal Armoured Corps
I not only volunteered myself but also a friend of mine, Hugh Fraser, who was on leave. He had been at Wellington with me. When he came back from leave I said, 'I hope you realise you've volunteered for hazardous duties behind the enemy lines,' and he said, 'Oh, have I?' We had both been trying very hard to get into the commandos, anything to get away from regimental soldiering.

Captain Oswin Craster
Oxfordshire and Buckinghamshire Light Infantry
Every time we volunteered to go somewhere else the colonel always tore it up and said we were rats trying to leave a sinking ship. Fortunately he went up to London one weekend, to see his wife, poor chap, and we managed to get in our applications, I and two other chaps, and volunteered for what we thought was going to Yugoslavia.

Lance Sergeant Ray Mason
Royal Artillery
The CO said, 'Unfortunately this has come from Corps and there's nothing I can do to stop you going. I've got to forward your name.' He gave me a railway warrant and said, 'You will go back and pack your gear, get the six o'clock railway train from Carlisle and get off the train at Oxford station.' I said, 'What do I do at Oxford, sir?' He said, 'You volunteered for this lot, you bloody well find out.'

I got to Oxford at about three in morning. Got off the train. I saw two other soldiers get off the train further up the platform. The train pulled out and there were we knowing nothing at all. Then out of the gloom an officer approached me. 'What's your name?' Told him. 'Wait there.' He went to the next person, same thing, then to the furthest one; and then the three of us joined up: a captain in the Royal Artillery, a corporal in the Royal Signals and me.

We were taken out to the station yard, put into the back of a fifteen-hundredweight truck, the canvas curtains were pulled down and the officer said, 'Do not speak to one another and do not try to look out of the back.' I think there was a military policeman in there with us. We were driven away and after about fifteen minutes stopped at a gate, some murmuring went on, the gate opened, then there was a further gate, then we were told to get out the truck, and we were in front of an enormous country mansion. We were taken in, given breakfast, the three of us, and then taken to a room and told to go to bed, we'd be called at ten in the morning. During the next two days we were interviewed.

Captain Selwyn Jepson
Recruiting officer, French Section, SOE HQ, London

They would come to the War Office by appointment and I would decide whether I would want to go on with them. I simply went with the cover that having languages and knowledge of France they might be valuable in the war effort. Then they would go away. I would then have to refer their names and addresses to MI5 for vetting. MI5 tended to be rather dilatory until I made a bit of a fuss and then I got quick answers from MI5, generally, simply, 'Nothing known against.' Not a very positive vetting, but enough for me. Anyhow, by the time I'd interviewed them I'd a pretty good idea of where their loyalties lay. For the most part they just hated Germany, hated the Germans and wanted to get into the war.

I interviewed entirely on my own. It was a job which put me by necessity on my own. There was nobody to help me. Help of any kind, even of the best sort, would have been an inhibitory factor. And it was entirely informal. The only time I put on uniform would be if I was interviewing somebody in the services. I never interviewed a civilian in uniform. Never. That would automatically put us on a different personal level. I had a desk but there was nothing on it. I think a desk is a form of protection for the person who is being interviewed, there is a barrier, a physical barrier, between them and the examiner, so I always sat one side of a very narrow desk. Then I decided it was too formal and threw out the desk and got an ordinary, folding, army-issue wooden table, which made it much easier. Then there was no sense of officialdom about it. The desk was a little bit official.

One wanted normal, natural people with the qualifications and the courage and the motivation. I had to watch out for the domestic situation, of course, so that there should not be too much looking back over the shoulder. In other words, people who were without strong family ties would be at an advantage, not somebody who was wondering what was happening with their wife or their husband or their children. They had to be individuals on their own and prepared to work on their own, or with whosoever it was necessary to have an association.

Francis Cammaerts
Civilian and former conscientious objector

Jepson subsequently said that he was quite sure that he didn't have any doubts at all that I was suitable material. I was a little surprised that he didn't talk much about my philosophical approach. The reason, of course, was that he wasn't telling me what I was going to be trained to do. He couldn't. At that time these were sort of vague talks, 'You could use your French in North Africa where there's going to be a problem.' That kind of suggestion was made but the idea that I would go into occupied France didn't even occur to me. I didn't know anyone was doing that sort of thing.

Signalman Roger Landes
Royal Corps of Signals
At the interview I met Major Lewis Gielgud, who was the brother of the actor, and he attacked me straight away in French. He told me what they wanted to do with me, to send me to France as a wireless operator, and that I could be very useful to them. I had to give an answer straight away.

Second Lieutenant Harry Despaigne
Duke of Cornwall's Light Infantry
I was interviewed by Gielgud who asked, 'Can you ride a motorcycle?' I said, 'Yes.' The second question was, 'How do you feel about going back to France?' I said, 'Why not?' He said I could have a few weeks to think about it but I said, 'I've no reason to think about it. Yes, I will go.' I thought I was going to be there next morning.

Sub-Lieutenant Harvey Bennette
Royal Navy Volunteer Reserve
I was shown into a room where there was a naval commander, an army major and a civilian, and introduced. I didn't get the commander's name but Major Reeves was the army fellow. He walked round me rather like a slave buyer at a slave market, walking round and round, and he said, 'Would you care to get into dangerous activities?' I said, 'I'll do anything that's wanted of me, sir.' He said, 'What about midget submarines?' I said, 'Well, I've never really thought about it.' He said, 'Ah, that makes you very suitable.'

Lieutenant Duncan Guthrie
Duke of Cornwall's Light Infantry
They asked me what languages I spoke and I truthfully said I spoke a little bad French. They noticed in my curriculum vitae that I had spent a couple of years, when I'd first left school, in the Ionian Bank in London, so they immediately thought I knew something about Greece. I didn't, except I vaguely knew the geography of Greece because I knew where the bank had

different branches. They said would I like to go to Greece and I thought, 'Well, that would be nice.'

Private Herbert Anderson
Austrian Jewish refugee serving in Pioneer Corps
I was told, first of all, 'You are not to talk to anybody about this. Not even your parents.' I was then asked whether I was prepared to do a dangerous job, and I said, 'Yes.' 'Would you like to do this job in uniform or in civvies?' I said I would prefer uniform. I'd already guessed what it would be. I was then asked which area in Austria I knew especially well. Now it was clear what they needed me for, so I said, 'The Tyrolese mountain chain.' I could of course have said Vienna but I don't think that was what they wanted. They wanted something that bordered Yugoslavia and Italy. But I did tell Kathleen about it and I did tell my parents, saying, 'Don't tell anyone else.'

Lieutenant John Ross
Royal Artillery
I was asked, 'Are you afraid of death?' My answer was, 'Yes.' I can't remember anything else about the interview whatsoever.

Lance Sergeant Ray Mason
Royal Artillery
I was told that I should be working outside the international law concerning soldiers and the only thing I could expect if I was caught would be a bullet in the back of the head.

Trooper Norman Smith
Northamptonshire Yeomanry
This is perfectly true, they said to me, 'Why do you want to join?' and I said, 'I don't know.' I thought I might as well be honest. Also I said, 'I'm terrified of heights,' and they said, 'But you're going to be a parachutist.' I said, 'I know, but I know if I can overcome the parachuting bit I can do the rest.' Much to my amazement they passed me.

Captain William Crawshay
Royal Welch Fusiliers
I was one of the volunteers who was required to pass certain tests in order to be selected, which was the usual kind of thing: 'How do you react to height?' and 'Do you wet your bed?' The usual kind of trick cyclists' – psychiatrists' –

stupid questions. But one was always forearmed. I saw a couple of chaps going in for an interview in front of me and they came out saying 'bloody shit, bloody shit' and I soon found out why, because I was asked this daft question, 'Did you wet your bed as a child?' I said, 'Yes.' He said, 'Do you still do it?' I said, 'No.' He said, 'When did you stop?' I said, 'When my father took me to a psychiatrist.' It was a simple one, that one.

Trooper Eric Child
Fife and Forfar Yeomanry
They had a series of drawings and you had to tell them what these things suggested to you. They suggested various poetry quotations to me.

Captain Dick Rubinstein
Royal Artillery
There was a three-day War Office-type selection board at a house in Hampshire. We were divided up into groups of about eight for the test procedure and at the end of the three days you knew those eight pretty well. In fact I think one of the most valuable things probably to the selection staff was that we each had to put in order, of the eight, who we'd be prepared to take with us into enemy-occupied territory.

Captain Tom Carew
Royal Artillery
We had to climb up a tree – I hate heights – to ropes between two trees and then you had to go along these ropes. It really wasn't my scene. And I got across one and then the other one and then a higher one and I looked down below and he said, 'You can do the top one if you want.' I called him a shit or something worse than that. 'That's the only fucking one I've got to do, isn't it? If I don't do that one I don't pass. You can't con me.' So I climbed up there, got stuck half way through, but had to take the risk and got to the other side. When we got down I said to Alistair, 'Did you do the top level?' He said, 'No, I didn't. He said it was voluntary.' Well, it was the only one you had to do and they never took him. I never heard of him again and he was much more suitable than I was. He was much more active, strong, intelligent, he was a really bright guy. And he wanted that job but of course he didn't realise that the top one was the only one he had to do.

Captain John Smallwood
Royal Armoured Corps
We were supposed to be a gang of thieves who had holed up in a building. The 'police' were down below, banging on the door, and we were told we had three

minutes to do something about it. I decided the best thing I could do was jump out of a window and escape, which is what I did. That was my answer, though I never knew what the official answer was. Another test was where again you were a member of a gang of thieves who had left some incriminating things in a house and you had five minutes to find them, stuff them into your pockets and walk out. Then you had to explain why you had taken each item. Why you had taken this, rather than that.

Lieutenant Aubrey Trofimov
Royal Artillery
I was locked up in a cellar and told to try and get out. In my case my architectural studies helped. I looked at the walls and I couldn't see anything, then I noticed some loose bricks at ceiling height and I scraped away and there was a convenient duct. I crawled along this duct where it led to a grate and I was able to get out. I thought I would have some fun and I proceeded very quietly along the side of the building to where a guard was and got behind him and took him in a grip and said, 'You're dead.' He played ball, I went into the main building and presented myself at one of the officers' doors and said, 'I'm here, I could technically shoot you.'

Captain John Smallwood
Royal Armoured Corps
When my wife, who was also in SOE, was interviewed by the same man, he said to her, 'What would you do if I locked the door?' and she said, 'I'd scream for help.' He marked her, 'Very vivid imagination.'

Captain Selwyn Jepson
Recruiting officer, French Section, SOE HQ, London
I was responsible for recruiting women agents for our work, in the face of a good deal of opposition from the powers-that-be, who said that women, under the Geneva Convention, were not allowed to take combatant duties which they regarded resistance work in France as being. It took me some time to find a proper answer to that and then I found it. I discovered that the anti-aircraft units always had ATS officers on their strength and that when it came to firing an anti-aircraft gun the person who pulled the lanyard that released the trigger was a woman, an ATS officer. Eventually it went up to Churchill who remembered me from the old days of the *London Magazine*. He growled at me, 'What are you doing?' I told him what I was doing. He said, 'You're using women in this?' I said, 'Yes. Don't you think this is a very sensible thing to do?'

He said, 'Yes, good luck to you.' And that was my authority. So in any arguments I said, 'Would you mind talking to Mr Churchill about it?' The one woman who was not against it was the woman known as the 'Queen Bee' who was the chief of the FANYs. With her connivance I dressed my recruits in FANY uniforms, which were very pretty and very nice and gave them complete cover because they could always be drivers or whatever.

Commandant Marian Gamwell
FANY Commandant
They were sent along to me to see if I would recruit them as FANYs. They couldn't have much FANY training – we had a training centre for the others – but they were sent to me and I had to see them in my flat, not at the office. The FANYs had a wonderful album of photographs of what they'd done in the first war and, well, I did my best to try and impress them with these. Of course they had to be very special people. They had to be faultless at French and at living in France. I only just had an interview with them to try and boost their morale, the ones I thought were all right, but it really wasn't up to me to turn them down. And they were good stuff. They had to be.

Flight Officer Yvonne Cormeau
Women's Auxiliary Air Force
After my husband was killed I joined the WAAF, the Women's Auxiliary Air Force. Well, going into the forces, one had to fill in a great number of questionnaires and when they asked, 'What have you as special qualities?' I put down my knowledge of German and Spanish and bilingual French. After a while this got through to the Ministry, of course, and then, as they were looking for people for SOE, I was interrogated. I received a telex from London asking that I should come down to town as soon as possible to see a certain Captain Selwyn Jepson. He asked if I was pleased with my work that I was doing and then he spoke about France. France at that time was divided into two parts, the northern part was completely occupied by the enemy and the southern part was so-called unoccupied, so we talked about that and he suddenly asked me if I would return to occupied France. I replied in the affirmative. I thought this was something my husband would have liked to do, and, as he was no longer there to do it, I thought it was time for me to do it.

Odette Sansom
French civilian living in England
I saw in a newspaper and heard on the radio that if people had photographs of a certain part of the coast of France, would they send them to an address in London. Of course I sent them to the wrong address. I think I sent them to the navy instead of the army, but in any case they reached where they should have been going. I was very surprised a few weeks later when I had a letter thanking me and asking me if it would be possible for me to come to London and have an interview. I thought, 'Well, it's probably to give me back my photographs.' So I organised to come to London and was very surprised by all the questions that were asked of me. Then I had a letter asking me to come back for another interview.

I came back and I was told, 'You would not know the way we do these things but we have made enquiries about you in this country and in France and we're very satisfied by what we've found.' I lost my temper. I said, 'Well, what do you mean? Why did you have to make enquiries about me? What do you think I am?' I was told, 'Oh, calm down, we're going to explain to you why. We train people here and we send them to the country of their origin, or if they speak a foreign language well we send them to that country, where they can use it and be useful to the war effort.' I could see that. I agreed with all that. I said, 'Yes, of course. I can see that.' Then I was told, 'Well, we think women could be useful, too.' 'Yes,' I said. 'I think women are very useful.' And that did it. I was told, 'So glad you think that way because we're going to ask you to be one of them.'

Captain Selwyn Jepson
Recruiting officer, French Section, SOE HQ, London
Odette was a shrewd cookie and she knew at once what it was about. She guessed and said, yes, she wanted to do it. And I said, in effect, 'Wait a minute, what are your domestic circumstances?' She said they wouldn't bother her. She had a husband and a couple of children but the husband didn't come into the matter very much and the children would be looked after by an aunt. When could she start?

I was rather doubtful about her capacity. Although she had perfect French and knew France, her personality was so big that I couldn't quite see her getting away with it. However good the cover story we gave her, I couldn't see her passing unnoticed. I had a little form that I wrote names and addresses on and, for my own guidance, made a comment at the bottom on the question of suitability. I remember very clearly on her piece of paper I wrote, 'God help the Germans if we can ever get her near them, but maybe God help us on the way' – because she has such a huge personality and will dominate everybody she comes in contact with. Not necessarily because she has a dominant nature, but because she just can't help it.

Vera Atkins
Civilian staff, French Section, SOE HQ, London
I've always found personally that being a woman has great advantages if you know how to play the thing right and I believe that all the girls, the women who went out, had the same feeling. They were not as suspect as men, they had very subtle minds when it came to talking their way out of situations, they had many more cover stories to deliver than most men and they performed extremely well. Also they're very conscientious – I'm not saying men are not. They were wonderful wireless operators and very cool and courageous.

Captain Selwyn Jepson
Recruiting officer, French Section, SOE HQ, London
The question of loyalty was always at the bottom of all thinking and all questioning. Where is the loyalty? There was one, Noor Inayat Khan, her mother was British and her father was Indian. She had perfect qualifications, amongst which was the fact that she was already in the services as a WAAF and was a wireless telegraphist, which meant that she could then be a ready-made wireless operator. And when I got down to the question of loyalty she said, 'My first loyalty is to India.' I said, 'I can understand that.' She said, 'If I had to choose between Britain and India I'd choose India.' I said, 'At the moment we have to choose what you feel about the Germans,' to which she said, 'I loathe the Germans, I want to see them lose this war.' So I said, 'Right, would you like to help to that end?' That was the only time that a loyalty was not directly British.

Vera Atkins
Civilian staff, French Section, SOE HQ, London
The sort of person who volunteered was in the main someone prepared to operate on their own with a considerable amount of courage and prepared to take the very considerable risks of which they were made fully aware. I think we assessed the chances of coming through at no more than fifty per cent.

Private Gordon Nornable
Gordon Highlanders
They said it was less than that, really. I was told it was less.

Training

Colonel Maurice Buckmaster
Head, French Section, SOE HQ, London
The training was very, very thorough indeed. As an example, the French Section had a place near Guildford, at Wanborough Manor, where the French Section recruits, male and female, gathered, about twelve in each group, and were trained for anything up to a fortnight in self-defence, in the use of arms, in the use of cover – moving around at night and so on – and all sorts of things which seemed to be a little remote from wartime activities. Like they must learn what the rules were in France about when you could get a cup of coffee or couldn't, that sort of thing; what a ration card entitled you to.

I used to spend quite a bit of time down at the training station with the man who was running it, a very marvellous colonel, de Wesselow. We used to sit up half the night talking about various people. We also used to test them out on how they reacted under a little bit too much drink. We'd give them an extra drink or two and see how they behaved. We would wake them up in the middle of the night with a sudden bright light and see what language they exclaimed in, whether they said, 'God Almighty!' or whether they said, 'Nom de Dieu!' Nothing but French was spoken, of course, the whole time.

That was the original training. Then after that there was the training in the rough mountains of Scotland and then finally, if they were accepted, they were parachute-trained at Ringway, Manchester. Then the decision had to be made what job they would undertake, whether they would be an organiser, in which case they would go for further training at Beaulieu, in Hampshire, for specialised training in managing and organising a group, or an arms instructor, which was fairly straightforward, or a radio operator.

Flight Officer Yvonne Cormeau
Trainee agent
They gave us some ideas about living and operating in France but they said, 'You've got to judge when you're on the spot. Things might change by the time you're there. All we can tell you is that there may be certain days of the week when you can't have certain drinks or foods in certain cafés, so don't

ask, just try and look out and see what is on the menu and advertised for those days. Please don't do too much dyeing of your hair or have very noticeable make-up and things like that because you'll fall foul at some time or other. Try and dress as they do locally as much as possible. If you're going to live in the country, don't have a manicure, don't have this, don't have that.'

Birger Rasmussen
Norwegian trainee agent
At our first place, Stodham Park, near Petersfield, we had a training sergeant, a British sergeant, who was quite good although he exaggerated tremendously. Apparently he was going to make us innocent young men tough. He told us some remarkable stories but even though we couldn't believe all of it I think it had some effect. For instance, he talked about what happened in Flanders, before Dunkirk, and he said, 'We killed so many Germans it was a problem because there were heaps of dead Germans and we had to rise up on our feet to look over them.' Then, I remember, he said, 'It was a terrible smell in the summer with all those dead German bodies.' And I said, 'Well, there's only one thing that smells worse than a dead German. Do you know what that is?' No, he didn't know. 'That's a living German.' I remember I couldn't help laughing.

Second Lieutenant Jens Anton Poulsson
Norwegian trainee agent
Some of us had military experience, military education if you like, some other boys had never seen a rifle or a pistol or done any military training at all, so we were a mixed lot.

Lieutenant Denis Newman
SOE instructor, Brock Hall, Hampshire
I trained a group of Danish sailors and gave them the course that I'd just been given on arrival at Brock Hall – basic weapon training, planning a small raid – and I gave them an exercise. The exercise that I'd worked out was to place charges on the masts at Daventry broadcasting station. I taught them how to make up the charges they would need and where to place them and how to approach the place without getting caught.

The boss at Daventry knew what I was doing and was against it from the word 'Go'. He was as helpful as could be, a very nice chap, to the extent of offering me a job after the war if I survived, but he said, 'We can't guard this place and when they know that you've attacked it successfully there'll be hell to pay.' I said, 'No, that won't happen because it's deadly secret. No one will know.' But he was right and they did know. People were cross that these Danish sailors could get in so easily and could have wrecked the place.

Stanislaw Kujawinski
Polish trainee agent
Quite a few in the initial stages had to drop out. Not because they wanted to, they just couldn't stand the pace.

Frederick Serafinski
Polish trainee agent
Someone in high spirits expressed that when he found himself in Warsaw, he'd blow the head off the first German he sees. Of course, he was sent back. As the liaison officer explained later, 'We don't want these sort of heroes. We want them to live and do actions.'

Second Lieutenant Robert Sheppard
Trainee agent
We were to be gangsters with the knowledge of gangsters but with the behaviour, if possible, of gentlemen.

Lieutenant George Abbott
Trainee agent
The second stage of the training was up in Scotland, which I would call a hardening course. At the first school there was quite a few exercises of map reading and marching around the countryside and so on and so on but the Scottish exercise was much tougher.

Lieutenant Robert Ferrier
Trainee agent
A course of about twenty of us, all officers, all more or less lieutenants, were sent as a party under a conducting officer by train to Arisaig House, in Scotland, which is a very isolated house, a very fine house, quite near Mallaig. We were welcomed by the staff with a large glass of whisky and we lived there comfortably for about three weeks. We used to have a piper piping around before breakfast every morning.

There were about six or seven special training schools around Arisaig, which was the headquarters. Some specialised in training one nationality. I was sent to Inverie House, which was just across the loch from Mallaig, owned

Inverie House, Knoydart, Scotland, where many SOE agents were trained.

by Lord Brocket. A lovely house with magnificent salmon and trout fishing, a river going right through the estate into the loch.

Captain Aonghais Fyffe
SOE security officer, Scotland
We knew that there were foreign nationals coming up because we were warned to keep them apart. They mustn't even see each other. Of course, the contours up there are such that each house is screened from its neighbour, it can't be seen. Camusdarrach couldn't see Garramore. You could put a battalion in there and they wouldn't be seen. That's why they were so ideal for training purposes: you could have five or six different teams working in the mountains there, day after day after day, and they wouldn't see each other.

Second Lieutenant Robert Sheppard
Trainee agent
We had all sorts of instructors, military most of them, regular soldiers; an extraordinary PT sergeant, strong as a bull, fit like a champion. And we had to catch up with this very sporting type of life right from the morning. PT training after just a cup of coffee and then a huge breakfast and then all the courses, lunch and again courses, map-reading, left alone in the countryside.

Private Gordon Nornable
Trainee agent
Major Sykes was an expert in small arms. I think he'd been in the Shanghai police. He used to go round seeing that the training was in order. He was once at a railway station up in the Highlands, Morar, I think it was, and he was in uniform and he was approached by the military police and they asked him what he was and he said, 'Troops Welfare Officer.' Rather amusing I thought. He looked like a country rector but he was a holder of a black belt. He was a very genial chap but of course the kind of chap who would probably go and get a terrible grip on you. I've seen that chap turn round with his back facing the target and hit the bull's eye from between his legs. I've seen him do that.

Second Lieutenant Brian Stonehouse
Trainee agent
I remember a sergeant giving us our first lesson in unarmed combat. We were all second lieutenants there, officers and gentleman, and he started by saying, 'The first thing you have to learn in unarmed combat is to grab your opponent

by the balls.' Then he stopped and said, 'Oh, sorry gentlemen, I forgot. Officers have testicles.'

Second Lieutenant Peter Lake
Trainee agent
It was the usual thing of giving somebody a clip on the neck, pulling his arm in such a way that the neck came into the right position for you, and knees placed in suitable vulnerable parts. The chap who taught unarmed combat was about six foot three, he must have weighed fifteen stone, and I was probably one of the smallest of the pupils there and he found it awfully convenient to pick on me to demonstrate his skills. I used to think it was not entirely convincing that a person of his huge physique should find it easy to twist me up in knots.

Second Lieutenant Joachim Rønneberg
Norwegian trainee agent
Sometimes, after having a lecture in silent killing and things, it was a bit difficult to sleep, especially once. We had been trained in using this fighting knife which was a terrible weapon actually and had been told that if you put it in here it doesn't stop until it comes up here and hits the bone. And having been a very, very quiet, innocent boy back in Norway, never been in fights at all, I felt, 'What are you doing? And what are they doing to you?'

Private Eric Sanders
Austrian Jewish trainee agent
There was a story of a soldier in another camp, who, going out, had forgotten to report to the guardhouse and the guard sergeant came up behind him and tapped him – 'Hey!' And having just had a whole hour of unarmed combat, he automatically turned round the way he had been taught and killed the sergeant, just because of this training.

Sergeant George Lane
Hungarian trainee agent
There were three very nice chaps there, Latvian sailors, and they'd joined SOE because they were very anxious to parachute into Latvia. They were very nice chaps – it was fairly difficult to understand what they were talking about but they worked very hard. And one day the CO said to me, 'Look, these chaps have been working so hard, I think it would be a good idea if I gave them a day off. Will you take them to Glasgow so they can have a good time? Give them lunch and take them to the cinema.'

I took them to Glasgow and they said, 'We don't want to go to the cinema. We want to go to a pub because we know some of the pubs here.' They were sailors, you see. So we looked in on some pubs, they didn't like them, and then suddenly they said in one pub, 'Oh, we like this one. This is very nice.' So we sat down, ordered drinks, and then suddenly a terrific fight started and I said to them, 'Come on fellas, we'd better get out of here,' and I stood up. Before I'd reached my full height a little fellow flew up to me and hit me and knocked me cold. The next thing I knew I was outside the pub and these three chaps were trying to make me come to. 'Come on, come on, you're all right.' So I stood up and said, 'Shall we go for lunch?' 'No, no, no. Let's go back home. We've had enough.' So I said, 'If that's what you really want,' and I took them back home.

I was very puzzled by the whole thing but next day I read in the paper about a fight in a pub where two people were killed. And I felt absolutely convinced that these chaps had been learning how to kill silently with their hands, that they'd practised on dummies and hadn't believed it worked, because they were completely relaxed and happy after this incident. It was something I could never tell anybody. It was something so extraordinary. I have no idea what happened to them.

Frederick Serafinski
Polish trainee agent
It was exciting and most interesting from the beginning till the end. We not only had to make tremendous physical efforts but also learn the art of blowing up things, using dynamite and so on, blowing pylons, railway lines, derailing trains, ambushes.

Lieutenant Robert Ferrier
SOE instructor, Scotland
Most of what we taught them on explosives was blowing up railway lines and trains. We took them over to Mallaig, to the terminus there. It was the end of the line from Glasgow via Fort William. By arrangement we were allowed to show the students how to drive a train, how to get underneath it and where to put the explosives if you wanted to blow it up.

Second Lieutenant Peter Lake
Trainee agent
We got to know the engine drivers very well, because they used to see us placing our dummy charges on the line and shout remarks at us as they went by, knowing perfectly well what we were supposed to be doing.

Lieutenant Robert Ferrier
SOE instructor, Scotland
We carried out exercises, gave them a little bit of practice at living off the land. They would be sent off for a couple of days with an objective, a task, to set some dummy explosives, and they would be given some basics: a little bit of sugar, some tea. The rest they had to get themselves. They had to catch some trout out of the river if they could. I think they used to try and steal some lobsters out of the fishermen's lobster pots in the loch. Kill game. They were allowed to kill one sheep by arrangement with a farmer. They had to sleep rough for a night. I think they quite enjoyed that. The trouble there was, if you got good weather it was one of the most beautiful places in the world but generally it is one of the wettest places in the British Isles. You reckoned that if you only got soaked to the skin once a day you were lucky.

Second Lieutenant Joachim Rønneberg
Norwegian trainee agent
Once we had a big scheme up on the railway viaduct just before Inverness. It was a huge viaduct with pillars about forty metres high and eight or nine spans and we were working on the middle of the highest ones, out in the girders. We went there and we didn't know it was guarded at all. We saw some soldiers moving around but they didn't see us and we had a notebook and we had a measure stick and we put in the cut and we did all the detailed drawings to find out how much explosive would we need and so on. And after we had finished we saw that there was a tea house on the other side, so we climbed up on the viaduct and went over and suddenly we were arrested. We were taken in to the commandant and we thought this was rather funny but he did not. He phoned Inverness and asked security people to come immediately: they'd caught two chaps on the bridge; they were in uniforms but had no identity cards and no country marks; they don't speak English very good; and there they were with this wonderful picture of the bridge. So we said, 'Please phone Aviemore number so-and-so and ask for Sergeant Forester,' hoping he should be first on his bike, and he did win the race and we were taken back home and told off.

Birger Rasmussen
Norwegian trainee agent
We made explosives with the correct charges for the big railway-bridge crossing the Firth of Forth, and at night, in pitch darkness, we had to climb down the steel structures placing magnetic charges all over. I remember Colonel Wilson, who was in charge of us, was very nervous, because he was

afraid that some of us would fall down. Trains passed over our heads and down below we could see vessels sailing on the Firth and when the job had been done and we climbed up again, I remember, Wilson was counting us. 'One… two… three… Oh, thank God.' Then we had two or three days' leave, we went to Edinburgh, and then in daylight we had to climb down again and remove the charges and that was much worse than doing it in darkness.

Private Stephen Dale
German Jewish trainee agent
At the end of the four weeks, during which time we only saw the sun on one occasion and it virtually never stopped raining, I'd really got to love Scotland, even the porridge, even with salt instead of sugar. The whole atmosphere, the whole country, was great.

Second Lieutenant Joachim Rønneberg
Norwegian trainee agent
We had a great time up there. We felt very much at home because the countryside was so similar to Norway. We had stags and hinds running about us, we had salmon in the river and we had great fun.

Ole Lippmann
Danish trainee agent
I think it was the best time of my life, playing all sorts of games, blowing trains, giving the poor people of Scotland a hard time because the trains were never on time because we had sabotaged them and so on. It was a lot of fun and we enjoyed it. It was hard but I have never been in a better physical state.

Second Lieutenant Francis Cammaerts
Trainee agent
The month in Scotland I would regard as being probably the most effective. You came out of it feeling ready for all sorts.

Second Lieutenant Peter Lake
Trainee agent
It gave one considerable confidence. And confidence was I think one of the most important things you could possibly go into any situation with.

Lieutenant Ernest van Maurik
SOE instructor, Scotland
From us they went down to Ringway, to parachute. Some didn't worry about it but at least two or three of them who I knew were worried. That led me to suggest to Jimmy Young that if I were to go down with one of the courses and do the parachute course myself and then come back, I would be able to say, 'There's nothing to it. Don't worry.' And that was agreed and that's what I did. Jimmy Young was forty-two, I think, and rather portly but he was so keen that eventually he came down and parachuted with me. The first day we trained. The second we went up in the plane, an old rattling Whitley, and lay on our bellies and looked through the hole. I had never been in an aeroplane in my life until I did that. I expect a lot of other people hadn't in those days. I spent most of the time sitting, waiting to jump, thinking, 'How the hell did you get into this?'

Private Paul 'Yogi' Mayer
German Jewish trainee agent
Before we jumped a group of twelve Poles went and they were instructed, 'If you see the green light, jump. But when you see the green light for the first time, it's only a check to see whether everything works. Have you understood? So when the green light comes on *you do not jump*.' We jumped then from Whitley bombers, two at a time. You had to swing in the hole and jump and then the next one swung in and so on. And they jumped when the green light went the first time, not understanding what it meant, and they all landed in Manchester.

Captain Oliver Brown
Trainee agent
Unfortunately, when we were there, we did in fact witness a fatal accident. It was a Frenchman. This chap came out and he got a thrown rigging line and just came down like a stone.

Lieutenant Robert Ferrier
Trainee agent
We started off, I think, with a slow stick of six, going out one by one very slowly. And then we eventually got rather faster and I think we ended up by doing a quick stick of something like ten. But what was really rather clever of them was that there were several girls on the course who were going to be parachuted into France, and they always made a girl go out first. So, of course,

it made us quite certain that we would have to go out. We'd have been ashamed not to.

Private Eric Sanders
Austrian Jewish trainee agent
When we went into the plane, the dispatcher, that's the man who would shout you out, or kick you out, had to hook the end of our chute to a metal bar on which it could wander. The point was that when you jumped that pulled your chute open and when it was open it would tear off. He made the joke, I'm sure he made it a thousand times, 'Sometimes I don't connect it properly. You'll notice if I don't.'

I was sitting very near the hole, the glory hole. I think I was the second on my side to jump and 'Yogi' Mayer was sitting a bit further to my left. And I, as I always did, began to sing out of sheer boredom and suddenly 'Yogi' Mayer said, 'I'm not afraid now, but I was afraid all the morning.' That was very honest and I began to think about this and I remember I was trying to think whether I was afraid, trying to be logical about it, and thinking to myself, 'Well, if it doesn't open it'll be so quick you won't even notice.' I had no time to think any further because it was my turn. He shouted, 'Number 1, ready! Number 2, ready!' and the next moment I was out.

I remember I looked round and I was quite flabbergasted to see about forty or fifty, I don't know how many, other people in the air in parachutes, and down below there were some six or seven people with megaphones shouting up 'Number 2, put your knees together!' I quickly went like this. Then after a while I realised that this could not possibly be genuine. This was just a trick to make us feel we were being supervised, because there were so many people in the air how could anyone know who was meant?

Captain Oliver Brown
Trainee agent
The only frightening one was the balloon drop. That absolutely terrified me because I can't stand heights. You don't get any sensation of height in a plane but immediately you go and drop out of a balloon you've got that hawser between the balloon and the ground, you've got a connection between ground and air, and you do get a height. Fortunately Charles Tice was up there in the cabin on that day and he said to me – of course I'd known Charles quite well by this time – 'Off you go Oliver, go when you can.' And I just sat on the edge there and I said, 'Well, for Christ's sake kick me up the arse, Charles, or you'll never get me out.' I'd have been there till today I think.

Birger Rasmussen
Norwegian trainee agent
Jumping from the balloons, we were in sticks of four. I was in stick Number 2 and the first four were all sent to hospital.

Lieutenant George Abbott
Trainee agent
After Scotland, if it was thought necessary, you were sent to some specialist training schools. For instance, there was one just outside Hertford, known as Station 17, which was a school in industrial sabotage. You were taught things that might appear obvious, that it is sometimes more efficient to play havoc in a planning office than blowing up something which might be repaired in a matter of a few hours. You were also taught advanced things in explosives.

Lieutenant Robert Ferrier
Trainee agent
The school in Hertfordshire, the school of industrial sabotage, was extremely professional, very well staffed, and we were taught there to sabotage and blow up much more complicated machinery than we'd dealt with up at Arisaig. Things like turbines and powerhouses, transformers, all kinds of electrical equipment, water turbines. We were taken round various pumping stations and I think we went to a powerhouse, just to see these engines working and be shown where exactly the charges should be placed. This was a very intense, very professional course. After that we went on a rather extraordinary course near Blandford in Dorset, which was the school for home-made explosives. We were taught certain ingredients that you could buy at a chemist's or an agricultural engineers and make up your own explosives, so that if in the field they weren't able to supply you with proper explosives you could in fact make up your own.

Lieutenant Denis Newman
SOE instructor, Brickendonbury sabotage school, Hertfordshire
The main parting demonstration for visiting dignitaries was to have an old car towed down the drive with a suitable length of rope, giving the driver some protection, and then a spigot mortar would be fired by a tripwire. It was a nice avenue of tall trees down the approach to Brickendonbury and these were pretty heavily decorated with bits of old car as a result of these demonstrations of the spigot mortar. It was quite impressive.

Lieutenant Robert Boiteux
Trainee agent
I was told to go to the Severn Tunnel in Bristol and spend the night in there to see how much damage I could do, and I could have done a lot had I been an enemy agent. Then I was sent to Portsmouth, I think, on an exercise to get a job in a factory. I got a job in a factory and I worked there for a week, in an aeroplane building factory, to find out what I could about where the different parts came from. Because, if we found, say, a factory that was making a certain part that was very important to the plane, and we could blow up that factory, then, of course, that would stop the building of the planes for maybe a few weeks or even a few months. The only thing I didn't like about the factory was that I had to get up at five in the morning.

Sergeant Ron Brierley
Trainee agent
There was a place at Henley-on-Thames called Fawley Court, a big house right on the Thames, obviously one of the stately homes that SOE had such a knack of acquiring, and it was the main radio and code school for operators.

Coding is quite a laborious business. Quite obviously you can't send messages in clear, not only would they reveal the point of your transmission but clearly give the enemy exactly what you were talking about and what you were doing, so everything had to go in code. The system under which we trained was basically the commercial Q code, which is the normal system of communication used in radio telecommunication work by ships and sometimes by aircraft, where you use a standardised system of calling. For example, you send out a signal 'QRK IMI' to enquire whether base is receiving you and at what strength. Base would reply, 'QSA 1, 2, 3, 4 or 5,' according to the strength of your signal. That's known as the international Q code and there's a whole series of three-letter combinations of letters, all commencing with Q, which indicate short messages like 'Send faster', 'Send slower', 'I missed that', 'Send me a bit more'.

But the actual message itself had to be coded, and we used a thing called the one-time letter pad. This was a pad on to which one wrote the messages. There were a whole series of five-letter groups of words printed on these pads, quite meaningless groups of five, and you wrote the message underneath the groups of five letters. You then had a silk square, literally printed on silk, where you took the two letters, the letter on the pad and the letter of your message underneath it, you applied them to this silk square, which was a

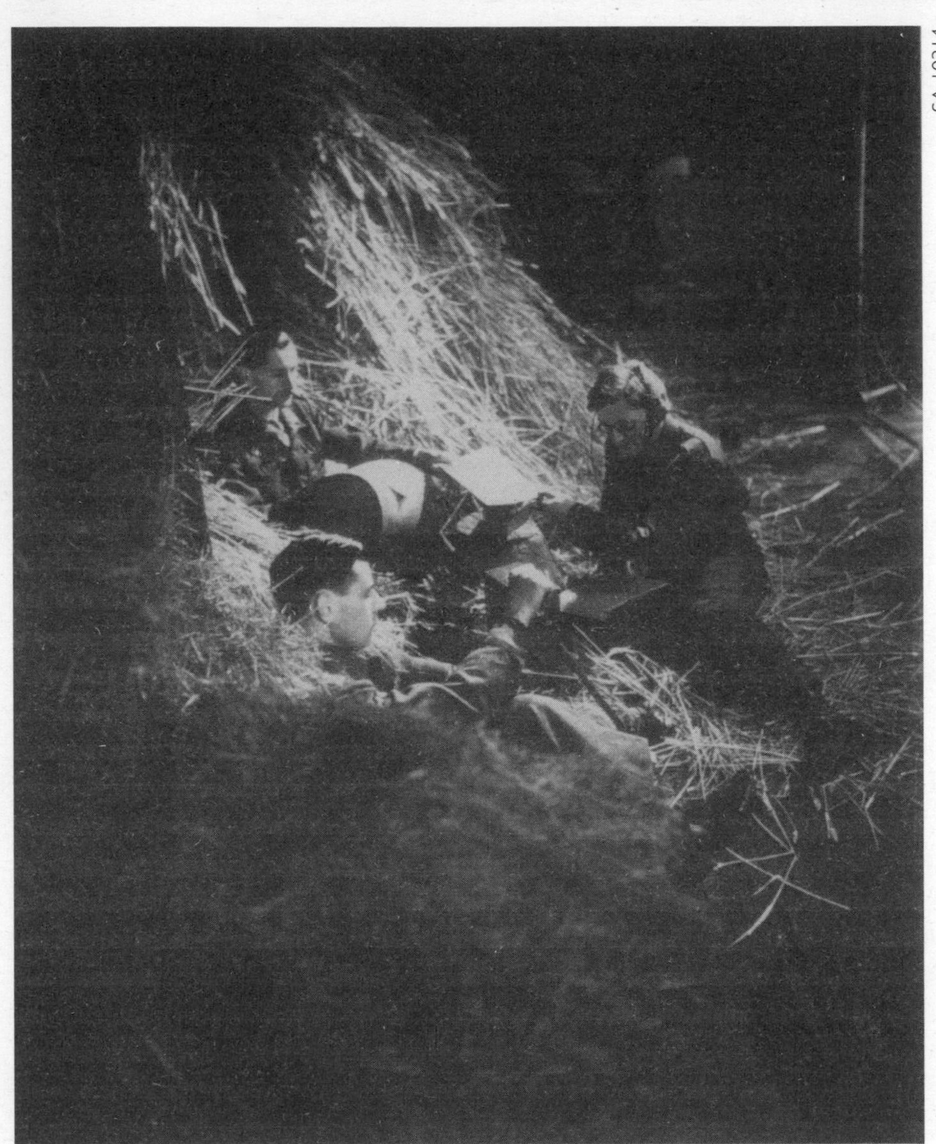

SA 10314

Ron Brierley, in spectacles and headphones, training on a wireless set at Milton Hall, Peterborough.

transposition thing, and you came up with a further letter and that's the letter you transmitted.

The only way you could break that code was by having the confirmatory pad, which was sitting back at one's base in England. It was a foolproof code and incapable of being broken. But it took time to construct one message because you had to write it all out on this one-time pad and take the silk square and transpose it and to get it into blocks of five and one thing and the other. So a comparatively short message could take you half an hour or so to code.

Captain Martin Lam
Trainee agent
We had to be given a poem by which we could transpose texts in case we hadn't got our one-time pads, these of course being the absolutely unbreakable form of cipher. For a poem you had to have twenty-six words and I chose a sonnet of Dante's:
**Tanto gentile e tanto onesta pare*
la donna mia quand'ella altrui saluta,
ch'ogne lingua deven tremando muta,
e li occhi no l'ardiscon di guardare.
The first lines have twenty-six words in them and I used the first letter of each word.

Sergeant Harry Hargreaves
Trainee agent
The poem that I remembered for this purpose was:
It is an ancient Mariner,
And he stoppeth one of three.
'By thy long grey beard and glittering eye,
Now where fore stopp'st thou me?'
I remembered that because, when I was at school, that was what I used for the hundred lines when I was a naughty boy.

*So gentle and so honest appears
my lady when she greets others
that every tongue, trembling, becomes mute,
and eyes dare not look at her.

Captain Henry Threlfall
SOE instructor, Beaulieu finishing school, Hampshire
At Beaulieu, it was our job to instruct parties of potential agents who were sent down to us from the country sections in London. We had parties of French, Belgians, Norwegians, Danes, Dutch; we even had some Spanish. We used to get singles, small or even quite large groups of students down. My particular job was talking to them about the German Army and Nazi Party organisation, how to recognise different types of German troops, how, if they were asked for information about German troops, to be able to give it, the sort of badges they should look for.

Lieutenant Robert Ferrier
Trainee agent
We learnt all the sorts of things that we'd love to have learnt at school. Secret inks. Codes. We had the gamekeeper from the Sandringham estate who taught us how to snare and catch rabbits and things and also what to do if you were burgling a house, what action you could take to try and disguise your scent from a dog. I'm sorry to be crude, but you crap in the corner. I don't know if that's general practice but it was what we were taught.

Odette Brown
Trainee agent
Suzanne and I and one of the Belgians, Molders, went in the dead of night to this house and tried to break in. They'd told us that there was going to be some place left slightly open, so that we could get in without actually breaking a window. Well, she and I had just located it, a window on a landing, when we heard the most unholy row. Molders had wandered off on his own and thought he was being very clever and had found a way in. What he had found was the flap of a coal chute, where the coal was delivered into the basement of the house. Of course, he wasn't familiar with this at all. He lifted up this thing, stepped into it and then, with this awful row, slid down and went straight into the basement, into the coal cellar. Well, of course, that awoke the household, all the lights came on and Suzanne and I just ran away. We disappeared and he was caught.

Second Lieutenant Tony Brooks
Trainee agent
They taught us about passwords and how to have safety signals. If you were passing a chap in the street and he kept his hand in his pocket, that meant,

'Don't talk to me, I think I'm being followed.' Things of that sort which were very important for keeping alive in an occupied country. Safety signals for what we called a letterbox, i.e. a house where you could leave a message, would always be the abnormal. If you had a windowsill with a flowerpot, the flowerpot would be at the side and probably cocked up a bit, so that if the Germans came to the door the person occupying the house would move the thing towards the middle, meaning, 'Don't, for Christ's sake, come in. The Germans are here.'

Odette Brown
Trainee agent
We did all sorts of practical things, like, for instance, learning how to pick locks and get out of handcuffs with a bit of bent wire. We went once to Southampton, once to Bournemouth, to learn how to follow people, how to follow each other. The one thing that floored me completely, and I tried very hard to get out of it but they wouldn't let me, was handling pigeons. We had to learn how to send off a carrier pigeon and put a little message on its foot and so forth. I'm very fond of birds but I can't touch feathers and I couldn't bear the thought of handling a bird with feathers and I kept going to the end of the queue when this man was showing us what to do. Trouble was, he kept spotting me and said, 'I don't think you've been through.' I said, 'Oh, it's all right, I know what to do.' And he said, 'No, no, that's not good enough,' and on two occasions I had to send off this rather fat pigeon.

Lieutenant Robert Boiteux
Trainee agent
There was a lot of stuff I thought was rubbish in the training. For example, they taught us how to bury a parachute. Now, imagine. You jump into France by moonlight, either the Germans or the French police have seen you jump, you're not far from a village. You're not going to spend half an hour digging a hole to bury your parachute. At least I didn't. I just folded mine up and threw it in the bushes. Another thing I thought was rather stupid: we should meet our wireless operator in a café and have an aperitif and he would offer me a cigarette, then give me a matchbox to light my cigarette and in the matchbox was a message. I'd open the matchbox and take out the message. Well, that seemed a bit stupid. All he had to do was to whisper, not even whisper, just talk. 'I've got a message from London. Your next dropping zone has been accepted. Everything's OK.' Nobody's going to hear him say that.

Second Lieutenant Harry Despaigne
Trainee agent
Passing a message in a café was so obviously wrong that we never did it in real life. Passing pieces of paper in newspapers and things like that. These are things you see on TV these days but in real life it doesn't happen that way.

Second Lieutenant Tony Brooks
Trainee agent
About two o'clock in the morning we were woken up by batmen and mess waiters we recognised but dressed as German troops with tin hats on and rifles with bayonets. We were thrown out of bed, told to wrap ourselves up in our blankets and marched out barefoot across the parade ground into the garage where Sturmführer Folliss was wearing his SS uniform. We were told to stand up and were harangued in broken Kraut, which became English, and taken through our training cover stories and I played it straight. I knew that the chap standing beside me was the batman who used to look after us, he provided Alka-Seltzers for us the next morning, and they all looked so stupid in their uniforms, they just didn't fit. Everybody knew it was Folliss but I played the game. This was a very valuable experience. Other people, in fact two on my course, said, 'Oh, Peter, for fuck's sake, let's get back to bed.' And I regret to say neither of those chaps survived. They were both caught and both died. Beaulieu, I think, was the most important part of the training and I took it very seriously. That's why I'm here.

Second Lieutenant Harry Despaigne
Trainee agent
When we were sent on another scheme, into the countryside, a long way away and had to give our addresses to the local police, we were more or less chased up by field security and, if caught, interrogated. And that was a bit more serious because you didn't know you were going on that scheme to be interrogated. You thought you were on that scheme just to use your wireless set and see whether you could make it work.

Private Eric Sanders
Austrian Jewish trainee agent
One day, at Anderson Manor, a man from the War Office turned up. He looked exactly the way a film would have described a man from the War Office: he wore a dark suit and a tie and had a briefcase under his arm. We were all invited into the big hall and all sat down and our commanding officer

told us that the War Office had decided, in view of the fact that if we were caught in enemy territory we had a very good chance of being treated as spies, we should all change our names to English-sounding ones. We were given a form, each of us, and we sat in that hall and had to change our names. And I can tell you something, Erich Ignaz Schwarz is not the prettiest name in the world but it is very difficult to change a name you've been used to all your life. But, by coincidence, my mother, who wrote almost every day, and if you write that often you have nothing else to write about but chit-chat, had written saying one of her nieces had said, 'If you want to change your name to a more English one, how about Sanders?' The man also advised us to stick to the same initials. He said, 'Sometimes, under pressure, you start writing your old name and you sometimes have a chance of remembering in time. It's a small thing but it helps.' So when all but two minutes of the hour had elapsed, I couldn't think of anything else and I wrote 'Eric Ian Sanders'. This name changing had one or two funny consequences. On the Monday I received another letter in which she wrote, 'Oh, by the way, I misspelt it. It was supposed to be Saunders.' And I wrote back, 'Dear Mutti, it's too late, my name is now Eric Sanders.'

Private Stephen Dale
German Jewish trainee agent
I was born Heinz Günther Spanglet. I changed my name to Stephen Patrick Dale. I chose Dale because it was unobtrusive and insignificant.

Private Eric Sanders
Austrian Jewish trainee agent
Helmut Fürst called himself Anderson, after Anderson Manor. Most people did what I had done and chose English-sounding names. Walter Freud refused. He actually said, 'I want the Germans to know that a Freud is coming back.' Sort of, 'It's my pride and I'm sticking to my name.'

Lieutenant John Ross
Trainee agent, Palestine
We were sent up to an establishment called ME102, on Mount Carmel, above Haifa, and that was a wonderful course. There was an awful amount of instruction about the German Army and in sabotage methods. We used to go and blow things up in a local quarry or go down to drive steam engines and learn what part to blow up or lay dummy mines on railway lines around Haifa. It was very good training. We did all kinds of fascinating things, like

learning how to carry limpets, which you swam out and plastered on the outside of ships.

Captain Geoffrey Chandler
Trainee agent, Palestine
I was taught how to drive a steam engine and how to sabotage it. The theory was you got into a marshalling yard, you turned the turntable the wrong way round, you then got into a steam engine and you drove it into the turntable. This is a skill I still haven't exercised, but still look forward to using. And we were taught to use enemy weapons and so on and I still dream of picking up weapons and not having a clue how to fire them.

Captain John Smallwood
Trainee agent, Palestine
I passed out top in demolition, which I always loved. I also made myself immensely unpopular by complaining. I found the instructors on some courses were people who didn't understand anything and certainly didn't know how to treat officers even though they were alleged officers themselves. I took grave exception to this. It was the attitude they had towards you. I expected a certain 'égal' as the French say. As an officer you expect to be treated as an officer, not as a lump of shit. I found some of them totally unspeakable; even Walter Mitty characters. One chap explained how he was the son of a gypsy with whom his father had had intercourse on his country estate – and this was the sort of person who was supposed to be telling us what to do. Even less did I think of the twenty-one-year-old lieutenant colonel, ex-heavy ack-ack, who was in charge and used to come up in the planes with us. He wouldn't jump himself but wrote little notes about our reactions. I found that disgraceful and disgusting. I took exception to the whole ethos there. The actual instruction was good. The demolition instruction was done by NCOs and that was first class.

Signalman Ed Lawson
Trainee agent, Palestine
When we were on Mount Carmel they had this system which was rather clever. You had to strip down to shorts and PE shoes and run over very long and difficult terrain that was more vertical than horizontal. There were a number of checkpoints and at these checkpoints you had a rubber stamp stamped on your back. Consequently you had to go to all the points because, when you got back, your own back was inspected for all the rubber stamps.

Captain Bob Martin
Trainee agent, Palestine
It was the toughest training that I've ever come across. The whole essence was physical fitness from the very beginning. Route marches and field work involved miles of walking. I remember one night they took us on an exercise down by the Dead Sea. Well, if you want heat, go there, and this was summertime. We were given one bottle of water and we had to do an overnight individual march from A to B without being seen and we couldn't use any tracks or roads because they were all patrolled by staff. It really was a tough march. Nobody to talk to, you had to do it on your own, and after about the first ten miles my water bottle was empty. When eventually I did get there, I think I got there about half an hour late but there were others still to come, I couldn't speak. My tongue was swollen; my lips were in a shocking state. That gives you some idea of the rigidity of the training.

Captain John Smallwood
Trainee agent, Palestine
Ramat David was for parachute training. We used to jump before breakfast, before turbulence set in, and after our first jump someone Roman-candled in front of us and landed with a nasty thump. A Roman candle meant that your chute hadn't developed spirally or hadn't developed at all or very exceptionally got equal pressure inside and outside and the thing didn't develop and there was little or no braking effect. We had to go back, have breakfast and then jump again. Morale was very low. We also saw a Polish officer shake out a Roman candle, which is one of the most impressive things I've seen. He shook it out about a hundred feet from the ground and landed safely.

Captain Jim Davies
Trainee agent, Palestine
They were damned good these RAF instructors. I remember when we were doing a training jump from a Hudson, we'd all got our harnesses hitched to the static line, about seven or eight people queuing up, and the corporals at the back were shouting, 'Get on! Hold on! Move! Watch the light!' We got to the door, shuffled, and the sergeant was there in charge. And the chap in front of me, poor bugger, he was very enthusiastic and got his hands on the sides of the door in the approved manner and he gave himself too much of a heave to get out. His pack hit the top of the door, the lintel, and he promptly sat down very fast with a bang, feet outside and his bottom in the doorway, still holding

on and wondering where he was. The sergeant reacted so quickly. He said, 'Get out!' and gave him a hell of a kick and away he went.

Captain John Smallwood
Trainee agent, Palestine
In my plane was one of the Greek Sacred Brigade and he wouldn't jump, he wouldn't jump and he wouldn't jump. They chased him round and tried to push him out – they were very good at pushing you out if you didn't want to go – but he wasn't going so they unhooked him. On the way back he suddenly screamed, 'Long Live Greece!' and jumped out of the plane but he was unattached so it didn't do him any good. He was killed. You are if you jump out at a few hundred feet.

Captain Neville Hogan
Trainee agent, India and Ceylon
I did my parachute training at Rawalpindi, got my wings, then went to Kandy. My gosh, we were roughed up in Kandy. You walked down a track and two instructors would jump out of the jungle and literally beat you up. If you were prepared for them and you put up a good fight, the whistle was blown and they stopped; but if you were caught unawares they'd really give you something to think about.

Lloyd Beresford Chinfen
Trainee agent, India
We were transferred to a place called Poona, south east of Bombay, a very mountainous area, and there our training mainly consisted of firearms training, explosives, unarmed combat, guerrilla tactics and long treks through the mountains with a very, very, very heavy load on our backs. We were always egged on by a captain who had fought on the Afghanistan border and who said if you made a mistake up there, you were dead. He always impressed that on us. 'Don't make any mistakes, you're dead if you do.'

Captain Aubrey Trofimov
Trainee agent, Ceylon
In Ceylon we were given two weeks' intensive jungle training. That was all. There I have to say I have a lot of criticism. We were not told about the conditions of living in the jungle, merely how to get from A to B by cutting through dense jungle and so on. We were given basic advice but we were not told about the diabolical insect life. We were not given enough advice that would have helped us medically.

Corporal Eric Child
Trainee agent, Ceylon
Jungle training in Colombo consisted of drinking gin or whisky in the trees and having monkeys throw coconuts at us.

Sergeant Jack Grinham
Trainee agent, Ceylon
We were supposed to have had three months' jungle training in Ceylon but it never materialised. The first I saw of the jungle was when I dropped into it.

Tools

John Brown
Wireless set designer, The Frythe, Hertfordshire
When I got to The Frythe I remember seeing a huge searchlight parked on the driveway just outside the mess, which I was told was an experimental loudspeaker sonic device to focus high-powered sound energy on the enemy across no-man's-land to drive him mad with supersonic sound. And I remember wondering what kind of madhouse I'd got into, because everything I came across seemed to me to be way-out ideas of the science fiction variety and not very practical.

Sub-Lieutenant Harvey Bennette
Test submariner, The Frythe, Hertfordshire
The Frythe before the war had been a hotel but it was well shielded from the road. Hangars had been built in the grounds and a tank about sixteen feet deep, about twenty feet long and about eight feet wide was built and filled with water. And here they were making two types of submersible craft. One was a thing called a Welman, which was a one-man craft that turned out to be totally useless because, when it was totally surfaced, the slightest wave made it impossible to see where you were going. It had no periscope and it had very limited range from its electric batteries.

The other thing they were making was a bigger craft called the Welfreighter. This was a four-man craft. Two of the men were to be agents or subversives and two were the captain of the craft and a mechanic who were both to be naval personnel. These Welfreighters were being made individually by hand in these sheds in the grounds of this lovely country hotel and they were lifted into the tank and tested and that was one of my jobs.

Welman one-man submarine at The Frythe.

Welman one-man submarine undergoing testing at Laleham Reservoir, Staines.

HU 56752

Wireless set factory.

And when they decided that everything that they had done experimentally was OK they put the task of making them out to a firm at Letchworth in Hertfordshire, which was not very far from Welwyn, a firm that in peacetime made municipal dustcarts.

John Brown
Wireless set designer, The Frythe, Hertfordshire
Captain Rickard brought me a briefcase and said, 'We need some way of communication with people abroad.' This was a large black briefcase with OHMS [On His Majesty's Service] on the front, a typical big civil servant briefcase, and he said, 'Could you put a wireless receiver and transmitter in that, which could operate over a few hundred miles?' This was the first clear idea of what they wanted me to do. I had a quick go at doing this job and then I realised what wonderful backup I had. I was told I could make full use of the people in the workshop, actually the conservatory of The Frythe. There was a very well-equipped workshop there with about half a dozen hand-picked instrument makers and precision mechanics. I found that I could make freehand sketches and they would have the parts made so quickly that very often, from a sketch that I had given them before going to lunch, the finished article would be on my bench by the time I came back from lunch, beautifully made. The kind of priority that any engineer dreams of.

Security was very tight. I remember being told that whatever I needed to know to do my job I would be told, enough and no more, that if I wanted to ask questions of anyone I should address my questions only to my immediate boss. If anyone asked me questions, no matter how familiar that person might be or how well qualified he might be to receive answers, I was to be at least suspicious because if he needed to know he would have been told. We had security people who used to make lunchtime raids or late-night raids into our laboratories, to see that we'd locked up the things we should have locked up. Now this was a near impossibility because you can't have a bench full of equipment and lock it up every night and it's a bit difficult to gather together all your sketches and put them all in a file every night. But there was a lot of security.

Sub-Lieutenant Harvey Bennette
Test submariner, The Frythe, Hertfordshire
You had an awful lot of people there, civilians as well as service people, who were incredibly brainy and they were all working on different aspects of various things. Extraordinary characters, who strutted about with books in

their hands and pencils in their pockets and wouldn't talk to you, all with their funny ideas about how things should be done.

Joyce Couper

Technician, The Thatched Barn, Hertfordshire

I was sent to The Thatched Barn on Barnet bypass. It was the most beautiful place with a swimming pool and everything. It was gorgeous. And we were confronted with wooden boxes, all nailed up, and given rolls of hessian and we had to wrap these wooden boxes in the hessian and nail them down all the way round and nail a label on them and pass them on. Of course I wondered what on earth I'd come into, doing this. We all had a grumble but we all got on with it and about a fortnight after that we were moved on to some very much more interesting things.

Jack Knock

Technician, The Thatched Barn, Hertfordshire

Everything was so meticulously done. Everything was so clean. The laboratory parts and the parts you used were absolutely scrupulously clean. You just did not take a chance. There was no concrete dust. Linoleum, half-inch cork liner, which you couldn't get in England, was used for our laboratories. Somehow we got it. So if anything dropped there was this softness.

We used to wear a suit, not of denim but of canvas. There were no buttons. Everything was done up with tapes. You didn't have metal buttons. No buttons anywhere. For shoes you wore shapeless felt bootees and you had a hat over your hair, a white hat, to stop any static electricity and you were careful where you took that off. I mean you didn't do a day's work and then just take it off where you were. You went to be cleaned up. A chap would brush you about with a dampish cloth. Great care had to be taken by everybody. You didn't go to work with a headache and think, 'Oh Christ, another one of these.' You sort of told yourself, 'Now come on son. Let's really be on the ball. Let's not blow our bloody hands off.'

Captain Peter Lee

Security Section officer, SOE HQ, London

They used to develop all sorts of nasty things that used to go bump in the night. For instance, this little motor scooter, the Welbike, a collapsible motor bike: the whole thing folded up and went into a parachute container and we used to drop it down to agents. Triangular nails which agents who were trying to escape from the Gestapo used to chuck out of the window of their cars and

HU 56740

Welbike fitted with a generator for charging the batteries of a wireless set.

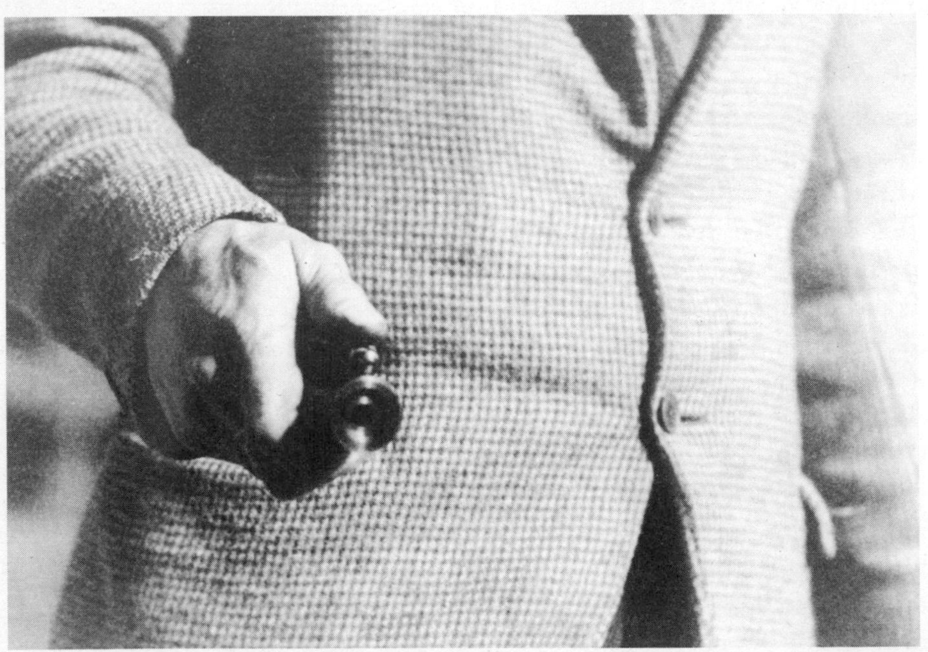

HU 56777

'Sleeve gun' developed for close-quarter assassinations.

puncture tyres as they went along. And explosive turds were really very exciting. Lumps of manure which blew up when you ran over them. They were wonderful.

Marjorie Hindley
Technician, The Thatched Barn, Hertfordshire
This horse had been sent for us to do a sample of its dung. We had other words but I'm not going to go into that. Three of us went down and collected it. Bare hands, no aprons, nothing. I was in my uniform, looking at this and wondering what the so-and-so we were going to do with it. I just couldn't believe that this was something we had to work with.

Jack Knock
Technician, The Thatched Barn, Hertfordshire
The horse dung would be allowed to dry or if it hadn't dried it would be helped along in a kiln until it was dry dust. Then we'd blow the dried horse manure on to the plaster cast until it looked like horse manure again. It was a very good imitation. It could take in anybody at a distance or even close to, except that the smell wouldn't be so bad, I suppose. We hadn't got round to producing the smell. They would just place these things in the middle of a road and something would go over them and would blow itself to bits.

May Shrubb
Technician, The Thatched Barn, Hertfordshire
Everything had to look authentic, no matter what you done. If a jacket came in pretty newish-looking you'd rough up the leather ends on the elbows, make them look old. Everything had to look old. If there was a man going out dressed as a bargee his clothes had to look like a bargee's clothes. It was no good putting him in a three-piece pinstripe suit. So we had to rub it down or do darns, make a hole and tear it all about and darn it roughly, so it would look old. Things like that.

Jack Knock
Technician, The Thatched Barn, Hertfordshire
We would be told what rocks there were in a locality, so you had your tinsmiths produce a tin rock, which we again smothered in glue, we used countless gallons of glue, and peppered with the rock of the locality. In the end you would finish off with a rock filled with everything: rifles, ammunition, revolvers, explosive this and explosive that, incendiary this and

incendiary that. And we used to pack these very carefully and we used to put them on the shaker, a machine that shook, and you used to stand around it and listen. If you could hear a rattle of any description you used to have to take it all out again and sort of repack it. We even went as far as that, to listen for rattles, to put it on a damned rattling machine. Now this will give you some idea of how religiously we took the job.

May Shrubb
Technician, The Thatched Barn, Hertfordshire
The first job I had was making tyre-busters. I think we must have done hundreds. A tyre-buster was three pieces of canvas, made like an envelope, and you had to keep stitching round. A detonator was put inside. They went to the art department to be coloured. Then they went to the dirtying shop to be dirtied, made to look like real stones. You would never pick them out. They just looked like stones. Pebbles.

Joyce Couper
Technician, The Thatched Barn, Hertfordshire
We used to do little silk maps to go inside handbags, between the lining and the bag, and to roll up and put inside fountain pens.

May Shrubb
Technician, The Thatched Barn, Hertfordshire
Jelly feet, we put the straps on them. Shoes of natives' feet. Imprints. They made them in the plaster shop of latex. The agents would strap them on their shoes so they looked like natives. That was for the Far East.

Joyce Couper
Technician, The Thatched Barn, Hertfordshire
They got dead mice and they scooped the insides out and sent the skins over to us. Rats the same. We used to have to fill them with plastic explosive and fasten them up again and those went out. That put the girls off and they let the men do that. It was pretty messy handling dead rats and mice.

Jack Knock
Technician, The Thatched Barn, Hertfordshire
French children or French men used to take the bicycle pumps off Germans' bicycles, because the Germans were great ones for using bicycles at one time, and then they would replace this pump that they had stolen with one we'd

made to the exact specification. They would let the German's tyre down, one tyre or two tyres, the German would come along, take his pump and the first pump he gave of course he would blow his hands off. It's an awfully dirty trick if you think of it. The same applied with the Germans' torches. You would remove the German's torch and put yours back in its place and the poor sod would again lose his hands when he switched it on.

You had a material that you put inside soap that would explode with contact with water. They could wash their hands a dozen times and nothing would happen but they washed their hands the next time and a piece would be exposed to the air and water and explode.

Some of the things we did could be termed atrocities. They couldn't be termed warfare – not blowing up people with torches. I didn't lose very much sleep about it but to my mind we were maiming people, we were taking away their hands or their arms, their means of sustenance. Quite honestly this sort thing was in my mind in those days. It was a hurdle to get over and one that I still remember. I still remember being in this shed, doing these jobs that I was doing, and knowing what was likely to happen as a result and not quite liking it.

Marjorie Hindley
Technician, The Thatched Barn, Hertfordshire
The whole reason for us being there was to be creative and to protect the people who were doing the awful stuff, trying to get at the enemy.

John Brown
Wireless set designer, The Frythe, Hertfordshire
Everybody worked all the time and there was no other subject but the problem at hand. I felt uplifted and motivated by keeping company with so many talented people. There was an atmosphere generated mutually between people that sort of drove the whole engine at full speed all the time.

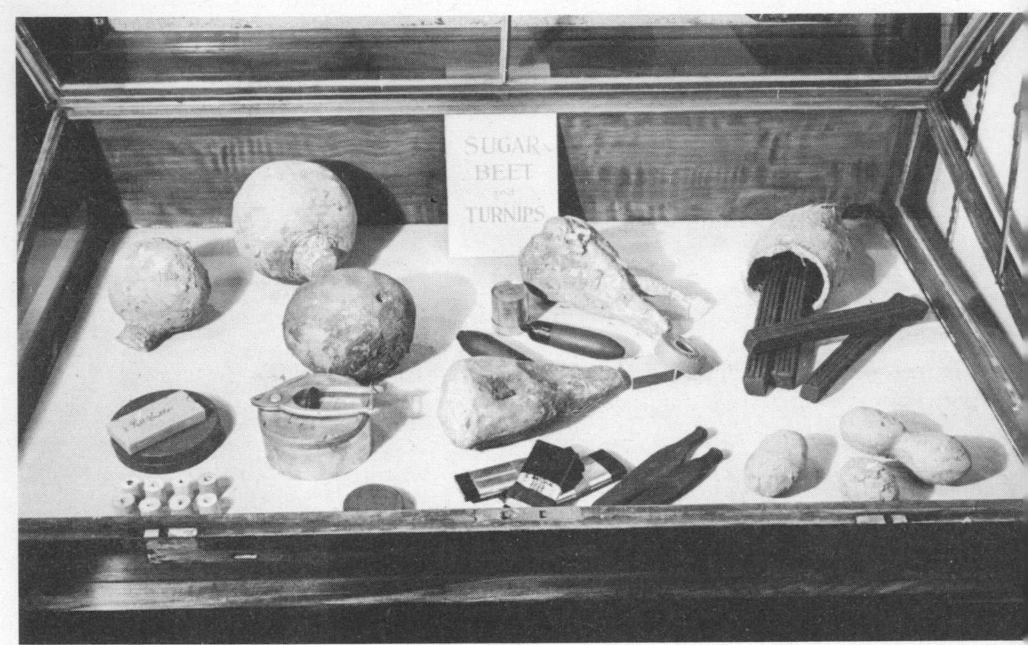

Fake vegetables concealing ammunition and other items.

Into the Fray

We heard the dispatcher screaming over the intercom,
'All the four "joes" are hit and the aircraft is riddled with holes!'

Getting agents and supplies into the field was a dangerous and difficult business. Sometimes shipping them in by sea to secluded entry points was possible. Occasionally submarines were used but few were ever available. From time to time, SOE set up its own small-boat, para-naval units: one, based in the Helford River in Cornwall, ran secret sorties to the French coast; another, the Small Scale Raiding Force, also active across the Channel, launched pinprick attacks and reconnoitred beaches.

Most agents, though, together with thousands of containers of stores, were delivered by air. Burdened with other commitments and reluctant to divert resources, the Air Ministry released aircraft and crews only slowly, but in time whole squadrons were assigned to 'Special Duties'. Early operations into Europe were flown mostly from England; bases in North Africa and Southern Italy were used, too, later in the war, while missions bound for the Far East would drop in mostly from India. Small Lysanders and twin-engined Hudsons proved effective for covert, short-distance pick-ups and landings but the majority of aircraft employed were bombers, like Halifaxes and Liberators, modified to make parachute drops. It was hazardous work and losses were high.

THE HELFORD FLOTILLA

Lieutenant Commander Gerry Holdsworth
SOE Naval Section, commander of the Helford Flotilla

I could get from Helford over to the Breton coast, let us say, by midnight, leaving our side about five-thirty in the afternoon, spend an hour ashore meeting my friends and delivering whatever it was, dynamite and things of that sort, stores, possibly collecting one or two people. And possibly after they'd been in England a fortnight, three weeks, perhaps received some SOE training, they might return to me and at the first opportunity I'd take them over again.

I didn't take much of a crew with me, a total of five of us. My second-in-command was Brooks Richards. First of all the crews needed to be good sailors and secondly it was essential that they be volunteers. Although it was not to be revealed to them what the complete object of the exercise was, it was very important that they should know that they would be in serious trouble if they came unstuck, either by the enemy or, indeed, if they were insecure, by our own side.

Sub-Lieutenant Robin Richards
SOE Naval Section

Gerry Holdsworth was a buccaneer, a strong character. He had been in the precursor organisation of SOE. Although he was in naval uniform and had a naval rank he was very informal in his methods, in the sense that if he wanted something he would use any method that he could to accomplish it. For example, the first contact operations on the north coast of France were carried out by Gerry and my brother, Brooks, in a thirty-six-foot seaplane tender they had scrounged from somewhere. It was very slow, did about fifteen knots at best and was armed with a tommy gun.

It was all very makeshift and Gerry gathered round him a number of what you could call quite rough characters. For example, there were a lot of seamen who had escaped from the Channel Islands and been recruited into the small craft personnel base at Lowestoft, people who were manning minesweepers and so on. One of the larger-than-life characters at Helford was a chap called John Newton, a red-headed Channel Islander, who had been, I think, a sort of amateur pirate before the war. Anyway he certainly made a living by smuggling. If you wanted something you simply said to him, 'What about a so-and-so?' and he would say, 'Leave it me,' and he'd find it. He'd knock it off.

I was involved in one of the 'Lardering' operations. The intention was to build up stores or warlike arms in sealed camouflaged containers on the north coast of Brittany. The operation that I was responsible for, I think it was known as 'Carpenter', involved two dories towing inflatable boats loaded with about a ton of these containers with arms, explosives and so on. We started from Dartmouth in a Fairmile gunboat. The gunboat dropped anchor, we landed our stores on one of the islets, tried to bury them, found there was no soil and simply had to camouflage them as best we could with seaweed and

HU 66772

Gerry Holdsworth, commander of the Helford Flotilla.

branches, got barked at by a dog, and by the mercy of providence managed to find our way back to our gunboat.

Lieutenant Brooks Richards
SOE Naval Section

We were a good deal occupied by how to give ourselves a little protection against machine-gunning if we were caught in the area where we had no business to be as fishermen. The only thing available to put round the wheelhouse was concrete. Well, of course, if you had concrete bolted on, slabs of concrete, it no longer looked like a fishing boat, so I wanted to get hold of non-magnetic armour. Non-magnetic because the only compass on the boat was right in the wheelhouse roof and if you put a lot of extra steel underneath it you made the compensating of the compass really very difficult. So I wanted non-magnetic armour and they said, 'Oh, far too expensive. That'd cost about £600.' However, a couple of well-bestowed bottles of whisky on the petty officer in charge of the naval side of dockyard repairs at Falmouth got us some non-magnetic armour put in place.

Well, we were barely twenty miles off the Scillies when we were due to be picked up by a British Beaufighter at the limit of the fishing area that boats from Newlyn used. At the right time an aircraft appeared and came in towards us, we fired the recognition signal but instead of firing the recognition signal back, as was expected, we were strafed from end to end by 20-millimetre cannon. It was in fact a German Focke-Wulf, which end-on looks very like a Beaufighter, and he came round and gave us a second dose. Fortunately, Gerry and I were able to take shelter behind the wheelhouse armour and consequently we were perfectly all right. One chap on deck was killed. He didn't die immediately but he was dead by the time we got into the Scillies. John Newton was outstandingly good in the prevailing bad weather in dealing with this dying man on the foredeck, staying up there, with the water breaking over them, right until we got back.

The Small-Scale Raiding Force

Lieutenant Brooks Richards
SOE Naval Section

A second SOE para-naval outfit in the English Channel was run by Gus March-Phillipps, one of the early small-scale raiding experts that we had. He'd set up a small-scale raiding group of his own, under SOE auspices, with a

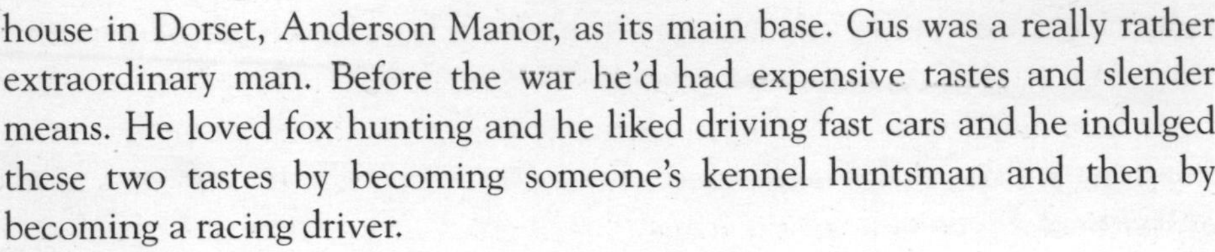

house in Dorset, Anderson Manor, as its main base. Gus was a really rather extraordinary man. Before the war he'd had expensive tastes and slender means. He loved fox hunting and he liked driving fast cars and he indulged these two tastes by becoming someone's kennel huntsman and then by becoming a racing driver.

Lieutenant Freddie Bourne
Coastal Forces, attached to the Small-Scale Raiding Force

I was dealing with the specialist force under Major March-Phillipps and a chap called Geoffrey Appleyard. March-Phillipps had all the dash and flair and the outward signs of a commando. Appleyard was much more of a thinker; I won't say he was the brains of the operation, but he gave a great deal more detailed thought to what we were going to do and planned it, whereas March-Phillipps set up the inception of the scheme. Then there was Graham Hayes and three or four others of like ilk, plus a couple of sergeants and the usual ordinary ranks, all well trained. All had been doing commando work anyway.

I was the naval link for them. I was their only means of getting to where they wanted to go. My boat was sort of attached to them. I was fully serviced by the navy, of course, at my Portsmouth base, but any operations were done through Appleyard and March-Phillipps and myself. I went out to Bere Regis and would be briefed out there as to what we were going to do, how we were going to deal with it and what my role was going to be. I came back, got the boat ready. That meant fuelling up, arming the boat, necessary anchors and things like that, and they'd arrive, say, at dusk – we had to choose the time of the month when the moon was at the right quarter or sequence – and we'd set off.

I was always alone. We were only a small boat. My crew consisted of about eight chaps and a dozen commandos. We'd get close and idle down in silent engines or reduce speed to a much quieter level, then anchor the boat, what, a quarter or half a mile off the rocks, anchor down and launch the dory and the commandos would push ashore. I'd keep bearings to see that we were not drifting, so that they could come back, because they'd come back on a reciprocal course, and eventually, an hour, two hours later, they'd come back with whatever information they'd gleaned or whatever captives they'd got. And all being well we'd embark them, put the dory back on board and sail back to Portsmouth, with the Germans hopefully none the wiser at that stage. Didn't always work out like that.

March-Phillipps, apart from his usual armoury of pistols and machine gun, commando knife, etc, always carried what appeared to be a very long cook's knife, a big carving knife, about eighteen inches long. He carried it down his trouser leg. And once, before we set sail, I was somewhat surprised to see one of the commando officers carrying what appeared to be a violin case or something similar. All was revealed when we went to sea. It was, in fact, a very particular type of bow and arrows. I thought, 'We've really gone back to the Stone Age now,' but in fact there was method in this, the reason being of course that it was a swift, silent killer. This particular officer was an expert marksman and it was in fact used. On getting ashore they came across a sentry who'd got a dog with him and they were both of them fairly quickly dispatched with the aid of the bow and arrows.

We did one raid off Port-en-Bassin and March-Phillipps was in command with Appleyard. It was right down in the bay south of Cherbourg. I don't know what they were after on this because it seemed to me a slightly odd place to go. Normally they would go for a rocky area and work their way up to wherever they wanted to get to, a village or something, whereas this was a flat, sandy beach. We anchored offshore about a quarter of a mile and they paddled the dory ashore. I was in the torpedo boat and so was Appleyard. Unfortunately, at that very moment when the dory was going to land, just coming into the surf, a German patrol came along the beach. Our party was challenged and the Germans opened fire at our people as they were just getting out of their boat. The fire was returned. We got nobody back. Most of them were killed, including March-Phillipps. We had to cut the anchor to get away. A bullet went through one of our engines, so that reduced us very badly, and we turned and made out towards the sea. One or two chaps tried to swim out, we heard them in the water, but they were too far off for us to do anything and by that time we'd got a searchlight on us and we couldn't rescue them. Later on we understood that they captured two or three of them alive. One was Captain Hayes and he was finally executed.

The Special Duties Squadrons

Major Peter Wilkinson
Staff officer, Polish–Czech Section, SOE HQ, London
We were delighted, early in 1941, when we were allotted a small number of Halifax aircraft. Any aircraft dealing with these particular operations, of course, had to be adapted for the purpose and when we got into modern aircraft like the Halifax it obviously became a clash of priorities between Bomber Command and special operations.

Major Douglas Dodds-Parker
Staff officer, Operations Section, SOE HQ, London
Portal [Chief of the Air Staff] and Harris [Commander-in-Chief, Bomber Command] had their viewpoint that every plane taken off bombing was one wasted. But I think it was shown, as time went on, that by helping Bomber Command, by putting, for instance, Rebecca, which was a guided beacon, into the field, we could often give them more accurate bombing targets. Also, of course, in my opinion, by sabotaging a lot of the targets they were after, we could do a better job and do less damage to our friends in occupied territory.

Major Dick Barry
Staff officer, Operations Section, SOE HQ, London
The Belgian section wanted a couple of chaps dumped here. The French section wanted umpteen chaps all over the place. The Norwegians worked by ship almost entirely. The Danes wanted someone. The Dutch wanted someone. You got a great list of operations and you scheduled those in order of priority and then had a daily conference with the RAF. As the thing developed, people were taking with them not just their wireless sets but a container load of, oh, all sorts of things – usually it was when circuits had got more or less established – arms, explosives, money, cigarettes, chocolates, all sorts of goodies. We had a standard equipment load, which the section concerned would order, as it were, and a packing station. So you would get an operation set up, which contained, let us say, a chap who might be an organiser, a wireless man and perhaps some other body, plus two containers' worth of equipment. And that was your operation. One was very busy and your life was entirely governed by the moon. During a moon period, when these aeroplanes were leaving, then you were very busy and you were probably up practically all night, two or three times a week. But then you had the slightly calmer period, in the dark half of the moon, when life became slightly more normal.

Odette Brown
FANY secretary, French Section, SOE HQ, London
The moon was something quite special. We were so used to keeping our work secret that if anybody outside SOE said, 'Oh, look, there's a lovely full moon,' or something, you thought, 'What do they know about the moon?' You got all suspicious. We were young but nevertheless the moon and moonlight had no romantic connotations for us at all. All it meant was pilots risking their lives and agents going out to reception committees and being in danger.

HU 60542

Pilots of 161 (Special Duties) Squadron, RAF, standing in the garden of Tangmere Cottage, Sussex. Squadron Leader Hugh Verity is second from left.

Squadron Leader Hugh Verity
Lysander pilot, 161 (SD) Squadron, RAF
When I was intruder controller in Headquarters Fighter Command, I could see plots of all the aircraft going across the Channel in both directions during the night and sometimes there were single aircraft on their own called 'specials'. I never had to inquire what they were doing but the senior air traffic control officer from Tangmere came to visit me one night and he told me that these 'specials' were black Lysanders that were going to land in France by moonlight.

This was the first I knew of this special type of operation and I thought that I would like to get involved in it, so I volunteered to join a Special Duties squadron at Tempsford, 161 Squadron. Every moon period, that's to say one week before and one week after full moon, all the Lysanders and their ground crews were detached from the main squadron to be based at Tangmere, on the south coast, because that was well on the way to our target areas in France. We had a very independent little show going there, with our quarters in Tangmere Cottage just on the other side of the road from the main RAF station. It was a discreet hidey-hole where agents could be brought without too many people seeing them arrive.

Barbara Bertram
Safe house hostess, Sussex
We were a little over ten miles from Tangmere aerodrome. Nothing would happen until my husband or the other conducting officers rang up to say they were coming, and as soon as I heard they were coming I had to arrange the beds to fit the number of people and do all I could about dinner. They would arrive about the middle of the afternoon and we would give them a cup of tea. Then they went up and had their final instructions and they were given a false identity card, false ration cards, lots of money and a revolver. While they were being given their revolvers and things the drivers and I would go through their luggage, looking at anything they'd bought in England to see if that was marked 'Made in England'. Hats, you had to confiscate, because they were stamped on the leather band inside. Gloves, you ripped off the snapper. Shirts and pyjamas and things, you rubbed very, very hard with Milton and either it rubbed the label out or it rubbed a hole in the shirt. Once I came across a beautiful pair of pink pyjamas and I was just starting on the Milton when the owner rushed at me and said, 'Don't dare do that. I bought those in Paris before the war.' He took them as they were. Some of them asked me to sew their poison capsule into their cuff, because they thought they wouldn't be able to withstand torture. I hated that job.

HU 59359

Westland Lysander of 161 (Special Duties) Squadron, RAF, on the ground at Tempsford, Bedfordshire. This aircraft was flown by Squadron Leader Hugh Verity on twenty missions to occupied France in 1943.

Squadron Leader Hugh Verity
Lysander pilot, 161 (SD) Squadron, RAF
We had the agents in the rear cockpit, facing aft, facing the tail, and they were equipped with microphones so that they could speak to the pilot and we asked them to let us know if they could see any night-fighters coming along behind. Sometimes the agents were too chatty. The pilot had to think what he was doing with his navigation and so on and had to switch off the intercom in order to have a little time to think. But most of the agents were no problem at all.

It was only natural, particularly just before take-off, going to France, that some of them would be a little over-excited or they would be unnaturally quiet. But their demeanour when they were picked up in France and were brought back to Tangmere for a night-flying breakfast, maybe with champagne, this was something else again, because they were so overjoyed to be free of the constant tension and fear of living in the clandestine world in France and bubbling over with stories about all their exciting activities. They really were quite exhilarating to be with when they'd just arrived in England.

Barbara Bertram
Safe house hostess, Sussex
When they came back, they generally arrived at our house at about half-past four in the morning, something like that, and we'd have to feed them and for some reason it got called 'reception pie'. I suppose once we'd had a pie of some sort. After that it was always 'reception pie'. People who'd never been to the house before would arrive at half-past four in the morning and their first remark would be, 'What have we got for reception pie?'

One night two of our pilots were killed. That was the worst night of all. I waited and waited and waited. Three planes went out. The second plane crashed at Tangmere because unexpectedly the fog had come right down to ground level. The pilot was killed but the passengers weren't. The third plane was sent off to Ford, quite near Tangmere, where there was a landing ground, and it crashed killing the pilot and the two passengers. Nobody rang me up that night till about seven and then I could hear from my husband's voice that something awful had happened. He simply rang up and said, 'Coming with two,' and that was all there were. We had 'reception pie' in awful silence and then at last I got him alone and was able to ask what had happened.

Wing Commander Thomas Charles Murray
Stirling pilot, 138 (SD) Squadron, RAF
I was offered the command of 138 Squadron, which was one of the Tempsford

cloak-and-dagger squadrons. Station 61, where some agents were trained, was fairly close to Tempsford and it had been the tradition when I arrived to have parties over there, and I went to one or two, but I'm afraid I put a stop to that – one of the first things I did. I reckoned it was a security risk. I knew that if I'd been shot down and they were twisting my goolies or doing whatever they were going to do, I couldn't rely on myself not to spill the beans. So, the less you knew, the greater the security. It was good for morale to meet them but completely unnecessary and, I think, a dangerous break of security, because you can't expect people not to give in under torture.

Pilot Officer John Charrot
Halifax observer/bomb-aimer, 138 (SD) Squadron, RAF
You would be put on a board saying that your crew was operating that night and so you would then get yourself ready. The captain, the skipper, would call you together and say, 'Right. We're doing an NFT – Night Flying Test – at two o'clock in the afternoon,' or whatever, and you would go up and do an hour round the aerodrome, circling, testing everything. The gunners would test their guns. And then you would land and have your meal and then assemble about an hour, an hour-and-a-half, before take-off in the crew room and then get taken out to your aircraft. Very different from Bomber Command because if a bomber squadron was going out there'd be twelve aircraft probably, all lined up. They had to go one after the other, together, and probably fly in some sort of formation to begin with, whereas we didn't. We were single aircraft going off at different times to different parts. Some might be going to Belgium, some to France; some might be going into Norway. So it was a much more individual sort of briefing and take-off than a normal squadron.

Flying Officer Peter Nettleton
Halifax rear-gunner, 138 (SD) Squadron, RAF
Five or ten minutes before we were due to take off, a large car, normally with drawn curtains, would drive up and the agents would get out. Mainly men but not exclusively so. We would then shake hands with them and that would be that.

Pilot Officer John Charrot
Halifax observer/bomb-aimer, 138 (SD) Squadron, RAF
We only operated about fourteen to sixteen nights in a month, as the moon was really essential, particularly for me, because you had no other lights in Europe at all. But if there was a moon you could pick up the rivers and

particularly the lakes and the forests. I mean, this business that I learnt at navigation school – dead reckoning and keeping a log of every twist and turn – was hopeless on this job. You really just had to watch the ground. We were flying, what, three hundred and fifty, four hundred feet? That's all. Having climbed up to six thousand to cross the coast in order to avoid the flak we would then drop down very low. Of course, it's very difficult going at a lower height because everything's going past so quickly, but it was the only way to do it really.

Closing in on the dropping ground, first of all there would be no lights there. They would wait till they heard the aircraft noise. So if you thought you were pretty near you would do perhaps a circle or maybe two circles at about five hundred feet. Then the first light would come on and it would flash a recognition signal that we knew of and they would know the return that our wireless operator would send from a hand-held lamp. Having established that, they would then get their other torch-men, as they called them, lined up, going across to tell us the wind direction – we had to go upwind – and when they were all set we would come down, if it was containers, to about two hundred and fifty feet. It was my responsibility to get the containers on the lights, so that they could quickly deal with them.

By this time I was in the nose of the aircraft all the time, telling him 'left, right, steady, steady' and the skipper would be calling out the height so that I knew that he was at the right height, because I had no idea of that where I was. And then, when it was all set, it was a question of red button first and then the green and off you go. The skipper used to slow the aircraft down by putting wheels down and maybe some flap, so that you were going much slower but not stalling, hopefully, because that would be it. And then as soon as I said, 'They're all gone,' then up with the flaps and up with the wheels and then we would just turn round and make our way home as quickly as we could, but still keeping low.

Squadron Leader Frank Griffiths
Halifax pilot, 138 (SD) Squadron, RAF

Six hundred feet was all right for a professional parachutist. He could disentangle himself if there was a foul line or something. But when you're dealing with a man who's only had, say, a fortnight's training, you want to give him eight hundred feet to sort himself out in case there's a thrown line over the canopy or something like that. Also the higher you dropped them the more inaccurate the landing.

Pilot Officer John Charrot
Halifax observer/bomb-aimer, 138 (SD) Squadron, RAF
We had a chute you could use as a toilet, a little chute, and we had these bundles of leaflets. It was usually the rear-gunner's job or the wireless operator's, they would tear the string off them and push them down this chute and they would float away. The pigeons we were much more careful about. They had their own little parachute, they were in a little cage made of cardboard and they had food and some water in there, and we used to try and find a nice quiet spot for these so that they would be all right. We would drop them and watch them go down and sometimes quite useful information came back, I gather. We didn't see that of course. But there'd be a little pencil in this cage and a piece of rice paper and they were supposed to get hold of these pigeons, you see, write a message and put it round their legs and send them back.

Squadron Leader Frank Griffiths
Halifax pilot, 138 (SD) Squadron, RAF
Sometimes you'd get terribly rude answers: the messages were from the Germans; they'd found them. Some, I'm jolly certain, got eaten in places where food was short.

Flying Officer Reginald Lewis
Halifax observer/bomb-aimer, 138 (SD) Squadron, RAF
My trips from Tempsford involved going down to the south of France, a couple of trips to Norway and one into Germany itself. That one always surprised me, because we had an agent dressed up in German uniform.

Wing Commander Ken Batchelor
Halifax pilot, 138 (SD) Squadron, RAF
I did a drop in Denmark where we bundled out not only the agents but a whole load of bicycles.

Flying Officer Reginald Lewis
Halifax observer/bomb-aimer, 138 (SD) Squadron, RAF
The squadron was operating as far as Poland and that was quite a long flight in wartime conditions. From the UK up to somewhere like Warsaw was something like fifteen hours, between twelve and fifteen hours. Apart from the danger of the flight itself it was almost at the complete endurance of a Halifax. They just couldn't hold any more octane. And a number of crews were lost, particularly over the Baltic, to night-fighter attacks.

Handley Page Halifax of 138 (Special Duties) Squadron, RAF, resting on its nose at Tempsford, Bedfordshire, having burst a tyre on landing and swung off the runway.

Sergeant Alen Neville Dent
Halifax flight engineer, 138 (SD) Squadron, RAF
We went two trips to Poland and the aircraft was virtually a flying petrol tank. The whole of the fuselage was taken up with tanks containing petrol. I had to keep a log of height, speed, direction and all that sort of business, petrol consumption. Flying across Denmark you would be flying below sea level and the altimeter would be reading nought. That was a lovely line shoot: that we were flying at nought feet.

Squadron Leader Frank Griffiths
Halifax pilot, 138 (SD) Squadron, RAF
Polish crews came in and they used to do the Polish work with us and they were marvellously aggressive. I sometimes questioned my own aggression after I had the Poles. They would go as briefed: fly across the Skagerrak, the tip of Sweden, to Bornholm island. Then in Poland they would navigate by the POW camps, because, in line with the Geneva Convention, they had to have their lights on, and they'd do their drops, as far as east of the Vistula, which was a long way to go, and come back. Now the British would come back the proper way, as briefed, but you'd be very surprised to come back and find that the Poles were about an hour ahead of you, because they'd come back through the middle of Germany, and they never had a bullet left. Having got rid of the packages to be dropped or the men, they would go on a shoot-up in Germany. And, of course, in many places the aircraft got hit and then we had to repair them. They were hard to discipline, they were difficult and yet you couldn't help but admire them. You'd have to say, 'Look, we want this aeroplane back tomorrow in good condition.' They would smile and you'd assume they'd listened, they'd understood, but they'd go off and do it again. But they were magnificent chaps. There was no turning back with the Poles.

Wing Commander Ken Batchelor
Halifax pilot, 138 (SD) Squadron, RAF
People were attacked, intercepted, here and there. I did a dog-leg to avoid the German airfield near Caen and of course flew right over the bloody airfield and we were at nought feet. It was very interesting over the housetops with the tracer bullets horizontal over and under your wings.

Pilot Officer John Charrot
Halifax observer/bomb-aimer, 138 (SD) Squadron, RAF
We were coming back, our usual route, close to Cherbourg. There was a bunch

of rocks there and if we were over those we knew we were on track. And this particular night we were heading for those and I said something about the rocks coming up and Griff suddenly screamed over the intercom, 'Terry! Port wing, quick!' He had seen an E-boat wallowing in the water, not moving, quite stationary, and he'd recognised it straight away that it wasn't a rock. They opened up and Terry opened up from the rear turret at the same time and I think we won the battle fairly quickly, fortunately. We just got away. After we'd survived this, Griff said, 'I think they're probably waiting for the navy, because the navy used to do the picking up and dropping of agents as well, on the Brittany coast.

Wing Commander Thomas Charles Murray
Stirling pilot, 138 (SD) Squadron, RAF
We were losing a lot of casualties over Denmark and, after a short time, I expressly forbade anyone to fly there above four hundred feet. Immediately our casualties went down to almost zero. I was rather proud of that. They'd intercept us with a Focke-Wulf 190, they used to dive down and try to come up underneath us, and the damned things used to fly into the ground because we were so low. In the end we felt pretty well immune from them.

Pilot Officer John Charrot
Halifax observer/bomb-aimer, 138 (SD) Squadron, RAF
In France they had these trains which were usually carrying troops probably but you couldn't always tell that on the back they had a gun, a flak gun, and this night we didn't pick it up and they started firing. But Terry, from the rear turret, was so quick that he knocked it out before much damage had been done until we heard the dispatcher screaming over the intercom, 'All the four "joes" are hit and the aircraft is riddled with holes!'

Squadron Leader Frank Griffiths
Halifax pilot, 138 (SD) Squadron, RAF
As a matter of fact, the expression he used was, 'It looks like a butcher's shop in the back!' None of the RAF crew was hurt, fortunately, but we turned round and came home. After we'd landed, the petrol was still pouring out of the aircraft and the medical officer on the station sent the casualties off to hospital. Then a medical orderly, who'd been told to clean up all the syringes and things we'd used in our first aid kit, found the ear of this man. This was nine o'clock in the morning and the ear was packed in ice, rushed down to the hospital and sewn on, and it was quite OK, he got his ear back. I don't know what his hearing was like but it was quite a gory do.

Wing Commander Ken Batchelor
Halifax pilot, 138 (SD) Squadron, RAF
If you were shot at and shot down you were often too low to bale out. Some people occasionally managed to crash-land and get away with it.

Flight Sergeant Brian Atkins
Halifax observer/bomb-aimer, 138 (SD) Squadron, RAF
We crossed the Danish coast at about eight hundred feet and flew towards Roskilde. It was a very bright moonlit night, almost daylight – very frosty and cold. We got over the reception area to drop our agent, who we had not had any conversation with, which was the norm, and then, shortly after we had made our approach run to drop the agent, we were attacked by a Junkers 88.

He made a run on us and missed. Our rear gunner opened fire and the pilot took as much evasive action as he could but there wasn't a lot of height for him to manoeuvre in. After about three encounters with the Junkers 88 he hit us and set two engines on fire. All this time our rear gunner was commenting in no uncertain terms over the intercom and was very wound up indeed and was doing an excellent job – he hit the aircraft.

The German fighter hit us again and the pilot said he'd have to make a forced landing. We couldn't bail out – we were far too low. Fortunately we made an excellent emergency landing in a ploughed field, the furrows of the field were parallel to the ascent and the hard frosty ground with no obstructions enabled us to get down safely. We were extremely lucky – the aircraft was on fire.

We got the agent out, Flemming Muus, who introduced himself to us in a matter of seconds. He was the chief agent for the whole of the Denmark resistance.

Squadron Leader Frank Griffiths
Halifax pilot, 138 (SD) Squadron, RAF
I was to drop this load off just north of Annecy, about halfway between Annecy and the Swiss town of Geneva. Most of the equipment, the military equipment, was for the Plateau des Glières, this very high plateau, which was an excellent place for the Maquis to hide out. It was high up, of course, and there were chalets and things, which the farmers used to occupy during the summer – take the cows up to graze.

On the third trip, one engine failed. At first it sounded like fuel starvation. I wasn't over-worried. Slapped it into coarse pitch, which means less drag, and the flight engineer started to try and sort things out. We seemed to be doing quite well on three and I even climbed a bit. Then I turned round and came back. I wanted to keep near the lake just in case things deteriorated, because, believe me, there's nothing worse than having a four-engined bomber which won't climb in the bottom of an Alpine valley in the middle of the night, even if it is a full moon.

The next thing that happened was the other engine on that wing went. That's No.2 engine. Well, we never got to the lake. I sent the crew to crash stations and then we hit the first house. In fact, the last thing the dispatcher said to me over the intercom was, 'All OK, skipper. Crew's at crash stations.' That was the last actually spoken message. Before that, this chap McKenzie, the co-pilot, who'd merely come for the trip because he was so keen, had wrestled with the escape hatch over my head and got that off. Then the aircraft broke up and I got shot out through this hatch and partly through the windscreen, with my seat attached and about a good half hundredweight of thick steel armour plating behind.

I ended up in telephone wires between two posts. Meanwhile, the aircraft had crashed and the crew was killed, though I believe Maden, the dispatcher, did get as far as a hospital in Annecy and then died. It's hard for me to say exactly what went on. There was a tremendous fire. Curiously, and perhaps now I should say unfortunately, we killed about thirteen Italians.

On my way up the street, there was a boy coming down on a bicycle. He was about fifteen, sixteen. He lived not all that far away, two to three hundred yards, and he saw me. I'd still got uniform on, to a degree. I'd got shoes on and I'd got RAF trousers on; but in fact I had always flown on ops in a peculiar thing which a Breton fisherman always wears, a blue vest with white lines across. But the blood coming from my face and the fact that I had shoes on, good shoes, were the things that made this boy stop. He said to me, 'Are you English?' I said, 'Yes. Where are the Boche?' He said, 'Oh, there are not many around here, they're Italians.' I said, 'I'm going to Spain.' – there was still at the back of my mind the escape lecture from that morning: 'Get moving fast.' I then promptly passed out.

Pilot Officer John Charrot

Halifax observer/bomb-aimer, 138 (SD) Squadron, RAF

If a crew were missing we'd assemble at the Red Lion pub. And the Poles, the Czechs the same, would line up a short drink on the bar and then one of them would just come along the bar and if it was a crew of six then these six glasses would be knocked over. The publican was such a nice chap, they would offer him money for the glasses but he didn't mind at all, but he had a job clearing all this up as you can imagine. But that was their way of saying farewell to some of their mates.

Squadron Leader James Wagland
Hudson navigator and station navigation officer, RAF Tempsford
I suppose it's fair to say you did enjoy doing it. It was interesting work. It was very different from bombing operations. You felt that with bombing operations you couldn't help but bomb civilians if you're going for a major target in a town. That's how it goes. It was just how it went here, in this country. But in these sort of operations you were dropping agents and supplies to help resistance boys to be more selective, shall I say, in their work.

Squadron Leader Hugh Verity
Lysander pilot, 161 (SD) Squadron, RAF
I thought it was fascinating, partly because of the skill required – it gave one a sense of achievement if you could pull it off successfully – but largely because of the contacts one had with the passengers who were amazingly interesting and stimulating people.

Wing Commander Ken Batchelor
Halifax pilot, 138 (SD) Squadron, RAF
It was one of the best jobs that one could have done.

1941–42

We were shoving the whole lot into danger, men, women, girls, boys, and not just them but a number of their friends. Anybody who had associations with them could be pulled in.

Long after being driven from mainland Europe, the British remained firmly on the back foot. In the Atlantic, German U-boats were inflicting heavy losses on British shipping. In North Africa, early British victories against the Italians precipitated powerful German drives that threatened to defeat the British there altogether. The summer of 1941 saw the Soviet Union enter the war, the United States followed in December, but many months would pass before either nation was able to make a decisive impact. With Japan's aggression in the Far East causing further strain, a quick return to the Continent was impossible and, to many, strategic bombing seemed the best means available of striking back at the Reich. SOE, unproven and untested, struggled to compete for resources, but it did what it could with what little it had.

France was to receive a significant share of SOE's attention and over a thousand agents would be sent there during the war. Early efforts focused mostly on making contact with local resisters, organising secure 'circuits' (*réseaux*) of trusted confidants and training men and women ready to fight. Progress was slow. SOE found it hard to prise vital aircraft from the RAF, while many agents, once in the field, found local support not always forthcoming. A good number of agents were also made quickly aware of how dangerous life in the field could be. More than a few were killed or captured.

Not long after sending its first men to France, SOE prepared a pair of Czech agents tasked with killing Himmler's hated deputy, Reinhard Heydrich, the Nazi Deputy-Reichsprotektor in Prague. Although the attack went in, reprisals were horrendous and stand as a graphic example of how such acts risked ruthless Nazi reaction.

Working partly out of neutral Sweden, SOE made Scandinavia an area of particularly unorthodox activity, while 1942 also saw SOE send its first team into occupied Greece. Working in uniform, the mission made contact with local guerrillas and led a daring assault on the important Gorgopotamos viaduct: perhaps SOE's most significant early success.

France

Lieutenant Tony Brooks
SOE circuit organiser
I was suddenly called in to Orchard Court. We had a wonderful old janitor, he used to be the doorman at the Westminster Bank in Paris before the war, and he said, 'Strip lad.' I stripped all my clothes off, my uniform and everything else, right down to my birthday suit, and then he handed me my imitation French clothing, made by SOE-briefed tailors. He folded my uniform and pressed it down and put paper round the brass buttons.

Outside Orchard Court was one of these terribly secret cars that SOE used, an enormous great American gas-guzzling station wagon, painted in sand and spinach but with civilian number plates and civilian licence disc, driven by an extremely glamorous girl in a very smart FANY uniform. We went off up Baker Street and up the Great North Road towards Tempsford. When we passed Hatfield she took her cap off and her long blonde hair rolled down right on to her shoulders. It cheered me up a bit and I thought it would be a good thing to remember when I was facing the firing squad.

Captain Ben Cowburn
SOE circuit organiser
We went to the office in London and were getting in the cars and were told, 'No, it's scrubbed. There'll be fog tomorrow morning.' This became quite common practice. We did our waiting and once we went as far as the airfield and were dressed and then it was scrubbed. It was rather irritating, that.

Lieutenant Brian Stonehouse
SOE wireless operator
I was taken in this limousine with the blinds drawn to Tempsford and suddenly it hit me, 'What the hell have I got myself into?' Suddenly I felt it was something I couldn't get out of. 'If only I can get out of this and go home where everything is normal.' That was the only time actually.

HU 473659

Twenty-year-old Tony Brooks, SOE circuit organiser in France, 1942.

Lieutenant Roger Landes
SOE wireless operator
I wanted to get there. I was getting more and more impatient. I think the waiting was worse than the jumping.

Lieutenant Robert Sheppard
SOE arms and sabotage instructor
I had no waiting. I was called for the mission. I had everything: the details of the mission, the documents, the papers, everything. Then came the day of the jump over France, which is always a moment of a little anxiety, although we were so well prepared that we had the impression that we knew everything which could come. The preparation, the drop, the dropping zone, the reception committee, etc, we knew all that quite well. We had been so well trained that it was not something new in our minds.

Lieutenant Brian Stonehouse
SOE wireless operator
At Tempsford all the FANYs were there and there was this big goodbye, Maurice I think was there and gave me a silver cigarette case and a nice watch, and then we got into the plane. It was a hot night, I had a bit of a nap and I woke up and said, 'What are all those headlights?' In fact they were searchlights over the northern coast of France, and then there was some firing, which was a bit scary.

Then the communication broke down behind the rear-gunner and the pilot and we had to go back to England and land at the first airfield. I remember we had to stay hidden in the plane so that the ground crew, who had to climb in, didn't see us. Talk about an anti-climax, with all this build-up of nerves and so on. The next day the three of us were taken to Henley and spent the day there on the river and the same evening we tried again.

Lieutenant Tony Brooks
SOE circuit organiser
We rumbled off and finally took off and there was a terrific bang as the wheels came up. The dispatcher said, 'Don't worry, that's just the undercarriage.' I slept and the next thing I can remember was this chap shaking me awake. He gave me a Thermos of black coffee and some sandwiches. Then I sat on the edge of the hole, watched the fields of France go by. 'Action stations, Go!' and out I went. I looked at the moon and saw the disappearing Halifax and the next moment I was looking down on the church spire of the village of Saint

Léonard-de-Noblat. Fortunately for me I was on the backward swing and I went into a tree and that broke my fall. I fell through the tree, hit the ground pretty hard, I saw I couldn't get my parachute out so I unhitched myself and crawled into a ditch. Scrooge suddenly appeared in a great white night shirt and a little bonnet on his head, clippety-clop, clippety-clop, because he was wearing his clogs: a farmer. His son appeared, similarly attired. I watched them. They hadn't seen me and he said to his son, 'Get all that parachute stuff down, take away any broken branches and hide the whole lot under the hay in the big barn. I'm going to look for him – he's probably injured.' I thought that sounded friendly so I whistled him up and he picked me up like a kid and looked after me. I spent the night there and I left the next day.

Lieutenant Roger Landes
SOE wireless operator
Because of bad weather, the pilot had to go down to two hundred and fifty feet to see the dropping zone and he asked me what I wanted to do: jump or come back to England. As it was my fifth attempt to go to France, I decided that I'd prefer to jump than go back again. I must have touched the ground within ten seconds.

Lieutenant Brian Stonehouse
SOE wireless operator
We circled over the countryside for about half an hour. Eventually the people on the ground got some sort of light and we jumped, way off from where we were supposed to jump. I slid down the side of a tree into a bunch of cows. We were welcomed by the receiving people on the ground but we were told immediately that the château where we were supposed to spend the rest of the night had been raided by the French police, so we had to leave the area as soon as possible. Also I had a hundred thousand francs on me, which was supposed to last me for six months at least. In those days it was worth quite a lot. But the French said, 'Oh, you can't walk around France with all that money on you. You just keep ten thousand and we'll keep the rest.' Of course I never saw the rest, the ninety thousand; I don't know what happened to that.

I walked to Loches and got a train at seven-thirty in the morning to go to Limoges. I got into this compartment, a first or second-class compartment, where the seats face each other and there's a door to each compartment. There was no one in the car except a French woman. After the train started we starting saying 'Nice day' and so on, and she looked at my shoes and said, 'Oh! I love your shoes. My brother bought shoes exactly the same as yours in London in '39.' Can you imagine how I felt? I'd barely been in France a couple of hours and I'd already been noticed because my shoes were conspicuous, because at that time you couldn't buy leather in France. So the first thing I did when I got to Lyons, I bought some shoes made of raffia. I think that was pretty terrible, actually, to send me to France with shoes like that. I had this beautiful suit that I was sent to France in, made to measure in London and aged artificially, sandpapered and put through a vacuum cleaner bag to make it a bit worn, but the shoes I didn't know about.

Lieutenant Harry Despaigne
SOE wireless operator
I went by felucca to Cannes. We left in a force 9 gale and everybody including the crew was violently sick. The wardroom where we were supposed to sleep got flooded so it couldn't be used by anyone for the rest of the voyage and we slept under the sails on the aft-deck. The thing that is vivid in my memory is the fact that when we were a mile or so from the coast we could smell the flowers. Even out at sea, the smell of the flowers.

I went overboard into a rubber dinghy, ripped my trousers from top to bottom, got ashore with one sailor and my luggage. When I got on the rocks I was so giddy having spent nearly three weeks at sea that I couldn't stand upright. I think I fell into the water again. We got ashore, we got through a storm drain, which went underneath the road, and then we went up some stairs to a house and spent the night there. Next morning somebody came to fetch me with a bicycle.

Lieutenant George Abbott
SOE circuit organiser
I was told, 'You're going to be landed by motor gunboat on the coast of Brittany and you're going to go to Paris.' We landed on 12/13 February 1942. The whole thing was a catastrophe from start to finish. The sea was very bad – we were supposed to land some equipment but that landed in the sea – and when we landed we were informed that the Germans were observing the whole operation. The chaps on the beach were in a panic and told us, 'Nobody lands, you have to re-embark immediately.' Nobody was able to re-embark: the sea was very rough; the dinghies collapsed and lost their oars. It was a complete catastrophe. The chaps on the beach said, 'They'll come back tomorrow night, you'd better hide.' We didn't understand how they had been able to go through the German lines but we understood that later. There was

a woman with them, Mathilde Carré, she was known as 'Cat'. At the end of the war she was very famous, or infamous. She considered herself as being the Mata Hari of the Second World War. She'd played more than a double game – she'd played a triple game. Anyhow, she was there on the beach with two other blokes and they went their way and we went our way.

We hid in this little hut and we were in pretty poor shape. Three of us had been in the sea. We were soaked, we were shivering, we were feverish, and it must have been eight o'clock in the morning when the naval officer said, 'I can't stick it any more. I'm in uniform, I'm going to give myself up.' Well, there was nothing much we could do. Either bump him off or let him go and we had no possibility of bumping him off and no inclination of doing so. He said, 'I haven't seen you,' and so on, so I said, 'Good luck to you, goodbye,' and he went. We stayed in our little hut. During the morning we observed lots of commotion on the beach, Germans in uniform, Alsatian dogs. Obviously they were looking at a lot of things on the beach, I assume the wireless sets and ammunition and explosives. In the evening we climbed the cliff and found a road and started walking into the night. We were going to try and reach a town, probably find a train and so on. We came across a farm, and we'd been told the Bretons were absolutely all of them pro-English but this particular one wasn't. He was a Breton nationalist and having given us something to eat and having put us up in this barn he called the Germans and we were caught.

Lieutenant Robert Sheppard
SOE arms and sabotage instructor

I remember the last dinner with Major Buckmaster, a very nice dinner with candlesticks and so on, a sort of last dinner in the civilised world. Then to the airfield, for the presentation of the crew, a Polish crew, and then into the plane with my companion, Robert Boiteux, 'Nicolas'. We were not supposed to work together but we were jumping together.

We had a little flak over the Channel and over Lyons and the trap opened and I saw the soil of France I had left nearly two years before. It made quite an impression. I was going to go back to the soil where my father and my mother were interned and I was wondering what had happened to them. Also this period of two years away seemed to have been a very long part of my life, much longer than it was in reality, and it was something to come back practically to my childhood. I saw the River Saône and the green light; 'Nicolas' jumped first and I jumped second.

When your parachute opens there is always a great moment of excitement. There is the silence, the bright moonlight. It is something very special, which one cannot forget. But then I was in the mission and I had to think fast: 'What was waiting for me downstairs?' I realised that with the wind I was going far from the reception committee and I saw a little village. I could not change direction, I was definitely going right into the village, and a few seconds later I fell into the roofs.

The parachute caught on telephone wires, I think. It was impossible to take it down so I had to turn the lock and leave it hanging on the wires and at that very moment a little window next to me on the roof opened and I heard a voice: 'Who goes there? *Gendarmerie Française*.' After all these studies, all this experience, all these adventures, I'd managed to fall right in the middle of France on the roof of a police station.

The two gendarmes took me to their home and they helped me to quit my flying kit, helmet and everything and they were quite ready to let me go. Unfortunately the noise they made inadvertently woke up the chief of the brigade. He realised that there was something wrong and at the very moment I was going down with the two gendarmes, to go away, they opened the door, other gendarmes caught me and the two gendarmes couldn't do anything. I couldn't really do anything. I still had my gun but I had this strange reflex, that I'd come here to fight the war, to help the French resistance fight the Germans, and I was not going to start my mission by killing a French gendarme. It was a sort of human reaction that I'm still really proud of. The reception committee was arrested because they tried to come near the gendarmerie – they'd realised something was wrong. 'Nicolas' got away by himself.

Captain Robert Boiteux
SOE circuit organiser

I hid my suitcase – I thought I'd better not walk with a suitcase – and all the way to Lyons there were police on motorbikes rushing down to this little village called Anse. They'd been alerted and were looking for me but all they saw was a little Frenchman walking along the road and they didn't take any notice. Just before Lyons I got a tram to go to the centre and people were talking in the tram, 'Oh, do you know what happened last night? There were some British people parachuted in.'

The thing was, I didn't know where to sleep. Although I knew France it was still dangerous to go to hotels. I went into a café and a prostitute came up to me, started talking and said, 'Would you like to come with me?' So I thought, 'Well, this is an opportunity.' So I went to her room, and I had a few hundred thousand francs in the belt round my waist, and I said, 'Look here, I've come a long way. Here's a couple of hundred francs, do you mind going to sleep somewhere else?' So she was quite happy, she went and fetched some other clients. I got rid of her and I was able to have a good night's sleep. Next morning I went and had a shave at a barber's place and I said, 'I'm looking for a room.' He told me where to go: a place called Place des Terreaux. They had notices in the window and I saw 'Room to let, *à la Croix Rousse*' so I went there. Two old ladies were letting rooms and I got a room.

I had no contacts. I didn't know what to do. I went straight to a restaurant and had a good meal. I'd had nothing to eat for three days except strawberries and cherries. As soon as I entered this restaurant whom should I see but two blokes from SOE having lunch. One of them I knew, I'd done training with him. So, according to our training, I went in front of the table, dropped my newspaper on the floor, picked it up, looked him in the eye – he recognised me – and I went to the next room and had a coffee. He followed me and put me in touch with the organisation.

Lieutenant Robert Sheppard
Captured SOE agent, Croix Rousse hospital, Lyons
My only aim was to try and escape, which eventually I did thanks to the sanitary organisation of the prison. I was supposed to have diphtheria and I was sent to the Croix Rousse hospital in Lyons, which was not a prison hospital, it was a public hospital, and put in a room guarded permanently with two gendarmes by the door. The window was locked with a special key. I managed with soap to take the print of the key and have it passed outside. I must say that all nurses, doctors and so on were extremely sympathetic to my case and ready to help.

One night I managed silently to escape, jumped through the window, went into the back courtyard, jumped on another little roof and over the wall of the hospital. It was about one o'clock and the chap who was coming to the meeting point was late and I had to wait two hours in my hospital shirt. Suddenly I saw his face over the fence and he arrived with a pair of trousers, a coat, everything except shoes, so I had to walk through Lyons in my socks to a safe house. The next morning I found 'Nicolas', Edward Zeff, the wireless operator, 'Gustave' and all our team, and went back to my task of instructor.

Lieutenant Tony Brooks
SOE circuit organiser
In 1942, when I went back, I had to use the whole of my circuit for my first parachute drop because there weren't any bloody volunteers to come and stick

their necks out to come and get the containers. It slowly came back as it looked as if we might win the war, but you've got to remember that we were kicked out of Singapore, out of Hong Kong, out of Greece, Crete, the whole lot. They wanted to back the winner and that's why they were not prepared to co-operate. They weren't pro-German but they were certainly not prepared to back us.

Captain Ben Cowburn
SOE circuit organiser
We'd ask them to try and find a field which would be isolated enough for a drop and then we'd ask them to choose a phrase, which would be read over the French edition of the BBC. Then I'd radio back and they'd listen and it would come through. And that was the first manifestation of power: you'd been able to give an order to tell this formidable British broadcasting company what to say. Then, of course, if the operation was on, we'd go to the field and wait and wait, and it wasn't a small, fast thing, it was a great big four-engined bomber that came over and dropped something to them. There again, the manifestation of power: this thing had come through, it had roared through the German defences and everything, and it was they that had ordered it. And you were somebody from then on.

Captain Robert Boiteux
SOE circuit organiser
We did blow up quite a few power pylons and they did amuse themselves blowing up the windows of shops belonging to collaborators, but there wasn't a lot done in 1942. You can understand that. If you're a gentleman with a wife and children, you've got to think of them. You can't stick your head up too much. It was all right for me. The British agents, they were all by themselves if they were caught.

Captain Ben Cowburn
SOE circuit organiser
We British officers who came to France secretly to organise resistance against the Germans had a job that was quite special. That is to say we had to recruit people who were living, well, managing to live, in their homes with their families and we were putting the whole lot in great danger. I remember many times when a man who was enthusiastic about joining would take me home, he'd have a pretty wife and a little girl, and he knew what the Germans did. We were shoving the whole lot into danger, men, women, girls, boys, and not

just them but a number of their friends. Anybody who had associations with them could be pulled in. So it was really a very, very heavy responsibility. It weighed me down quite a bit.

Lieutenant Harry Despaigne
SOE wireless operator
At Marseilles, going out of the Saint-Charles station, on the steps there down to the street, I was tapped on the back, turned round and saw a chap in uniform and dark glasses. He said to me, in French, '*Que fais-tu là, mon petit cochon?*' – 'What are you doing there, my little pig?' It turned out to be an old school-friend of mine who was still in the Vichy Air Force. He said, 'I met your mother a fortnight ago and you're supposed to be in England. What are you doing here? If you don't do anything against France, I'll give you forty-eight hours to get away.' I said, 'Give me two hours and that'll be enough.'

I went to Arles. Two friends carried my wireless set past the control at the station and from Marseilles to Arles and they got me into a hotel there. The hotel threw me out after three days, they said they couldn't have a British officer staying there, it was too compromising, so I left and I went to live in a flat near the theatre. One day, the lady I lodged with, a hairdresser, came back at lunchtime and said, 'Today I was doing the hair of the wife of the commissaire of police. I said, "What a pity it is that the Germans are here," and she said, "Ah, but you know there is a British officer here? You know, that tall chap with the dark, wavy hair?"' I disappeared within five minutes and went to Nice.

Lieutenant Brian Stonehouse
SOE wireless operator
My cover story was that I'd been a fashion artist and drawn for *Vogue* in Paris just before the war. Being an artist, no one can pigeonhole you. You can go anywhere. You could either be bohemian or be a successful artist. It's always been like that anyway. As an artist you can't be categorised and in that respect it was very good as a cover story. You could walk around with your paintbox and do little sketches of the countryside and so on. And by that time the transmitters were fairly small, so mine was built into a box of paints, all colours, and some of the heavier tubes of paint had the spare valves inside. It was made to carry around on public transport. I was never allowed to carry it when I was in France. The courier always did that.

Lieutenant Roger Landes
SOE wireless operator

With Bordeaux being down in a valley my first contact was not successful. I could hear London calling me but they couldn't catch my messages, my set was not strong enough. Then the resistance found me another house, in the hills above Bordeaux, a small village occupied by the Germans, and I started to work my wireless set. I thought it was a very good idea because the Germans would never have thought that anybody would work so near them. I worked in that house for about six months without interruption, without being discovered by the Germans.

Lieutenant Brian Stonehouse
SOE wireless operator

A lot of the time, especially in the summer, was spent on café terraces, because there you weren't conspicuous. All Frenchmen spend half their lives on café terraces. You had to know what to order and the price of things and so on to be inconspicuous. So I found out what was available, what were the habits, the ways of doing things, because I hadn't been told that in London.

The safest place to work, to transmit, was not from a château or anywhere isolated in the country but from apartment buildings in a big city. You could be pinned down in a château much too easily, whereas in an apartment building they could pin down the building but not the apartment. That's how I got caught, mind you, because I didn't follow those rules.

I'd been at the château on the air for several hours and I'd been spotted by the vans that follow the beam to the transmitter. Château du Hurlevent was eight miles outside Lyons, in the country. Monsieur Jourdan had been keeping an eye open for any strange faces in the vicinity and he'd seen someone so he immediately turned off the mains. That was a pre-arranged thing with me if anything fishy was going on outside. 'Christiane' was sitting with me when this was turned off. She was feeding me messages, coding or decoding messages, and she said, 'My God, it's the Germans,' and I said, 'What do you mean the Germans?' She said, 'I forgot, I walked past them on the way here.' That was pretty awful, because, if she'd told me when she'd arrived that she'd passed these Germans, we'd have had plenty of time to pull my aerial down and escape, because the castle wasn't surrounded by then. She wanted to kill herself, she told me, because she felt so awful about that.

I pulled the aerial down, but inadvertently left a little insulating porcelain thing hanging from the ceiling, and hid the transmitter at the bottom of a lift shaft and Monsieur Jourdan put the lift down and jammed it there.

'Christiane' and I tried to get out of the back of the château, which overlooked the garden and the valley of the Rhone. We got out on to the back terrace and sat down pretending to make love, because we'd seen a man come around the far corner of the château. Then another came with a gun and we were caught.

They beat me up then but they still hadn't proved that I'd sent transmissions from the château and I thought, 'There's nothing much they can do because it could have been from somewhere else.' But then they found this little porcelain insulator from the aerial hanging in one of the rooms where I'd been working. Then they found my radio set at the bottom of the elevator shaft.

Lieutenant George Abbott
Captured SOE agent, Fresnes prison, Paris

What the Germans did was very simple. They took a chap, in my case a chap that had been in London only twenty-four hours before, they arrested him, they interrogated him on the spot, he was transferred to Paris and he was put in a cell by himself. He was locked up, his shoelaces were taken, his braces were taken, his tie was taken off, his watch, cigarettes, everything. He was given some kind of so-called food that he couldn't eat, because obviously he hadn't been accustomed to that type of food, and they kept him locked up for three weeks before anybody saw him. They let him stew in his own juice and they starved him. After three weeks he was taken out again, asked the same questions. There were two possibilities there. Either he was going to stick to his own story without making the slightest deviation or he was going to say something different. Well, if he was going to say something different, the chances were that possibly he wouldn't get beaten up.

Lieutenant Brian Stonehouse
Captured SOE agent, Fresnes prison, Paris

After three days of interrogation, I decided to say that I was English. It was a mistake in retrospect but at the time I thought I was going to be executed and I would have liked my family to be able to trace, after the war, what had happened to me under my real name.

At this point the questions were asked in German, translated into French, and I replied in French. So now I refused to speak French, so they had to get an interpreter to ask questions, first in German, then in French, then in English, so I had time to think up an answer. My whole motivation in interrogations was to stall, to gain time, never to say 'I won't say anything' but invent. I used to invent all these tall stories and think, 'This story's good for another two weeks, because it'll take them two weeks to check up on the truth of what I've said.' I also used to invent people. 'Can you describe so-and-so?' 'Yes, I worked with so-and-so,' and I'd describe what he'd looked like. First I'd describe the person who was interrogating me. It's extraordinary how they don't recognise the description of themselves, but I had to have a face I could tie in with my description.

I was never hit. It's one thing I don't understand. I was threatened, I was starving, people would eat in front of me, I may have had a couple of smacks, but I was never tortured. I always expected to be.

Lieutenant George Abbott
Captured SOE agent, Fresnes prison, Paris
After three weeks I was taken out. Their approach was, 'Well, we know everything. The other chap has told us everything.' I said, 'Well, I don't know what he's told you. My story, there it is, you have it. This is what happened, this is the truth, I'm so-and-so, this is my rank,' and so on and so on. They locked me up again for three months. Then they took me out, we went through the same thing, and after that they said, 'All right,' and locked me up and left me to rot for practically one year.

Lieutenant Brian Stonehouse
Captured SOE agent, Fresnes prison, Paris
On New Year's Eve, in Fresnes, my interrogator said, 'Well, you know, this is it. You'll probably be shot as a spy.' I was never actually officially condemned and I was never in court but I expected from then on to be taken out and shot.

Czechoslovakia

Lieutenant Colonel Peter Wilkinson
Staff officer, Czech–Polish Section, SOE HQ, London
In September or early October 1941, Colonel Moravec, head in London of the Czech Intelligence Service, told me that he had it in mind to undertake an operation. And what we agreed with Moravec was that we would provide the weapons and training for two or three of his men to carry out a spectacular assassination. Heydrich, if possible. It presented no great difficulties because SOE had a sort of general mandate to conduct operations against members of the enemy armed forces and Heydrich, the new Deputy-Reichsprotektor, was,

after all, a high-ranking officer in the SS and a perfectly legitimate target. We had no reason to know officially who was to be the target. Our job was merely to arrange for the equipment and for the transport of high-grade assassins from the United Kingdom to Czechoslovakia and who they chose to bump off after they got there was Czech business and not ours.

Captain Ernest van Maurik
SOE instructor, Scotland
I think it was the only course I took that wasn't F Section. There were two courses each of twenty men and they were Czech Army in exile. They were disciplined. They were mostly warrant officer types. It was quite a different ball game to F Section, who were, I wouldn't say a rabble, but one was a waiter from Soho, others were this and that. These Czechs were all soldiers and they more or less called to attention when you appeared. And of course I didn't know what they were doing. Neither did they. We did a lot of shooting and I had a couple of sergeants who would take that. They didn't really have to teach them how to shoot. I did have to teach them demolition, explosives, which they didn't know, and I also hiked them over the hills, but they were pretty fit.

Sub-Lieutenant Robert Clark
Trainee agent, Scotland
I didn't know what they were doing when I was there but I found out afterwards. They were all training to be agents and the most famous of them were the two Czechs who went in and killed Heydrich. They were the most unlikely-looking heroes, and they certainly were heroes, you could ever imagine. Ordinary working people without any flamboyance.

Lieutenant Colonel Peter Wilkinson
Staff officer, Czech–Polish Section, SOE HQ, London
They were a very typically Czech pair. They were very, very solid citizens. The sort of NCOs who one would have given anything for on active operations: utterly reliable, apparently utterly fearless and absolutely devoted to their cause. I could not have admired them more.

There were several false starts, I think two or three, and at the end they were getting slightly nervy, which wasn't surprising being held in a holding house in London. My friend, Alfgar Hesketh-Pritchard, who had taken over charge of the Czech section, and I thought it would be a good idea to take the two of them to the theatre, which we did. We chose what we thought would

Jan Kubis and Josef Gabcik, the Czech agents trained by SOE to assassinate Reinhard Heydrich.

HU 47379

Heydrich's car after the attack.

be a fairly easily understood general revue, because they didn't speak much English. But when the couple on stage were indulging in passionate embraces, these two thought it screamingly funny and roared with laughter, and during the more jokey parts of the performance they remained stolidly glum. Finally, at half-time I think, Hesketh-Pritchard and I said, 'Well, we should really get them out of this before somebody hits them,' so we went off and gave them a slap-up supper at the Criterion, I think it was.

Captain Ernest van Maurik
Staff officer, Air Operations Section, SOE HQ, London
Subsequently I was in the Air Operations section of SOE, laying on operations, and we always had, I remember, for a long time a high priority code-name on our board going to Czechoslovakia. I didn't realise it but those were the assassins on their way. And then there was a pause before they laid on the ambush.

Lieutenant Colonel Peter Wilkinson
Staff officer, Czech–Polish Section, SOE HQ, London
I don't remember there were very detailed operational plans on the British side. First of all, I don't think we would have wanted to know them, for security reasons; and secondly, I don't think there was very much that we could have added to the local knowledge possessed by the Czechs. Both Hesketh-Pritchard and I had lived in Prague but obviously the Czechs themselves knew far more about it than we did.

I think the original plan was that they should be armed with Colt Super .38 pistols and they were certainly trained to be Deadeye Dicks with them. We had always taken the view that a sub-machine gun was really far too bulky to carry on an operation of this sort. However, for some reason or other, a Sten gun was included in their load list, probably at the personal request of one or two of the chaps. I would certainly not myself consciously have sanctioned it if I'd personally approved the load list, which I don't think I did.

The plan, as far as we knew it, was that in some way Heydrich's car was to be held up and at that moment one or both of them should throw one of these special bombs against the side of the car. The bombs had been designed to cause the bodywork of the car to fragment and not to fragment themselves, like a Mills bomb: they were an adaption of a bomb used in the Western Desert to attack tanks. And of course it was extremely successful. Although the Sten gun jammed, the car did slow down and the second chap did throw a bomb, which exploded against the side of the car, and, as a result,

HU 47377

The church of St Cyril and Methodius, Prague, where Heydrich's assassins were finally cornered.

K 9332

Smoke rising from the burning village of Lidice, Czechoslovakia, destroyed by the Germans after Heydrich's assassination.

a piece of poisoned clothing or something got into Heydrich's wound, from which he died.

Captain Peter Lee
Staff officer, Security Section, SOE HQ, London
I remember to this day when the news came through that we'd got Heydrich. The night he told me, this old boy, General Lakin, was sort of doing a fandango round his office in Baker Street. He was so excited about Heydrich's assassination.

Lieutenant Colonel Peter Wilkinson
Staff officer, Czech–Polish Section, SOE HQ, London
I remember being agreeably surprised when the radio news came through that Heydrich had been assassinated, but it certainly wasn't something I was biting my nails over day to day at my desk. Our job was over when we dropped the fellows inside. Thereafter there were an awful lot of other things on our plate.

George Hartman
Czech Jewish civilian, Prague
After the Protektor, Heydrich, was assassinated by the Czech parachutists, the Germans eventually caught those people. They were surrounded in an Orthodox church in downtown Prague, surrounded by Nazi tanks and artillery, and for about two or three days there was a battle in the middle of Prague. Eventually they all committed suicide. The Germans didn't get a single person alive.

Jan Hartman
Czech Jewish civilian, Prague
There were huge pictures in the papers of the bicycle that was found, of the trench coat that was found. The bicycle and the trench coat were exposed in a shop on Wenceslas Square, the main square in Prague, so people would see it. It was very much publicised as the Germans made it clear that others wouldn't get away with it.

Frank Bright
Czech Jewish civilian, Prague
Recrimination, and of course Lidice, where they killed the population and sent the children away, was the result. It was pretty awful because we knew they were going to take reprisals.

Jan Hartman
Czech Jewish civilian, Prague
Every day the newspapers published the names of people who had been executed. And the assassination very much affected the transportations. Then there was one transport after another. You knew you wouldn't get away any more.

Frank Bright
Czech Jewish civilian, Prague
Somebody else would take his place who would be just as awful. Unless you could wipe out the whole of the Gestapo building, it wouldn't really matter. Whatever happened, the Jews would always suffer in the end. From that point of view there was no benefit. But any German SS who got killed, that was a plus.

Scandinavia

Major Henry Threlfall
SOE officer, Stockholm
I went to Stockholm with the object of seeing what could be done to cause trouble to the Germans in various ways from this neutral outpost. The briefing was really rather vague because it wasn't quite known what could be done. One chap, a former Unilever colleague of mine, had tried to do something early in the war and had been caught by the Swedes and put in prison. He hadn't been a member of the legation staff, as I would be. I was appointed a clerk to the naval attaché, that was my cover, which wasn't a very good cover, but that's what I was told and off I went, and I found there an extremely good and very lively-minded SOE base. There was a man called Peter Tennant, the press attaché, who was the inspiration for a good deal of it. There was an extremely able man called Turnbull who was working into Denmark and there was a Norwegian section, too, which was a very active one indeed because they were able to get people across the land frontier between Sweden and Norway.

Peter Tennant
SOE officer, Stockholm
When I arrived I had no idea what a press attaché was supposed to do. Nobody told me what to do so I had to find out. Obviously I'd got to try and

influence opinion so I met the people who could influence opinion in both directions. One of the ones who influenced Swedish opinion in the German direction was the Swedish explorer Sven Hedin. He was a remarkable explorer, a Jew, and he had been decorated by the Kaiser, by Hitler, and had honorary doctorates from every German university you could think of. I thought, well, I really must meet this man and see what it is that makes a Jew kick in this direction, so I went and had tea with him one day with his two old sisters who ran a flower shop beneath their flat. And there was this little pear-shaped man who really looked like a professor or a country chemist or some worthy little character like that: little moustache and pince-nez spectacles.

We went over the whole thing and he said, 'I suppose you've come to ask for my good offices in making peace.' I said, 'Nothing in the world would ever persuade me to ask for your good offices. I've come to find out what you think and how you can possibly be a pro-Nazi Jew.' He said, 'My friend Goering is very pro-Jewish and I can tell you that we have a great plan for a Jewish home in the empty quarter of Arabia. It's all ready.' I said, 'Have you asked the Arabs about this?' He said, 'That's all been fixed. Don't you worry about that. Germans don't do things that are not properly planned.' I said, 'How very interesting this all is. So you're convinced that the British are going to lose the war?' 'Oh, yes, obviously. I'm sorry about it but that's what's going to happen.' I said, 'Well, I bet you we won't. I bet you five pounds.' He said, 'I'll take you on. How very British to be so sporting.' So I bet him five pounds and we never met again.

Major Henry Threlfall
SOE officer, Stockholm
In Sweden, the Social Democrats, who were out of power, were very friendly to us but the general attitude was rather unfriendly, rather pro-German and extremely strict in guarding their own neutrality and not getting dragged in, in any way. In fact there was a most ludicrous thing, there was a camp for Norwegians who'd escaped from Norway across the frontier into Sweden, an internment camp, and these wretched chaps weren't allowed to play football. Football was physical training and physical training could have been interpreted by the Germans as pre-military training and that would have been a breach of Swedish neutrality. The Swedes did carry their neutrality obsession to great lengths.

Major Andrew Croft
SOE officer, Stockholm
We had tremendous problems with the Swedish police. We nicknamed them the 'Svestapo'. One of them was caught in the naval attaché's house,

up in the roof, listening in to conversations between the naval attaché and his guests.

Peter Tennant
SOE officer, Stockholm
I had a wonderful character called Wilfred Latham as my No.2 and expert for radio stuff, he'd been a rubber planter in Malaya and was sent out to me to help with SOE. And one adventure we had with the Swedish police was when I got very annoyed with the way in which the legation was being watched by the security service. We had a barn on the other side of the road overlooking the legation and they used to go and hide there, or walk up and down disguised as nursemaids with prams and so forth, wearing policemen's boots. It was the most ridiculous charade. So I said to Wilfred one day, 'I tell you what we're going to do, we're going to photograph these chaps. I want you to go round the back, take them by surprise, photograph the lot and get back here with the film.' So he said, 'Fine,' and he did it. They tried to catch him and seize the camera, he got back to me, we got the most wonderful photographs of these fellows and I went straight down town with the film to the press. The press was delighted because I told them that this was the Gestapo, not the Swedes, watching the British Legation. Well, I got this into the papers and it came out as a bombshell.

As I was walking back from town, I suddenly saw the French military attaché's little Citroen being driven in a very erratic way towards me and in it was my minister, Victor Mallet – he was a very bad driver – purple-faced. He saw me and stopped and said, 'Peter, what have you done now? You've gone and compromised me. Go straight back to the legation and stay in your office until I come back. Günther has asked to see me.' Günther was the Swedish Foreign Minister who was the wettest of the wet. About an hour later, Reggie Sutton-Pratt, our military attaché, rang up and said, 'We're all having drinks next door. Victor wants you to come round and see him. You're not being fired this time.' The residence was just round the corner from the office and I went round and there was Victor, who had this way of losing his temper with me and then patting me on the back and saying, 'Dear old chap, sorry about that.' He said, 'Look here, I'm terribly sorry about this. You were right, it was Günther who was red in the face this time. He told me that these people you photographed were not the Gestapo at all, they were the Swedish secret police. It's an absolute disgrace.' I said, 'Of course it's a disgrace.' Well, Günther had said he'd seen the head of the police, he'd told them to call them off and that it must never happen again, and we avoided the secret police after that.

Major Henry Threlfall
SOE officer, Stockholm
I got hold of a young Swedish sailor who said he was perfectly willing to do something because he disliked the Germans very much, so he was equipped with some explosives and a time pencil. He was on a German ship, which was going from Stockholm through the Kiel Canal with the eventual destination of Hamburg, and one of the things which obviously would have been a very good achievement would be to block the Kiel Canal which the Germans used freely. So he quite correctly planted his explosives inside the stern of the ship, actually on the plates of the hull, as I'd told him to, and set the time pencil and it went off. Unfortunately the weather was very cold and this time pencil, which worked through chemicals eating through a copper wire which then released a spring and an explosion, was slow in working and the ship just got out of the Kiel Canal before it went off. The ship did sink, the explosion blew a hole in the stern and water came in, no one was drowned actually, and this chap came back and reported to me. But it happened outside the mouth of the Kiel Canal, which was a great pity. They lost a ship but the Kiel Canal wasn't blocked.

Peter Tennant
SOE officer, Stockholm
Some of the pamphlets we managed to distribute on the Swedish railways, on transit trains to Norway, for the German troops, were fake copies of Nostradamus's prophecies, seed catalogues and so forth, inside which were instructions as to how to fake various illnesses which would make it possible for you to escape service on the Russian front. These were very popular.

Also we had itching powder which we distributed to the laundry ladies in the Grand Hotel, where all the German delegations used to stay, so as to make life difficult for them – it was put in their underclothes and on their lavatories. And then the girls in our office did some enterprising things by collecting French letters, which were neatly packed in German Army packaging, and filling them with itching powder and packing them back again and then getting them nicely distributed back through the German Army.

The black propaganda we produced was quite considerable. There was a whole series of German stamps with Himmler's head on, which, with the help of various German refugees and some fifty thousand addresses, we smuggled back into Germany. It was thought that this would have a serious effect on Hitler's carpet-biting propensities.

The great thing I always thought with SOE was that you could make use of opportunities. There was no point in having too fixed plans, leave plenty of initiative to people to do things their own way. I tried to get SOE to invent a bomb, which you could insert into a piece of iron ore, which would then set the thing alight or blow it up after so many bumps from loading from a ship, but this proved absolutely impossible. So I said, 'Well now, instead of actually trying to do it, let's pretend we've done it and sell the blueprints and part of the bombs to the Germans.' So we were able to induce them to take an interest in this and they bought the blueprints and little pieces of evidence of the bomb, which were quite insufficient. I think it was for some dramatic sum, about 200,000 kronor, which paid for a lot of SOE activities at that time.

Ronald Turnbull
SOE officer, Stockholm
Occasionally we had to send funds through in the form of diamonds to the underground in Denmark. They would send me a little tin full of diamonds, cut diamonds. I used to look at them occasionally, admire them.

Reginald Spink
Staff officer, Danish Section, SOE HQ, London
Denmark was criticised in those days because it was not offering any resistance and in consequence it was rather disregarded in SOE. We had to fight for any facilities, training facilities and so on. Even an aeroplane to drop people, when we got a few to drop, was difficult to get. However, the head of the section, Commander Hollingworth, and I used always to argue in answer to that criticism that the Danes would come along when the time was ripe. We could in the meantime organise quietly, unsuspected by the Germans, and we in fact recruited a number of Danes mainly from the seaman's pool up in Newcastle.

We found a man we thought would be a very good leader in Denmark, an organiser. His job would not be to start blowing things up but to build up an organisation quietly in Denmark. He was trained and he and his wireless operator were dispatched finally to Denmark at the end of December 1941 and we encountered disaster from the start, because his parachute didn't open and he was killed. That was Bruhn. He had just finished his training as a doctor and he was to have been our great man in Denmark, our great organiser.

The whole thing was blown from the start, the Germans knew all about it, so we had more or less to start all over again, this time in the knowledge that the Germans knew we were operating there. That threw us back many

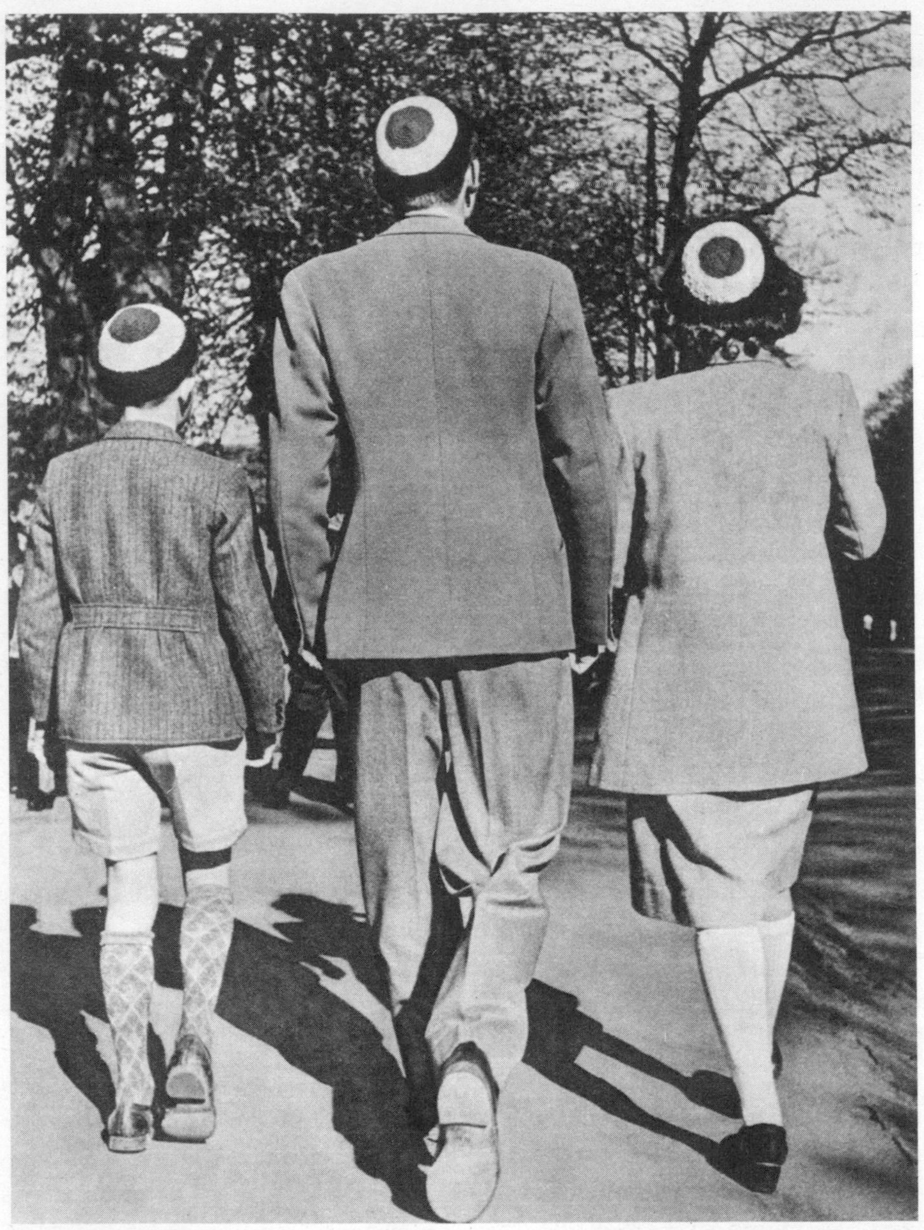

HU 47381

Civilians in Denmark wearing caps in the colours of the RAF roundel: a mark of passive resistance.

months. It was not until well into 1942 that we really got going and we had further accidents on the way. We had to withdraw one or two people and others were killed. Bruhn's successor, Rottbøll, was killed in a shooting with the police.

Major Henry Threlfall
Staff officer, Scandinavian Section, SOE HQ, London

A dreadful problem arose one day. We had dropped a party into Denmark who'd landed perfectly safely, I think there were three of them, and gone to ground. Then one of them, things went to his head and he started forgetting all about his cover and the need for security and keeping a low profile in a German-occupied country. He was actually endangering the lives of anyone who associated with him because he was making himself far too prominent.

In the end this got so bad and warnings didn't seem to have any effect on him that they sent over a proposal, quite seriously, that he be executed, because he was a danger to the whole organisation. Ralph Hollingworth, the head of the Danish Section, got this signal – he probably went as white as a sheet when he got it – and came in to me. The head of the Scandinavian Section, a man called George Wiskeman, was away, so I was taking his place. Hollingworth came in and said, 'What do you think?' and I said, 'I'll attend to it,' and looked at everything that the Danes themselves had said, and I said, 'Well, I'm sorry, there's nothing we can do. We've got to agree.'

Hollingworth was a man of immense character and the interesting thing, which is very dominant in my mind to this day when thinking about it, is that he took the blame himself. He didn't blame this chap; he blamed himself for having chosen an agent who didn't stand up to the strain. He was a most extraordinarily honest man, this Hollingworth. He was intensely worried and took this enormously seriously as you can imagine. After all, we weren't used to signing people's death warrants. So I had to take it on myself and say, 'Yes, he should be executed.' So he was. He was shot. He was taken out into woods in the northern part of Zeeland, if I remember rightly, and shot and weights were tied round his body and it was dumped in the lake. But the deed was done; the danger was eliminated. One was at war and one had to do these things and put up with them however much one disliked it.

Ronald Turnbull
SOE officer, Stockholm

We would have been better to wait and choose more Bruhns. Practically all of the seamen ended up being killed because there was no intellectual element whatever in them. They were just rough seamen and whilst it looked good to say, 'We put six men into Denmark,' most of them started blowing themselves very quickly and very few of them developed from what they were into something more intelligent. I wouldn't like to generalise, they were all very brave, but they were sent to their death without having the background.

Major Henry Threlfall
SOE officer, Stockholm
The Danish General Staff were purporting to work with the Germans. In actual fact they were supplying us with everything they could. They used to send over to Stockholm enormous lengths of microfilm, concealed usually in tubes of toothpaste in the luggage of travellers going across from Copenhagen to Malmö or Helsingør to Helsingborg.

Jutta Juncker
Danish resistance worker
I got into delivering and carrying around a lot of different intelligence stuff. We'd get the times when ships were sailing from Germany, up and down, through Danish waters. We got maps of all the air sites and where German soldiers were posted and knew who went to Norway and who came back. We got drawings of a V1 that had fallen on Bornholm.

Major Andrew Croft
SOE officer, Stockholm
Two German air force generals on a certain day each week went up on the train to northern Norway, to Bardufoss and Bodö, two aerodromes used for the bombing of the Murmansk convoys. These two generals had a special reserved carriage, of course, and, when lunch came along, they left their briefcases in the carriage and went along to the dining car next door. The Norwegians realised this and two of them boarded the train and pinched the briefcases and got off the train, because the driver had been persuaded to slow down at a certain point, and within about forty-eight hours both briefcases were on my desk. They were all about the meteorological bases in Spitsbergen, East Greenland and elsewhere in the Arctic.

Beatrice Jackman
Civilian translator, British Legation, Stockholm
There was a Danish doctor who invented a little tiny silver thing like a double-ended bullet, really, and in there microfilm was placed and the

couriers then inserted that into their anatomy and that was brought up to Sweden. And in the legation in Sweden there was much sitting on waste-paper baskets all over the place until they arrived on the scene and then they were opened and somebody in the legation would develop the films.

Ronald Turnbull
SOE officer, Stockholm
I remember one person had a very big backside. He was a great carrier.

Major Andrew Croft
SOE officer, Stockholm
There was masses of information coming in. There were also certain people who were doing commando operations. There was one party, for instance, who attacked the *Tirpitz* with 'chariots' – human torpedoes. The weather was unusually and rather tragically rough and the chariots had to be scuttled and the chaps had to escape over the border. One was killed, shot by the Germans. Another was wounded. I was able to represent the story that they were captured by the Germans and had managed to escape, so, that being so, the Swedes let them go. Actually they hadn't been captured but the story was good enough and we got them back home. There was a lot of that sort of thing. One wasn't always successful in hoodwinking the Swedes but if one could create a good alibi story, one was successful.

Major Henry Threlfall
SOE officer, Stockholm
There was a rather precarious air service between Leuchars airfield in Scotland and Stockholm. Planes could only fly by night when there was ten-tenths cloud cover because you had to pass over the German fighter belt protecting Norway. Personal communications like that were extremely unreliable and sometimes six weeks would go by without a single flight and then you'd manage to get two or three through. It was a highly uncomfortable flight. You flew very high, as high as they could in those days. I went off in January in the midst of an appalling cold wave. I don't think I'd ever been so cold in my life, even though I had a fur-lined coat on. They gave us sandwiches when we were about halfway off and you couldn't eat them because they were frozen solid. It was all very primitive. All sorts of people wanted to go and priorities were a very thorny problem. That was one of the things that we had in our hands and had to settle.

Ronald Turnbull
SOE officer, Stockholm
We invited Niels Bohr to come out because he was vitally important to the whole business of nuclear development. They wanted him to work on the atomic project. I knew him from when I was there before the invasion. He was, as they say in Danish, very 'English-friendly'. Both Churchill wanted him and also the Americans.

No particular effort was made to hide him or disguise him and he was moved through very quickly. It was he who caused most of the trouble by saying that he didn't want to get on to the plane without his son. We had to point out to him that there was only room for one in the bomb rack and it was impossible. But we did put the son on the very next flight.

GREECE

Brigadier Eddie Myers
SOE officer, commander of Operation 'Harling'
In Cairo one day, a friend of mine, who had been at the Middle East staff college with me a few months previously, came into my office and asked how he could get hold of a few parachute-trained sappers to be dropped into Europe somewhere to blow up a bridge. He didn't specify where. I told him that I happened to know – it was part of my job to know – that there were no parachute-trained sappers in the Middle East at that time. And he looked at me and said, 'Well, what's that badge you're wearing?' It was a parachute-trained badge, a parachute on one's arm. I said I'd learnt at the combined training centre at Kabrit. Well, one thing led to another and a week later I was in Greece.

Our first attempt, this small party of volunteers, nine officers and three wireless operators divided amongst three aeroplanes, Liberators, was abortive. These were the only three Liberators which SOE had in Egypt flying for them at that time and they had to be serviced and got ready for another flight and it was two nights later before they were ready to go again. On that second attempt I was determined that we didn't come back because otherwise we were going to miss the moon – the moon would be too late in getting up – and there'd be a month's delay. The whole idea was to cut the railway line to Piraeus before the battle of El Alamein, the breakout by Montgomery, so I was determined that we should drop that night at the second attempt, signals or no signals. We dropped on the lower slopes of Mount Giona, very

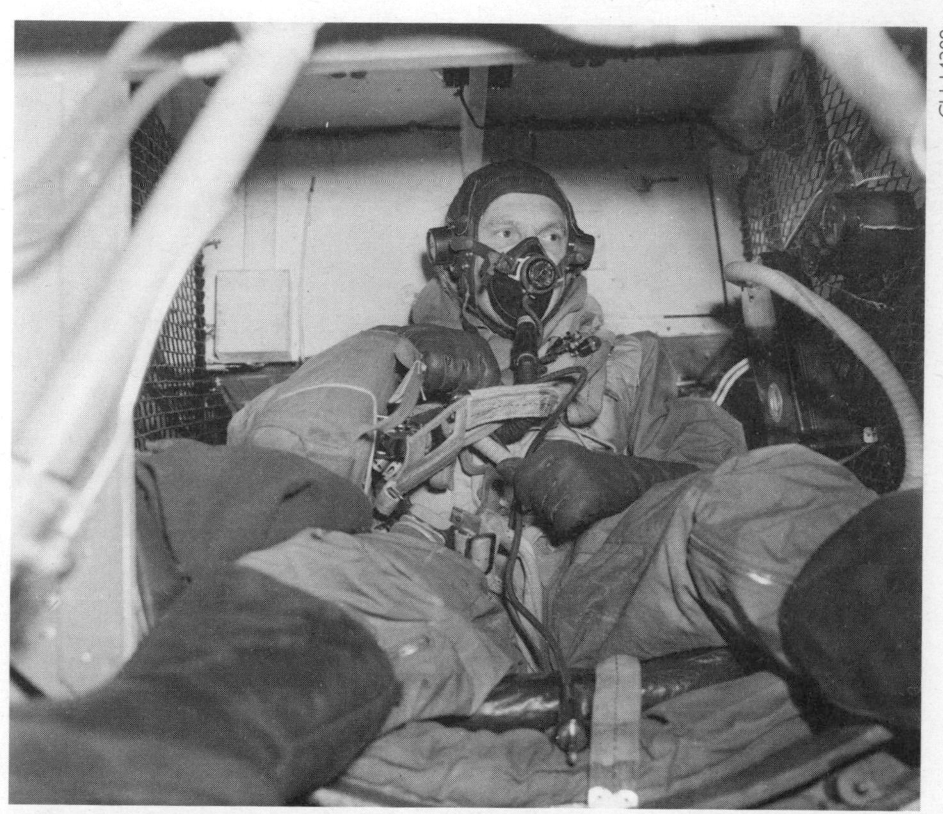

CH 14389

A passenger travelling in the bomb bay of a De Havilland Mosquito, flying between Leuchars, Fife, and Sweden.

knobbly surroundings, rock and all the rest of it, and I landed in the middle of a fir tree.

Major 'Monty' Woodhouse
SOE officer, Operation 'Harling'

The object of the mission was to link up with guerrilla bands who were known to be in existence in the Greek mountains and to attack the railway line through Greece, which was one of the lines of communication and supply from central Europe to the German Afrika Korps in North Africa. We were offered the choice of three major viaducts on the railway line as targets and it was Myers's responsibility to choose which we would attack. My principal function was to round up the guerrillas who were said to be active in the mountains and form an assault force that could wipe out any garrison on the chosen bridge and make way for the demolition.

We were briefed in advance, not very fully. We were told that there were two guerrilla bands available who would be willing to co-operate with us. Neither of them was actually in the location where they were said to be so that even after we arrived in Greece it took several weeks before we could bring the guerrillas together to the target. We were given the names of the leaders of the two bands. One was a Greek colonel called Zervas. The other was a civilian lawyer called Sephariadis. We were not told anything about the political background of either of them or of the resistance movement in general and we did not appreciate in advance that these two guerrilla forces were antagonistic to each other.

The Sephariadis force, which later became known as ELAS, was under communist leadership. The Zervas force, which we later came to know as EDES, was a mixed bunch politically, rather right of centre, certainly not as homogenous in its political outlook as the ELAS force. But one thing that the two leaders had in common, at least to begin with, was that none wanted the King of Greece back in the country, and this was something of which we were totally unaware in advance. We were equally unaware that it was a cardinal feature of British Government policy that the King of Greece should be restored after the war. None of this political background was revealed to us at all in advance. We had to learn entirely on the spot after we arrived.

Zervas was nominally in command of the attack on the bridge. I say nominally because in fact the plan of operations was worked out by Myers after a reconnaissance of the three target bridges which he made himself. He worked out the plan of attack and the timing of the whole operation before either Zervas or the ELAS guerrillas arrived on the scene at all. And my first function when I had brought them all together was to translate Myers's plan of operation to Zervas and the leader of the ELAS band, whose pseudonym was Aris Veloukhiotis.

Brigadier Eddie Myers
SOE officer, commander of Operation 'Harling'

I decided that we should send a small force of our amply strong number of guerrillas, the andartes, about a thousand yards north and a thousand yards south of the bridge itself, in order to stop enemy reinforcements coming up by rail. This was a force of about a dozen andartes, each with an officer or a Greek engineer who knew how to lay explosives and cut the railway line before they withdrew or, if reinforcements came up by rail, to stop the train coming right on to the viaduct.

The next party of chaps to be organised was the actual attacking force. It was a fast-running torrent, melted snow coming down from the mountains, which divided the garrison on the north side of the viaduct from the south, so we had to have two attacking forces, each about forty-strong, one on the north side and one on the south side. That left us with about thirty or forty chaps as a reserve in case anything went wrong. Then our explosives, which we'd prepared, were strapped on to the backs of mules to carry them down from the mountain to as near as we could get them to the bridge. By eleven o'clock at night, which was our zero hour for the attack, we were all in our positions.

At about a quarter past eleven all hell was let loose at both ends of the viaduct and after half an hour or a little more a message came back from the north end of the viaduct that they weren't doing too well. They'd been beaten back by the Italians. They had rather too many automatics and our chaps were unable to get through the barbed wire to overpower them. From the shouting going on at the far end, the south end of the viaduct, it was quite apparent that they were doing all right, so we decided to put in the whole of the reserve, then and there, on the north end of the viaduct.

After the battle had been going on for well over an hour, Zervas began to get anxious that we would soon be running out of ammunition and I decided that we must take a risk. So I went forward by myself, with a bodyguard, an andarte, and signalled across the river to the chap in charge of the demolition band, a New Zealander, Tom Barnes, to take the demolition party in and start fixing their explosives.

About one or two o'clock in the morning, Tom Barnes whistled on his whistle that he was ready to blow the bridge. The whistle was for everybody to take cover. Almost simultaneously, the Very signal, which we'd prearranged to send up when the north end of the bridge was captured, went up in the air, so the viaduct was entirely in our hands. A few seconds later the demolition of the viaduct took place and I was able to see, from a few yards from one end of the viaduct, two spans lift up into the air and come down in entangled pieces.

I was able myself with my bodyguard then to run along the top of the viaduct to the jagged end and shout to Tom Barnes. He had some explosives still left and one pier of the two steel piers was still standing, although one at least of its four legs was cut. He had enough explosives hopefully to bring down that pier and to put some more explosives on the fallen spans. I told him to carry on with it, to get on with it as quickly as possible. There'd been a loud explosion from the north end indicating that our small party of chaps a thousand yards north of the viaduct had stopped a train coming from the north with enemy reinforcements, as I'd had every reason to predict would happen. The train had stopped without being derailed and there was quite a bit of a battle going on.

I shouted to Tom Barnes to be as quick as he jolly well could because I could only give him about another twenty or thirty minutes. He prepared for the second demolition, for which, at the end of about half an hour, he was ready and he blew his whistle again. Everybody took cover and a bit more of the bridge came down. The general withdrawal signal was sounded and we all made our way up the side of the mountain down which we had come the previous night.

The Heavens were on our side. It started to snow, obliterating our tracks. We got to our forward rendezvous, just about daylight, in dribs and drabs, climbing up the mountainside, and we got to our final rendezvous deep in the fir forest some time that afternoon. We'd been on the go for the best part of forty-eight hours without any sleep, we'd come down from a mountainside of about 4,500 feet to a few hundred feet above sea level, fought a battle and gone back again, and I for one was very nearly exhausted. And that was the end of the battle for the Gorgopotamos.

Major 'Monty' Woodhouse
SOE officer, Operation 'Harling'

We particularly asked both Zervas and Aris Veloukhiotis to order that no prisoners were to be taken because we had no facilities for holding prisoners. We were guerrillas, we just had to scatter and get away as best we could, we couldn't possibly look after Italian prisoners. Disastrously Aris disobeyed this order and took one Italian prisoner and the following day he still had this man alive with him. By the evening of that day the Italian was dead. He was killed on Aris's orders, by the youngest guerrilla in Aris's band, who was ordered to cut his throat: a deliberate act of Aris's to blood the young man and strengthen his attachment to the ELAS band.

Brigadier Eddie Myers
SOE officer, commander of Operation 'Harling'
The effect of the Gorgopotamos, being one month late, didn't have any direct effect on the outcome of the Battle of El Alamein at all but it had a great effect on Rommel's supplies later because it cut for six valuable weeks all supplies going that way. They had to go other ways, down Italy and so on. From the Greeks' point of view, to hear that Greek andartes, aided possibly by British soldiers, had blown up an important viaduct on the railway right under the noses of the Axis, even though they were only Italians, was a tremendous morale booster and also to the resistance forces themselves and in their future recruiting. From the point of view of SOE it was the first major success in the field literally anywhere. It was a tremendous publicity event for SOE and resulted in it being recognised by people from Churchill downwards as something worth backing. Although we were a month late so far as the tactics and planning of the operation were concerned, we had achieved something that was tangible and obviously of great tactical help to the Allies, to British forces, in the Middle East. As a result, SOE got its status raised to enable people like Churchill to prise, without undue difficulty, a few more aeroplanes for supplying SOE operations, not only in south-east Europe, out of the grasp of Bomber Command, who thought that they could practically win the war unaided.

1943

The engine driver must have seen the sparks from the fuse because he put on his brakes, but he was a bit too late. The explosives went off just under his engine, derailed it and tipped it over on to the embankment.

By 1943, the tide of the war was beginning to turn. The input of American men and material was making itself felt, particularly in driving the Germans from North Africa, while the Soviet Union was dealing heavy blows to German forces on the Eastern Front. The Red Army's success at Stalingrad, where the German Sixth Army surrendered in February, was the catalyst for a steady German withdrawal to the west. Eventual Allied victory in North Africa, meanwhile, opened the way to thrusts into southern Europe. After British and American forces invaded Sicily in July and mainland Italy in September, the Italians sued for an armistice.

With the British and Americans deciding on north-west Europe as the place to launch the second front against Germany, priority was placed on preparing in Britain a massive invasion force. Consequently, SOE continued to struggle for resources, though now it was doing work of real importance. Nineteen forty-three opened with what was arguably SOE's outstanding sabotage operation of the war: the attack on the Norsk Hydro heavy water plant at Vemork in occupied Norway. The operation was launched to frustrate Nazi Germany's atomic bomb plans, for which heavy water – deuterium oxide – was essential. Today it seems that Germany's scientists may have been on the wrong track, but no one knew that at the time or could have predicted which side would develop the weapon first.

From the spring, SOE poured further uniformed teams of liaison officers and wireless operators into the occupied Balkans, particularly into Greece, Albania and Yugoslavia, to find and work with more groups of guerrillas and harass the enemy's garrisons. Impressed already by reports of significant guerrilla activity, Allied commanders were anxious to harness

and encourage it as a means of tying down Axis units, accelerating Italy's defeat and deceiving the Germans into believing that the Allies might open a major front there.

As British and American forces prepared to invade Sicily and Italy, striking success was had in Greece with the destruction by SOE of the Asopos viaduct and a concerted campaign of ambushes and further demolitions. Across the Balkans, however, SOE efforts to maximise resistance were also complicated by the degree to which Balkan guerrillas were divided by politics and motivated less by a desire to kill Axis troops than by a wish to secure post-war power. This was particularly the case in Yugoslavia, where SOE came to support, simultaneously, both Draža Mihailović's royalist 'Chetnik' guerrillas and Tito's communist-led partisans.

Nineteen forty-three was also a year of disasters. In France, where, after the Allies landed in north-west Africa, the Germans had taken full control of the whole country, SOE increased its efforts to build circuits, prepare for the invasion and carry out sabotage, but casualties were high. Some agents were lost to poor security and to the enemy's efficiency at detection and interrogation; some fell victim to a colleague's double-dealing with the enemy. Perhaps the worst of SOE's troubles took place in Holland, where dozens of Dutch agents parachuted straight into German hands.

Norway

Lieutenant Jens-Anton Poulsson

Norwegian SOE officer, commander of advance party 'Grouse'

We were going to be sent home to establish small resistance groups in Norway in the Telemark area and the planning for this went along and we were actually sent out to Station 61, near Tempsford, to go back home. But all this was changed in the autumn of 1942, because the importance of the heavy water suddenly got first priority.

My radio operator Knut Haugland and I were called to London and told about a British Army mission that was going to go by either parachute or glider: the 'Freshman' force. And at a meeting in Baker Street we picked out the place where the gliders could land and thrashed out all that technical stuff about how to receive the gliders and so on and what we would do afterwards. 'Freshman' was going to blow up the heavy water apparatus and part of the electrolysis plant, they were going to come in two gliders and each glider had a team that could if necessary do the job alone, and we had to be a reception committee. We had to be on the radio, we were going to put up lights and after the gliders had landed we were supposed to take the British forces down to Vemork and say goodbye.

When we left, Haugland and I, to go back to Tempsford, I remember Colonel Wilson took me aside and said, 'This operation is very, very important because if the Germans get that heavy water they may be able to destroy some part of London' – or words to that effect. And I didn't believe him. I thought he'd just said that to make us eager to do a good job. I knew nothing about atomic bombs and so on. I didn't hear about atomic bombs until after the war, when that bloody thing exploded over Japan.

Major Joe Adamson
Staff officer, Norwegian Section, SOE HQ, London
The advance party was to receive a considerable body of qualified British commandos who were to arrive by glider. This operation unhappily ended not only in disaster but in a tragedy of great proportions. Bad weather forced the towing aircraft to turn and one of them to crash. Down came the gliders, well short of target, and the soldiers who were not killed were executed by the Germans.

Lieutenant Jens-Anton Poulsson
Norwegian SOE officer, commander of advance party 'Grouse'
I think we were told the day after the tragedy what had happened, and a couple of days later we were told that a new party would come and join up with us, so we had to stay on. We went further back into the mountains, because the Germans had a large search in the Rjukan valley, and went on to the Vidda. Then we moved to a hut called Svensbu – it belongs to my family actually – and we stayed there and we waited.

Major Joe Adamson
Staff officer, Norwegian Section, SOE HQ, London
Well, the Government turned to SOE to ask what we could do. The target unhappily was already, as they say, blown, because of maps found on some of the dead soldiers. Anyway, it was our job now, so we set to work and we picked the best collection of men from our numbers that could be expected.

Lieutenant Joachim Rønneberg
Norwegian SOE officer, commander of Operation 'Gunnerside'
I was working up in Scotland as an instructor, when suddenly, one day in

November '42, I was called up to Major Hampton. He said he had just got a telegram from London asking if I could take on a job in Norway and if I could pick five of the unit to go with me. I remember, I said, 'Well, it's easy to pick the people to some extent.' There were so many good ones to choose from – that was the difficult bit. I asked, 'Do they need to be skiers?' And they didn't know because they didn't know anything, where we were going or when we were going. They just knew that it was an operation that had to be done as quickly as possible. Well, I picked out the five I wanted and talked to them and said, 'I have been offered a job, I don't know what it is yet. Do you want to follow?' And everybody, of course, oh, they cheered. That was great. And I knew I had a good team. A very good team indeed.

Lieutenant Jens-Anton Poulsson
Norwegian SOE officer, commander of Operation 'Swallow' (formerly 'Grouse')
'Gunnerside' was supposed to join us in December, before Christmas, but the weather was very bad and they didn't arrive until the middle of February '43. In the meantime we had to fend for ourselves. To stay alive we needed wood and we needed food. Before Christmas we had a very bad time and we had to eat reindeer moss, or rather Icelandic moss. We mixed it with some oatmeal we had. It was only a few times we tried that. So we were dependent on hunting and the day before Christmas I shot the first reindeer. In all I think we shot fourteen reindeer, which was our main source of food. We used the contents of the stomach as a vegetable. The reindeer did the preliminary cooking for us so we just mixed it with blood and used it with the meat. We used everything from the animal, everything except the skin and the feet.

Lieutenant Joachim Rønneberg
Norwegian SOE officer, commander of Operation 'Gunnerside'
We went down to London and we got new weapons and some of the items that we hadn't got before. We got new information, the latest information from Vemork, saying that nothing had been easy during the black moon period but we will hope for the best. Then we went down to Station 17, where they had made the charges and had the models and had helped the commando troops. I don't know what they expected to meet when they were welcoming us down there. Instead of thirty-two or thirty-four British commandos they got six innocent young Norwegian chaps.

We were invited upstairs to see where we should live and sleep and told to come down in about half an hour for a drink before dinner. And quite naturally when you are planning an operation like this and you get new weapons you will take them out and look at them. You have been told during your training that your gun is your best part – and it definitely is in a tight situation. And round me I heard people taking loading grip and pressing the trigger and everything – 'click, click, click' all round the place – and everyone seemed happy. And I took loading grip and pressed my trigger and it didn't say click – it said 'bang!' and there was a big hole in the wall and I saw five shocked friends. The one who was most shocked was myself. I couldn't understand what had happened. In came a batman looking very scared indeed and also the adjutant, a lieutenant colonel, asking, 'What the hell is going on?' And I said, 'We have just come from Chiltern Court and we have new weapons and I have tried mine and it works!'

The attack should have taken place on Christmas Eve, 1942, but due to the weather we had no chance of flying in December at all. Next we flew in January, in the moon period of January, but we didn't succeed in making contact and we returned back to England. By now they had already started nicknaming us 'the permanent furniture up at Station 61' because they never got rid of us, but we couldn't do anything about it. Our next chance was on 17 February.

Wing Commander Ken Batchelor
Commanding Officer, 138 (SD) Squadron, RAF
Wing Commander Corby, an old friend of mine, who was in charge of air operations at Baker Street, came down to see me one day to say that the Germans were after an explosive a thousand times as powerful as anything yet known. Of course there was no mention in those days of heavy water or the splitting of the atom. If we had heard details at that time it would have been as unbelievable as when people reported they had seen an aeroplane flying at Newmarket without a propeller, which was of course our first jet aircraft. I'd just taken over the squadron a month before and this was just one of the rare occasions when it was stressed how important it was. I had a splendid chap, Gibson, who I had known on the squadron before and who'd done a number of trips to Norway, and I briefed him to do the trip because it was obviously something very important. What the explosive was we had no idea at all.

Pilot Officer John Charrot
Halifax observer/bomb-aimer, 138 (SD) Squadron, RAF
To see these six people arrive at the aircraft – they were huge. They were all carrying a tremendous amount of equipment, which they dumped of course in the aircraft – they didn't come in a car, they'd come in a big lorry – and the

ground crew loaded up all their containers. I think they probably had the maximum, which was twelve. We set off and it was a lovely night. The station navigation officer came as the navigator, I was up in the nose all the time and we went across the North Sea, made a very good landing where we wanted to, just near Stavanger, and then went off to where the dropping site was to be. And that was where it got difficult.

Everybody was looking out. The rear gunner was a great help. At one time he said, 'You know, you're talking about fluffy clouds. I'm not sure. I think these are the tops of mountains not fluffy clouds you're going over.' So it was as bad as that. But it had been agreed with Rønneberg and Gibson, before we started, that they would do a blind drop because it was essential now that they got there and destroyed this heavy water plant, so we circled around and then Joachim said, 'This is very close. I can recognise certain features. Go round again and we'll do the drop, we'll go first, then go round again and send the containers down.' So they all went quite happily and the rear-gunner reported, 'All parachutes opened,' which was useful to know, and then we dropped the containers.

Lieutenant Joachim Rønneberg

Norwegian SOE officer, commander of Operation 'Gunnerside'

Everybody came down all right. But war is a question of luck and immediately after we had landed up on the Hardangervidda we saw one of our packages being carried away with one of the parachutes. We ran after it and after about half a kilometre, probably more, we came to an open patch of water, the outlet of one of these thousands of lakes, and there was the package. It had gone through the water and the parachute had tried to pull it up on the other side but the wind wasn't strong enough. In that package we had rucksacks for half the party with sleeping bags and weapons and food for the first five days. Had the wind been a little bit stronger we would never have found it and there wouldn't have been an attack on the heavy water that month or until another party had come and taken over.

Lieutenant Jens-Anton Poulsson

Norwegian SOE officer, commander of Operation 'Swallow' (formerly 'Grouse')

After 'Gunnerside' had been dropped they met a poacher and they took him prisoner. They had to. They used him also for pulling one of their sledges. They took him with them to within four or five kilometres from our place and left him there with a guard. We talked it over, what we were going to do with him. We ought to have shot him but we didn't. We knew the operation was very important. On the other hand it's difficult just to shoot a man, to kill him.

Lieutenant Joachim Rønneberg
Norwegian SOE officer, commander of Operation 'Gunnerside'
He was interrogated and we went through his rucksack. He was about forty years old. He was a hunter by profession. He was unmarried. Nobody was waiting for him. He hadn't been home for two months. Those was the sort of answers we got out of him and you can see why we asked liked this. We had our orders. Professor Tronstadt had told us, 'Whatever you do you must do the job. Whatever problems you hit against, think of the job. That is your main responsibility.' Well, we talked it over and I remember one of my friends, a very great fellow, he was always ready to give a helping hand and try to solve problems, and he thought, 'Well, now, Jo has enough problems, I'll take one of these dirty jobs.' Imagine the situation. We were standing outside this hut, in brilliant sunshine, a few degrees of frost, clear skies, calmness all over the place, with this tremendous problem inside. And he said quietly, 'I'll shoot him for you.' That was the biggest offer he could make in my favour, to help me, to take on the job. But I said, 'That's not the problem at all. We can't have this man lying on the stairs when the owner comes in the spring.' So we told the man, 'Well, you have written a declaration saying that you are hunting illegally, you have a weapon illegally and you are selling on the black market, we are adding that you have been guiding us on this mission, and you have signed it. So if you don't keep your mouth shut you will be shot by the Germans, because if anything happens to us we will see to it that this declaration will end up with the Germans. All right, you are free. You go and hunt for another week and earn more money.' And he left – three days before the attack. We managed to forget about him, fortunately, otherwise we wouldn't have slept at all.

Lieutenant Jens-Anton Poulsson
Norwegian SOE officer, commander of Operation 'Swallow' (formerly 'Grouse')
We started out at eight o'clock in the evening. The weather had changed dramatically. There was a warm wind blowing, the snow was melting, the water was running on the roads and so on. We went on to the main road, followed it, left the road before Vemork and came down on the road again on the other side, so we bypassed the inhabited area. Then we followed the road to the place where Helberg had found it was possible to cross the gorge and we left all our winter equipment, skis and what have you there. We were in

British battledress and had only the prepared demolition charges and our weapons. 'Gunnerside' had Thompson sub-machine guns, 'Grouse' too.

Lieutenant Joachim Rønneberg
Norwegian SOE officer, commander of Operation 'Gunnerside'
We could hear the humming of the machinery and we saw it faintly in the moonlight. It was slightly overcast, so it was excellent weather for us to work in. When we had to walk downhill the snow was up to our waists, and when we came further down and had to make a short-cut round the houses it even went up to our arms. You had to sort of do front crawl to get out of the snow and downwards. The whole time we heard the humming from the target, hoping that in about two hours' time it would be quiet.

We watched the guard being relieved and saw them coming up, two of them, finished with their guard duty, up and into their hut. We were lying just in cover outside the fence and we waited there for about an hour. Of course we were tense but the situation was very calm at the same time. It was like being on a training scheme in England or Scotland. Everybody was talking calmly, we were eating biscuits and raisins and chocolate.

Lieutenant Jens-Anton Poulsson
Norwegian SOE officer, commander of Operation 'Swallow' (formerly 'Grouse')
We waited until we were sure they were back in their guard hut and then Rønneberg gave the order to start. He and his demolition party went for the heavy water room – actually they had to use a cable tunnel to get in. The covering party took up their pre-planned positions. Hauklid and I, for instance, advanced to twenty yards from the guard hut.

Lieutenant Joachim Rønneberg
Norwegian SOE officer, commander of Operation 'Gunnerside'
I had one set of charges and a friend of mine, who was outside, he had another one and I had one man guarding me. We came to the opening and looked through the window and saw the man who was on duty down in the high concentration room, a Norwegian workman. He was reading the instruments and writing the log and so on. We managed to get down and open the door and said, 'Hands up.'

I was about halfway through putting on the charges when the window out to the yard suddenly broke and I saw my covering man pointing his gun immediately at the window. What he saw was the head of one of our friends. They had lost us and decided, 'Well, we have orders to do the job if something

The Norsk Hydro heavy water production plant at Vemork, Norway, which was attacked by Norwegian SOE agents in February 1943.

uncertain happens.' They hadn't seen us, didn't know where we were at all, so they were just as astonished as we were when they saw us.

We thought it would be very nice to know that we'd succeeded, so we decided to cut the fuses to half a minute, all the two-minute fuses, I think it was eight of them, and saw that all of them were burning. We lit one each. And by the time the Germans realised that there was a drain in the flow of the high concentration room, all the heavy water and the half-made, quarter-made and ten per-cent made were out in the river Mono. There was only fresh drinking water from top to bottom in the factory.

I remembered Tronstadt telling me, 'If you need somewhere to lock up the Norwegian guard, you can put him in the toilet and the key for the toilet is on the left-hand side of the door.' And I remember, when I left, seeing the key. That was the sort of information we had. I am quite certain there was not one operation during the war with such good information and knowledge of the target as we had on ours. That was part of our success, of course.

We climbed down the same way, down to the riverbed. It was very steep but we went very quickly. And along the railway the snow had blown away and the ground was frozen so we left no marks at all. The Germans hadn't seen anybody. When we came up to our equipment depot, the first car came from the garrison at Rjukan – there were about three hundred soldiers down there. They were on their way to Vemork, to take us, of course. We followed a parallel road to the main road and the whole time we could look down on the road, fifty metres below, and see all the traffic going that way.

Lieutenant Jens-Anton Poulsson
Norwegian SOE officer, commander of Operation 'Swallow' (formerly 'Grouse')
Up on the plateau it was much colder, there was a hard wind blowing, and there we started to move. We were not afraid of being followed by the German forces. They wouldn't have been able to move at all up there. It was rather hard work against the wind.

Lieutenant Joachim Rønneberg
Norwegian SOE officer, commander of Operation 'Gunnerside'
We came up on top and could put on our skis and start on our way, going towards the mountains. We had a brilliant sunrise. The mountain on the other side is two thousand metres and it was reddened in the morning sunshine with a very light layer of immaculate skies hanging over. It was marvellous: everybody was there; not a shot fired during the attack; the Germans not knowing where we came from, how many we were and so on.

We were a lucky team, definitely. We felt our enemy now was the Norwegian winter and the Norwegian mountains and we felt that we could compete with them as long as we would respect the weather and their superiority when conditions were bad. And that was no problem at all.

We had about four hundred kilometres, five hundred kilometres, to go to Sweden. We crossed all the main valleys going east. We had to avoid Lake Mjøsa because it would have been rather difficult to cross. When we'd planned it, it should have been done in December and the lake would have been frozen. Between Oslo and Mjøsa there were lots of German locations and so on and up at Lillehammer you had the German headquarters for southern Norway, so we had to go a bit north of that to cross into Sweden. It took us about eighteen days. When we got to Sweden we had to present ourselves as refugees. We took off our British uniforms and we reported to the Swedish authorities in woollen underwear, a jersey, a white snow suit with no marks at all, no weapons.

We had been in our uniforms for a very, very long time and we smelled tremendously, I think, and the de-lousing in Sweden was an experience, too. We were taken to a hospital then invited downstairs and told to take off all our clothes. We had to present ourselves for a shower as men born and two nice Swedish nurses with a bucket of strong soap and a floor brush started up here and worked downwards, and I don't know who had the greatest fun, the nurses or me.

We had come from occupied Norway. We had come from war-battered Britain, with blackout and bombing and things, and now we came to neutral Sweden with lots of things in the windows of the shops, no blackout, lights in the street. It was like coming to heaven, more or less. And I remember the first day in Stockholm we went to the opera and saw La Traviata and I remember we were sort of punching, pinching each other to be quite certain that we were not dreaming.

Greece

Brigadier Eddie Myers
Senior SOE liaison officer
Arriving back at Zervas' headquarters in early January, I found a long message from Cairo, congratulating everybody on the success of the Gorgopotamos and inviting us to stay on and organise the whole of Greece, helped by a large number of additional officers who would be sent from the Middle East by parachute with wireless operators.

Corporal Eric Child
SOE wireless operator
As we flew over Salonika on the way into Greece I could hear pitter-patter, pitter-patter, against the fuselage of the aircraft and I said to the dispatcher, 'Just my luck, it's bloody raining.' He said, 'That's not rain, that's ack-ack fire.'

Major Brian Dillon
SOE liaison officer
I'd asked them to drop me at about six to eight hundred feet, which was sufficiently high for the parachute to open. By the time I jumped out – it was a brilliant moon – we must have been thousands of feet high. I could see half of Greece in the bright moonlight. I had time to get my compass out of my belt, take a bearing on some signal fires I could see on the horizon, put it back in my belt and button it up before I landed, so we must have been pretty bloody high. I landed in a tree on the edge of a cliff. The parachute fortunately caught in the tree. I shinned down and had to leave the parachute up the tree, which you're not supposed to but I couldn't get it down.

Walking down this track there was a wire apparently stretched tight across the track. I thought, 'Mines! It's a minefield!' I didn't think why there should be a minefield on top of a mountain. Anyway, we explored this wire and followed it. Do you know what was on the end? A goat. Sudden relief. Eventually we discovered some bodies sat round the remains of a fire so I shook one and a bearded figure jumped up and shoved his rifle in my face. It was a partisan. One of them spoke English and said, 'Ah, we were expecting you, but we thought nobody had dropped so we went to sleep.'

Major Guy Micklethwait
SOE liaison officer
I tried to get into the Peloponnese but luckily the pilot said no, the signals weren't satisfactory. Actually we discovered later that there were Germans sitting there waiting for me. I was very angry at the time – I wanted to get out. It was a good thing I didn't.

Sergeant Bill Weatherley
SOE wireless operator
On the fifth attempt we got in. We flew over and we saw a few lights and we hoped it would be our reception committee. I got out of the plane and I remember distinctly looking around. It was quiet but God it was cold. I saw the old Halifax flying away into the distance, you could still see the exhausts,

and one felt very, very lonely. There were stacks of white chutes all round and I hadn't a clue as to which one was Geoff, which one was Simonides, which one was my radio or what. All I knew was that down there were some bloody dangerous-looking mountains covered by fir trees. I had a good landing, I sat up and released myself, I took my whistle out and I gave a plaintive blow into it that echoed all round Greece. Next thing I knew there was a fellow came up to me, with a beard down to his waist, covered in ouzo and breadcrumbs and bits of cheese, and he stank to high heaven. He grabbed hold of me and was kissing me. One of the local reception boys.

Major Ken Scott
SOE liaison officer
I was going in with two other sappers on Operation Washing, which was the demolition of the Asopos viaduct. The drop went very well. It was a clear night. We saw the flares. We were told, 'That's the dropping zone, we'll do one dummy run and then we'll come in. When the green light flashes, off you go.' We all three arrived safely with our stores.

The original plan was to get a combined force of guerrillas to attack the bridge, neutralise the guard and then the sappers would come along and place the explosives and do the demolition. That was the original plan and Eddie Myers turned up in the village two or three days after we landed to talk with Arthur Edmonds, to finalise the plan and to talk to the guerrilla commanders on how it should be done. This is when the whole thing came adrift because the guerrillas had decided that the target was too difficult for them to attack. So Eddie and Arthur with our support decided that the only way of doing it was by stealth, that somehow or other the Brits had to find a way to the bridge and do it as a stealth operation.

It was very heavily guarded. Because the Italians guarding the Gorgopotamus viaduct further north had failed, the Germans took over the guarding of all the main viaducts. They had concrete pillboxes, they had heavy and light machine guns and they had searchlights. So the conclusion from the Greek point of view was not at all unreasonable: it was a hell of a difficult target to attack. Imagine a river running through a mountain range into the most tremendous gorge that you can envisage, a gorge that was a thousand feet deep with vertical cliffs and at the bottom the river was perhaps twenty or thirty feet wide. It was that sort of gorge. And as the gorge came out on the plain it widened a bit and the viaduct had been constructed halfway up, approached from two railways on each side. As a defensive viaduct it was virtually impregnable. The technical side of it was fairly straightforward, we knew what to do with the explosives; but we had to get to the bridge.

We decided that it was not possible to approach it from the plain. The only way was to come down through the gorge, which was regarded by everybody as impassable. In the course of the river winding its way down to the plain there were numerous waterfalls thirty or fifty feet high, pools twenty or thirty feet deep. These were the things that we had to negotiate. We used fallen trees. We used rope ladders that we made. We handed the explosives down on the end of parachute cords. We called Cairo for more rope to help us down these waterfalls, which was another reason why we had to delay the operation for a month because we just couldn't get there. We had prepared all our charges, we had wrapped them in gas cape, we waterproofed them as much as we could; but we had to get the explosives and ourselves down the waterfalls.

I remember vividly turning round the last corner in the gorge and seeing the bridge for the first time. It was way above us, three or four hundred feet above us, the most enormous steel arch and only about a hundred yards away. We were so close to it. One could see the German guards all walking about on top. There were we down on the bottom, waiting for the light to fade and for the moon to appear, and we waited there until perhaps ten o'clock at night before putting in our attack.

Gordon-Creed was doing the scouting at the base of the bridge with his rubber truncheon, and Harry McIntyre and I were on the bridge fixing the charges. It took about a couple of hours. We had to place the charges, fix them firmly, connect them all up with primer-cord, fix the detonators, fix the primers, tape them all up, ignite them all and withdraw. It took about two hours and the searchlights were flying on the bridge the whole time, going from pier to pier, and whenever we were illuminated we had to lie flat or stick on the girders.

We'd hauled up three hundred pounds of explosives on the end of a bit of string and that in itself took quite a long time. We had to haul these up and fix them and haul more up and fix them. It was quite a lengthy operation for two chaps stuck on these girders three hundred feet above the river. Then Harry McIntyre and myself climbed down the scaffolding, got hold of Gordon-Creed, who said, 'By God you've been an awful long time,' and went down to the river and back up the waterfalls. And when we'd got ourselves about halfway up the waterfalls we saw this tremendous flash and then heard this enormous bang and I said, 'She's gone.' And she had gone. Didn't see it. We saw the flash and heard the bang but didn't see it.

News of the demolition was spread along the railway by the local stationmaster. And we heard later, after enquiring, that all the German guard had been shot under orders from the German commander. The bridge was cut for about three months and at a valuable time, just before the invasion of Sicily.

Sergeant Bill Weatherley
SOE wireless operator
The Asopos operation was a wonderful achievement. Donald Stott, who had led it, was put up by Eddie Myers for the VC. He didn't get it, because no shots were fired, but he got a DSO. And there were Germans around. Geoffrey Gordon-Creed in actual fact had to get rid of one, dispose of him. He hit him on the back of the neck with his cosh and knocked him straight over the edge, into the gorge.

Major Nicholas Hammond
SOE liaison officer
I was on Mount Olympus, in a village, say, a thousand feet up, fairly high, and the Germans attacked us. They aimed at this village, which they eventually destroyed. Well, when we saw them coming we simply walked higher up the mountain, and when we were up two thousand feet or three thousand feet we went round the side of the mountain and went away. We didn't fight the Germans when they came up because their armament was far superior. They came with heavy machine guns and mortars and things and we just took evasive action and just disappeared into the woods. So did the villagers, on the whole.

Sergeant Bill Weatherley
SOE wireless operator
If you walked into a village that had never seen a Brit before, they would flock round you. 'Have an ouzo!' And never, ever, when we were anywhere near a village did we have to live out in the open, under the skies, because they would drag you in and give you a bed, they would clear their mules out and put down fresh straw. They gave you whatever they had, even if it meant denuding their shelves or going without themselves. They really went out of their way. I think we were a peculiar phenomenon to them. Most of them had never seen a man from Athens never mind a foreigner.

Sergeant Ray Mason
SOE wireless operator
We were more or less living off the country. We had a few spare rations tucked

away in various caches around the area but we didn't get to those too often so we lived mainly as they did, on maize bread, olives, cheese, a bit of goat meat occasionally. There wasn't much spare food around. People were hungry and starving and dying of starvation in some parts of Greece. We had certain comforts dropped into us, perhaps occasional bottles of Scotch and a few sweets, tobacco, cigarettes and that sort of thing, but not much in the way of food.

Corporal Ben Kerevan
SOE wireless operator
The Greeks very soon found out that the red container was the one with the comforts in and they went for that first and if you weren't quick they had the red container hidden under the bushes or somewhere and you just didn't get your comforts. Sometimes we lost it and sometimes we didn't. The Greeks were very helpful of course but they were also very helpful to themselves. They wanted parachutes and whatever they could get. They made all kinds of things out of the parachutes, they made clothing and they used the webbing for harnesses for the mules and they took the cords to pieces and used it as cotton. They liked anything that dropped out of the skies. If the containers contained arms, they stole arms. If the containers contained explosives, they stole explosives. They just stole containers ad lib and that's it.

Sergeant Ray Mason
SOE wireless operator
I sympathised with the lot of the villagers. It must have been horrific up there. I mean even peacetime living must have been pretty awful. It's such a barren country. They scratched a living from patches in the mountains to grow their maize, their corn, to make their bread. They kept a cow or two, a few sheep. There were a lot of goats up in the mountain ranges amongst the trees; the goats of course devoured everything in sight. And I could understand them being in sympathy with the communists who promised them that things would be better when peace came. For those villagers, things could never have been any worse. This of course is where communism makes it mark, on the basis that you've got nothing to lose but your chains. At the same time many of the younger people, the Greeks, knew nothing about communism really. They just thought that life would be better, as they'd been promised, if they joined ELAS-EAM and the andartes generally and helped to liberate the country.

Colonel 'Monty' Woodhouse
SOE liaison officer
ELAS of course was very suspicious of the British presence. They took it for granted that the purpose of the British presence in Greece was to ensure the restoration of the King at the end of the war. We had no notion what British policy was but we gradually realised that Churchill did have strong feelings about the Greek monarchy, and that the communists had an understandable point in regarding us as being a sort of outpost of Churchill's policy of restoring the King to Greece. But whenever the subject came up in discussion and argument we noticed that what everybody seemed to want was a plebiscite on the subject of the monarchy. Well, that seemed to us a perfectly reasonable idea, because if a plebiscite showed the King was wanted, well, that was fine. If it showed he wasn't wanted, one couldn't believe he would want to come back. Early telegrams that Myers and I concocted in about January 1943 more or less took it for granted that a plebiscite would be held after the war. These telegrams caused a storm in London between SOE and the Foreign Office. The Foreign Office first of all said it didn't even know that any British officers were in Greece. What were they doing there? Why had they been sent? And why were they talking about seditious things like plebiscites?

Major Nicholas Hammond
SOE liaison officer
It was decided to give one hundred per cent support to the ELAS movement even though we knew that it was trying to create a monopoly and liable to attack any other movement. The object of this arming and enlarging of the resistance movement was to create a diversion for the invasion of Sicily. We were told in May and early June to set up a number of demolitions of the railway line and to attack the road system.

I blew one main bridge at Litokhoro before the invasion of Sicily, when we were creating diversions. I went down with some of my fifty ELAS people and a couple of mules carrying my explosives. I had devised a method of using what we called limpets. They were shaped like a bowler hat with a thin side where the bowler hat is open and when the thing exploded it blew inwards through the weak part. They had magnets on them so you could stick them on the side of a ship – they were used for blowing ships. I brought these to blow the girders of the bridge.

I went on to the bridge with my bowler hat limpets and stuck them on the various parts I wanted to blow and was arranging the simultaneous firing cords when a train came along. It had German troops on it and equipment.

Unfortunately I wasn't ready. I lay on the embankment and it passed overhead without any of them seeing me. Then I went back to the bridge and completed my preparations. I used a time-delay pencil, which meant that you pressed it and it fired the detonator three or five minutes later. I pressed my detonator and then ran down and hid in a hollow and there was a big 'Wham!' and the explosives went off. We knew from the noise and everything that the bridge had fallen and then we went off into the hills.

The Germans, when they came to the bridge, found that one of these limpets hadn't exploded. They thought these were used only at sea and thought the operation had been conducted by a party landed from a submarine in the Bay of Salonika, so there were no reprisals against Litokhoro as there would have been if they'd known the attack came from inland.

Major Ken Scott
SOE liaison officer

We came to an unguarded railway bridge near the town of Lamia. We fixed our charges at night and waited for the first train to pass. By luck we got an ammunition train. The thing went on, a pyrotechnic display, for about four or five hours.

Sergeant Ray Mason
SOE wireless operator

A troop train appeared less than a mile behind the pilot train. We just froze along the embankment. I was under a small bush and the train came past, it seemed to be going at quite a rate, then all of a sudden jammed on its brakes, sparks came out of the wheels, slowed down and stopped. And at the back of the train, when I looked up, I could see on a sort of platform a couple of guards with machine guns, talking and smoking. Everything was quiet and I was just lying below them. I could hardly breathe, you know, thinking that they were going to see me and which way shall I run. We stayed there for about ten minutes. Then there were a couple of toots in the distance and thankfully the train just moved off.

So we didn't get that troop train at all but we stayed and attempted another train. Major Scott attached a piece of safety fuse to the explosive charges and waited till we heard the train approaching and at the last minute lit the fuse and ran. The engine driver must have seen the sparks from the fuse because he put on his brakes, but he was a bit too late. The explosives went off just under his engine, derailed it and tipped it over on to the embankment. Then all the guerrillas who were supposedly helping us opened fire on the train. There was no response from anybody on the train. It was quite empty. It was goods, mixed goods.

I could see no sign of Major Scott so I walked down to the place where I'd last seen him, called his name quietly but there was no sign of him. I thought perhaps he'd been shot by these guerrillas opening up because he hadn't got much time to get away. I walked back up the length of the train, still looking around, and as I got to the end of the train a machine gun opened up on me, much to my surprise – these sort of fireflies whistling around me. I dropped to the ground and waited for a bit. Finally I crawled away and started back, quite on my own, the way we'd come down and after about half an hour of struggling through the brushwood I was confronted by a figure pointing a pistol at my head and it was actually Major Scott. He'd heard me coming up and thought I was somebody after him.

Major Brian Dillon
SOE liaison officer
One of the things was exploding mule shit. Exploding mule shit consists of a plastic explosive, which you can mould like putty, with some glue on it and dried mule shit sticking to it and a detonator stuffed in and you just chuck it down the road. The easiest way to do it was to find some old woman going to market and say, 'Here you are, my dear, here's a dozen. Just drop these on your way up the road.' They weren't terribly powerful, they would blow the wheel off a truck, but they irritated the Germans. And what was good to see was that the Germans had fatigue parties of soldiers sweeping the roads, sweeping the shit off, because they were covered with mule shit.

Sergeant Bill Weatherley
SOE wireless operator
We had two telescopic Lee Enfield rifles – I liked shooting, I made international level, represented both Hong Kong and the British Army – and we used to go down, put a white brick on the road, zero in on the white brick from up in the hills among the pine trees and wait for a truck to come round the corner. We'd shoot through the windscreen, wait for the people coming to look for him to come round the corner, have a go at those for a little while and then just turn round and saunter away.

You'd do whatever you had to do wherever it had to be done, but you'd let the locals know or you would do your damnedest not to carry out any job anywhere near any inhabitation. I mean, if you had villages ten miles apart, whatever you were going to do had to be done five miles from either. If it was down on the plains you would give them the benefit of the doubt and you wouldn't do it because there were more villages down on the plains. But up in the mountains, that road going up through the mountains, there were occasions when you had quite an area of road you could play around with. If you went down to the railway line you didn't really think of the consequences. You had to do the railway or the bridge or the gully or whatever it was, so you did it.

Major Brian Dillon
SOE liaison officer
We had an identification book of German units. 'Number such and such on a tank indicates it belongs to such and such a division.' So we built up a picture of what reinforcements had come into the country and that was fed back to Cairo. One way of observing was to give a small boy some chocolates and say, 'When you go around the market place and you see a German tank' – the German soldiers were quite good with children – 'please tell us how many wheels it's got, what number it's got on its side.' It was a very good way of finding out.

Another thing we did was to ambush a truck to get a prisoner. I made a bit of a cock of it. Geoff was on one side of the road with a rifle and I was on the other side of the road with a Sten gun. Various trucks came. What we wanted was a single truck, we didn't want a whole column, and a single truck came along, Geoff put a shot through the windscreen and it stopped. I went to spray the near side of the lorry with the Sten gun and it jammed. Geoff fired another shot. A body that I thought was dead fell out of the cab. In the meantime the truck drove on. I managed to reload the Sten and fired another magazine into the back of it but it disappeared round the corner. And then there was the biggest bloody German in the world on the other side of the bush, my Sten gun was empty and it was the only time in my life that I've pulled my pistol out. He said 'Kamerad, kamerad' and we got our prisoner.

On cross-examining him he confirmed that they were expecting an invasion. They'd all been warned that they might be ambushed and all this kind of thing. He said he was very worried that he'd been taken prisoner by the Greeks and we said, 'No, by the British.' He said, 'Well, I won't get my throat cut.' We said, 'We can send word to your next of kin and all that by radio, and have you any problems?' We were being very fatherly – he was only a private soldier. 'Yes, I have big problem. What about my needles?' 'What do you mean, needles?' 'I have the syphilis.' We arranged needles for him and he became a sort of camp follower. We used him to wind the gramophone up and fetch water and make fire and do things. He was quite a harmless chap. He was a Czech in the German Army.

Colonel 'Monty' Woodhouse
SOE liaison officer
The 'Animals' operation in June and July 1943 achieved its full effect. It convinced the German High Command that the Allied landings after North Africa were going to come in Greece. Hitler had ordered massive reinforcements down to south-east Europe, some of which never arrived but some of which did arrive and were locked in there by the destruction of the lines of communication. Furthermore Hitler went on believing that Greece was the ultimate target even after the landings had begun in Sicily and Italy. But as we had succeeded in deceiving not only the Germans but also the communist leadership that Allied landings in Greece were imminent, there were serious political consequences.

Brigadier Eddie Myers
Senior SOE liaison officer
When 'Animals' was over and resistance was at its peak, I signalled to Cairo, 'And when is Greece's turn coming for liberation?' I was horrified to receive a signal, 'Not until early 1944 and possibly later.' How was I going to keep ELAS and EDES from each other's throats when they had nothing to do but prepare for further sabotage operations at some indefinite future date? I signalled that this, combined with the political question of the future of the King, must be tackled and I must be given a more definite policy, otherwise we were bound to have civil war in the mountains even before the end of the war, and that I wished to come out and was prepared to bring a delegation of EAM-ELAS with me and I'd be glad to take this opportunity of bringing representatives of the other organisations also. And this I did. We built our airfield, we organised representatives of the three parties to come out to Cairo and we duly arrived in early August.

Then all hell was let loose because my delegation of andartes started asking for seats in the government and a public declaration by the King that he wouldn't return to Greece until, and as a result of, a plebiscite in his favour. When Churchill and Roosevelt heard of this they were extremely worried, and I think it was Eden himself, the British Foreign Secretary, who said that if we acquiesced to these sort of demands by the resistance movement it would be tantamount to inviting the King of Greece to sign his abdication. This was in short the beginnings of my troubles with the Foreign Office and I was summoned home with the head of SOE in Cairo, Lord Glenconner, to explain why we had allowed this sort of situation to develop. It was most unfortunate. We merely stated the facts but the facts ran absolutely contrary to what HMG's long-term policy was. Although the military, from the CIGS personally downwards, fully supported all that I'd done, the Foreign Office disliked it all so much that it led to my never being allowed to return to Greece.

Major Brian Dillon
SOE liaison officer
At the time of 'Animals', we all thought that the invasion was coming, never mind the Greeks. In fact I was told on being briefed, 'You won't be there very long, old boy.' I thought I'd be there for a couple of months. In fact I stayed there for eighteen.

Albania

Captain David Smiley
SOE liaison officer
We were parachuted into northern Epirus, right up in the north of Greece, with the object of walking into Albania where nobody had yet been from SOE. So we walked into Albania, made contact with the resistance and spent the next nine months with the communist partisans. Several teams were dropped into us and the SOE network expanded and eventually a brigadier was sent out.

Captain Marcus Lyon
SOE liaison officer
I went and saw Brigadier Davies and he said, 'We're going to Albania.' I thought, 'Where the hell's Albania?' In those days no one had ever heard of Albania.

Lieutenant John Orr-Ewing
SOE liaison officer
I was to go to Albania so I started learning Albanian with somebody called Fanny Hasluck, who had been the toast of the Balkans in her time. I don't remember much. I remember, '*Mali është i bukur.*' It either means the mountain is beautiful or the girl is beautiful. Very dangerous thing to say if you got it wrong because you'd have your throat cut.

Captain Peter Kemp
SOE liaison officer
We dropped in from Derna, in North Africa, in Halifaxes. I had to make two runs. The first time, the first evening, one of the engines caught fire just after we'd taken off. Luckily we were able to land quite easily. The second night we were able to drop.

Captain David Smiley
SOE liaison officer
There were moments of intense danger, one was sometimes in pain, one had illnesses and things which you couldn't do much about. It was a mixture, what life in war is like: moments of boredom, moments of extreme excitement and danger and sometimes great fun, having barbecues and parties in the mountains with all the partisans and everybody.

Captain Peter Kemp
SOE liaison officer
Our instructions were to stay in uniform. I don't think it would have protected us much if we'd been caught, because Hitler by then had given the order to shoot all parachutists, but it was supposed to raise the morale of the locals.

Corporal Willie Williamson
SOE wireless operator
We all carried a capsule, it might have been strychnine, and if we were going to be captured we had to swallow this. I couldn't bear the thought of taking that out and swallowing it.

Lieutenant Michael Lis
Polish SOE liaison officer
We were caught by a German patrol and we had a few Albanians with us and had to retreat up the mountain. They were running like goats, the Germans were advancing slowly, they were not pushing too hard but they were after us, and George Seymour and I would stop behind rocks every fifty yards or so and shoot back. At a certain moment George turned round to me and said, 'Michael, it's not because we are so brave. We are just out of breath.' And that was perfectly true: the natives could run much faster than us.

Captain Peter Kemp
SOE liaison officer
If there was a serious attack by the enemy, it was very difficult indeed to get the radios away. It wasn't so bad with the Italians because they behaved in a much more gentlemanly fashion. They would bomb us and shell us for a day or two beforehand, giving us plenty of time to get all the heavy stuff away. The Germans were no gentlemen. They would turn up about a company strong with machine guns and mortars in the early hours of the morning, with no warning, and you were very lucky if you got yourself out. You couldn't hope to get any of the equipment.

Corporal Willie Williamson
SOE wireless operator
We were bombed out of this village. We had stacks and stacks of landmines in this cottage and we ran from the cottage to the bottom of the valley carrying these landmines and I remember one partisan caught it. His leg was severed and there was a lump of lead sticking out of his stomach, and the poor soul, he was saying, '*Ujë, ujë, ujë*,' which is Albanian for water, and nobody gave him water and he just died.

Captain Marcus Lyon
SOE liaison officer
We moved away from the road so that we wouldn't suddenly be overtaken by the Germans. A few days later they did a big push and we had to take to the mountains with the Partisan 4th Brigade. Nexhip Vinçani was the brigade commander: he was a very good man, he wasn't really a communist. Alan Palmer said, 'We must eat as much as you can before we go,' so the partisans made a huge omelette out of a hundred eggs for everybody, we ate this and then we marched over the mountains. We went very close to where the German posts were, very silently, with instructions that anybody who made a noise would eventually be shot, and we marched through the snow for forty-three hours without stopping, but we got out.

Lieutenant Michael Lis
Polish SOE liaison officer
All the time in Albania we were helping both sides. There were missions with the partisans, the communist partisans, which were in southern Albania and other missions with the nationalists, which were led by various competing chieftains. It was inevitable to support both sides. It was inevitable for the war effort.

Captain Peter Kemp
SOE liaison officer
Many Albanians took, from their point of view, the very reasonable attitude that the Germans were bound to leave anyway because they were obviously losing the war. They weren't in fact giving the Albanian population a bad time unless they were themselves attacked. If they thought that the Albanians in the villages, in the mountains, had organised or collaborated in an attack on a convoy, an ambush, they would take very serious reprisals indeed, burning villages and murdering the inhabitants with the bestiality for which they were only too well known in the war. So the Albanian attitude was, 'Why should we risk these things when the end result is going to be the same because the Germans are going to have to get out?' Later on, it got worse, particularly in the northern areas, where they were very anti-communist, because they said, 'Why should we risk our lives fighting the Germans in order to give the communists, who will be much worse than the Germans, control over our country and ourselves?'

Captain David Smiley
SOE liaison officer
We picked up some very good interpreters in Albania. They were all caught by the communists afterwards and I think they were shot, poor devils.

YUGOSLAVIA

Major Basil Davidson
Head, Yugoslav Section, SOE HQ, Cairo
In Yugoslavia, there was, to begin with, a resistance which was not communist, not left-wing, but which was in support of the King of Yugoslavia, who was in London, and of the Royal Government. They had a leader called General Mihailović, who became the Minister of Defence in that Royal Government, and was himself in Yugoslavia. He was leading the Chetniks and we supported the Chetniks as far as we possibly could. We sent parachute drops, munitions, officers, wireless operators.

Captain Charles Hargreaves
SOE liaison officer with Chetniks, Serbia
The only instruction I was given was to do anything I could to harass the Germans and to try and encourage the Chetniks to do everything they could.

HU 64787

Albanian tribal chief with his SOE-issued Sten gun.

I was told the area in which I'd be operating and given the name of a Yugoslav commander on the ground. I also combined my drop with another British officer who was going to another area. We flew from a place called Derna, in the Western Desert, but it took us about four attempts before we were able to drop because of weather conditions, getting lost and the correct signals not being shown.

Squadron Leader William Griffiths
Liberator pilot, 1575 (SD) Flight, RAF
Electrical storms were extremely bad there. On one occasion, I remember, we were flying up to Yugoslavia and the weather was such that we had St Elmo's fire, which really gave the aircraft a most ghost-like appearance against the cloud, like a flame going through the air. It was rather frightening. You get little flickers of light and fire that goes from propeller tip to propeller tip which gives the effect of each propeller being a kind of Catherine wheel. You also get little flames of electricity darting from the control column on to other metal parts of the aircraft. It was quite alarming but in many ways a beautiful thing.

Captain Charles Hargreaves
SOE liaison officer with Chetniks, Serbia
On our fourth trip we finally arrived over the dropping zone and found all the fires burning and all the right signals. It was right in the middle of an enormous forest – just a clearing. It was a beautiful night with a full moon and luckily no wind. So, when we did drop, in fact, the aim was marvellous, because I landed right in the middle of one of the bonfires.

The Chetniks were very friendly indeed. Lots of kissing. They're very emotional and they grasped you in their arms. I think quite a large number of them had made an oath not to cut their hair or shave until the country was liberated, they'd been living in the woods for rather a long time and they looked rather spectacular. They had a form of national dress which most of them were wearing, really a uniform, and they had these things called *šajkačas* – funny woollen hats rather like the Cossacks used to wear – and were draped with three bandoliers.

It was really the most marvellous contrast having come from the Egyptian desert and the heat and the flies and the unattractive surroundings, to be dropped into this most beautiful countryside, fresh and green, birds singing. It was really such a complete contrast as to be unbelievable. The country in which we were was very, very wild indeed and there was nothing much in the

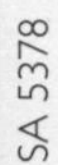

Captain Charles Hargreaves in parachuting kit prior to being dropped into occupied Yugoslavia.

way of roads. The houses were rather like English Tudor cottages, made of beam and brick, to the extent that when one went through a doorway the ground had been hollowed out and there were rushes or bracken on the floor and the furniture was of the most basic type – wooden stools.

The people lived a way of life which vanished in England five hundred years ago, practically. They were very kind, very good people. They'd give you anything. I had one unusual experience going into one house. It was a very hot day and we'd been walking for a long time and we were sat down and made a great fuss of and two of the daughters came in and removed our boots, washed our feet and dried them with their hair. It was really quite biblical.

Captain Robert Wade
SOE liaison officer with Chetniks, Serbia

You never knew when your enemies were going to pop up because there were all sorts there. The most difficult people were the local gendarmerie. You never knew whose side they were on. And the Bulgars, they were ghastly people. They took no prisoners. They took great delight in bayoneting people.

Captain Mike Lees
SOE liaison officer with Chetniks, Serbia

It was intended that I should drop just north of Prishtina and then move south into Macedonia to replace a Major Morgan who had dropped blind and been captured. I had a wireless operator and two young engineer officers with me. One was to be with me, to help with sabotage. The other one was to go to Major Sehmer, to whom I was dropping and who needed an engineer. So there were four of us and the drop was very simple. We didn't, like so many others, start and then come back again. We took off from Derna and we flew six or seven hours. I remember I had a stinking cold, which was rather unpleasant.

We found the fires and dropped and gathered together and were embraced by the Chetniks, as was the usual procedure. They were exactly like one would have imagined a guerrilla resistance movement in the mountains. Peasants were helping with collecting the canisters, there were twelve or fifteen canisters dropped with us; they were brought in by the peasants on ox-carts.

The following morning, the situation became dangerous. Reports were then coming in about a German column and a Bulgar column moving in our direction. We moved around the mountains that day, we moved into another peasant house the following night and lay down to sleep and the following morning I was woken by a peasant woman coming through the door. We were all there together, Sehmer and Djurić and all the British and a great number of Yugoslavs sleeping on the floor – the room was packed – and the peasant woman was saying, 'Go quickly! Go quickly! The Bulgars are here!'

Everybody disappeared through the door at enormous pace. There were probably only about thirty Chetniks with us that night. None of them was armed with more than a rifle and they were therefore in no position to form a defensive line and fight. By the time I'd got my boots on most of them were out and then I suddenly remembered that I had brought a bagful of gold sovereigns, two thousand sovereigns or something of that nature. I looked round and there was the saddle of Djurić's horse with the bag on it in a strongbox. I had to shoot the lock off the strongbox to get the bag of gold out.

By the time I'd done this, I couldn't go out through the door because there was a machine gun already covering it, I could see bullets splattering against the wall. So I dropped out of the window at the back and made my way down to the forest. I found John Sehmer and I said, 'What's happening? Where's Djurić?' He said, 'Djurić is ahead and the others are with another party.' But it transpired later that four of the mission hadn't got into the forest but had got hit in front of the house. My wireless operator, one of the engineers and two of Sehmer's mission were killed. In fact two of them were wounded but they were shot on the ground by the Bulgars.

Captain Robert Wade
SOE liaison officer with Chetniks, Serbia

We came over the crest of a hill and crossed over a little culvert. Immediately on the right was a maize field and before you could say 'snap' the machine guns were going. The other side was an open field – hopeless. Everyone ran into the maize. I've never run so fast in my life and I've never seen so much maize mown down. You could see it being cut down like that. I came to a ditch and I was as thirsty as hell and it was absolutely filthy but I remembered that my uncle had said from the first war that if you ever drink out of a dirty ditch, strain it through a handkerchief. Well, I always carried a handkerchief and I had a suck out of this. It was pretty filthy but it was wet. I crawled up on to the bank on the other side and thought, 'I'll just wait here for a minute or two.' It was bright moonlight and very still and I got under a bush on the far side and I just waited to see if any of the other chaps were coming on after me. Nothing happened. I waited a bit longer and then suddenly I saw a bloody great bastard of a Boche with a machine gun walking up the other side of the stream. I thought, 'I've got a pistol and it's ready and pointed,' and if he'd pointed his gun at me at all I'd have had a go. First, I hope. I lay absolutely motionless, camouflaged in the shade of this bush – the stream wasn't more than three or four yards across, no distance at all. He just went on and looked and strolled on down. I let him get out of sight and then went back.

Major Archie Jack
SOE liaison officer with Chetniks, Serbia

We were walking along the main road and making notes of the signs on the various German trucks and lorries passing us, so that we could signal back to SOE this information because you could then establish which divisions they belonged to. Another chap and I were going down the road dressed as peasants and Ljubo and another orderly were following on a footpath parallel to and above the main road with a horse loaded with our belongings. We joined up when night fell and had another six miles to go to a safe house for the night. We came down to a village where there was a small bar with people drinking inside. I skirted round it and continued up the path but Ljubo felt he wanted a drink so he entered the bar, not having noticed some German soldiers seated at a table. They, of course, spotted the tommy gun on his shoulder and pounced on him. Ljubo ran out of the door, pursued by the Germans, who sprayed him with light automatic fire. He was badly wounded and, rather than be captured, committed suicide by pulling a grenade on himself. The other orderly, also wounded, managed to join us and we ran off into the night pursued by gunfire.

Captain Robert Wade
SOE liaison officer with Chetniks, Serbia

We were ambushed just outside a village. I was trained in the cavalry and when you're doing cavalry drill you have one tank, or a 'point' as it's known in the cavalry, right out ahead of you. Not just twenty yards ahead, but two, three or four hundred yards ahead of you, and a chap backing him up. Dear, oh dear, we had none of that and we walked straight into it. We were quite a strong bunch, must have been forty of us, probably fifty, and I was up front with everybody else and we just crested a ridge and they opened up with everything. I hit the deck, bloody quick. There was a sort of slightly sunken road, not very deep, about two feet; otherwise it was absolutely sheer open to the enemy. I crawled down this and some Yugoslavs said, 'Come this way, captain. We'll go and outflank them.' So I followed these chaps and we'd no sooner started to cross an open area and they all got popped off, all five, right ahead of me. So I thought, 'Well, you can't do it on your own, Wade – return!'

My word, it was awful. Another thing I will never forget. These poor chaps, they were peasants, you see, they weren't trained. But grand people.

Captain Robert Purvis
SOE liaison officer with Chetniks, Serbia
The party I was with, I really have got the highest regard for them. They were really most loyal and helpful in every sort of way. They were simple peasant folk most of them. Georgevic, who I associated with mostly, though he wasn't really the area commander, had been in the regular Yugoslav Army and he and I got on awfully well together. We managed to converse in German, which was a special asset. Dealing through interpreters was difficult and I didn't really have any command of Serbo-Croat, having had only half an hour's lesson in Cairo before I went.

Captain Mike Lees
SOE liaison officer with Chetniks, Serbia
We were living, as far as we were concerned, with a straightforward guerrilla resistance force. The people of the area, real mountain peasants living in isolated holdings, were pure individualists and, in so far as they thought about politics, which they did, they were absolutely royalist to a man. This was the real Serbian heartland. From their viewpoint it was unthinkable that the royalist dynasty would not return after the war in Yugoslavia and these people were in absolutely no way tempted by communism or by any other change. What they wanted was to keep their land, to keep their way of life. They weren't ambitious for a better way of life. They didn't want anything more. What they wanted was to be able to live their peasant life on their own holdings.

Major Archie Jack
SOE liaison officer with Chetniks, Serbia
The whole bulk of the central area of Serbia, pretty well up to the Sava, was in Mihailović's hands. As one went from village to village the peasants spoke of nothing else except Mihailović – 'Draža Mihailović this' and 'Draža Mihailović that'. They absolutely worshipped him. He was the commanding figure of the Serbian resistance and of their future. He was the Serbian national hero.

Captain Erik Greenwood
SOE liaison officer with Chetniks, Serbia
They wanted more arms. Their troops were either unarmed entirely or had ex-Yugoslav Army rifles, one or two captured German rapid-firing weapons

General Draža Mihailović, commander of the Royalist Chetnik guerrillas.

and a few home-made hand grenades. So what they said they wanted was more arms, a lot more ammunition, and they said they could have as many troops as we could provide rifles for, really; there was no limit to what they could embody. So they said. Now what they were going to do with them was another matter.

Major Basil Davidson
Head, Yugoslav Section, SOE HQ, Cairo
Unfortunately the Chetniks took the view that it was up to us to win the war against the Germans and up to them to win the war inside Yugoslavia against the Yugoslav communists, who had meanwhile formed a much stronger and more effective resistance, known as the partisans. And that caused great difficulties.

Sergeant Alexander Simić
SOE wireless operator with partisans, Croatia and Slovenia
I was the first natural-born Briton to be dropped in officially to contact the partisans. We took off from Derna in civilian clothes, almost a comic opera outfit. We had riding breeches specially made, riding boots, a checked shirt, underwear with the labels ripped out in case we were captured so that they wouldn't show where we were coming from, a flat cap and a leather coat. And of course we had Schmeissers and Beretta pistols and I had two wireless sets. I went with two Canadian–Croat communists, older than myself. One was in his late forties and the theoretical communist of the two. The other had been wounded fighting with the International Brigades in Spain.

We had chosen a place called Šišan Polje, a very large area, about eighteen kilometres wide, where we thought we had a good chance of getting away and burying our gear and contacting local people. But as it happened there was a very strong mist and the pilot cruised around and said, 'I can't see anywhere to drop you. You've either got to drop now or we go back to Derna.' We said, 'No way are we going back to Derna.' So we dropped.

We looked around for Paul Pavlić, who had disappeared. He'd dropped about a kilometre ahead of us. Peter and I roved around very quietly until we heard dogs barking in a nearby village. We couldn't tell if it was friendly or enemy-held or what. All of a sudden we came across a very ragged peasant who said, 'Oh, where have you been, brothers? We've been looking for you all night long.' Apparently Paul had made contact with the partisans and had a party out looking for us. We were then taken to the headquarters of a local division where the commandant was very suspicious. In fact I was told

An SOE wireless operator in Yugoslavia with the remains of his damaged set.

afterwards that he thought he might have us shot. At the partisan GHQ in Croatia we were met by the commandant, who greeted Peter and, to my intense surprise, cuddled him, kissed him. It turned out that they'd fought together in Spain.

We had a meal and then eventually we were taken to a wooden cabin to spend the night, very rough bunks, and in the middle of the night I had a nightmare of explosions and flames and screaming, terrible screaming. I woke up to find that the arsenal that they'd built, a long wooden workshop where they repaired all sorts of captured weapons, had exploded. A young lad, in preparing some anti-tank mines from captured shells that they'd taken from German defence wiring, had dropped one and it had exploded and sent all the others off and the whole lot went up. All their gear, all their equipment, had all gone and there were about forty wounded and killed. There was screaming, young lads screaming with pain. It was a terrible experience for the first night we were there.

Next day I had to go round the detachment and I was amazed at what I saw. They had these long big wooden huts, all built from trees felled around them. They had a garrison of two hundred troops. They'd got a bakery, an agit-prop department with printing presses, a hospital: all concealed, camouflaged. I couldn't believe my eyes. I wrote and enciphered about a dozen messages explaining my reactions and gave a general impression of what I'd come across, of these men and women. They all wore these funny little hats with red stars and all were very interested in the Allied effort. 'When are we going to start the second front?'

Captain Robert Wade
SOE liaison officer with Chetniks, Serbia

The army of Mihailović was completely peasant-based and they hadn't got much discipline. Whereas Tito's lot, ruthless though he was, they behaved like the Brigade of Guards by comparison. I mean, no drilling, but when they were told to keep their distance they kept their distance and they were properly led and you could see the difference.

Sergeant Alexander Simić
SOE wireless operator with partisans, Croatia and Slovenia

The Germans chased us for five weeks. We couldn't even light a fire. There are great deep dells in Slovenia, very, very deep dells, where we used to hide at night. We were desperately hungry and we came to a village that turned out to be pro-quisling and they wouldn't give us any food. I said, 'For God's sake, you've got food, people are eating bread.' 'No, no, we've got no food.' We offered to pay and they refused and I said, 'Well, I'll bloody well shoot them, I'm not going to starve. God Almighty, they're collaborating with our enemy, I'm entitled to use some force.' But the partisans said, 'You mustn't do that, it'll give us a bad name.' They told me that Tito had said anyone would pay with his head that was found guilty of atrocities or ill treatment of the civilian populace.

Lieutenant Colonel Peter Moore
SOE liaison officer with partisans, Bosnia and Slovenia
I was dropped into the Yugoslav partisans. My first impression was one of surprise at the way the charcoal gas truck, which took us on our way to Jajce, moved openly in broad daylight along the road, leaving a plume of dust for many hundreds of metres behind it. Although we stood ready to bale out at the sound of a hostile aircraft, it was clear that the partisans had a firm grip on the countryside in the liberated areas and that the air surveillance effort must be limited. I learnt, however, on arrival at Tito's headquarters, that a similar truck had been machine-gunned from the air a day or so earlier. By this time the partisans moved relatively freely on the roads and had day-to-day control of considerable areas. They wisely did not attempt to stop incursions by armoured columns but melted away into the woods to strike elsewhere, at the enemy's exposed communications. It was beyond the Germans' resources to maintain themselves in such areas. At that time the partisan forces in Slovenia were absorbing large numbers of new recruits and immense quantities of equipment surrendered by the Italian Army in September.

Captain Erik Greenwood
SOE liaison officer with Chetniks, Serbia
The Chetnik officers told me that as soon as they were adequately armed to beat off any attempts to burn down villages or take hostages, they would indulge in any sort of action against the Germans that I cared to suggest. The two main things that I had in mind were the blockage of the Danube and the effective destruction of the equipment at the Bor copper mines in eastern Serbia, the largest copper mines in Europe. We talked interminably about how to achieve these things: organising at least a thousand men to take the town of Bor, to give us enough time to destroy the operating equipment, the generating equipment, the crushing equipment, the haulage equipment and so on; and also to undertake similar action on the Danube to block the river. But there was always a waiting period: 'Well, we must have more arms before we can do this.' We were constantly being put off.

Captain Robert Wade
SOE liaison officer with Chetniks, Serbia
We recced a bridge, we made a plan and we got all the ammunition and explosives prepared and wrapped up in parachute material on wagons. There was a hell of a lot of us, I can't tell you how many, and we got to within spitting distance of the job and then this chap said, 'Oh, we can't do it.' George More was absolutely furious and so was I. The chap said, 'Come on, we'll go and find some women.' We said 'Bugger off. We're not having any of that sort of damned nonsense.' We'd really thought we'd got it this time and got right to the job practically and they'd called it off. This was a trick, you see, to get more and more planes in.

Major Archie Jack
SOE liaison officer with Chetniks, Serbia
Reprisals meant a lot to them because it was their own people, not necessarily relations or even friends, but people from their own locality who were being taken out and shot. What one's got to remember is that the Germans arrested a huge number of Serbs and stored them away in prisons so that they could just be shot when required. They didn't have to go out into the countryside and arrest them; they were already in the prisons. And they would display huge posters saying that these people had been taken out and shot.

Captain Charles Hargreaves
SOE liaison officer with Chetniks, Serbia
Sometimes they would be quite prepared to do small things, perhaps to ambush a train or a convoy, but nothing very big, nothing that would have involved too much German loss of life. After one had been living with them for some time, you did notice that they were often very depressed because, so far as I could see, their main intention was to secure control of the country after the war. They were more interested in that, really, than in fighting the Germans.

Major Basil Davidson
SOE liaison officer with partisans, Bosnia
The first time I came under fire in Yugoslavia, though by no means the last, was when I was crossing the Bosna River in August '43, going from central Bosnia to eastern Bosnia and on to the Vojvodina with a non-combatant group of wounded, nurses and recruits. The Bosna river is not very wide, it's only about two hundred yards wide, but it's a flood and you have to ford it.

Captain Erik Greenwood with a band of Chetnik guerrillas, Yugoslavia, 1943.

The local Chetniks had advised the Germans and the Germans brought up an armoured train from Doboj, sat it along the railway behind us and mortared this little column as it proceeded across the river. So I myself feel that anyone who's going to tell me that the Chetniks were fighting the Germans has got to stand truth upon its head. Some did, here and there, but very few, very little. Some revolted, some regretted it, but the commanding officers, and this is what counts, were all of them determined not to risk their lives or their movement, for what it was worth, in fighting what they regarded as a hopeless struggle against the occupying forces.

Captain Mike Lees
SOE liaison officer with Chetniks, Serbia
They were just fighting for their king and for their country. In so far as there was any collaboration, it was purely pragmatic.

Captain Charles Hargreaves
SOE liaison officer with Chetniks, Serbia
On more than one occasion, having captured some partisans, they were very put out when they found that there was a British officer with the Chetniks because they had had a British officer with them, too. So there we had two British officers fighting each other.

Captain Mike Lees
SOE liaison officer with Chetniks, Serbia
After we'd derailed a train and were marching back, we came near a village and were fired on. A man called Vlada was alongside me and pulled the pin out of a grenade. It was one of these new American grenades where you had to hold the top down as well as holding the flange in, and it exploded. He was killed and I was extremely lucky because I was alongside him but I didn't get hit by it. That was one occasion when we were attacked by the partisans.

Captain Charles Hargreaves
SOE liaison officer with Chetniks, Serbia
Often when one went into a village or a town the local commander would get all the people together and address them against the partisans much more than against the Germans. There was very little doubt that what they were more interested in was control of the country, and I think they knew very well that, with the growing strength of the partisans, their chances were growing less all the time. But it was really rather pathetic because they trusted the

British absolutely implicitly. So often, they said, 'We know that you're going to help us and that with your help we shall win the war and eventually we'll all go on a marvellous victory parade in Belgrade.' They were really quite convinced that the British would help them to win. We were never ever given the slightest indication that support for the Chetniks was going to be withdrawn.

Captain Robert Wade
SOE liaison officer with Chetniks, Serbia
On 13 December 1943, I had this message from Cairo saying, 'Decode the next message yourself.' When the next message came in, it was, 'We are dropping the Mihailović missions and if you think you can walk to the coast, do so. If not, stay put and we'll try and do the best we can for you' – to save us getting our throats cut.

We got pretty elated the first night that we met the partisans and we said we ought to send Cairo a pretty good New Year's greeting over the air. It said something like, 'We cheated the Chetniks, buggered the Bulgars, fucked the Germans to reach the partisans at such-and-such a date.' I said to Bill, 'I won't sign that, it's a bit too rough,' but he did and he sent it off. But it caused a little trouble in Cairo. They didn't understand our joy at meeting the partisans who we thought would conduct us to the coast. We more or less thought, 'We've made it, chaps.'

Captain Mike Lees
SOE liaison officer with Chetniks, Serbia
So there we were. It was highly embarrassing. We sat at our headquarters and I personally got rather bored. And it was Peter's idea; Peter said to me, 'Well, look here. It's getting really very boring and I don't want to leave Yugoslavia without seeing some action.' So, encouraged by that, I said, 'Christ, yes. That's a jolly good idea. Let's go and blow a train.' And Peter and I went off and blew a train on the line just north of Leskovac.

This was the most important line in the Balkans and it was terribly heavily guarded. They had temporary blockhouses erected every couple of miles and in between they had sentries, mostly civilian sentries, who stood on the line and if they saw anything untoward they'd tap the line and that carried a signal right the way up to the blockhouses. So there was no possibility of doing what was done with most guerrilla operations against railway lines, where people just went down in the dark and put a charge on the line and went away and in due course the train came along and ran over it.

But I'd developed a technique whereby I used to move up to about fifty yards from the railway line in the dark and then lie up. There were a lot of trains travelling on that line, sometimes trains every ten minutes or a quarter of an hour, a massive number of trains, and I'd wait for one train to go through which would show me the sentries and show me any blockhouses there may be. Then, when the second train came, I'd wait until it was about six hundred yards away and then I'd run. I'd get to the line ahead of the train, put the charge up against the line and put the dummy fog signals on and then run like hell and the charge would blow.

On this particular occasion I misjudged the distance to the line. I ran and I ran and I ran and I only got there by the skin of my teeth. And I slammed the charge on, clamped the fog signal on and literally jumped over backwards and fell down to the bottom of the embankment, thank God, when the charge blew straight over my head. In fact it was a very nice derailment. It punched the train right off.

Captain Charles Hargreaves
SOE liaison officer with Chetniks, Serbia
When it was clear that there was no further help coming for the Chetniks, some of them turned very, very nasty indeed and I think in many ways some of us are still lucky to be alive. It was only due to the goodwill of the more senior Chetnik officers who protected us that we were able to get away with it. During that time everything deteriorated very much indeed and we were almost entirely on our own with no food and no support and no help. One was just wandering around the country from place to place. One got no shelter. And this is what really led in the end to my capture.

I was living in an abandoned house at the top of a mountain with a Polish officer and one or two Poles with him who acted as our bodyguard. Then at first light one morning we heard some shots which rapidly came nearer, then a mortar opened fire and hit the house in which I was. After that everything happened very quickly. The Germans suddenly appeared and disarmed us. I was taken outside where I found that the Polish officer had been killed. The Germans proved to be perfectly decent and straightforward, there was no brutality at that particular time, and the German officer spoke some English.

Later I was taken by road to Belgrade and into a big office building. I was taken downstairs to quite a modern sort of jail and all my clothes were taken away, everything removed, and I was put into quite a small cell right next to the heating equipment for the building. It became absolutely like an oven and I was kept there I think for about two days without food, no water, nothing at all. By that time I was almost completely dehydrated. Then I was taken out and I was given a shirt and a pair of trousers and taken upstairs to some very elegant surroundings, a very nice office room, where they had some restraints on the wall for putting your hands and arms into. I was asked quite a lot of questions. One's answer always to begin with was, 'According to the Geneva Convention all I've got to tell you is my name, rank and number, which I'm very pleased to do.'

I was taken down to my cell again and left there. A considerable time went past. Occasionally I was taken up for interrogation and there was a fair amount of brutality. I was hung up by my arms in such a way that I could just take the weight of my body on my tiptoes. That immediately brought on terrific cramps in your leg and you couldn't stay there so immediately you had to put the whole weight of your body on your arms again. I think I spent forty-eight hours like that before they eventually put me back in my cell. Another thing they did was to put a bucket on my head and beat it with pickaxe handles. What that was supposed to achieve I don't know.

It seemed to me that one of the things they were trying to do was to create this tremendous contrast between their own civilisation and sophisticated atmosphere and myself, filthy dirty, bearded and stinking to high heaven, starving and chained up to this wall, to make you feel as though you were beyond any form of human consideration. I always insisted that I was a British officer and I always said, 'Whatever you do to try and hide whatever is happening here, it's going to become known and you're going to have to pay for it.'

Eventually they told me that I'd been convicted of being a terrorist, that I had had sabotage equipment with me, and that I was to be executed and I'd be sent to another jail first. I can remember very, very clearly feeling very, very strongly, 'When the time comes I hope I can behave properly and not faint or do anything stupid.' But there was no point in making a demonstration or anything because who was to see it except the Germans?

I ended up in Buchenwald. No one had told me anything about concentration camps or anything like that and I rather stupidly thought that I was going to just an ordinary prisoner of war camp. From a distance I could see people moving about and when we got to the camp proper I saw these extraordinary-looking people, scarecrows, in the most awful physical condition, and I knew at once that they weren't British and I didn't know where the devil I was.

FRANCE

Captain Fergus Chalmers-Wright
SOE agent
I was shot across the Channel towards Brittany. Then the MTB stopped and a little rowing boat was lowered. I already had one leg over the gunnel, preparatory to dropping into this little rowing boat to be rowed to the coast, when the sky was lit up – we'd been spotted by the Germans. So, with a remarkable piece of navigation, we turned round 180 degrees and went back to England.

It was then decided that the best way for me, since I'd done no parachuting, was to walk it, through the Pyrenees, which I did, with a guide who dropped me at the frontier. There was a little village but this was in the prohibited area, an area on the northern flanks of the Pyrenees. People had to have special papers from the Germans to go there. However, there was a little man there, I suppose he was a smuggler, and I asked him, 'Can you get me through?' He put me in a little mud-floored hut, through the windows I could see the German patrols at the frontier, and he said, 'I'll see what I can do'. After a day or two he came back and said, 'I've found a way. The adjutant of the local gendarmerie is willing to help you.'

I spent the whole evening trying to pierce this man's mind. Was he genuine or not? Ultimately I decided I'd risk it and the following morning, before dawn, we walked into this little town and there was the adjutant at the door of his gendarmerie. He took me up to his room and I told him I was a British officer, I had a mission in France, would he help me? He said, 'Yes, I will help you. Did you see that group of people down in the hall? They're criminals who are going to be escorted to Perpignan to serve their sentence. I'll put you among them.' He called in one of his aides who opened his satchel and I put in there all my money, my identity cards, everything, and climbed in a bus with these other chaps.

When we reached the frontier of the prohibited zone, of course, there was a very strong German guard with dogs. They came into the bus to inspect everybody's papers and when they reached me I did my best to look like a common criminal. The gendarme said, 'Oh, he's one of ours, he's on my list,' and in due course we arrived at Perpignan. He opened his satchel and returned all my property. I gave him a little present for his wife and from there I just made my way to Paris.

Lieutenant Harry Rée
SOE circuit organiser
They decided to drop me right over the other side of France, near Tarbes. I insisted on being dropped to a reception committee. Some people were dropped blind but my French wasn't all that good and I certainly would have messed things up suddenly arriving in France and walking into a village. So I insisted on being dropped to a reception committee and there was a fairly good circuit round Tarbes so they agreed to take us and pass me on to Clermont-Ferrand.

It was a disastrous drop. Several of the parachutes containing arms and things landed in electric pylon wires. We found the cage with our luggage in it and with the wireless set belonging to the radio operator and we took these out and hid as much as we could but it was hopeless. No sign of anybody to receive us. It was maddening. Just dogs barking. Worrying. So we decided we must make for the woods and hide for a bit and we walked through streams like boy scouts to stop us being trailed by dogs. We walked up into the woods, we went I suppose a couple of miles, carrying these damned suitcases and wearing overcoats and far too many things. It was a pretty nasty experience. We passed farms where the dogs were and we laid up in the woods at dawn.

I heard a dog barking and scuffling and I thought, 'Oh, God. The damned Germans, they've found us.' But then the dog appeared and it obviously wasn't a tracking dog, it was a lovely mongrel, and a sort of peasant followed it and I looked up and said, '*Bonjour*,' and he said, '*Je ne vous ai pas vu*' – 'Haven't seen you!' We had a conversation. I said I was an escaped prisoner. He was obviously on the side of the resistance and he said, 'Would you like any food?' and I said, 'Like anything I would.' He came back with some ham and bread and wine from the farm where he worked.

Lieutenant Jacques Poirier
SOE circuit organiser
I was dropped two hundred kilometres away from the place where Harry Peulevé was in fact waiting for us. It was night, I didn't have any idea where I was, but finally, after various incidents, managed to take a train. On the Sunday morning I arrived in Brive-la-Gaillarde, in Corrèze, went to the supposed rendezvous, it was in fact a *magasin*, a shop, but the shop was closed and there was no way for me to get into contact with Peulevé. Therefore, being a Sunday, I spent my first morning in France in church. I felt a church was safe enough and I sat through about four masses. After that, during the night, I went to sleep in the hills around Brive-la-Gaillarde to make sure that

I was not discovered. The next day, the Monday, I came to the shop and Harry Peulevé was there, completely amazed to see me because he had heard the plane but since nothing happened he thought the plane went back to England.

Flight Officer Yvonne Cormeau
SOE wireless operator
Slowly but surely my chute opened and I didn't even feel the jerk on my shoulders. It was only three hundred feet so it wasn't a long drop. I took off my jumpsuit immediately and handed it to the French people who were meeting me. I only had a handbag, with my money in, which was strapped behind my back, cushioning the lower vertebrae of the spine so that the shock wouldn't damage anything. I was dressed in what I thought was normal for France: a black coat and skirt with a silk blouse and black shoes. My ankles were bandaged, as I was in shoes and not jump boots.

Lieutenant Robert Maloubier
SOE arms and sabotage instructor
I jumped and I just landed and this chap came and said, 'That's you?' and I said, 'Yes, that's me.' 'OK, join me.' We went to a nearby farm, myself with my packages full of chocolate and cigarettes and all this. This farm was lit at one o'clock in the morning but it was right in the middle of the countryside, far away from Louviers. There was a huge table and ladies cooking all over the place and they had everything you could think of: pâté, hams, heaps of butter, bread, wine, cider. And I'm bringing chocolate and cigarettes and preserves because I was going to starve! Of course, by that time, the people in the countryside had too much to eat because the transportation didn't work and they couldn't export what they had. I feared for my liver and my stomach when I was in Normandy. It was incredible what people could eat.

When the curfew was lifted, we got the containers and stored them. A French driver and myself went down to Rouen, to a garage, which was actually a sort of depot for the *réseau* [network] and we stored everything I'd brought: the containers, a new radio set, a few Bren guns and Sten guns, plastic explosive, plus money. There were so many Germans, especially in Rouen, the rear base of Rommel's army, that I was really upset, I was really uncomfortable. Charles told me, 'You'll get used to it. First of all, don't do anything. Stroll around Rouen until you get used to the uniforms.' And this is what I did.

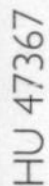

Yvonne Cormeau, an SOE wireless operator who parachuted into occupied France in 1943.

Captain Peter Deman
SOE agent, DF (Escape) Section
There was a reception committee for me, there was a chap who pushed a bicycle into my hands and said, 'Good luck,' and I was very happy to go. I was glad to get away from this crowd. I didn't think it was very healthy to be in a field in occupied France with a twin-engined bomber standing on the ground and about twenty guys chattering away like mad. I got on my bicycle and went to this tiny little station, the train arrived and I made my way to Brittany, to Rennes. I'd taken all the precautions. I was quite satisfied I was not followed. I mean, you can't take many precautions cycling around a deserted road nor sitting on a train, except being observant. The kind of training we'd had involved running in and out of stores with two entrances and so on. Well, you don't have that in the middle of the countryside, nor do you have it on a train. Just be observant and inconspicuous. Frankly, if I was asked today to say what should an agent be, I would say, 'Observant and inconspicuous.' I don't think that truth will ever change.

Lieutenant Harry Rée
SOE circuit organiser
They'd got some contacts up in the Jura, right over in eastern France, where there were some Maquis starting up in the hills. Would I go up there and contact these groups and try to organise them, get some *parachutages* – parachute drops – and start arming them? It was about the time that the Germans had started calling up French young people to go and work in Germany. Those who didn't want to do so and were against the Germans would get themselves false identity cards and go up into the hills and join the Maquis.

Lieutenant Robert Maloubier
SOE arms and sabotage instructor
I started training people all over Normandy, small groups in farms and districts, training them how to make plastic explosive charges and bombs and use pistols and Sten guns and be able to gather information about factories, plants, power stations and all that.

We had two targets to destroy. One was Rouen power station, which is a huge, huge power station built on the bank of the Seine. It had actually been raided two or three times by the RAF but unfortunately it's by the foot of a huge hill and the weather was so bad that the Mosquitoes couldn't hit it. We attacked the sub-station, which was on the other side of the Seine, made up of switches and about five or six very huge transformers which were actually feeding the Rouen industrial area. After that, a steel plant, which was actually one of the largest in France. We attacked it and destroyed the pumps and one of the big electric motors and some of the machinery there was put out of action for at least six months. They were actually manufacturing the undercarriage of the Focke-Wulf 190, which was very important.

Then there was a submarine tender, which was being refitted by the French, which always managed to get through the blockade by the navy and get to the Atlantic or the Channel and not only refuel but also supply the submarines with whatever they needed. There were about fourteen Frenchmen, technicians, working on refitting this ship. One of these chaps belonged to our *réseau* and was provided with a charge, which he managed to stick on the side of the ship, and the ship was sunk.

Lieutenant Harry Rée
SOE circuit organiser
There was an RAF raid on Besançon. It was rather funny to feel yourself bombed by one's own side. We came out of the house and watched it and sheltered under a peach tree. Next day I took the train up to Montbéliard – it hadn't really damaged the line all that much – and learned the raid had obviously been more on Montbéliard than Besançon and that they'd been trying to get the Peugeot works there. We all knew that the Peugeot car works had been turned over to making tracks and engines for tanks for the Germans, so it was obviously important that the factory should be, if possible, put out of action.

The damage in Montbéliard was pretty nasty, I suppose a few dozen people had been killed, but on the whole the morale was amazing on the part of the French. They said, 'Jolly good to the RAF. Obviously you can't make omelettes without breaking eggs.' But I was seeing Rodolph Peugeot the next day, at a friend's office, and I said to him, 'Wouldn't it make more sense if we organised sabotage inside your factory rather than having the RAF come again, because they are pretty well bound to come again?' He said, 'Of course,' and that he'd put me in touch with some people, some foremen inside the factory, who would be interested in the idea. I sent London a long report about the Peugeot business and said to them, 'Can you arrange with the RAF not to come and bomb the factory again while we continue to sabotage it inside?' Evidently Buckmaster and the SOE people had awful difficulty with the RAF in getting them to agree but in the end they said, 'If you can send us monthly reports of the sabotage undertaken and we're satisfied that it's doing a useful job, we will lay off.' Well, this was a wonderful job for an ex-conscientious objector, to stop bombing by blowing up machinery.

The first sabotage was about the beginning of November and they decided they'd blow up a whole transformer house where all the electricity came into the factory. About five men were involved, Frenchmen who worked in the factory. They had their pistols in the pockets of their overalls and they had their explosives, plastic blocks with room for a detonator, in their pockets too. There was a wonderful carelessness about the whole thing. They were playing football with the German guards outside the transformer house – somebody had forgotten to get the key – and in playing football one of them dropped his plastic block of explosive and one of the German guards who was playing football pointed it out to him. 'You've dropped something, sir, I think.' He put it back in his pocket. That was absolutely typical. The transformer house blew up and after that they went on throughout the whole of the rest of the war fixing these magnetic plastic blocks to machines and enormously reducing production. They also arranged for production figures to be produced which we sent back to London.

Flight Officer Pearl Witherington
SOE courier

The job of a courier was terribly, terribly, terribly tiring. It was mostly travelling by night. We never wrote and we never phoned. Any messages were taken from A to B and the territory we were working on was really very big, because apart from Paris we had Châteauroux, Montlucon, down to Toulouse, from Toulouse to Tarbes, up to Poitiers. It meant mostly travelling by night and the trains were unheated.

One of the jobs I did regularly was going from Toulouse to Riom near Clermont-Ferrand. I'd leave Toulouse at seven o'clock at night and get to Riom at eleven o'clock the next morning absolutely frozen stiff to the marrow and having had nothing very much to eat. Then I went into the safe house, to the people who received me, where there was no heating either.

Lieutenant Francis Cammaerts
SOE circuit organiser

Whoever I stayed with, I told them I was English. The penalty for putting up an Englishman was that you were executed and so was your family, or deported if you were lucky. So I never felt I was justified in accepting hospitality in a home where they didn't know I was English. As I never used a hotel or a lodging house that meant a lot of people knew I was English, but it was two-edged, because the fact that I was English was an enormous encouragement to them. They were tremendously excited by meeting and being the friend of the people who stuck it out.

In hotels and lodging houses you had to fill in a form and sign it and if you were using a series of different names your description was fairly easy to follow. To find that you were going under false names was very easy for any police force. Also the Germans and the French Vichy police knew that public lodging places were the vulnerable spots. It was the same with railway stations. It was very often sensible to get off at a little railway station and cycle into the main town rather than go with the train right up to the main railway station.

Lieutenant Harry Rée
SOE circuit organiser

Active resisters were a very small minority but the majority of the French people listened to the BBC. The BBC and de Gaulle via the BBC had an enormous morale effect, I think, on the French. So on the whole you could be pretty certain that anyone you didn't know, if you asked for help in a difficult situation and said you were English, would help. They might be frightened and not help you for very long but they would certainly not give you up.

When I left England my wife was due to have a baby, our first, early in May. And we'd arranged with the message people that from 5 May to 10 May, they would send out a message, either '*Clement ressemble son grand-père*' or '*Clementine ressemble sa grand-mère*' or both, to tell me whether it was a boy or a girl or twins. I was up in a little peasant's cottage, a really very tumbledown place, on 5 May with a funny little man who had been training for the priesthood but had then given it up. He was about eighteen years old. He took me out to his parents' house and we had the wireless on – they were not resistance people but they had the wireless on and they listened to the news – and we were sitting round the fire and the message came through. He knew I was listening for that message, they knew nothing at all of course, so when it came through we couldn't really get up and open a bottle. It was a girl. The message came on 5 May and she came on 5 May. It was all very quickly done.

Captain Raymond Neres
SOE agent, DF (Escape) Section

I was in the DF Section, which was the clandestine communication section of SOE. The organisation was set up to produce a chain of safe houses, from the Belgian frontier right down to the Spanish frontier, in which one could conceal shot-down airmen or Allied politicians or military people who wished to join the Allies outside Hitler-controlled Europe. My main occupation was going round the country checking up on safe houses, contacting new people who would help us and choosing guides to accompany especially shot-down airmen, who normally didn't speak a word of French and had to be escorted down to the Spanish frontier.

Once I was with an airman who didn't speak a word of French, who was covered with freckles and had ginger hair. I can't imagine anybody who looked less French than him and yet we travelled from Lyons to Perpignan with controls on the trains. I remember we had to change trains at Narbonne and had breakfast in the restaurant at the station and suddenly three Gestapo men came and sat down at the table next to us. I had to make a sign to the boy not to say a word – they were in civilian clothes and he wouldn't have realised. I was always amazed that the Gestapo men didn't become suspicious (a) by his appearance and (b) by the fact that here were two people having breakfast who never said a word to each other.

Lieutenant Harry Rée
SOE circuit organiser

I was coming away from a village, I'd taken some explosives from a cache there and had them in my saddlebags on my bike, these *sacoches* things, and I was stopped by some gendarmes outside the village. They asked for my identity card and I showed it them and they said, 'What have you got in your *sacoches?*' I said, '*Oh, des affaires de nuit*' – just a few night things – and I leant down and pulled out a towel. The explosives were in the bottom. And my leg started shaking and one looked at me and saw this leg shaking and said, '*C'est vrai? Vous avez froid?*' – 'Are you cold?' I said, 'Yes, it is a bit cold this morning, isn't it?' He said, 'OK, go on.'

Lieutenant André Watt
SOE wireless operator

I had a tendency, and other people had a tendency, to find that it was too easy and that you were tempted to do things you shouldn't, such as meet others or go to nightclubs. Things like that. Every now and again I felt that it was necessary to pull myself up and remind myself what should be done and what shouldn't be done and try to think if I'd done anything that could have been bad security.

Flight Officer Pearl Witherington
SOE courier

I was terribly, terribly careful and very much awake to what was going on around me because you never knew, wherever you were, in a train or a restaurant, if anybody was listening. An occupation is really one of the most awful things because you're just not at home. You have to be careful of everything.

Flight Officer Yvonne Cormeau
SOE wireless operator

The identity they gave me, with cards and all that, was quite good, but as soon as I arrived and showed these papers to my boss, he told me, 'Look, the quality of the paper is far too good, I'll get you some new cards.' So those were changed. I went out with ration cards, too, but again the paper was a bit too good. Paper had deteriorated in France.

I'd left my wedding ring and engagement ring in England but my finger was unfortunately marked by the wedding ring after a certain number of years. One very observant woman told me, about three months after I got to France, 'You're married, aren't you? There's a shiny line on your finger.'

I must admit to butterflies floating in my tummy the whole time. You had to be careful. You had to have eyes in the back of your head. The life was totally different to anything I'd experienced previously.

Lieutenant Roger Landes
SOE wireless operator

During the first six months we managed to find about twenty different grounds to receive weapons and ammunition. Also we started to build a resistance group. At that time Claude de Baissac was in charge and he made contact with a French officer who brought him about three thousand men all around Bordeaux and promised him in a few months he could build it to thirty thousand. Everything went well until June 1943 when we heard that the group in Paris with which we were in contact had been caught by the Germans. A wireless operator had been forced to work for them. And of course with the group in Paris knowing we were in Bordeaux we started to have difficulties. Also there were many in the resistance being arrested and we didn't know why, where the leak was. Then I found out that a French officer had betrayed us and had started to work for the Gestapo.

Lieutenant Robert Maloubier
SOE arms and sabotage instructor
In 1943, lots of organisations were destroyed by the Germans and lots of people arrested. It was 'the bad days'.

Captain Robert Boiteux
SOE circuit organiser
I was nearly caught by the Gestapo because somebody was caught and he'd put my address in his little notebook. He was caught, this man, and of course they went through the book and went to all the addresses they could find.

I had three flats, so I could go from one to the other, and this particular flat I just kept as a depot for my explosives. I used to go there once a week with a suitcase to take some explosives to teach the French people how to use them. One morning I went there about ten o'clock, opened the door and saw the landlady there talking to a man. I thought, 'Oh, this could be the Gestapo,' so I shut the door very quietly and went away. I had a few jobs to do and I thought, 'Oh, I'm being a bit nervous for nothing' – I had heard from the landlady that the owner of the building was going to do some repairs and I thought that that was probably the owner going to have a look round.

I went back about twelve o'clock but as I put my key in the door I couldn't open it. 'Ah,' I thought, 'the landlady's worried and frightened and she's put the bolt on the door.' I knocked on the door. 'Madam Gutmann?' Knocked a few times and slowly the door opened and a man appeared, short, stocky build, and I thought, 'Hello, Gestapo.' I took a step back and he came out and slammed the door behind him. He made a step forward, I made a step backward and I got to the head of the staircase – it was on the third floor, this flat – and then he went to hit me. Well, I saw it coming, I was featherweight champion of Kenya for three years, and I just ducked, he fell and as he fell I kicked him in the head, in the face. He got hold of my shoe and at the same time another man, who was hiding behind the door, came out and started shooting.

I ran down the stairs, a spiral staircase, it's very hard to hit a man running away, and I got into the street. This particular part of Lyons is very old – you crossed the street and you went down some steps and you found yourself in another street – so of course they never got me. I lost my hat and my shoe. I went to some friends who were working for me and the man was a shoemaker. He gave me another pair of shoes and that was the end of that.

After that they offered a reward for me. They published a photo of me and offered about £20,000 reward. I went to Paris, I had an uncle there, and he made me a nice hairpiece, I grew a moustache, and I went back to Lyons thinking, 'I'm quite safe now,' walked down the high street and all at once a woman called, 'Monsieur Robert! Monsieur Robert!' I thought, 'I'm supposed to be disguised.' She crossed the road. 'Oh, Monsieur Robert, you do look well.' Of course I looked well, I looked ten years younger.

Lieutenant Harry Despaigne
SOE wireless operator
I had to move out of Montauban because the Germans were after me. I was very vexed that they only put five thousand francs on my head. I thought I was worth much more than that.

Flight Officer Yvonne Cormeau
SOE wireless operator
You never knew, man or woman, who was prepared to give information to the Gestapo. Sometimes it was a personal vendetta between two families. Other times it was just for money.

One day I met 'Hilaire'. I'd gone to meet him, to give him messages, instructions, from London. And as we got near a very small village, cycling, we saw on the shutters of a house, which served both as the schoolroom and the town hall, two identikit-type drawings of ourselves. So we looked at them, looked at each other, we didn't say anything and we split up. I went back north and he went south.

Captain Fergus Chalmers-Wright
SOE agent
We arrived in Lyons and there I was put up in a safe house and I was very well fed. After a while I said to my host, 'Look, I don't like being kept such a long time.' There was something not quite right about the exchange of passwords in Paris that stuck in my mind and I said, 'Tell all the people with whom you're in contact that unless they come and see me I'm returning to Paris.' A man came along, furious. He said, 'If you do that, we wash our hands of you.' I was equally furious. I said, 'But why am I being kept here?' I had a bedroom on the first floor, I was facing the window and he sat on a chair with his back to the window, and there we were, hammer and tongs at each other, each one very angry. And then in anger he twisted his head and I instantly recognised his profile. Months before, in an office in Baker Street, while I was talking with an officer there, somebody had walked into the room and started looking at the map on the wall, and his profile had registered on my mind. So I said, 'OK, I'm with you.'

Lieutenant Harry Rée
SOE circuit organiser
I went off about four to see this schoolmaster and I knocked on the door and a man in civilian clothes, whom I didn't know, opened up and he said, 'Put your hands up,' and produced a pistol. I said, 'Don't be an idiot, it's very dangerous to play with firearms like that. For Heaven's sake put it away.' Then he pulled out his card, which said Gestapo or *Sicherheitsdienst*, and I said, 'Oh, I beg your pardon,' and put my hands up. He said, 'Come on inside,' and I said, 'What's happened? What's happened?' and he said, 'Jean's been arrested and we discovered some arms here. What have you come for?' I said, 'I came to borrow a book. He's an old friend of mine, a teacher.' He said, 'Oh well, never mind. Come and sit down here and we'll wait till I'm relieved and then we'll just go along to the Gestapo to clear you and it'll be all right.' And I knew that if I ever got inside the Gestapo I'd never come out, because although my French by that time was fairly fluent they could have questioned me and it would have broken down. So I realised I had to get out before he was relieved.

I sat down and we discussed things a little. He said, 'Are you a Gaullist?' I said, 'No, no.' He said, 'Everyone's a Gaullist these days, aren't they?' I said, 'What about a drink?' He said, 'Do you know where the wine is?' I said, 'Oh yes, in the cupboard there.' I brought the glasses down from the cupboard and as I was walking behind him with the bottle I hit him on the head with it. He was wearing a hat actually, it was stupid of me, I didn't hit him anything like hard enough, and he stood up, turned round and fired. And as he fired I remember thinking, 'Good heavens, how extraordinary' – I was by that time hitting him – 'they must have blanks in there,' because the pistol was sort of pointing into me.

We went on and we had a real fight. He tried hitting me on the head with the back of the pistol and did and then he dropped it. He sort of pushed me down some stairs into a cellar and I managed to push back up again. Then he got my head into one of those bloody grips, a sort of half-nelson, and I remember it going through my mind, 'If you're ever going to see your daughter, you've got to get out of this one.' I put my hands right back and pushed them up into his stomach and he let go, then he fell back against the wall and said, '*Sortez, sortez*,' and I didn't ask twice. By that time he had got my identity card but I didn't think of getting it back off him.

It was pouring with rain. I left my bike, I didn't think I'd take my bike, didn't feel like biking, and stumbled across the fields. The man whose house it was, the schoolmaster, had told me, 'If ever you want to get away from here, out the back, straight across the fields, takes you to the next village.' There was a river I had to cross and before I got to the river I was getting very wet from the rain and I put my hand inside to see if it was going through and it came out covered in blood. And I thought, 'God, they weren't blanks.'

I swam across the river, it wasn't terribly wide but it needed swimming across, and got to the village where I knew there was the grandmother of some people I used to stay with. I thought they often went for Sunday lunch and there'd probably be someone there. I went to this little villa and knocked on the door and the son, a very nice factory owner, opened the door and he was horrified, seeing this bloodstained, bedraggled figure at the door, on a Sunday afternoon, about six o'clock. He said, 'Oh God. Come in.' They put me to bed and got a doctor and the doctor examined me. He said, 'Well, there is a hole, a bullet hole. It goes in just above your heart and comes out the other side and the lung might be affected so you've got to get into hospital in Switzerland straight away.' About three nights later a group of resistance people took me across the frontier. I was a bit weak and I gave myself up to the Swiss and they arranged for me to go into hospital.

Captain Robert Boiteux
SOE circuit organiser

I was caught at three o'clock in the morning by the police. They said, 'What are you doing this time of the morning?' I said, 'There's a train to Marseilles at three o'clock and I'm just going to the station.' Well, they searched me and they found a knuckle-duster in my pocket. 'Aha, *mon ami*. Come with us to the police station.' As soon as they mentioned the words 'police station' I just turned round and ran. They didn't catch me – I ran very fast. They were on bicycles actually and by the time they'd got on their bicycles and got their revolvers out and started shooting, well, I'd done a hundred yards.

Lieutenant Robert Maloubier
SOE arms and sabotage instructor

I took this motorbike and unfortunately was caught by the German field police. It was nearly curfew time and on top of that I had taken a member of our network. He was on the pillion and when the German car overtook me and stopped in front he jumped off and disappeared. So I was in a bad position. I said, 'OK, I've got my papers, I've got everything, I'm good, I'm first-class,' and they said, 'What about the chap who was on the pillion?' I said, 'He was hitch-hiking, I took him with me,' but they didn't believe me.

One German took me to the car. There were about four of them in the car. And very, very fortunately the gendarme who was supposed to ride the motorbike couldn't start it – I'd closed the petrol tap. He said, 'I can't start this damned thing. You ride it and we'll drive behind you with full lights on.' One of the German Feldgendarmes took his place on the pillion behind me with his Luger on my neck, which was uncomfortable. There wasn't much I could do, I couldn't escape by a side road because I didn't know the roads, so I drove out with four gendarmes in the car just behind me and one with his pistol on my neck.

When the car drove to the Feldgendarmerie, I stopped in front. I did whatever the gendarme behind me was telling me. Then he left me and started walking towards the Feldgendarmerie and I used the motorbike as a weapon. I threw it as hard as I could. Well, he fell down with the motorbike on top of him and I started racing like hell the other way. They all started shooting of course and I got a bullet through me, in the liver, in the lung, but I carried on running, racing, until I got in the open.

I was in the small suburbs of Rouen and I ran under a railway bridge and I got lost in the fields near the Seine river. They fetched some ammunition and dogs, police dogs, to chase me. There was a small canal and the dogs lost my scent. I had to walk across this canal, which was very, very cold indeed, up to my chest, and after that I just lay down right in the centre of a field. That was good security. I didn't forget that in some cases it is much better to be right in the open than being in bushes. I knew that the dogs and police would go around this field and look in the bushes. The dogs didn't scent me and the Germans didn't find me, and I didn't die. Later, doctors told me, 'You should have been dead but this dip in icy cold water saved you, because it stopped the internal bleeding. If you had a bullet right through your liver and right through your lung in hot weather, you shouldn't have survived.'

I walked back home, which was about fourteen kilometres, at five o'clock in the morning when the curfew was up. I was a real ice-block, covered with ice, stuck with ice. I could hardly move. I went to my safe-house in Rouen after having watched the bridges to see that there were no German check-ups, no roadblocks, and this old, old doctor belonging to our *réseau* came to see me. I managed to get word to Claude Malraux and say that I'd been hit and that I'd left the motorbike on the spot. The morning after, they went to the police and reported that the motorbike had been stolen.

Captain Raymond Neres
SOE agent, D/F (Escape) Section
I was travelling by a train between Pau and Bayonne and I was arrested at a place called Oloron where the train had stopped and the Gestapo boarded the

train. They examined everybody's papers on the train and they came across me and there, according to the papers, I was only eighteen. I was in fact twenty-one and therefore looked a little older than eighteen and they thought I was trying to avoid forced labour in Germany, which then was applicable to all Frenchmen between the ages of nineteen and thirty. They took me to a Gestapo headquarters in Biarritz and kept me for a week and then I was moved to the citadel at Bayonne, where I was declared a hostage. If any of the inhabitants of Bayonne had tried to kill any Germans, I would have been on the list of hostages to be shot for that.

After two weeks I was taken to Bordeaux and a much more formidable prison and I was kept there and interrogated six times. Then at the end of nine weeks suddenly the door of the cell was flung open, my name was called and I was hauled out. That's the only time I was really frightened. I thought that they'd discovered that my papers were false and that I was really for the high jump. On the contrary, it was just to tell me, with a charming smile, that they had made a mistake and that I would be freed from prison three days later.

I'd managed to convince them, very fortunately, that I was not trying to cross the Pyrenees and escape from France. I was dressed in the most ordinary manner, with plain shoes, not mountain boots or any extraordinary gear that one would need to cross the Pyrenees, and I was carrying a large number of books, I'm a great reader, and I think that saved me more than anything. I had biographies of various people in my luggage and the head of the Gestapo asked me what I was supposed to be doing and I said I was a student at Grenoble University, which was on my identity card. He started asking me questions about history, first of all whether Charlemagne was German or French, to which I parried by saying he was neither because neither country existed at that time, and he laughed.

The most dangerous thing of all, actually, was the release, because they had lost my identity papers. They gave me my suitcase back but not my identity papers and I said, 'Where's my identity card?' and they looked so surprised that I realised immediately that they'd lost it. They said, 'Oh, here it is, here it is,' but it wasn't there at all, of course, so I had to go all the way back to Annecy without any papers. And there I was nearly caught, because, when I got out at Annecy station, there was a German control post at the exit. Of course, I couldn't go through it, because I had no papers, so I hopped on to the train again and dashed out the other side, ran across all the lines and hurdled over the barricade at the other side of the station. All the people on the train must have watched me, but fortunately nobody called the Germans.

Wing Commander Hugh Verity
Air Liaison Officer, SOE HQ, London
I was pretty confident that Henri Déricourt was one of our best men in France, finding fields for us and laying on our landings. He was Buckmaster's air transport officer in the field and, as he was a pilot himself and had been attached to us at Tempsford for some time, he was quite a friend. It was a very serious shock when I discovered that he had been working fairly closely with the German counter-espionage people in Paris and had given away a lot of our secrets. Certainly during the time that I was doing landings on his fields I had every confidence in him.

Lieutenant Harry Despaigne
SOE wireless operator
I was receptioned by Déricourt, who provided bicycles for us to go back to Angers. We agreed to meet him next day on the Champs-Elysées where he tried to find out what was my mission and where was I going and when was I going, to which I gave him no answer whatsoever. You're not supposed to be interrogated by people who are only just supposed to receive you. I just wouldn't talk and I left Paris the same day.

Lieutenant André Watt
SOE wireless operator
Apparently we were known to the Germans, where we lived and who we were, everything, because apparently Déricourt had given all that information to them. Once or twice he would sometimes meet me at a brasserie and we would have a drink or something together and it's possible that he did it purposely to show the Germans who I was and where I was, so that they would recognise me. I never had any indication or any thought that that kind of thing was going on. He had a terrific personality; he was always jovial, full of fun and so on. No indication whatsoever that there was any pressure on him. No indication whatsoever that he was in contact with the Germans.

Wing Commander Hugh Verity
Air Liaison Officer, SOE HQ, London
We had to kidnap him in France at pistol-point almost and bring him back and tell him that he was accused of being a double agent. I was present at that interview. We were all sitting around in comfortable armchairs and Buckmaster told him that he'd had reports that he was working with the Germans in Paris. Déricourt was very deadpan and said, 'Well, of course I

have to co-operate with the Germans and give them some black market oranges from Spain and be friendly towards them, so that I can get on with my work for you.' But in the event, one discovered later, from German archives, that he was in fact in close touch with the Germans in Paris and had given them a lot of useful information.

Lieutenant Robert Sheppard
SOE arms and sabotage instructor
I was directed to come home to HQ together with Edward Zeff, who was a wireless operator. We prepared to go back but there was no Lysander at the time and we were ordered to go back through Spain again. London knew that I had already gone through Spain so I knew what we were facing and could have helped the others. Everything went on well: we had a day's rest in Perpignan and in Amélie-les-Bains and in the evening we went out to the Pyrenees. After one hour's walk, or less, we were caught by the *Grenzpolizei*: the German frontier police. Edward Zeff and myself, we'd tried to run away. I had a couple of bullet holes in my coat. One of our chaps was shot through the head.

I had decided with Edward Zeff that in case we got caught we would not speak a word of French and we had prepared a cover story of two shot-down airmen going through an escape line, and when we were arrested we stopped speaking French. We spoke English between us, English with the Germans, and could not understand a word of French. We went to the prison in Perpignan and then to the prison of Fresnes, near Paris. No special interrogation for weeks, then interrogation a month or two later. I kept to the story of, 'No, I'm in the air force.' I knew in London a friend of the family who was a gunner in the Royal Air Force, Andrew Fry, and before I left I knew he had disappeared, shot down in the Channel. So, knowing him well, I entirely took over his personality, name, family and everything.

I was in a cell with three Frenchmen. Now, imagine, the life in a cell, twenty-four hours a day all together, the three Frenchmen speaking French, and I was not supposed to understand the way they were talking about me, their jokes. They were all extremely nice. Now, what would you do in a cell in order to pass the time? 'This poor Englishman doesn't speak French, we're going to teach him French' – and for nearly a month every day I had my French lesson. It was an extremely difficult thing to stay serious and learn, with a very, very bad English accent, all the words they taught me and to remember exactly the next day not to know too much.

Lieutenant George Abbott
Captured SOE agent in Fresnes prison, Paris
Time was measured by the sounds you could hear outside. For instance, Sunday and Saturday were far worse than the weekdays because there were practically no sounds outside. On Sunday afternoon you could hear the crowd shouting in the stadium in Fresnes but there was no sound in the prison except prisoners trying to communicate between themselves. There was in the prison a very old system of central heating, which was not operating, but they could communicate by the ducts by knocking against the walls using a very elementary code. 'A' was one dot. 'B' was two dots, two taps, and so on. You could hear these sounds and you could even hear the voices but I never communicated with anybody. What guarantee did I have that the chap next door to me is not a stool pigeon? And I'd made up my mind from the beginning, 'The only way I'm going to get out is as a dead body, they're going to shoot me.' I was convinced of that.

Lieutenant Robert Sheppard
Captured SOE agent in Fresnes prison, Paris
One day I was taken for interrogation and I realised in the car with the Gestapo that there was something on. They carried on talking English to me but in a much rougher way than they used to when they thought I was a pilot. And one of them, just before arriving, told his friend in French, but I understood, 'He's going to see if he can't speak French now.'

I arrived in this house and the Gestapo said, 'Show him, show him, and see his reaction.' They opened the door and what should I see but Edward Zeff. I knew it was Edward Zeff but his face was absolutely swollen like a huge football, absolutely blue from knocks he'd received. Head cut, hands cut, mouth bleeding. He looked at me and said, 'They knew me, I had to tell them.' I was then taken away. They told me, 'We know everything about you. You are "Patrice". You see what happened to your friend? The same thing will happen to you if you don't behave the proper way.'

The Gestapo kept me three days in this interrogation house. They wanted to know all sorts of things which I didn't want to tell them. They especially wanted to know what I did after my escape and precise things on the organisation of SOE. And just for fun I suspect, because I had really not much to tell them, they pulled one of my toenails out.

Odette Sansom

Captured SOE agent in Fresnes prison, Paris

I could have told them what they wanted to know, just like that. They wanted to know where our radio operator was; they wanted to know where another British agent who had arrived some time before had been to, and now was. I'm not brave or courageous, I just make up my own mind about certain things, and when this started, this treatment of me, I thought, 'There must be a breaking point.' Even if in your own mind you don't want to break, physically you're bound to break after a certain time. But I thought, 'If I can survive the next minute without breaking, this is another minute of life, and I can feel that way instead of thinking of what's going to happen in half an hour's time, when having torn out my toenails they're going to start on my fingers.'

On Armistice Day, when I had been in prison since April, at ten o'clock in the evening I was taken out of my cell and taken down to the courtyard of the prison. There was a car waiting with two men in uniform and the man who tortured me, who was not in uniform, said, 'Well, as you are so devoted to your country, I thought you'd like to go to the Arc de Triomphe on 11 November and see the German guards standing there.' We went, believe it or not, round and round the Arc de Triomphe. I said to him, 'You like what you are doing, the job you are doing. You are a sick man. You like doing this.'

Lieutenant Robert Sheppard

Captured SOE agent in Fresnes prison, Paris, and Saarbrücken, Mauthausen, Natzweiler and Dachau concentration camps

Then came the time to go to Germany. We were called one day for what was called a transport and we were informed that we were going to a camp. I was mixed up with French and different types including Edward Zeff, who joined me in a separate cell in order to get ready. I had time to send a note to my fiancée stating that I thought that my difficulties were over because I was going to be sent to a camp. Just this little letter, a little piece of toilet paper, written with a little piece of pencil. 'I can now give news. I have been through the worst interrogation of the Gestapo but they have probably decided not to shoot me and I know that I am going to be sent now to a camp in Germany.' I had no idea what the camps were like.

We took the train at Gare de l'Est and arrived at Saarbrücken. There we were surrounded by SS guards and immediately the atmosphere changed. Knocks, shouts. We were entering the world of the German concentration camp, which we didn't know. It was really entering a new life. We were absolutely shocked by the way they behaved. In the afternoon they called me out of the rank and they said, 'Ah, you are the British officer?' – '*Du bist der britische Offizier?*' I said, 'Yes.' They started slapping me in the face, and said, 'Now you get undressed.' After a few weeks or months in camp, getting undressed was nothing at all; but just imagine for us, just coming out of normal life, getting undressed suddenly in the afternoon, and I was absolutely naked. They said, 'Take this shovel.' I took this wooden shovel. 'Come with us.' And they had all the camp watching. There was the latrine, which was in fact a huge hole in the ground with two perforated planks, and they simply told me: 'Go down.' And for two days, my job was to empty the whole thing with the shovel and two buckets, with people still using the thing. I think they simply had ideas like this. 'Ah, a British officer. Put him in the shit.'

After a certain period, corpses, bodies, dead, you don't see them. It is horrible to say that, but you live with it, you don't see it. Someone's dead, you just walk over them. It is just part of the normal life of the concentration camp. This is the horror of it. They wanted us to be beasts and they nearly, nearly reached it. No more dignity; no more human behaviour. But the worst part is this daily life, when you wake up in the morning and you don't know if you're going to be alive in the evening. All the way through I wanted to keep my dignity as a British officer. I thought, 'I don't want them to destroy my personality, I want to be something,' and this helped me right through the concentration camps. With friends like Brian Stonehouse, although we were miserable, we were starving, we were dressed like clowns, we always wanted to keep dignified in front of everybody. It was the last part of our duty in the war, showing people that we were still there. I think many of our friends and comrades from the camps of all nations remember this. I think it was a way of keeping the standard high. Difficult sometimes.

Holland

Patricia Stewart-Bam
FANY staff, Air Liaison Section, SOE HQ, London
Holland went so terribly wrong. They had the right sort of flashing and the right signal from the field, because it had been taken from the agents under duress, and the supplies were dropped. I was never aware of any of the Holland business until much later on when it was generally known in the Air Liaison Section that the agents that were giving the messages were under suspicion and that everything must be very, very carefully watched, double-watched. At

that time they didn't know it was all being done under duress. It was a very successful counter-operation by the Germans.

Lieutenant Stanley Eadie
Signals officer, SOE HQ, London

I went into the signal office. Something had come up about the Dutch Section and Mac said, 'I've tried seeing the person in charge. You can try if you like. It would be good if you did.' Neither I nor Mac liked what was happening in the messages that were coming in. They didn't have their security code done properly. The security code was a quirk in the message: it might be that the twelfth or thirteenth letters were interposed; it wouldn't look bad at all on paper but that was our means of knowing that the agent was all right. Well, with the Dutch section we were seeing that some of these security checks were not there.

The Germans knew that we were having security checks so instead of having one security check, which we started out with, we had two, the idea being that if an agent was picked up and being tortured, he could reveal his first security check but not the second one. So if a message came in with no security checks, it might be all right as the agent hadn't bothered putting them in; and if it came in with both security checks, then that was all right; but if it came in with one security check only, that should have been alarm bells. But the major in charge of the Dutch section refused to accept it. He thought there was no problem at all and they'd just forgotten to do it. This was his attitude and we couldn't get anywhere with him. We couldn't prove anything, everything appeared all right from the messages except that some of the security checks were not there, and this major just pooh-poohed it. There was nothing we could do. We had no proof. We just had this gut feeling that there was something wrong.

Robin Brook
Director, Western Europe Section, SOE HQ, London

Once the thing had been thoroughly penetrated at the centre, the Germans were able to pick up incoming Dutchmen. And those Dutchmen, when they found that other Dutchmen were already working for the Germans or they were told that they were, etc, sooner or later gave in, not necessarily to torture, but to pressure; but torture if necessary. And against this combination, very few could, or did, hold out.

Then finally, on our side, we made in retrospect an almost equally fatal contribution, by assuming that success in operations was just a success for the Dutch and ourselves, whereas the success of the air operations, we realised far too late, was in itself suspicious. We should not have been so willing to accept that.

Squadron Leader Frank Griffiths
Halifax pilot, 138 (SD) Squadron, RAF
We aircrews were suspicious. People seemed to get a very easy run in and then the aircraft would disappear on the way out. Not all of them, but it was a rough ride out. Also the torches were excellent. Typical Germans. So bloody perfect, you know. Whereas with others there'd be weak batteries or they wouldn't be in a straight line and so on and so forth. But people used to remark, 'God, these Dutch are efficient,' and all the time we were dropping to the Germans.

Pilot Officer John Charrot
Halifax observer/bomb-aimer, 138 (SD) Squadron, RAF
The Germans were so well organised that they knew when an aircraft was coming to Holland, they knew where it was going to be, but in order not to spoil things for themselves they didn't shoot every aircraft down as it got over the dropping point, they just decided on the odd one. It wasn't until after eighteen months that someone really realised that there was something going wrong.

Squadron Leader Frank Griffiths
Halifax pilot, 138 (SD) Squadron, RAF
They'd briefed the anti-aircraft guns that they had on these receptions, saying, 'The aircraft will come over and he will identify the place. Don't shoot at him the first time, wait until the second'. I think that is what saved us, coupled with the fact that I used to drop first time if I could and then they didn't open up. The second thing was, they had fighters waiting to get us as we went back up the Zuider Zee.

Pilot Officer John Charrot
Halifax observer/bomb-aimer, 138 (SD) Squadron, RAF
We were dropping just at the bottom of the Zuider Zee, the south side of it, and we had a party waiting for us. We got to the dropping place. It was such a lovely night, really clear, and I could see the lights from a long way out while we were over the water and I said to Griff, 'Look, I can see the lights. They've got them alight already. I think I'm right on track, you're at the right height. We'll just go over and drop straightaway.'

So we went over the lights, I pressed the buttons and the containers went down and we then speeded away as soon as we could, which was the usual procedure. Wheels came up, flaps came up and we got away as fast as we could. But because we'd gone straight over and not diddled about they weren't prepared. They were prepared for the aircraft to circle, so they could get a good aim, I suppose.

Coming home, Griff must have had a premonition because normally after going to Holland we would cut out as quickly as we could to the North Sea, close to Amsterdam, but he said, 'No, I fancy going the way we came in.' So I said, 'All right,' and we went back the way we came in, in between the two islands, Texel and Vlieland, and on the way there we saw two fighters going across our path and Griff said, 'I think we've done the right thing.'

We reckoned that twelve aircraft from 138 Squadron were lost, which was about eighty-three crew, for a careless mistake back in London: not finding out that they had been sending warnings that they had been captured.

1944

We dropped off two people here, two people there, with instructions to wait until there was a non-armoured vehicle and then simply empty their Sten magazines into it once and depart. That stopped the column.

The long-awaited second front opened on 6 June 1944, when Allied forces began landing on the Normandy coast. More than forty SOE-run circuits were still active in France at the time of the invasion. These were supplemented by several dozen 'Jedburgh' paramilitary teams: inter-Allied missions, each of three men, charged with carrying out actions and guiding, arming and encouraging local resisters. Particular importance was attached to hampering German attempts at moving troops and armour to attack the bridgehead.

Elsewhere in Europe, many SOE activities were coordinated as far as possible with what was happening in France. Missions across the Balkans, for example, did what they could to keep German forces busy, although keeping Balkan guerrillas focused on the fight was not easy. Fear of reprisals continued to play a part, but as the year wore on and the Germans began to withdraw, SOE found guerrillas everywhere increasingly preoccupied with civil war and politics.

Difficulties were also encountered in Poland. British assistance to the Poles, channelled largely through SOE and the Special Duties squadrons from bases then in southern Italy, reached a peak in 1944. It was not enough to save those in Warsaw who rose against the Germans that August. The Red Army had advanced as far as the city's gates and could have intervened, but the Soviets had little time for non-communist Polish resistance. They would also have little patience with British and Polish parachutists found in its midst.

In Italy, as Allied armies continued to fight their way northward, SOE again supported local partisans and sought to assist the Allied advance by

harassing enemy garrisons and communications. No. 1 Special Force, SOE's Italian Section, dropped several teams of uniformed officers and men to work with guerrilla bands across the northern mountains.

In the Far East, where Japan's rapid conquest of Burma and Malaya in 1941–42 had pressed the British back to India, SOE – known there as Force 136 – was making less progress and significant guerrilla successes would come only in the last six months of the war. Few Europeans could exist easily behind Japanese lines and making and maintaining contact with locals willing to resist was hard. The difficulties are illustrated well by the experiences of Operation 'Gustavus': a small SOE team working with Chinese bands in the Malayan jungle.

FRANCE

Wing Commander Hugh Verity
Air Liaison Officer, SOE HQ, London
I was responsible for SOE's air operations room covering all special duties air operations into Western Europe and Scandinavia. During the time that I was doing this job, which was the first six months of 1944, the amount of air effort devoted to the secret armies of Western Europe, and in particular the Maquis of France, multiplied many times at Churchill's direct intervention. He got Bomber Command to switch a large number of four-engined bombers, in particular Stirlings, from other squadrons into carrying loads of arms and other material to the Maquis in preparation for D-Day.

I remember in the early months of '44 we could have over one hundred four-engined bombers out in a night, parachuting supplies to the resistance and the Maquis in France, as well as keeping going the resistance movements in other countries in Western Europe and Scandinavia. This was a tremendous load of weapons and ammunition, as well as blankets and food and boots, medical supplies and things like that. And of course parachuting in leaders and radio operators and arms instructors and all these people to make the Maquis into fighting forces.

Squadron Leader Thomas Seymour-Cooke
Halifax pilot, 138 (SD) Squadron, RAF
I sat next to Francis Cammaerts at dinner at Station 61 and he was complaining that he wasn't getting away. I said, 'Well, I'll take you next time,'

so I took him and a lot of trouble I got him into, too: we went over a defended area and were shot up. When we were hit he was saying, 'What's going on? What's going on?' and of course there was the smell of cordite and we said to him – this was the drill – 'Nothing, nothing, everything's all right.' We carried on. The next thing he knew, having been reassured once or twice again, he was hastened towards the hole and pushed out into the night without so much as a by your leave.

The starboard inner engine had started to glow, it may have been on fire anyway, and then it started to get bigger and bigger and bigger and then in the end I told the rest to bale out. The aircraft was in a spiral and I had to come back to the cockpit to see if I could fly it down because I couldn't get the hatch open. I saw then that the wing was on fire and the altimeter was spinning round and round and round, so I went back down and beat it open with my hand and got out that way.

The impression I'd got then was that Europe was an absolute maze of people to help us so we started to knock on doors. I was the only one who spoke French so it fell to my lot to say, 'We're English airmen, we're trying to escape. Can you help us?' The answer was usually that they'd slam the door in your face. You can't blame them, really, because they stood to be killed. Or, on one or two occasions, 'Come on in,' and then I heard them telling somebody, 'Nip down to the gendarmerie and let them know we've got a couple of English airmen up here.' Well, that might have been good, it might have been bad, but we took it as bad. Eventually we got in touch with somebody in the village of Beaurepaire and they put us on to the Maquis, the FTP, communists.

They sheltered us, but they were doing odd little sorties out. The first time they went out to a farmhouse and bullied this farmer, frightened his wife out of her wits and bullied the child and they were laughing and joking about this and all they did was pinch cigarettes and bread and things like that. After a while I said to them, 'Well, why don't you go and do a few raids and blow a few bridges up and things like that?' That wasn't very popular.

Captain Francis Cammaerts
SOE circuit organiser
The plane was shot down over the Drôme and I landed near a farmhouse. I knew, having been there before, that the chances were that nine out of ten people would welcome me with open arms and that one out of ten might be frightened and send me away and that one in a thousand would ring up the police. I walked straight up to the farm and knocked at the door. I said I'd had an accident and they said, 'Well, you're five miles from the road,' and I said,

'Yes, you may have heard an aeroplane.' 'Oh!' they said. 'You're an airman.' And they rushed downstairs and the farmer shouted to his wife, 'Go and get the wine out and we'll make him an omelette!'

Captain Cyril Watney
SOE wireless operator
Immediately after dropping we were being driven back by Jean Verlac to his farm. Suddenly there were about three police with torches and they stopped the car. They wanted to know who we were and then they said, 'Oh, you've just collected the English.' He said, 'Yes, yes.' 'Well, let's see them.' And they swung their torches on George Hiller and said, 'He's not English, he's French.' Then they turned the torch on to me and they said, 'Oh no, he's English all right.' They wanted to stop us but Jean Verlac said, 'Well, where do you get your cheese from, in your headquarters? You get it from us, the Verlacs. We always give you the cheese free of duty; you don't have to give your ration cards for our cheese. And if you stop us for any longer you're not going to have any more. I'll have to stop your cheese.' So they let us go on. That gave me a bit of a shock.

Major Robert Boiteux
SOE circuit organiser
I received a man in Marseilles and he broke his legs. I didn't believe him. I said, 'Don't be bloody silly, how can you break both legs?' But he had broken two legs. We took him to the doctor and the doctor said, 'Oh, no, no, no. I won't have anything to do with it. I'm sorry. If the Germans catch me they'll shoot me.' So I pulled out my gun and said, 'Look here, the Germans might shoot you in two or three weeks' time. If you don't do this job, I'm going to shoot you now.' So he chose to fix up our friend.

Captain Cyril Watney
SOE wireless operator
I went to Figeac and was going to stop the night at the flat of a woman teacher in Figeac School. She was also in our resistance group. So I stayed there and at about five o'clock in the morning her daughter, Pierrette, who was five years old, came in and said, 'The Gestapo are here, they're in the road.'

The Gestapo came to the door, she opened the door and they said, 'Is this number seven?' and she said, 'There are no numbers in this road. We haven't got any numbers. You have to go to the end of the road and count the houses.' The road was quite long. She came back and told me and we put her daughter in a pushchair, hid the radio under the coal bin in the cellar and took her off and walked through the Gestapo, because they'd gone up to the end of the road.

We found another house, which was run by a woman, Marie, who looked after a residence for women schoolteachers. She was very pro-English. She gave me a very good meal and while I was eating the meal the Gestapo arrived. I got up and stood behind the front door. Happily I remembered the tricks that they'd told me in Scotland and I was breathing through my mouth – if you breathe through your nose the sound of the valves in your nose can indicate that somebody's there. And I stood at the back of the front door while she opened it.

She refused to let them in. They couldn't come into her house because it was only for schoolteachers; she would never allow a man through her threshold; no man would ever come in. She was a very strong-willed person. She must have been eighty years old but she was very strong-willed and she stopped the Germans from coming into her house at all. I had my automatic but I don't what I'd have done. So they went off and then a friend came with his van, which was run by charcoal, and he said he'd take me off to a farm outside Figeac. Well, we went off. On the road to the village they'd just shot three Frenchmen who apparently looked like me.

Captain Jacques Poirier
SOE circuit organiser
From 1942 – mid-'42 – people were beginning to be more on the Allied side but that didn't mean they would do something. You must remember, too, that SOE particularly was not advocating a great mass of resistance in France. What they were interested in was to get, the day of D-Day, a well-trained group who would help tremendously the armed forces to disembark in France. Very often we had to discourage even some people who wanted to join the Maquis because we didn't have enough arms for them. We were not looking for a really great army. We were looking for small, adaptable and well-trained groups. All that meant that until the end of 1943 the resistance was really not a considerable amount of people. In 1944, things changed.

Captain Roger Landes
SOE circuit organiser
Before leaving for Bordeaux I'd had my briefing of what to do in France in 1944. They told me that the landing was very, very near. They didn't tell me exactly where it would be but I had a good guess. In my briefing the order was

to try to stop the Germans reinforcing the landing beach and to put all my activity on the Route Nationale 137, following the west coast of France, going up to Normandy.

I asked to be sent back to Bordeaux because I said I had something in hand, knew the district very well and, knowing where the danger was, I would be able to rebuild some things. At the beginning Colonel Buckmaster said, 'No, you can't go back to Bordeaux, it's too dangerous for you.' But in the meantime they had sent a French officer to take over and he'd been arrested by the Gestapo, so after a while they decided that I could go back to Bordeaux and rebuild an organisation. Within a week of my return I had managed to make contact with the headquarters in London and had an organisation of about ten groups, about five hundred men, and could organise nearly straight away about twenty dropping zones.

Major Robert Boiteux
SOE circuit organiser

A man who was organising the resistance in Marseilles came rushing down on his bicycle and I was introduced to him. I said, 'What about these three thousand men you've got?' He got a pencil and paper and started scratching his head, wrote down one name, scratched his head again, wrote down another name. Took him about twenty minutes. He wrote down fourteen names. There were no three thousand men; there was no Maquis.

'Right, where are we going to train these men?' Nobody volunteered to give up their house or lodgings. We found a man who wanted to be in the resistance, the manager of the local zoo, and he let us use one of the cages, the bear cage, which was divided in two. Halfway along the bear cage there was a fence, an iron fence, to separate the bears from us and I was doing the training in the bear cage with the bears looking through, very nosy and very interested, as if they wanted to learn. Eventually of course we got more people and more places and I got a few drops.

Captain Jacques Poirier
SOE circuit organiser

I was told that someone from the Savoie would be coming to visit me to see if I was prepared to give him a job in the resistance. I gave him a rendezvous in the basement of the shop and I told all the people, 'When this man comes, he will give the password. If it is OK, let him come down.' To come down you had a little ladder to the basement and I was waiting there. There was a little table in front of me and I had a gun on the table. Someone turned up and said,

'Your visitor is here,' and I saw a pair of shoes, then the trousers, then the body, coming down.

When the face turned up, it was my father. Needless to say, I was surprised. But because we had another chap there and I didn't want him to know that he was my father, I said, '*Bonjour, Monsieur*,' and my father understood immediately. He said, 'How do you do?' The other man left and when the door was closed we fell into each other's arms. But we had quite a big problem. After a while I told my father, 'Look, I am the boss here. I'd love to have you to help us but I want to remain the boss. I know it's difficult between father and son, why don't we sleep on it and tomorrow morning you tell me your decision.' The next morning my father turned up and said, 'Good morning, sir,' and that was the beginning of our relationship during the war, a relationship quite different to the one of a father and a son. But my father was a great help to me during that period.

Captain Peter Lake
SOE arms and sabotage instructor

I would spend three or four days in one Maquis and I would try to assess what their needs were, both in training and of course in armament. In between each trip I would generally return to Siorac. That tended to be our headquarters but it wasn't always Siorac: the thing was to be always on the move. This was being constantly interwoven with drops being arranged for them.

We came into a clearing where there were quite a large number of men who were obviously living in the open air. They all looked very fit. And the first thing that I noticed was that they were not young men, as I had rather expected to find. In fact most of them were refugees from Spain and particularly from Catalonia. I spent several days in that Maquis and instead of being able to give them tuition in the use of plastic explosive and the use of the Sten gun, in French, I found that I had to do it largely in Spanish, assisted by a few words of Catalan. A lot of them had already been extensively trained in subversive methods and moving around the countryside without being seen. They were in fact very well field-trained. A lot of them, as I discovered subsequently, had been heavily engaged in the Spanish Civil War and knew a lot about fighting. They weren't afraid of anything or anybody.

Captain Francis Cammaerts
SOE circuit organiser

It is commonly believed that we had a directive not to work with the communists. This is totally untrue. We were told to work with anyone who would be prepared to do what we were trying to do, which was to get the Germans out. Within the guerrillas fighting in the south of France, which became a very important part of the resistance, there were two major groups: the Secret Army and the Francs-Tireurs et Partisans. The FTP were thought to be communist but in fact weren't communist, although their actions were sometimes guided by the communist party hierarchy, and they received a lot of the material sent out to my organisation. Both because of their tradition and their nature, their policy was immediate action and they recognised that if you didn't have action, people weakened or fell out because they got bored. Often the non-communists criticised them because they took an action which was overt and in or near towns, which might result in hostages being taken: one of their initial needs was to make the young recruits prove themselves by shooting a German in the streets. On the other hand, when it came to getting things done, the communists were often the most effective people to turn to. In one case, when I wanted a hydroelectric station knocked out, a group of non-communist members of my organisation were preparing something very slowly and when I went to visit them one day they looked rather shame-faced because they said the job had been done. The job had been done in fact by a communist group who had stolen their explosives and weapons and done the job for them.

Major Ben Cowburn
SOE circuit organiser
In a good many cases I'd get some stuff and the communists wouldn't get any, so I'd slip 'em something. It didn't matter at all. They'd go on a job with me all right. They didn't try to make me a communist.

Captain Harry Despaigne
SOE wireless operator
We had some communists with us but at one time they decided that they wanted to go away and London gave us the order to let them go and take with them their side arms, so they went away with their rifles and a few rounds of ammunition. But some of them knew where some of our caches were and one day we had a slight fight. Some of my people went to the cache to get their arms and they found the communists there, pillaging the thing. A few rounds were fired and there were dead on both sides.

Peter Lake (left) and Jacques Poirier, SOE agents in France, 1944.

Captain Cyril Watney
SOE wireless operator
I saw a car and went up to it very slowly and saw one of the heads of the communist group asleep at the steering wheel. I put my revolver close to him and snatched his revolver away, at which he woke up, and I told him that, if he moved, I'd shoot him, I'd kill him. I told him to stay in the car and we were going to collect our parachute drop. When we'd received our parachute drop, I told him he must never come back and try and pinch our parachutes again.

Captain Harry Despaigne
SOE wireless operator
Among my own people, we had communists to start with, we had socialists, royalists, Bonapartists, Right, Left and what have you. We had Jews, Muslims, Protestants, Catholics, unbelievers; we had Russians, French, Yugoslavs, British and Americans. We were really a multinational thing.

Captain Roger Landes
SOE circuit organiser
By the end of May, my organisation was quite big. I had about four thousand men, fully armed and fully trained, in sixty groups in south-west France.

Captain Peter Lake
SOE arms and sabotage instructor
We all knew that D-Day was not going to be very far ahead and the difficult thing was to keep them in a state of preparedness without them literally going over the edge.

The Jedburghs

Sergeant Ron Brierley
SOE wireless operator, Jedburgh Teams 'Daniel' and 'Jeremy'
The object of a Jedburgh team was to have a small group of three people to be essentially a staff organisation to a militant fighting resistance group. It was known in France there were lots of these small groups of Maquis or resistance people who were keen to come out into the field but they needed several things. They needed arms. To get arms, they needed communications, guidance and leadership and liaison, and that meant somebody from the UK who knew what was available and what could be done in the way of support.

And they needed coordination, so that, as and when D-Day came along, that would be the time that they would become efficient active fighting units.

Captain Aubrey Trofimov
SOE officer, Jedburgh Team 'Guy'
The resistance was in many instances working blind. They were attacking the Germans to the best of their abilities or making life uncomfortable for the Germans but in many instances this didn't necessarily fall in with what was required by the Allied landing forces. We were not in any sense spies. That never came into our brief. We were paramilitaries. It was a coordinating role, making sure that the vast potential on the ground was being put to a really useful purpose. Otherwise we could have got into a situation where they were doing things that might have been harmful or slowed down the progress of our troops.

Captain Dick Rubinstein
SOE officer, Jedburgh Teams 'Douglas' and 'Douglas II'
Most of the teams were for France, so, of the hundred Jedburgh teams, probably there were ninety French officers. There were about three or four Belgians, half a dozen Dutch and one or two Danes. With them went a British officer or an American officer and the third one was the radio operator. We came together, these three hundred young men, at Milton Hall, near Peterborough.

Major Oliver Brown
SOE instructor, Milton Hall, Peterborough
The Americans who came to us were serving officers, soldiers. Bloody undisciplined soldiers, too. They'd take orders if they wanted to. They were extraordinary. I just can't describe them. They were so impatient it wasn't true. They wanted to go. They didn't want to be trained.

Captain Tom Carew
SOE officer, Jedburgh Team 'Basil'
I got on very well with the Americans. I really liked them. We had a lot of rapport. There was no bullshit with them.

Sergeant Norman Smith
SOE wireless operator, Jedburgh Team 'Brian'
To this day I can see them. At this time we had our old battledress, two pairs of boots, cellular blue pants and cellular blue vests. We had an army

groundsheet that had a collar on it and you wore that as a mac. These Americans came in their gorgeous uniforms: they'd got their lovely peaked caps, they'd got rain-covers, they'd got sun-tanned shirts, they'd got brown shoes, they'd got gaberdine uniforms, they'd got macs. They'd got everything and they used to show us all this gear they'd got. And they were getting £45 a month's pay. We could just not believe that such people existed.

Major Oliver Brown
SOE instructor, Milton Hall, Peterborough
We got the American carbine and a lot of American equipment, which we were very grateful to get because it was very much better equipment than ours; we supplied the demolition side, which was very much better than the Americans. We really worked very well together.

Captain Aubrey Trofimov
SOE officer, Jedburgh Team 'Guy'
The Americans, who were part of OSS, the Office of Strategic Services, wanted to remain as such. They were cooperating but they were not coming under SOE. This had rather an amusing side effect in that we had wonderful breakfasts with all these American bits and pieces. And because the French came into it, of course, we were able to get Algerian wine with dinner occasionally.

Captain Dick Rubinstein
SOE officer, Jedburgh Teams 'Douglas' and 'Douglas II'
When the Jeds were looking for their hundred Frenchmen, de Gaulle said that he couldn't provide a hundred but he did point out that there was more or less a French Army in North Africa which had got caught up in the politics of the immediate collapse of France. The North African forces had remained loyal to Pétain, they were not trusted, in fact they had fought in Syria, and at first I can understand that the British probably didn't want too much to do with the French in Africa. However, times changed, progress was made and de Gaulle said, 'Send your recruiting officers to my *Infanterie Coloniale*.' A hundred came forward immediately. They were very proud, regimental soldiers. They weren't fed up with what they were doing like the Brits and the Americans. They were older than us, they were more experienced than us, many of them had fought in France in '40, but they thought that unless they did something silly, like join SOE, there wouldn't be an opportunity for them to take part in the liberation of their country.

Major Oliver Brown
SOE instructor, Milton Hall, Peterborough
As far as the French were concerned, they were too steeped militarily. Obviously you couldn't behave as a military officer when you're dropped as a civilian in France, but you just couldn't turn them into civilians. They were military men and a lot of them had been entirely military for the whole of their lives. I mean, their fathers, their grandfathers and everything else had been in the North African Army and they just couldn't change.

Captain Dick Rubinstein
SOE officer, Jedburgh Teams 'Douglas' and 'Douglas II'
It took us about three weeks of our four-month course at Milton Hall to stop being shy and silly and get on with learning French. You would have three chaps having a drink, an American, a Brit and a Frenchman, and the conversation would be in French and the Frenchman would occasionally say, 'Not like this, like that.'

Sergeant Ron Brierley
SOE wireless operator, Jedburgh Teams 'Daniel' and 'Gregory'
We all lived together. We messed together, worked together. We did our PT, played our games. We learnt about explosives and did all sorts of exercises. And you made friendships and gradually people sorted out their teams. In the end there were ninety-three teams formed at Peterborough to go to France.

Sergeant Roger Leney
SOE wireless operator, Jedburgh Team 'Jeremy'
There was very much an emphasis that teams had to work. A team with three people, two officers and a radio operator, had to be very compatible. At times, trial teams were formed and if people didn't get on with each other, well, they changed. As far as I remember, you were allowed to say if you were stuck in a team and you didn't like one of the other members.

Sergeant Norman Smith
SOE wireless operator, Jedburgh Team 'Brian'
I was asked by Major Johnson, a regular Tank Corps man from Sandhurst who'd fought in the desert, and a French colonel, who we'd been out on exercises with, would I like to go with them? That was how I got into Jed team 'Brian'. They were lovely. Great people. The French colonel was the son of a French field marshal and had been in the Foreign Legion and he and I shared

a great hatred of anything physical. He was a funny little man, very, very thin, and whenever we came to doing physical training and had to leap over these horses without using our hands, he'd say, 'This is dangerous. We're not going to do this.' I said, 'You're dead right.' We used to duck out on anything we could. He'd got an MC in the desert, trying to get into a German tank with his sword.

Sergeant Neville Wood
SOE wireless operator, Jedburgh Team 'Gilbert'
We were all eager to get going and have a crack at the Jerry. Morale was very, very high.

Sergeant Alf Holdham
SOE wireless operator, Jedburgh Team 'Jude'
I was only nineteen and raring to go.

D-Day

Elisabeth Small
Civilian secretary, French Section, SOE HQ, London
Before D-Day there were two messages which had been arranged. One was a message 'B' which was to tell all resistance workers to be prepared that D-Day was coming soon. The 'A' message was that the invasion was on the way. That night I was on duty. Major Morel came in and he said, 'Come on, get off your bed.' I said, 'What's happened?' 'Nothing at all,' he said. 'I want you to type the "A" message, the airborne are en route. So that's something for your grandchildren.'

Flight Officer Yvonne Cormeau
SOE wireless operator
When finally the message came that the armada had sailed there was terrific rejoicing and we were up all night cleaning what weapons we had. They had been hidden under the beehives. We thought the bees would be good and protect them. This was of course out of doors so we'd had to first put a lot of soft soap on them so that they would not rust and then we'd had to get hold of the man himself, the beekeeper, to move the little hives a bit. We got all the stuff out, took it into the kitchen and spent the night cleaning these weapons.

Major Roger Landes
SOE circuit organiser
Straight away, the same night, we cut all the railway lines, we cut all the communication lines, telephone lines, and we blew up a lot of bridges, electric transformers, so that no Germans were able to leave Bordeaux and the district there and reinforce the Normandy beaches.

Anne Ponsonby
FANY *wireless operator, Grendon Hall signals station, Buckinghamshire*
I remember that first day, when the first landings were made, we got messages *en clair* from the French saying, '*Vivent les Alliés, Vive la France, Vive la Grande-Bretagne*.' Messages like that. It was terribly exciting, it really was, because we knew they had actually landed and that the resistance knew that. That was fantastic.

Captain Oswin Craster
SOE officer, Jedburgh Team 'Stanley'
We got the news of D-Day and then we hung around. We thought we'd never go. Some of the teams were shipped off to North Africa, about a dozen teams, and they jumped in from there. We hung around. At Milton Hall there's a picture, a very bad picture, of Earl Fitzwilliam in his hunting pink with a very, very red face. When a team was alerted it meant they were going; and someone, one of the Americans, of course, scrawled on this picture in chalk, 'NA', for non-alerted.

Sergeant Jack Grinham
SOE wireless operator, Jedburgh Team 'Stanley'
Teams would be assembled, they'd go away to London for briefing and away they went. We didn't know where they were going except that it was France. We'd gone down to London for briefing, we'd had a few lectures, we went back to our billets, and then in the afternoon Captain Craster came dashing in. 'Get your gear together, we're going.'

Captain Oswin Craster
SOE officer, Jedburgh Team 'Stanley'
We went from Tempsford in the evening. It was still daylight and I remember looking at the sun shining on the church and wondering whether I'd ever see that again.

Major Oliver Brown
SOE officer, Jedburgh Team 'Alastair'
We had a hell of a trip. First of all we went slap over Cherbourg and they threw everything at us. We followed that by going over Lorient and they threw everything at us there. We then flew straight down the Loire to Orléans and got tagged by a German fighter. They didn't realise until the plane got back to England that he had actually hit us.

Captain Duncan Guthrie
SOE officer, Jedburgh Team 'Harry'
Just before we arrived at the DZ, a message came back from the pilot. He was awfully sorry, he couldn't find the point we were supposed to be jumping and he was going to go home. I sent a message back. 'Come off it, does he know where he is?' 'He knows where he is but he can't see the DZ.' So I said, 'Well, nobody's meeting us. I don't want to go through all this again, let's go. It doesn't matter if it's not quite the right place.' I'm sure that was the right thing to do.

Sergeant Jack Grinham
SOE wireless operator, Jedburgh Team 'Stanley'
I must record my feelings as we were told to drop and I went through the bottom of the plane: 'Well, you're on your way now. You can't go back. Make a man of yourself and get on with it.' I was quite thrilled to be going out and doing just that.

Major Oliver Brown
SOE officer, Jedburgh Team 'Alastair'
I got a hell of a bad drop. I banged my nose and had half a thrown rigging line and only just came out of the spiral when I hit the ground. Luckily a Frenchman was running towards me from the reception committee and I actually landed on him. Not with my feet, but I sat on him. He was a good, fat, rotund one and I think this just about saved me, as I damaged my leg very badly. He was unconscious for forty-eight hours. I'm six foot six and weigh about eighteen stone.

Sergeant Glyn Loosmore
SOE wireless operator, Jedburgh Team 'Andy'
I came out of the aircraft, I reached up for my straps and I could see the aircraft going away and I hit the ground, very, very quick indeed. It was a hard

landing but I wasn't hurt. But the other two, Parkinson had broken his leg, got a bit of bone sticking out, and Vermeulen had twisted his ankle very badly. Poor Parkinson was calling for me, 'Loosmore! Loosmore!' My code name was 'Lundy' but with his broken leg he couldn't think of that. People thought he was saying, '*Doucement, doucement*' – 'Gently, gently' – which was quite a useful mistake for him.

Sergeant John Ellis
SOE wireless operator, Jedburgh Team 'Minaret'
The aircraft we went in was a rather vintage Halifax that had an engine put into the fuselage to drive all the auxiliaries and it was very, very hot in there. Due to all the heat, Hartley, that's Major Sharp, fell fast asleep and when we got to the DZ he was quite a bit fuzzy and so we had to help him out through the hole. The dispatcher took one loop of his harness and I took the other loop and we just held him over the hole and when the light turned green we dropped him. When I landed he was completely wide awake and chirpy and greeted me and shook my hand and said, 'Welcome to France.' Three days later I got a message back from Algiers: 'Could you please tell us anything about the state of the aircraft when it left you, because it hasn't returned?' It was believed to have exploded in mid-air.

Captain Aubrey Trofimov
SOE officer, Jedburgh Team 'Guy'
We were dropped at a place called Courcite, which is south west of Alençon, a big market town. I actually landed on a road and it nearly knocked me out, because I had my carbine just underneath my chin and a pack with all our emergency equipment, and the butt of this carbine came up and hit me on the chin. We assembled on the dropping zone and my throat was absolutely parched, possibly with the excitement, the fear, etc, and I said to one of these Frenchmen who was in the reception committee, 'I'd give anything for a drink.' He brought out a flask and offered it me and I took a swig. He said it was coffee. It was about fifty per cent coffee and fifty per cent Calvados. I thought he was trying to kill me. It just scorched its way down. I've never forgotten that or what I nearly called him.

Sergeant Gordon Tack
SOE wireless operator, Jedburgh Team 'Giles'
The French were ready for us but were badly organised. We brought with us quite a lot of arms in containers. A container of rifles is very heavy and they

didn't have the sort of transport necessary to take the arms away. They were still there next morning in daylight, loading them on to the one or two old trucks they had brought with them. What did disappoint me was that we had brought with us rucksacks with our personal kit, cigarettes and things like that. They had carefully gone through all that and stolen all cigarettes and anything else that was worth stealing, so for the whole of that period there I had one shirt, which I washed out on sunny days.

Sergeant Ron Brierley
SOE wireless operator, Jedburgh Team 'Daniel'
It seemed, after all the training we'd had about utmost security, that we'd dropped into bedlam because of the number of people shouting and running about all over the place. You felt like you were in the middle of Piccadilly Circus almost but we were assured the nearest Germans were about thirty miles away or something, so nobody seemed too worried. Then we were taken away from the dropping zone and to a safe farmhouse, I established contact with London on my first attempt the following morning and we were in business.

Major Thomas Macpherson
SOE officer, Jedburgh Team 'Quinine'
Activity started at once. I felt that we had to demonstrate to this group that we had not come to enjoy ourselves, that we were expecting action from them and that they were going to become active resistance. So I decided, on the very first night that we were there, that we would achieve something. I discussed this with Bernard and he on the map indicated a particular rail bridge that he thought was accessible without running across patrols and there was only one main road to cross. I prepared demolition charges – he had drawn me a picture of the bridge – and we took almost the full active strength, about half a dozen men, and Bernard, myself and Michel de Bourbon and set off. It was not a terribly good thing militarily to do and it was the only action that I ever did of that nature which I had not previously reconnoitred in detail, but it was so important to show them activity. Anyway, it went like a breeze. We set the charges, put on a short time delay and got back across the main road before we heard this reassuring explosion. It put great heart into the Maquisards that were with me and they never looked back from that.

Captain Dick Rubinstein
SOE officer, Jedburgh Team 'Douglas'
We would report locations of anything that looked useful, like guns or tanks.

They were only moving by night, so, if they were in a location at the start of the day, they'd stay there all day, and there was a possibility that you'd get an air strike down on them.

Sergeant Gordon Tack
SOE wireless operator, Jedburgh Team 'Giles'
There was a château just outside Châteauneuf where the U-boat officers used to go with their French girlfriends for long weekends and R&R after they'd done a trip. We knew about it and I got the map reference and transmitted it back to London and they sent across three planes and bombed it on a Saturday night or a Sunday night when it was full of U-boat officers.

Sergeant Jack Grinham
SOE wireless operator, Jedburgh Team 'Stanley'
A convoy of about 120 vehicles had stopped near the village of Bussières-les-Belmont. They'd come there overnight. The locals let us know, I went up on the emergency schedule to England and told them about it and the American air force came over, four Mustangs, and shot the convoy up. I remember watching them coming in at very, very low level, going along the convoy, and they killed about 120 German soldiers. There were two locals killed, probably by exploding ammunition. One night, one of the soldiers from this shot-up convoy staggered into our camp. He was caught and the following day the Maquis made him dig his own grave, shot him and buried him. He was not beaten up or anything like that. I think he was questioned and then I saw them lead him away with a spade and not long after I heard the rattle of Sten guns. They'd taken him down a farm track nearby. I saw the bloodstains afterwards and a little stick where they'd buried him.

Sergeant Neville Wood
SOE wireless operator, Jedburgh Team 'Gilbert'
Quimper's in a valley and we were in the hills all round with the German Army tied up inside. They kept coming out with a thirteen hundredweight truck, machine gun mounted on top, trying to get out and we were determined they wouldn't. They'd mortar the area for about four or five minutes and then come up with the machine gun truck and try to break through. And they did that one day and one of the shells landed outside the house I was in and all the glass in the room, the pictures and that, shattered and splintered and I got hit in the eye. It just sliced across the lid. I saw a

Members of the French resistance being instructed in the use of a Sten gun, Haute Loire, 1944.

French doctor afterwards and he sewed it up. He said, 'You're very, very lucky. An eighth of an inch or less and it would have sliced your eye open.'

Lieutenant Robert Maloubier
SOE arms and sabotage instructor
Almost every night I used to blow up a bridge. Even if the Germans were very fast at repairing them it took them two or three days. They came with an armoured train and landed a team of workers and rebuilt the bridge.

Major Robert Boiteux
SOE circuit organiser
I had Maquis on both sides of the road – about two hundred men. And at six o'clock in the morning, one of them, on the other side of the road from where I was, went to get some water from the pump by the side of the road. The Germans came along, three lorries of Germans, and they shouted, '*Halt! Was machen zie?*' and the man, instead of saying, 'I'm just getting some water,' ran away. Straight away they shot him. Then of course the firing started.

I had a bomb in my hand, one that explodes on contact, filled with plastic explosive. I was crawling towards this lorry on the main road, I was going to blow it up, and all at once I felt as if someone had thrown a stone at me, on the arm. I thought, 'That's funny. Who's throwing stones?' It didn't hurt any more than that. I kept on crawling and all at once I felt another one on my leg and I put my hand on my leg and it was covered in blood. I thought, 'I'd better get out of this,' and went back. Eleven of my men were killed, most of them youngsters. They were all kids, eighteen, nineteen.

Major Thomas Macpherson
SOE officer, Jedburgh Team 'Quinine'
A messenger came over that told us about the northward movement of the Das Reich Armoured Division and the Second Motorised Division, heading up towards the beaches and coming through the edge of my territory on two roads. There was almost a continuous stream of tanks, armoured cars, trucks and so on going up that road and what one had to do was stop them from time to time, make them de-bus, make them waste time. Now there were various ways of doing that and this was possible because it was quite heavily wooded, and there were tracks through the wood almost parallel to the road itself, so we could move people. We dropped off two people here, two people there, with instructions to wait until there was a non-armoured vehicle and then simply empty their Sten magazines into it once and depart. That stopped the

column. They had to get out and go and see what was happening. I myself, with two, went up the road further and started felling trees across it, brutally by explosive. Just a bang and the tree would fall down. They were not major obstacles but the southernmost two or three of them we booby-trapped, so that would delay them further. They had to look at each tree. The first one, I'm glad to say, was booby-trapped. They tried to push it aside with an armoured car and blew the front off the car. After that they were suitably cautious.

Captain Cyril Watney
SOE wireless operator
As the Germans started off, with their tanks loaded on lorries, we used bazookas and anti-tank guns to try and shoot the lorries. We didn't shoot the first lorry, we'd let the first lorry go by, but one would shoot the second and then the whole thing would stop and the men would jump off, with their machine guns, shooting. By the time they got to the northern part of the Lot, over two hundred lorries, with their tanks, were off the road completely.

Sergeant Roger Leney
SOE wireless operator, Jedburgh Team 'Jeremy'
I remember going up towards Vichy and running across the site of where there had been an ambush. The Germans had got prams, wheelbarrows, horses and carts, very few motor vehicles; there were dead horses all over the place. The resistance had boxed them in a country lane and just demolished the lot of them. There was about a mile of chaos up this country road.

Major Tony Brooks
SOE circuit organiser
Das Reich, chaps in black uniforms, were driving along the road from the outskirts of Montauban, where I had my headquarters for the southern zone, and going into town. I was cycling along, minding my own business, and I was overtaken by a lorry with about twenty Germans from the Das Reich in it and a chap with a rifle on each side of the rear door tarpaulins. And a chap went by the other way driving one of those enormous gazogènes and was able to make an enormous backfire – it was very easy to get a 'bang!' out of the back – and without the truck even coming to a standstill there wasn't a Das Reich soldier in it. One chap was facing this way, one chap facing that way, back to back, looking down the street. I got off my bike and just stood there, didn't try to run away or anything. They ignored me completely and after about ten

minutes they all started shouting, '*Schnell! Schnell!*' and climbed back in again, but they were so nervous that they were being ambushed by the resistance. You had a crack regiment, like the Das Reich, absolutely scared out of their pants, and that went on the whole time.

Captain Harry Despaigne
SOE wireless operator

We had about a dozen fights around us, which more or less stopped the Germans from using the main road from Carcassonne to Toulouse. Then one day, in July, they came over with about three thousand men and as many reinforcements, four or six planes and some armoured vehicles and we had a battle lasting all day. They started bombing our first camp and more or less razed it to the ground and all our wounded were burnt and thrown on the manure heap. I think I saw three bodies, carbonised, with no heads. The heads were cut off. They were apparently only wounded but the Germans had killed them.

Flight Officer Yvonne Cormeau
SOE wireless operator

We couldn't really send couriers on the road any more – it was too dangerous for them – so 'Hilaire' got himself a little car and papers that he was an inspector of tobacco. We'd been told the Germans were coming on the roads to the east and west so we took one due south, hoping to escape them. We hadn't gone fifteen kilometres when we were face to face with a personnel carrier. We were stopped and told to get out of the car. Then they put us in a ditch with two soldiers. Both had a pistol, one in my back and one in Hilaire's back. The *feldwebel* was telling somebody on the radio that he'd stopped a tobacco inspector and a woman, the woman had a district nurse's card on her, what was he to do with them?

My perspiration was coming down and the flies were sticking in my perspiration and I couldn't move, because if I'd moved they would have shot me immediately. Waiting, waiting. Then the crackle came again. He came back to us – '*Achtung!*' – and we tried to straighten up. 'Get in the car' – which we did at once. Suddenly he asked me what was in the case, which had been thrown on to the back seat, which, of course, was my radio set. I opened it. I knelt on the seat and showed it to him. He asked me what it was. I said, 'Radio,' which, in German, means X-ray as well as radio-set, and, in view of the fact that I was meant to be a district nurse, he thought it was an X-ray set. He said, 'Go,' and we got out very fast. The engine was already running.

Captain John Smallwood
SOE officer, Jedburgh Team 'Citroen'
We had a thing called a *gazogène*, a coach using charcoal as its fuel, which was burnt at the back as it buffed along. We had flags all over it, masses of ammunition and tons of stuff. We used to ring up from village to village and ask if there were any Germans there. I did 150 kilometres in France, in uniform, in occupied country, without any danger at all, and we were able to do that by just ringing up from village to village. 'Any Germans there?' 'No.'

Suddenly I saw in the middle of the road a German with a slung Schmeisser putting his hand up, saying, 'Stop!' We had a light machine gun in the front and started opening fire on them. They had a patrol and they opened fire too. Three chaps on our machine gun were all wounded so we broke off into the fields and vineyards round there. We did a counter attack and dealt with a few people. They were German Army signallers from Avignon, rolling up the cable along the road, and they were as surprised as we were when we met them. There were eight of us and we had four wounded, two seriously.

Sergeant Harry Verlander
SOE wireless operator, Jedburgh Team 'Harold'
We went off to a nearby village, to a restaurant, for a meal. Everything went reasonably well. They put the cars in the garage in the village and we sat down in the restaurant. And at that time my French was pretty minimal. I'd learned just a little at school, not a lot. We'd practised in our training and I was beginning to follow conversations but I couldn't make conversation, I'd join in a bit too late. So I was told to keep quiet and not to speak in the restaurant.

We sat down, the three of us in the team and three or four other people, and we hadn't been there long before a group of Germans came into the restaurant and went over to another table. We carried on with the meal and were enjoying it, because we hadn't had a proper meal, and there was quite a buzz of conversation going on. Suddenly my mind went completely off what we were doing, what was going on, and I just looked over to the major and said, 'Pass the bread, please,' quite loudly. And it was as though everything went dead silent, there was no noise and it echoed round and round the room. It seemed for a while that there was no other noise at all. We were in civilian clothes and the major had his gun stuck in his belt, under his jacket, at the back, and he put his hand behind his back and reached for his gun and we looked towards the Germans. Suddenly the Germans stood up, one of them lifted his glass and said, '*Prost!*' and carried on. We quickly did the same. Picked up our glasses, '*Prost!*' and carried on. It was quite scary at the time.

Captain Cyril Watney
SOE wireless operator

George Hiller, André Malraux and Colonel Collignon and a driver went off in the car. I was about seven kilometres away that night and we couldn't warn them that a German armoured division had put their headquarters in Gramat. Of course, when they were driving through Gramat, a sentry saw them, shot at them and killed the driver of the car, which somersaulted and overturned on the edge of the road.

Out of the car got André Malraux and he received bullets in his legs and he fell to the ground. George Hiller got out next and he had a Sten gun. He dropped this on the road and as he bent to pick it up the Germans shot him in the stomach with a dumdum bullet. Then Colonel Collignon managed to get off while they were watching Malraux and George Hiller and he escaped. The Germans then took André Malraux off for questioning. George Hiller, they thought, was dying or dead and they saw that Collignon had got into a little wood and they put a sentry on either side of the wood to prevent his escape. Collignon waited, because he knew at some time the sentries would want to get together, to just have a word together, and when they did get together he shot them both. Then he walked and ran the seven kilometres to the Maquis where I was.

He told me that George Hiller was smashed up. At the time I was lucky enough to have a Bugatti car, a coupé, with a Bren gun on the roof and I got into it and we drove to Gramat. Just outside, by the sign where it says Gramat, I saw George Hiller on the ground. We stopped the car and I ran out and picked him up and we carried him back to the car and drove the car to a village we knew was uninhabited and put him in the church minister's house, which was empty. I had to get on to the radio to London to try and get supplies of anti-gangrene tablets and all the required things for an operation. I wanted those dropped immediately. Then we had to go and try and get a surgeon. Then we had to operate.

Having no gas or any type of injection to give him to relieve the pain, I held his chest and shoulders on the table and two other resistance people held his legs while the doctors were trying to clean him out. He had two handkerchiefs and his tie among other things all stuffed into the hole that was made in his stomach by the dumdum bullet, and, of course, they had all coagulated and got stuck in with the blood. All that had to be taken out and cleaned. It was a particularly disagreeable thing to hold your friend while this was going on, and, as the wound was being cleaned, I could see something which upset me. He had got his bottom lip between his teeth and, with the pain, he had bitten right through his bottom lip and his teeth were joined through the lip. After about an hour and a half they considered the operation was satisfactorily completed and we got a bed and a nurse and guards and we left him in that house. After a month he was getting very much better and they sent a plane and we loaded him in so that he could be flown back to Britain.

Sergeant Gordon Tack
SOE wireless operator, Jedburgh Team 'Giles'

The Germans knew that we stayed in farmhouses. We answered that by getting up at dawn and did a forced march eight or ten miles away in rough, wooded country, and stayed there until late in the day when we moved to another farm, where we would stay another night and then do the same sort of thing. During training we'd had to do forced marches all the time, we did nine miles in seventy-two minutes, that sort of thing, so being chased by Germans was no problem. But if they found any evidence of our occupation, they killed the farmers. They normally shut them up in the farmhouse and set fire to the farmhouse or shot them. In one instance they found one Sten round, just an ordinary 9-millimetre Sten round, amongst the straw of the haystack where we'd slept, and on the strength of that they killed a whole family and burned the farm down.

Captain Peter Lake
SOE arms and sabotage instructor

The whole of the Dordogne and Corrèze were buzzing with elements of the Das Reich Division and of course that was when most of the damage to the local population was done. The Maquis did what they could but it really wasn't very much because with a Sten gun or a Gammon grenade you can't do a great deal against the tanks of those days. There were a few engagements but I don't think many of them made much difference to the Das Reich Division, quite frankly.

That was the time when the Germans went into Oradour-sur-Glane. We didn't hear about it for a very long time. They also destroyed a village called Rouffignac; that was much nearer where we were operating. One hadn't quite realised how severe they would be. They hadn't been too bad up to that point. It was only after 6 June that they became serious. There had been isolated shootings and the odd isolated farmhouse that had been set on fire and the inhabitants taken away and shot. But we hadn't had villages dealt with in the same way until after 6 June.

Sergeant Harry Verlander
SOE wireless operator, Jedburgh Team 'Harold'
I saw Oradour-sur-Glane not long after it had happened. We were driven there by a group of Maquis. It was pointed out to us where women and children had been put in the church and hand grenades had been thrown in. There was a garage where all the men had been put and machine-gunned. All the animals apparently in the village had been shot and killed. Everything that moved had been killed. There was a strange quietness about the place. We didn't stay very long. It was still quite an active area for the Germans.

Captain John Smallwood
SOE officer, Jedburgh Team 'Citroen'
The local French commander came to me and said, 'I want to shoot three Germans.' I did a Pontius Pilate and said, 'It's nothing to do with me.' 'You misunderstand me,' he said. 'I know I can shoot them. What I want is the authorisation of an Allied military officer to shoot them. We want revenge.' So I became a war criminal and said, 'Yes.' I wanted to avoid the responsibility and they did shoot them. They were going to shoot them publicly and then the Americans arrived and stopped them, so the French took them round the corner into a field and shot them there. I couldn't have stopped it but I'm not proud of it.

Major Oliver Brown
SOE officer, Jedburgh Team 'Alastair'
We were reconnoitring possible ambushing areas and a German came down the road on a bicycle and a girl from a farm below came across the road and he fell off his bicycle. She didn't knock him off but she was a little bit in the way and he literally got out his pistol and shot her. Killed her. We saw it and later on, actually, we caught him. We handed him to the father of the girl that he'd shot and we never asked any questions. She was about seven years old.

Sergeant Alf Holdham
SOE wireless operator, Jedburgh Team 'Jude'
A French woman and her husband were brought and found and convicted as being spies for the Germans. Their demise was short and sweet. I executed them. The French gave me the proof that they were spies and they offered me

the chance, as an English agent in with them, of executing them. Well, you can't very well turn it down, otherwise you would lose face, as you might say, and so I executed both of them, with a tommy gun, one shot apiece. They were blindfolded. Strangely enough they did not protest their innocence. In fact, just before I shot the woman, she shouted out, '*Vivent les Anglais!*, *Vivent les Anglais!*', so she knew I was English.

Captain Aubrey Trofimov
SOE officer, Jedburgh Team 'Guy'
The Americans were breaking through very rapidly and they suddenly had reconnaissance advance parties that were really getting quite close. So I thought, 'Well, the thing to do is to try to find out what the Germans are doing, where they're putting out their last-ditch posts and such like.' I couldn't do it in daylight, in uniform, so I became a farmer's assistant. They got me a *carte d'identité* and this enabled me, in civilian clothes, to go into the town of Gorron at night, but obviously I had to sneak round back streets and so on because of the curfew.

Well, I managed to get quite close to two or three of the German positions that they were taking up with machine guns and other equipment. And on the way back, on that very first night, I ran slap-bang into a patrol. They were mainly very young soldiers, led by a young NCO, and I had to think very quickly. Because of the curfew I shouldn't have been there so I pretended to be drunk. In fact I leant against a wall and started retching. They just went by. They were in retreat and morale was very different. Had it been a month or two earlier I think it would have been up for me because I was carrying a .45 Colt in my pocket, which is quite a heavy pistol, and if they'd frisked me they'd have very quickly come across that.

There was then another incident where I wanted to contact a gendarme who knew the area very well on the side of Gorron where the Americans were likely to come from. I decided to risk it in daylight and go and contact him because time was getting short. I set off to go to meet him and suddenly, to my horror, as I came round a bend, there was a German regiment resting by the roadside. There was no other way for it, I had to walk through this and I had to obviously not show any panic. I put on a slight limp because being young they might have thought, 'Why is he not in a labour camp?' and I kept my head down and tried to look like a sort of useless young fellow. Fortunately I had my beret right down on my head and I was wearing very old clothes. As I walked through I could feel the sweat on the back of my shirt and thought, 'Everybody must see that I'm panicking,' but I managed to get through to the

A member of the French resistance taking cover during battles with German snipers, Dreux, 1944.

other end. I've never been so happy to see a wood and get into it. I really had to pull myself together for three or four minutes because it was the most extraordinary feeling, being right amongst them with no weapons, nothing, and in civilian clothes.

Sergeant Ron Brierley
SOE wireless operator, Jedburgh Team 'Daniel'
We literally ran into an ambush by retreating German forces. We were in three vehicles and got very badly shot up. We were moving in daylight, moving across open country and just ran into a German machine gun. Ken Bennett and Albert de Schonen were both quite badly wounded. We managed to scramble out and got into a ditch nearby. Poor old Albert took out a cigarette and was inhaling on this cigarette when he suddenly noticed that smoke was literally pouring out of his chest. Pretty gruesome. He was in a pretty bad way. This was obviously a delaying action on the part of the Germans and we managed to get away without too much difficulty.

Captain Harvard Gunn
SOE officer, Inter-Allied Mission
The Americans landed at St Tropez, by sea and by gliders, to very little resistance really and they started to move northwards and I went down to see them. It's rather grand to say 'I went through the German lines' because there wasn't really a line, but anyway I contacted them very early on. They produced a column, called 'Miller's Flying Column' and that went up to the north and got quicker and quicker and quicker. There were pockets of resistance on the way but basically the Germans realised that the war was over.

At one stage we were on a road, with a precipice on one side and cliffs on the other, and there were a few shots and this whole column was held up, suddenly stopped. I had a little tiny Fiat and I drove up to the front and the commander said, 'We're under fire.' I said, 'You can't be under fire, there's nobody there.' I went out in front of the column and I shouted in German, echoing down this valley, that if they came out with their hands up they would be safe, but if they stayed where they were they would have no chance at all of ever getting home. There was complete silence and after a bit there was a rustling of bushes and a pathetic little group came struggling out with their hands up, falling over, boys about sixteen, seventeen. Terrified. In fact the first one out was crying with terror.

Major Thomas Macpherson
SOE officer, Jedburgh Team 'Quinine'
I got a message from Captain Cox, another Jedburgh, who was west down the Loire, to say, 'We have made contact with the German headquarters but they won't surrender to the FFI, the French, because they're afraid they'll have their throats cut. Will you come and see what you can do?'

We had captured a German Red Cross car, a French Citroen painted white with a huge Red Cross on it, and I said,'Right, we will go unarmed and we will drive just straight through the German lines and see if we can get to this place.' We drove through the night. We were shot at by machine-gun fire twice on the road but focusing on a fast-moving car with its headlights on towards you is not easy and they didn't hit us, though it was slightly unnerving. We arrived with the dawn at this place on the Loire and met up with Captain Cox and the local French resistance commander. They said that they had told the German Commander that a British regular officer would be appearing and he had therefore agreed to attend at the local schoolhouse at ten o'clock.

Just after the meeting started an American colonel turned up, too, which was fine because the great problem in my mind was, 'If these guys surrender, what do we do with them?' We got the German commander to surrender his force, which he said numbered 23,000, on two conditions. One was that they should be handed over to the Americans; the second was that until the Americans had an adequate guard for them they should be allowed to keep their personal weapons. That was agreed and he dictated a signal from his headquarters that went out to all his units on the spot, telling them to cease fire, cease all military operations and to allow British and American officers access.

Captain André Watt
SOE wireless operator
Patton's Third Army came into the outskirts of Troyes. I was told that they were just a few kilometres away and, since I was the only English-speaking person, Yvonne said, 'Well, come on, the two of us will go.' So the two of us went and made contact with the Americans about twenty kilometres outside Troyes. We just had Citroen cars and they were there with their great big Sherman tanks and they said, 'All right, you go through first and we'll follow you.' They were very correct, I must say. It was very hot at that time and the French were coming out with bottles of wine to give to them and they refused all the bottles of wine and said, 'No, no, water, water.'

Major Jacques Poirier
SOE circuit organiser
At ten o'clock in the evening, playing my little General de Gaulle, standing up in a car, I entered the town of Brive. I'll never forget that for the rest of my life. Everybody applauding, it was something fantastic. Brive was liberated.

Captain John Smallwood
SOE officer, Jedburgh Team 'Citroen'
I had the immense pleasure of liberating Toulouse. Not that I had anything to do with it, as the Germans were all gone. I was kissed by everybody. Great fun.

Sergeant Roger Leney
SOE wireless operator, Jedburgh Team 'Jeremy'
I was driving this Citroen and, as Geoffrey Hallowes and I arrived at the outskirts of Vichy, we were both in need of finding the nearest toilet. We spotted this French pissoir in the middle of the square. Geoffrey got out of the car in his kilt and battledress blouse and a Gordon Highlanders' bonnet with a big Gordon Highlanders' badge and shot across the road and disappeared in this thing. A couple of French women spotted him and shouted at him, 'Ah, Scotch officer!' and they started clapping. Then a crowd collected. There was Geoffrey, scarlet in the face, trapped in this thing by a crowd of cheering French people. By that time I had lost the urge, seeing this French crowd, so I stayed in the car. We then drove on in and went into this sort of spa place and there was an orchestra playing, a sort of palm court atmosphere. When the leader of this orchestra spotted Geoffrey, he stopped the orchestra and after a bit of consultation broke into '*It's a Long, Long Way to Tipperary*' on strings and piano. I was gawping around at this lot and people were clapping. Geoffrey dug me in the ribs and said, 'Stand to attention you fool, they're playing the national anthem.'

Sergeant Jim Chambers
SOE wireless operator, Jedburgh Team 'Bunny'
They rounded up these ladies who'd associated with the German troops and put them on a chair on the truck, shaved all their hair off, and then – they had these brands in the fire – they branded them on both cheeks with a swastika. There were lots of cheers and jeering and pushing and prodding. It was quite a happy occasion for those that were watching. The hairdresser made quite a show of it, dancing round and snipping bits off here and there, till he eventually shaved the whole lot off. Horrifying, really.

EA 33756

A member of the French resistance poses with his Bren gun in Chateaudun, 1944.

Major Roger Landes
SOE circuit organiser
A lot of women who they thought were collaborating with the Germans were working for the resistance at the same time. I saw about half a dozen cases like that, mostly prostitutes who were working for us, even giving us shelter when we had nowhere to go. They used to shelter us in one of the brothels.

Lieutenant Colonel Francis Cammaerts
SOE circuit organiser
How do you define collaboration? The chap with a little shop at the corner who sells a packet of cigarettes under the counter to German soldiers: is he a collaborator? The chap who runs the Peugeot factory at Besançon and is sending all his produce to the German Army, but when Harry Rée comes along and suggests that they reduce their production by sabotage, he accepts: was he a collaborator at any time? The French themselves got this terribly mixed up because people had different roles and the roles didn't always fit in with what their conception of resistance really was.

Captain Aubrey Trofimov
SOE officer, Jedburgh Team 'Guy'
There was a tremendous witch-hunt immediately afterwards. Equally we found there were vast numbers of people going around with armbands on saying they were members of the resistance. Where had they been when we were there? Some of them may have been genuine but a lot of them weren't.

Sergeant Leney
SOE wireless operator, Jedburgh Team 'Jeremy'
There were a lot of people who got on the bandwagon who had not been active in the resistance. They were suddenly appearing in old uniforms: either those they had before the war or their uniforms from when they had been demobbed from the French army, borrowed uniforms or whatever. They were only in it for what they could get out of it.

Sergeant Gordon Nornable
SOE arms and sabotage instructor, Inter-Allied Mission
'The Mothballers' they called some of them. They'd got their uniform out of the drawer and put it on and were strolling about.

Sergeant Ken Brown
SOE wireless operator, Jedburgh Team 'Paul'
We were told we could start making our way to Paris and somehow my officer had acquired a Renault. I wasn't by any means an expert driver but I was deputed to drive. I forget where we stopped the first night but it was very amusing because Hugo came rushing out of his bedroom when we had just retired, saying, 'There's a woman in my bed!' We were thinking, 'Well, lucky Hugo!' but obviously she was trying it on to get a lift to Paris. I think a lot of collaborators were anxious to get out of the area as quickly as they could.

Captain Stephen Hastings
SOE officer, Inter-Allied Mission
As there was nothing for us to do, we decided to go to Paris and report to SOE. It was a very interesting journey. Most of France was by that time in the hands of the Maquis. We were in Dijon for the liberation there – what an experience. And I remember we picked up a woman, dressed in American Army kit, by the side of the road, about a hundred miles from Paris. She turned out to be Mrs Ernest Hemingway, Martha Gellhorn. She was doing a job as a war correspondent and she was very glad to get a lift. She was clearly without fear but she was also without a sense of humour. I remember parting in Paris over breakfast because somebody had made a remark about her eating jam and bacon at the same time as an unacceptable American habit, for which we were accused of being arrogant British officers.

Captain Tom Carew
SOE officer, Jedburgh Team 'Basil'
I went to the Champs-Elysées where our officers were and I'd only been there a few days and we were rounded up straight away. De Gaulle had given the orders that all British officers, every British person who'd been with the resistance, would be sent home, cleared out of France.

Captain Cyril Watney
SOE wireless operator
They told me that de Gaulle wanted me to leave France within forty-eight hours and they would send a bomber to fetch me from Toulouse airport. I think the reason was that he was extremely insular in his wish for success in France and that France, as an entity, must become a great country again. He was still upset about the early part of the war, where France, unlike Britain, crumbled under the German onslaught.

Major Roger Landes
SOE circuit organiser

When de Gaulle visited Bordeaux in September 1944 I was presented to him and he told me, as a British officer, I had nothing to do with France and to go back to England within twenty-four hours. I told him at the time, I said, 'Excuse me, *mon général*, I only receive orders from my headquarters and I will leave France when I have orders to leave.'

In the afternoon I was sent for by one of his French ministers and he told me I had twenty-four hours to leave France. He was shouting at me. I didn't know who he was. One of my bodyguards put his gun in his stomach and said, 'If you don't shut up I'm going to pull the trigger.' He turned very pale and said, 'Do you know who I am?' I said, 'No.' He said, 'I'm the War Minister.' I said, 'Well, *monsieur*, first, you should introduce yourself, and also, if you wanted to talk with me, it would be better to talk privately, not in front of the public.'

I didn't leave France straight away. I didn't want to accept de Gaulle's ultimatum. I left Bordeaux but I went to the south of France to a town called Dax and there I took about six weeks' leave doing nothing at all. Then I decided to come back to England. In the meantime, the French War Minister reported me to Duff Cooper, who was the British Ambassador in Paris, saying that a British officer had tried to kill him. Of course that report went to the Foreign Office and I was sent for by the Foreign Office to explain what had happened. They said, 'Well, you were not the only one to have trouble with de Gaulle at the end of the war. Forget about it.'

Odette Brown
FANY secretary, French Section, SOE HQ, London

The agents came back. Some of them wrote out their reports and handed them in. Some of them would want to dictate it to a secretary and it was typed and handed in. I collated all the reports and I met them as they came into my office. I very much remember George Millar coming back – he was 'Emile' in the field. He came into my office and handed in his report and said, 'Can you possibly find me a quiet corner somewhere where I can sit and write a book?' I managed to find a little attic or somewhere in Bryanston, which was horribly cold but he didn't seem to mind, and he sat and wrote his first book. He wanted to be the first person to write about the thing. It was called *Maquis*.

Lieutenant Robert Sheppard
SOE agent captured in France, held in Natzweiler concentration camp
One day we saw four girls, well dressed, arrive. They were four girls of our SOE organisation.

Lieutenant Brian Stonehouse
SOE agent captured in France, held in Natzweiler concentration camp
They were all rather pale, in civilian clothes. You never saw any women in the camp and I couldn't understand what they were doing there. They hadn't make-up on but you could tell they'd been in jail for several months. One of the girls had a ribbon in her hair, a sort of defiant gesture. It was very touching. One of the girls had a fur coat on her arm; later on, one of the SS guards walked back up the camp with the fur coat over his arm. They all had their clogs on, which was usual for France. From an inmate's point of view they looked in good condition, pale and sallow. They were executed that evening. I saw them go through to the end of the camp, to the bottom, to the bunker where the crematorium was. One of the girls Pat knew. He recognised her. I didn't know any of them but I made a description of them as soon as I got back. It was so accurate that they were recognised.

Lieutenant Robert Sheppard
SOE agent captured in France, held in Natzweiler concentration camp
Everything was the same as before. They had simply disappeared. That was May, June, 1944, the very moment of Overlord and the landing in Normandy, but we didn't know about it. We were disappearing in the fog. We didn't know about the landing. We knew much later and we hardly believed it. Paris was liberated in August and we didn't know about it.

Yugoslavia

Sergeant Alexander Simić
SOE wireless operator with partisans, Slovenia
I was doing a 'sked' one evening, having a lot of trouble with 'DF'ing, because the Germans used to try and DF us, direction-find us, and also with static and atmospherics. I'd encoded a lot of messages and it had taken a hell of a long time to get through them – I'd had to keep changing my crystal to get a different wavelength – and about six o'clock in the morning I'd had enough. I'd got through everything, got through all the traffic, and I thought, 'Well,

I'm going to relax now,' so I did what I shouldn't have done, I switched over to the short wave Forces programme. And to my immense delight I heard, first of all, '*Down in the jungle something stirred*' – that funny little thing. I couldn't believe it, you know, and I wasted quite a bit of valuable juice from my accumulators on it. Then all of a sudden that was cut off and they said, 'Here is an announcement. The second front has started.' They said that four thousand ships were taking troops and equipment and the RAF was sending over planes and bombing the enemy coastal defences and so on. And I got it all down and rushed out and told them and they went absolutely berserk! They fired off all this valuable ammunition. They came and hugged me and kissed me. I can see it now.

Captain Maurice Sutcliffe
SOE liaison officer with partisans, Croatia
By the time I fetched up in Yugoslavia I was very tough and fit and all ready to get involved in what I thought was going to be a very dramatic and fast-moving war. In fact it wasn't fast moving except on rare occasions and it was fairly different to what I had any idea that it would be. I'd imagined people to some extent living in caves and rushing down, putting demolitions on railways and so on, but it was really very much more organised than that. I had no idea when I went into the country that it would be such a huge organisation, the partisan movement.

Captain Basil Irwin
SOE liaison officer with partisans, Bosnia
This little outfit I was with, the 16th Division, I should have thought it must have been about three thousand people. When you get three thousand people moving about in a group in the hills and the mountains, local food doesn't exist in that quantity, and at times their operations were based on the necessity to capture food, capture arms. And they had of course this terrible problem with all the wounded. What to do with them? It was said that rather than let their own wounded fall into enemy hands it was better to shoot them. We had a lot of wounded with us and we were never actually in the position that we ever left or had to leave our wounded behind. We always somehow broke through with them and they were dragged along in carts and on horseback.

Captain Robert Wade
SOE liaison officer with partisans, Montenegro
I saw a partisan chap who'd had his hand blown partly off with a grenade.

HU 67565

An SOE mission in occupied Yugoslavia.

They gave this chap a slug of alcohol and just held him down and did the operation. There was no anaesthetic there at all. I mean, if you were wounded, you had the operation straight, and if it hurt it bloody well hurt and that was it.

Captain Basil Irwin
SOE liaison officer with partisans, Bosnia
One of the toughest battalion commanders they had was a young girl, tough as hell. Women and men, they were all together. Women were expected to do exactly the same as men. You'd see them carrying exactly the same loads of ammunition, guns and anything else.

Captain Maurice Sutcliffe
SOE liaison officer with partisans, Croatia
Partisan girls were amazing. In a company-sized unit of maybe eighty or ninety people there were maybe twenty or thirty girls.

Captain Robert Wade
SOE liaison officer with partisans, Montenegro
We were walking with partisans along a mountainside goat path with a sheer drop on one side and a sheer mountain going up the other. When it came to the hot spot, where the Germans were dropping a few mortars across, orders came back and everybody obeyed impeccably. They said, 'Four metres between people, eight metres between people,' and as you got toward the hot stuff the line just filtered out and you just walked through it like Russian roulette more or less. If you were hit you just took a damned great tumble down the side of the mountain. It was a really good show. It was brilliantly done.

Major Basil Davidson
SOE liaison officer with partisans, Serbia
We not only sent very large quantities of military munitions and medical supplies, we also performed other services of which perhaps the most important of all was to evacuate the wounded to Italy. Partisan warfare was very fluid and mobile and you had to move from A to B very fast and you can't move from A to B if you have to carry with you hundreds and hundreds of wounded men and women. So the only way you could handle the thing was either to risk their being executed by the Germans or to evacuate them by air. And I'm very proud to say, and I think all of us are very proud to remember,

that we did evacuate many hundreds of wounded. I myself evacuated wounded from the area where I was, which was far inland, from an airstrip within sight and sound of Belgrade where there were three German divisions. And that got rid of the wounded, because the wounded, if they were found by the Germans, were invariably shot, with their nurses and with their doctors. They were shot out of hand.

Captain Maurice Sutcliffe
SOE liaison officer with partisans, Croatia
We had perhaps a total of thirty aeroplanes in, two or three a night, until the Germans made night attacks on the aircraft as they tried to land on our strip. A strip sounds rather like a prepared airfield; it was just a few fields put together. We'd pile them in. There were no stretchers or anything. We'd put straw on the bottom of the aircraft and then people would just get in. They were never strapped in. In an old Dakota we'd get maybe twenty-six, twenty-eight, very seriously wounded people. I mean, they'd lost both legs, lost both arms. I was just one location. There were five or six, maybe seven different locations throughout the country doing that sort of thing. We certainly lifted out from my own little strip maybe 250 people – 250 lives that would have been lost.

Captain Basil Irwin
SOE liaison officer with partisans, Bosnia
One of the great things that impressed me was the extraordinary courage and ability of the pilots who used to come in. They never reconnoitred these fields. They came in at night, didn't circle but used to come absolutely straight down on to the ground, just putting on their landing lights when they were about twenty feet off the ground.

Captain Maurice Sutcliffe
SOE liaison officer with partisans, Croatia
The air force was trying to knock out the German war effort, the oil fields at Ploesti in Romania and the manufacturing areas on the north side of Vienna. Those were the two main targets and we were very much en route and whenever we saw a vast formation of aeroplanes going over, one of my operators would say, 'Right, we've got some guests for supper tonight.' And of course, right enough, over the next few days you'd find a few airmen trickling in. They would then spend anything from a couple of days to several weeks with us. If there were too many of them we'd try and move them on somewhere where we knew there was a strip operating.

Major Basil Davidson
SOE liaison officer with partisans, Serbia
Once the German retreat had started, it was important to know what German units were coming through and how much was coming through and one of my jobs was to go into Novi Sad. Novi Sad was then the capital of Hungarian-occupied Yugoslavia and through it was coming the retreating German Army, being driven hard by the Russian Army on its heels. One would sit in a café, in civilian clothes naturally, with a partisan friend also in civilian clothes, and we would be chatting and drinking coffee and so on and hoping to see, round the edge of one's paper, what was going through the square. One would then go back to one's hidey-hole and put it into code for one's wireless operator. He would then send it back to base.

Captain Basil Irwin
SOE liaison officer with partisans, Bosnia
When the Russian advance got nearer, the Yugoslavs stopped us evacuating their wounded. The only reason we could really gather was that they wanted to be able to demonstrate to the Russians when they arrived, 'Look at what we've suffered.' On the other hand they had the idea that the Russian Army, when it did arrive, would have all the facilities that one would have thought of a Western army. But of course, when the Russians did arrive, it was quite a different matter. They arrived on foot and with horse-drawn guns and transport and they were living off the land.

Lieutenant Commander Alexander Glen
Naval intelligence officer, attached to SOE, with partisans, Serbia
It was bloody silly. We'd captured a small German unit with motor-bicycle sidecar things and a little scout car and a motorised twenty-millimetre Oerlikon-type anti-aircraft gun. We must have been three or four partisans, three or four Brits, it was quite a nice wide road so we drove off in those things, really racing against each other, came round a bend and the road beyond had been blown. There, on the other side, was a machine-gun post, manned, and that was our first meeting with the Russians. They didn't shoot. God knows why not, we'd literally hurtled round in German equipment. The opposite happened. They got up, came across, great huggings and kissings and whacks on the back, etc. Their unit had just crossed the Danube that morning in company strength.

Captain Maurice Sutcliffe
SOE liaison officer with partisans, Croatia
The leading elements were very good. They had modern equipment, vehicles, looked fairly well dressed. But the follow-up, they were terrible. I mean, they were a rag-tail, desperate-looking lot of people who stole everything they could find and made themselves terribly unpopular. I think the Yugoslavs were very disillusioned with the Russians, almost straight away.

Captain Basil Irwin
SOE liaison officer with partisans, Bosnia
It was quite extraordinary because they treated us with no hostility or suspicion but they treated the partisans like dirt. Partisan officers, wherever they could, had got uniforms and jackets made and put on some golden stripes or something for rank. And it was such a shock to the partisans, who thought here was the welcome they were giving to their brother Slavs and the great Russian Army and so on, to be really treated like dirt by them.

Greece

Major Brian Dillon
SOE liaison officer
On 6 June we invaded Normandy. I thought it would be a good idea to let people know in the surrounding villages. They didn't have radio; they didn't have newspapers. So I got on my horse with two companions and rode off round the villages giving them the news. By the evening we got to the village of Dhesfina. It was a village we'd always been a bit suspicious of but the ELAS detachment commander said, 'You're quite safe, Major Brian. I've got men here. Rest assured, you'll be safe.' So we went to bed.

Fortunately we got up, as always, very early in the morning and I was sitting having a cup of coffee on the veranda and I saw at the other side of the square a German helmet and a rifle pointing straight at me. I opened fire and Henrik, my Polish groom, opened fire and we took to our heels. I said, 'Towards the sea' – an instant decision – and towards the sea we ran and that deceived the Germans. We got down to the sea and found a very old man with a very old boat, thank God. He rowed us across the bay. We'd escaped.

The ELAS battalion were very upset that I had very nearly been caught through their own idleness – I was on very good terms with them – and the remainder of the battalion did a forced march overnight and ambushed the German party as it left Dhesfina. They killed about twenty-five Germans and burnt about forty vehicles – really put up quite a smart show. The Germans were even more angry by now and the commandant at Levadhia dispatched an SS battalion to punish the village of Dhesfina. The officer in charge had a Greek map, which he couldn't read properly. He got to the village of Distomon, which was between Levadhia and Dhesfina. It was entirely innocent, had nothing to do with any of this; the villagers were going about their work the normal way. The Germans surrounded the village and killed every man, woman and child and burnt the village to the ground. A mistake – and I've had it on my conscience forever. If I hadn't gone to Dhesfina it would never have happened.

Major Ken Scott
SOE liaison officer
The reprisals on villages in northern Greece were absolutely horrific. They would take all the men from a village and shoot them in front of the women. They would burn all the houses. They did the most horrible things.

Corporal Ed Lawson
SOE wireless operator
We came to a high plateau overlooking Lidoriki. We unloaded the mules. The mule drivers wanted to light a fire but I didn't want them to. I didn't know where the Germans were and I suspected that there was a very large number in the immediate area. Darkness fell and suddenly we saw many, many fires in Lidoriki and soon the whole place was ablaze. There was only one area of darkness – the cemetery. How many Greek civilians died I have no idea. I had previously heard of where atrocities had been committed, Greek villagers, men, women and children, locked in churches and set on fire, but here I was witnessing a whole town blazing in front of my very eyes. One couldn't help but feel responsible for this. I kept thinking about the parachute containers lying alongside of the house. I was terribly upset about Lidoriki.

Major Jim Davies
SOE liaison officer
We heard rumours about Kalavrita, that it had been destroyed by the Germans, so we thought we ought to go through it and we did. It was really horrific. It was still smouldering from being burned and bombed. People had been murdered, driven into the church, including women and children, and the church had been set on fire. People had been shot against the walls.

SOE mission on the march in Macedonia, 1944.

HU 67325

Corporal Ed Lawson
SOE wireless operator

We suddenly came to the tail of a long column of partisans. They were the first real partisans I'd seen and the most striking thing was they were terribly young and very, very cheerful. As we passed them on the track we finally came to their leader who sat on a magnificent chestnut horse. He was a most striking figure of a man and he was called Captain Nikki. He was tall, slim, had fair hair, a fair beard, he had a highly polished Sam Browne belt; he wore a khaki service dress officers' tunic, khaki riding breeches, highly polished brown boots and a German-type Afrika Korps hat. He asked us where we were going. We said Agnanda. He said he wasn't going to Agnanda but we could travel with him and this we did. He offered me a ride on his horse and I said, 'No,' because amongst his group he had some women partisans who were walking and I didn't think it was fitting to ride on his horse while these women partisans walked. As we walked along we heard almost directly overhead an aircraft engine and the partisans melted into the trees on either side of the track. The plane was a Fieseler Storch, an observation plane.

Nikki was tremendously popular with his partisans. We came to a very large village where obviously they knew of him and the fact that he was so well equipped showed he had got a lot of arms by actually operating against the Italians and the Germans. There was a tremendous welcome and I couldn't help thinking it was rather like Robin Hood and his band of outlaws. It seemed like the hero returning from the foray with some of the goods. This village obviously hadn't been hit by the Germans, as so many had, because there was a large hall where a meal had been prepared, of lamb, maize bread and retsina wine and we really had quite a feast. After the meal they all started to sing *The Internationale* and they looked at me and, although I don't know the words, I joined in. I sang as lustily as the rest, they were all singing in Greek of course, and this seemed to give me great kudos, the fact that I'd been able to sing it or was prepared to even join in. I must point out I'm not a communist. We spent the night with these communists and I really felt that these were the sort of people I'd expected to meet, brave and dashing, very much like outlaws but on the side of the right.

Colonel 'Monty' Woodhouse
Senior SOE liaison officer
The communists were permanently suspicious of our intentions. They did believe that our main objective was destroying ELAS.

Major Jim Davies
SOE liaison officer
Arthur and I were to take all these explosives by mule train and hide them in a cave and we quite expected that ELAS would shadow us, which they did. Of course they were very keen to get their hands on three tons of explosive. They shadowed us for part of the way and then made their appearance and the officer in charge said he'd like to talk to us and warn us that if we continued on the route we had chosen we were risking being intercepted. He advised us to go with him on this other route.

Well, we knew that this was a trap. We told him we knew what we were doing and where we were going was our business – this was Arthur, who spoke very good Greek – but this fellow didn't like to break it off. I suppose he'd had orders, too, to guide us round this alternative way where we would be waylaid. Anyway, we told him to go away and get lost and he still stuck there with his chaps looking on and then Arthur hit him on the jaw, floored him. He got up and shook himself and he and his men slouched off. He didn't know that Arthur had been a boxing blue at Oxford.

Well, we found our cave all right and I loaded all the stuff in. John was very anxious that the store should be made secure but this was pretty difficult. The only thing Arthur and I could do was to put up a fence in front of the mouth of the cave and notices with 'Keep out' and 'Danger of Death' in Greek. And before I'd finished loading them in I put in two or three booby traps, so the thing was highly dangerous. And it didn't happen when we were there, but, later on, the Greek guerrillas thought perhaps that we hadn't booby-trapped it, that they'd get away with it, but of course they didn't and I'm afraid a number of them were blown up.

Corporal Ed Lawson
SOE wireless operator
Dennis Nicholson came and said, 'We are being made prisoners by Aris Veloukhiotis.' We couldn't believe this, but sure enough an escort was provided. They didn't take our wireless set off us, they didn't take our pistols off us, but they marched us away from Agnanda with this escort of partisans around us. It was the most sickening feeling, to think we'd come to help these

people and now we were their prisoners. All we knew was that the British hadn't supplied them with arms but had been flying over to drop arms, food, etc, to Zervas every night and that had made us very unpopular indeed. We marched all day and we were very apprehensive because we didn't quite know what was to happen and we had the distinct feeling that they were going to shoot us. They put us in a deserted church that night, which was cold and miserable. Later on there seemed to be a slight change in atmosphere and Aris said he was going to free us.

Captain Bob Martin
SOE liaison officer
This crowd arrived. It was Aris. They were all mounted on horses. They all wore Astrakhan hats, Cossack-style, and tight uniforms. Aris himself had a big beard. He was only a little man, about five foot six. A messenger arrived at the monastery in the afternoon to say that Aris wanted to see me, so with my interpreter off I went. We shook hands but I felt straight away that I knew the type. His hand was podgy, wet, and sitting on the bed were his two lieutenants and they were holding whips.

The first thing Aris said to me was, 'Well, of course, Captain Martin, from now on, I am in charge of the Peloponnese. Therefore all orders will come from me.' I looked at my interpreter and I looked straight back at him and said, 'I'm very sorry, but they are not the orders that I have from the C-in-C Middle East.' He said, 'I don't care what the C-in-C Middle East says to you. You will obey my orders.' So I said, 'Well, Aris, let's leave it this way' – he could have put me in jail or even shot me, I suppose – 'let me go back and report what you've said to mission headquarters.' He said, 'You can do what reporting you like, but from now on you are under my command.'

The decision was then taken to close down our mission, at least as far as I was concerned. A pity, really, because it was going so well. I quietly told the family I was with and the few who had been giving me intelligence, because there was no doubt in my mind that within a very short time Aris would find out that these people had been helping the mission and that would be that. Of course, from the time Aris arrived, they were telling me that so-and-so disappeared last night, hadn't come home yet. I had to take these people out with me, which was a very, very grave risk, because we really shouldn't have got involved to that extent. But I just couldn't see myself leaving a woman and two children and Pops, an old man in his seventies, a Greek American, who'd been a tremendous help to me. I just couldn't leave them behind. My mind was made up – they were coming out with me. At least they could go into a refugee camp. They had to volunteer to come but of course none of them wanted to stay there with Aris, so off we went.

Colonel 'Monty' Woodhouse
Senior SOE liaison officer

I came out of Greece temporarily in the summer of 1944 to go to London to report to the British Government on the state of affairs in Greece. I had several meetings with Eden who was then Foreign Secretary and one meeting with Churchill at Chequers. At that time, the Government and Churchill in particular were thinking seriously of breaking off relations with EAM and ELAS, denouncing them as disloyal allies and so forth and trying to withdraw the whole of my force of British and Allied officers and other ranks from Greece.

I was very anxious to persuade them that this would be a mistake. It would leave the communist-controlled EAM and ELAS free to carry on as they wished, with no incentive to be cooperative with the Allies when they tried to come back to Greece at the end of the German occupation, and it would probably bring about a takeover of the country by the communists as soon as the Germans left. I made this point to Eden, who asked me to go and meet Churchill and explain the same point to him. But Churchill was obstinately opposed to it. He had become very embittered against EAM and he wanted to make a clean break with them and treat them as a hostile force.

I had a long talk with Churchill at Chequers, at which I tried to persuade him that the policy he was set on would be a great mistake. But I didn't gain the impression that I was making any headway until finally, knowing that Churchill had a strong sentimental streak, however ruthless he might appear on the surface, I used one argument which I had held back because I didn't think it was fair to use until the last opportunity. I said to him, 'If you do what you are threatening to do and break off relations with EAM and denounce them publicly, as you say you intend, I very much doubt whether any of my officers will get out of Greece alive.' He brooded on that briefly and then put his arm on my shoulder and said, 'Yes, young man. I quite understand.' And that was the last I ever heard of his intention to break with EAM and publicly denounce them. He never did so and the matter was never raised again. And as I left Chequers late in the afternoon his last words to me on the doorstep were, 'I am very impressed, and oppressed and depressed,' which was a very characteristic Churchillian expression. He could never resist the opportunity of a good phrase. But in the end I think he was won over and it certainly was not a waste of time going to see him.

Major Ken Scott
SOE liaison officer

'Noah's Ark' was a major planning operation in which the British liaison mission in Greece was trying to persuade the Greek guerrillas, during the German withdrawal from Greece, to make it as hazardous as they could, to deal with road and rail communications and kill the maximum number of Germans. That was the object of it. What in effect happened in the end was that we, the British, blew a few bridges, organised the ambushing of convoys, but without much Greek support.

Colonel 'Monty' Woodhouse
Senior SOE liaison officer

I don't think the final operations give us much cause for satisfaction and pride. We didn't inflict as much serious damage as we might have been capable of doing, but by that time, certainly in the case of EAM and ELAS, their sights were set on the future and not on the immediate present. There certainly were determined efforts by some units of ELAS to fight the Germans as they withdrew, just as there were on the western side of Greece by the EDES units which, despite earlier contacts between Zervas and the German high command, did put up a serious attack on the German retreat, but it was a very mixed picture. There were obviously a lot of Greeks in the resistance who were tired of the whole business of occupation, not surprisingly, who were only anxious to see the Germans out of their country and who didn't see any good reason why they should delay them in going.

Major Brian Dillon
SOE liaison officer

Athens was eventually occupied by the British, the parachute brigade got through, the Germans withdrew and for about a month the wine flowed and girls did what girls do and everybody was terribly happy. Then the civil war started, which was a whole new ball game.

It was an awful, shambolic business at the end. Dick Turner, an escaped Australian soldier who'd joined us and stayed right through, he could have got evacuated any time, but he volunteered to stay. It was then getting towards Christmas and I said, 'Dick, there's nothing more for you to do, we could get you home for Christmas.' He handed in his kit and got on a truck to go down to the airfield, was ambushed on the way down and he was shot through the head and I had to write to his widow. He'd survived everything till then.

POLAND

Lieutenant Colonel Henry Threlfall
Head, Polish Section, SOE HQ, Southern Italy

We had, of course, a very large number of Poles in Britain and a very large organisation in Poland, the Polish secret army, which started as soon as the Germans occupied Poland and the actual resistance of the Polish Army finished in 1939. It was a very widespread and very well-organised body and we had good radio communications with them, because the Polish Government in London were in constant radio communication with their underground representatives in Warsaw, and so a great deal of information flowed to and fro. We were obviously concerned with doing what we could to help this secret army, both with recruits and with materials, and the Section was flying operations from this country, dropping agents and equipment, radio sets of course and weapons as well. The Polish Section was a very big country section and had a huge stock of recruits available.

Captain Robert Ferrier
SOE instructor, Scotland

The Poles were magnificent. Very, very good. They were mostly trained soldiers, young trained soldiers, and, I think, probably officers, although we never knew their ranks and we never knew their names. I can remember one particular course of about fifteen Poles who came just before D-Day. Their discipline was superb. They were very good people to work with. They took to the course like ducks to water. And I always remember, at the end of the course, we marched with them from Inverie House down to the jetty, to pick up the boat to go away, all singing *Lili Marlene*, which of course was a German song but nevertheless the best song in the war, and they presented all of the instructors with a little gold parachute to wear in our berets. They were magnificent and I've always wondered what happened to them. I have a nasty feeling that they may have been dropped into Warsaw.

Stanislaw Kujawinski
Polish agent

When we parachuted into Poland there were five planes. One was shot down on the way, so four planes, Halifaxes, got there with people. I was parachuted at a place called Wiszkow, something like twenty miles from Warsaw, and was picked up by the Polish underground there and then.

Adolf Pilch
Polish agent
We had to be dropped between two rivers and unfortunately only one man, the first one, was dropped on the spot. We three were dropped over the river, in the forest. We couldn't find the first one and we couldn't find the second one. The second one, unfortunately, his parachute didn't open and he was killed.

Stanislaw Kolasinski
Polish agent
We had a reception committee and we were helped to a train next morning and in the train I was arrested by the Germans. I didn't have sufficient papers and I was informed that at the next station I would be taken from the train to a German post, which I was. Through the window I saw some of my friends, who I'd jumped with, going to Warsaw all right.

The commanding officer of the German post was a captain and he started a three-hours' long interrogation. Where was I working? What was I doing? Name of my father? Mother? How did I get to work? Which bus number? He said, 'You are a Jew.' Very moved I was by that accusation and I said he could check. A lower-rank German officer took me to the next room, looked at my genitals and found that I was not cut in any way and came to the interrogation room and said, 'He is not a Jew.' So they said, 'You are free and can go to Warsaw.'

Adam Benrad
Polish agent
We had a very, very uneventful flight. I was very, very calm. I jumped last and I didn't have any difficulties, landing practically standing up. It was the easiest thing that ever happened to me. People contacted me and transferred me to Lublin from which, after a day or two, I was taken to Warsaw. I was allocated a room with an old lady in a northern part of Warsaw. She used to tell me about the conditions in Poland, what to expect, how to behave. She used to bring me German-published newspapers in Polish to read. And eventually when my quarantine was up, after two weeks, I was told to go and contact somebody else, which I did, and a man allocated me to western Poland. Again I had to go to a certain address, say a certain password, and I was conducted all along the line and eventually I finished with a partisan unit, a guerrilla unit.

Stanislaw Kujawinski
Polish agent
I was allocated to the Polish underground army in Lublin to work as a signals officer and I was given papers and tickets and everything else. A young lady assisted me. I went from the main railway station in Warsaw, with false papers as a worker for the German forces, with an armband on my arm, with a ticket enabling me to travel with the Germans. In Poland the Germans had their own separate compartments and Poles couldn't travel with them, so I travelled with German soldiers. At Lublin I got off the train and I got picked up by somebody there and taken to a house near Maidanek, a concentration camp, within probably five hundred yards of the main gate. Every morning I woke up, there was this funny smell, a sweet smell, and it made me vomit every morning. Gradually after a few days I found out that this was a concentration camp. People knew what was happening there. They were burning these Jews and other nationalities on big piles and that's where this smell came from, the sweet smell of burning bodies. One day I was looking through the window and they were marching probably a thousand people or more, in concentration camp clobber, marching them into the main gate. I saw that with my own eyes. They were surrounded by Germans with machine guns and dogs.

Adam Benrad
Polish agent
There was this uneasiness, maybe not fear, seeing the Germans in the flesh. But there was elation that you were in the midst of something. Something was going to happen here. Whether in a few days or in a few weeks you would be fighting again.

Benon Lastowski
Polish agent
You walked along the streets and you were sure that everybody knew you came from England. It seemed so obvious to me that everybody noticed it, that it was almost written on my head. There was a feeling that somebody would come and say, 'Hello, how is London?' But that was only for the first few days. Later on, you just felt like everybody else.

Stanislaw Kujawinski
Polish agent
We changed our quarters fairly frequently but sometimes the Germans came

looking for us just after we had left. Zenon got fed up with it and said, 'We're not running away from them. Let them come.' And he sort of made me – he couldn't tell me to do it – transmit without any interruption, all the time, to give the Germans the chance to find out exactly where we were.

He set an ambush just in front of the village, I was inside the village working on my transmitter, and the Germans started coming towards us. The ambush was shielded by a small wood alongside the road and we could see one, two, three German vehicles drawing near. The vehicles were allowed to come as near as possible and then it started. To the surprise of the gendarmes and the German radio signal team hand-grenades were showered upon them. One of them was a Gestapo officer who could speak Polish, and in the mêlée, when they were all running around, he pretended to be a Pole and started shouting, 'Shoot the German dog,' and that sort of thing. But he was a stranger and he was in civilian clothes and somebody realised that he was a German and they shot him, of course. He had handcuffs in his pockets, several pairs of handcuffs, and that meant that he was on to a sure thing, coming just to arrest a radio operator in a village.

We didn't take captives. What would we do with them? Several of them escaped and they were running through the villages and they were that frightened that they were taking their hats off in front of the village women. They were really scared. There was eighteen killed. Eighteen bodies we dug into the woods. One of our soldiers was slightly wounded. We emptied all the cars, took everything out of them. There was a lorry as well. We put it all in one place and just burnt the vehicles. We salvaged some good receivers and they were ever so good. Sometimes we got to a village and could put up the receiver and the BBC news could be heard from one end of the village to the other.

Lieutenant Colonel Henry Threlfall
Head, Polish Section, SOE HQ, Southern Italy

The Poles in Warsaw revolted, came out into the open, on 1 August 1944. The Russians had reached the suburbs of Warsaw, across the Vistula, and the Poles were anxious to *do* something and drive the Germans out of Warsaw, partly in order to be able to say 'We did it ourselves', partly in order to clear the way for the oncoming Russians. But militarily it was a mistake. They hadn't got the equipment, the number of people and the weapons and ammunition they needed to deal with the very large German garrison of Warsaw and the enormous number of troops which the Germans rushed up as soon as the rising broke out.

They had a certain success at first, they killed an awful lot of Germans without a doubt, but their losses were appallingly high. The Germans rushed in troops, blew up the place bit by bit, split up the area the Poles held into small areas and gradually reduced them one by one, and bombarded the whole of Warsaw and knocked it to the ground in the process. The Polish Home Army was installed in different redoubts, communicating by the network of sewers, and sending us desperate appeals for help and there was an enormous amount of to and fro as to whether it was possible to help them at all. We started off sending planes but the losses were very heavy and it got more and more difficult to send any help.

Sergeant Alan Bates
Halifax observer/bomb-aimer, 31 Squadron, South African Air Force
In Brindisi we were briefed to go to Warsaw. They told us all about the uprising. We didn't usually take much notice of the news on the squadron. We might possibly have heard that the Warsaw uprising had happened, I think we'd heard that, but there was a Pole there who gave us quite a detailed talk on it and he got us all going as a matter of fact. He was so emotional about his town and his compatriots being in the situation they were in and that they'd got to have help.

Sergeant John Harvey
Halifax navigator, 148 (SD) Squadron, RAF
You went off singly. You didn't dare go in formation. You were a straggling of a squadron, going off at two-minute intervals. You were safer on your own.

Sergeant Alan Bates
Halifax observer/bomb-aimer, 31 Squadron, South African Air Force
You could see Warsaw from miles away, burning away, searchlights coming up and just a mass of tracer, like a little ball of tracer, rising to about the height of the searchlight intersections, so some poor devil was getting it.

Sergeant John Harvey
Halifax navigator, 148 (SD) Squadron, RAF
It was Dante's Inferno. There were blazing fires all over. One Liberator flew into a church steeple. Just disintegrated. Another one blew up over the target.

Sergeant Tadeusz Ruman
Liberator air-gunner, 1586 Flight, Polish Air Force
There were Germans on the roofs. They were firing at you, with revolvers, guns, over the rooftops. You could see them.

Sergeant Alan Bates
Halifax observer/bomb-aimer, 31 Squadron, South African Air Force
We had to go in at about four hundred feet, which is about the height of the Post Office tower, a little bit higher than that, and we had to throttle back, put the flaps down to reduce speed so that the parachutes wouldn't tear off the canisters. There was somebody caught in the lights so we thought we'd better nip in quickly. They burst into flames and disappeared and then the lights switched straight on to us. We crept across the target – I suppose we must have been two minutes in the lights – and you could see people firing at you, see blokes sitting with a machine gun on the roof and having a go at you. But mainly it was just a mass of tracer bullets coming straight up.

I was sitting in the nose and I'm afraid I had to turn round a couple of times. How we weren't shot to bits I don't know. We lost an engine and the hydraulics all went. Once we'd dropped our supplies we climbed to about five or six thousand feet and then the aircraft just shuddered and suddenly stalled and dived to starboard. And it really did dive. Being right up in the nose I got stuck to the ceiling. There was nothing I could do about it. I was stuck to the ceiling, looking down, and saw Warsaw coming back at me.

I didn't know at the time but the skipper had bailed out. Poor old Bob Burgess was left to cope all on his own and he just hung on to the stick and managed to pull it out eventually. Of course he wasn't taking up any time to talk to us on the intercom so we really didn't know what was going on. The G-force was just the opposite then and I was stuck on the floor and I couldn't have got off the floor if I'd wanted to. My eyeballs were almost popping out.

Jerzy Lando
Polish Home Army, Warsaw
They would throw down supplies and particularly PIATs, anti-tank weapons, very, very effective against tanks. They were most gratefully received. And at first when we saw these things parachuting and there was some food being thrown, that was just too wonderful for words.

Tadeusz Ochocki
Polish Home Army, Warsaw
We did get quite a lot of weapons and ammunition and food supplies but I would say the Germans got about three-quarters and we got one-quarter. That's my estimation. But always when the planes came from the West, well, the morale went up, you know. 'Somebody's still with us. Somebody thinks about us.' But otherwise it was a hopeless situation really.

Jerzy Lando
Polish Home Army, Warsaw
They were very brave and they did their best, but as time went on a lot of these supplies fell into German hands and then the German anti-aircraft fire got so accurate that they didn't have a chance.

Jerzy Gach
Polish Home Army, Warsaw
When the Germans opened fire the sky was completely full of shells and tracers. You could see the tracers. I could see a plane getting hit and the flames from the engine and the plane fell not far from us, so I went to see. It was still burning. The crew was dead. They pulled one out. Imagine. He had a Smith & Wesson in his pocket, in his trouser-leg pocket, the handle was burnt and the pistol when I touched it was red hot.

Sergeant Tadeusz Ruman
Liberator air-gunner, 1586 Flight, Polish Air Force
My last operation to Warsaw, five aircraft went, four were lost. We came back on two engines, crash-landed and asked the mechanics, 'Who came back?' They said, 'You're first,' and we said right away, 'If we're the first, we're the last.' We had one wounded on board and a big hole in one engine.

Sergeant John Harvey
Halifax navigator, 148 (SD) Squadron, RAF
Our squadron was mauled, terribly mauled. Warsaw and back was a long flight.

Lieutenant Colonel Henry Threlfall
Head, Polish Section, SOE HQ, Southern Italy
Several times the operations were stopped by the air force because they said, 'This is not a practicable proposition. We can't ask the crews to do this. It isn't

worth it. The losses are too high compared with the small amount of success, the small amount of containers which actually get into the Polish resistance's hands'. And I was fighting a desperate battle to get them to do more and it was a very difficult and unpleasant and exhausting and heart-breaking period of my life.

There was a magnificent air force officer, Air Vice-Marshal William Elliot, who was commander of the Balkan Air Force, with his headquarters in Bari, which was the unit in southern Italy responsible for supporting the resistance movements in that part of the world, Italy and the Balkans. He was a most understanding, fair-minded and just and helpful man, one of the best I've ever come across, and I had a great admiration for him. We got on extremely well. But he had to talk like an airman and say, 'Look at the losses we are suffering, the difficulties of pinpointing, the demands of other areas which want support, where Tito's partisans and the Italian partisans are clamouring for support as well from my limited number of aircraft and crews. As the airman responsible for this job I have to allocate my aircraft and crews where I think the best return is available.' And Warsaw wasn't it. Whereas all I could do was to say, 'This is politically an immensely important thing. It means an awful lot to the Poles and to the whole of Europe, this resistance of the whole population of Warsaw.'

June Darton
FANY staff, Polish Section, SOE HQ, Southern Italy
The terrible thing was that the Russians, who were our allies, so-called allies, stopped about twelve miles short of Warsaw and let them all be slaughtered. It was something so desperate, so desperate, and that was one of the tragedies of the war.

Lieutenant Colonel Henry Threlfall
Head, Polish Section, SOE HQ, Southern Italy
Right up to the end of July the Russian radio beamed at Poland was encouraging them to rise against the Germans. But from the moment they did so, they became a scruffy lot of bourgeois fascists who were only looking after their own interests and had not got the interests of the great Russian people at heart, so they were constantly being criticised. All the efforts that we made, the Allies made, from Churchill downwards to get the Russians to do anything met with this criticism, that it was a fascist body that had revolted and that it didn't merit any help.

The Russians did say one thing that may have had a certain amount of truth in it. They did maintain that it was only the forerunners of their troops at the end of a long advance who had pushed through as far as that, and that they hadn't got any forces big enough to bridge the Vistula and make an assault in the face of German opposition. There may have been some truth in that. One tries to be fair about it. But there's no doubt that the will was certainly lacking.

Sue Ryder
FANY staff, Polish Section, SOE HQ, Southern Italy
You would have been thought a traitor if you'd said, 'Was it a good thing? A wise course of action?' Though several of them knew that it was a bloodbath, that it wouldn't succeed, that the Russians wouldn't move across the Vistula, they nevertheless thought that their honour was at stake. One or two of us discussed it with them and said, 'This is absolutely ghastly.' We wouldn't have dared say, 'There isn't any hope,' but we said, 'The casualties are going to be appalling.' But the Poles said, 'No, it's something we've got to go through with, whatever the outcome.' It was something they had to show the world, that they were going to rise against the Germans.

Lieutenant Colonel Henry Threlfall
Head, Polish Section, SOE HQ, Southern Italy
It lasted two months before the Germans finally won, when the Polish army in Warsaw, the underground army, had literally no ammunition left at all and so they surrendered and they were all marched off into captivity. It was certainly the two months of my life that I would least like to go though again, without any doubt. The strain was enormous. Partly the actual strain of being busy and having things to do, and partly the emotional strain, because we were very fond of our Polish allies and had the greatest admiration for them and it was our job to help them. We did that to the best of our ability but of course what we were up against were the facts of the case.

Major Peter Kemp
SOE officer with Polish Home Army
When the Russians overran the part of Poland where we were, in their great offensive from the Vistula to the Oder, we had instructions to hand ourselves over to the nearest Russian divisional headquarters. We found out where they were without too much difficulty and we expected, as Allies, a warm and friendly reception with lots of vodka and caviar. We got something very different. We got a reception from the NKVD, which today would be called

MH 4457

Polish grave in a deserted Warsaw street, 1944.

MH 4473

Warsaw after the Uprising, 1944.

the KGB, and were put into a very unpleasant prison in Chestahova, which the NKVD had taken over about forty-eight hours earlier from the Gestapo.

There were six of us and there were three bunks on each side of this filthy cell with straw, very dirty straw. I've never had so many different forms of animal life on my body as I did by the time I came out of that. And we had nothing to eat. They gave us a small piece of bread and some warm water with a few grains of barley floating in it each day. There was a bright bulb, a naked bulb, shining in the cell, day and night, which didn't make it any easier to sleep. They took all our books away from us. But for some extraordinary reason they left us two packs of cards and we played bridge solidly. Four of us would play bridge and the other two would sleep, day and night, for all that month that we were there. I've never played bridge since, but it certainly kept us sane.

They used to come and haul us out from time to time. Or rather they used to haul Bill Hudson out, chiefly in the middle of the night, or at any time of day or night, to ask him stupid questions like what was our wavelength to London and who did we communicate with in London. Bill took a very good attitude indeed. He said, 'This is a disgraceful way to treat Allies. We are in uniform, we have identity cards, I am a full colonel and I am not going to talk to any Russian officer under the rank of full colonel.' So every time they wanted to interrogate him they had to find somebody and dress him up as a full colonel. It was very effective. It was the sort of thing the Russians understood. If we'd sort of cringed and tried to be nice to them we'd have had, I think, a worse time still.

After a while – I think they were keeping us on ice until after the Yalta decisions had been made – they put us in an aeroplane and flew us to Kiev. Then they put us on a train, an overnight journey, to Moscow, and handed us over to the British Military Mission, who were so sorry for us that I, at least, nearer died from alcohol poisoning in the next two weeks than I ever did from enemy action.

Stanislaw Kujawinski
Polish agent
The communists established this Polish Government in Lublin and they started giving orders and said that all officers must join the Polish Red Army. And I couldn't, because I was an officer of the real Polish Army, with the real Polish Government in London, and I was sent from London as an SOE officer. So I carried on doing my job with my sergeant, my faithful sergeant.

On 22 November we were working in a barn. Unita was sat on a bicycle with the back wheel lifted up and a dynamo underneath. He was operating the pedals and I was keying the radiograms to London. We had quite a few radiograms yet to do when all of a sudden a Russian company – I don't know how many there was – rushed into the barn and surrounded and arrested us. Of course they got our equipment and the bicycle.

I looked young, like a boy, and my sergeant was a middle-aged fellow, so they initially thought he was the main culprit and started beating him up something terrible. But I could speak Russian and swear, and the Russians are as good swearers as Spaniards, and I sort of started swearing. 'Why are you kicking him? Have you gone mad?' And they stopped doing that. Then, of course, they realised in a bit that I was the officer and he was the sergeant.

From there they took us to Lublin. I was put in the cellars of a big house and in that cellar there were already six or seven prisoners. Some of them were beaten terribly. They were blue. They brought them into these cells and just chucked them in because they couldn't even walk.

Adam Benrad
Polish agent
When I was arrested by the Russians I had a few knocks. It didn't warrant taking poison. After all, I was only twenty-four. You can take a lot of punishment when you are twenty-four.

Frederick Serafinski
Polish agent
I was actually arrested by the Polish communists because they knew me from my time with the partisans. They had the records of who was doing what and where and of course they found me. They just asked me to come to the police station, to ask me a few questions. It took six months.

Adam Benrad
Polish agent
In the same cell where I was, there were four parachutists from London.

Stanislaw Kujawinski
Polish agent
We were known to the Russians. When they'd come, we did not hide ourselves, they knew who was what and why, they had soon got to hear that I was the SOE officer operating the transmitter, so they knew and I couldn't say that I wasn't. It was all an open book to them. All they wanted to know was

why I was working against the Red Army. Luckily for me I said I was not working against the Red Army, in no way, and I wouldn't have worked against the Red Army, because I was thankful that the Red Army had come and pushed the Germans out of Poland. All I was working against was this new Polish Government in Lublin because the Polish Government was in London and I was loyal to that. These new people were just nobody. I was quite courageous but I thought that was the sort of thing to say to a Russian officer.

We were taken to a bigger cell and in the bigger cell there were three fellows sat behind a longish table. There was a middle-aged man in civilian clothes in the middle and two second lieutenants on each side of him. They put us on chairs at the back of the room and there was a secretary to start with but he sort of vanished. It took them about half an hour to read all the reports and things and they sentenced us straight away, there and then. I was sentenced to death for belonging to the underground AK Army, the Home Army. That was the first sentence. The second sentence was that I was sentenced to death for not reporting as an officer to join the Polish Red Army. And I got five years on top of that for possessing radio equipment, which sounds silly but that's how it was. My sergeant was given the death sentence for belonging to the Home Army and five years for being in possession of radio equipment. And that was the trial.

In Lublin they were shooting them down in the cellar in the back of the head. That's what happened to Szczepanski and Rossinski and the other eleven who were taken to the death cells. But from there I contacted my wife. Someone took a letter, a piece of paper. My wife worked all the time through her acquaintances, all sorts of channels, to get me out of the jail. She also got my death sentence altered to ten years. Through certain channels she paid some money, she was in a position to do it because she worked in the Ministry of Provisions, and they helped her to get my sentence altered. And all the time she tried to get me out of jail altogether and in the end she got me out, on 27 December 1945.

Italy

Captain John Ross
SOE liaison officer
Suddenly we were told that they were opening up Italy for British liaison officers and that we were going to go over. We went down to our headquarters in Monopoli to be briefed, which was really pathetic. The staff there knew

virtually nothing about the area we were to go and work in, which was around Belluno and the beginning of the Dolomites, and they had very little idea of what the resistance movement was doing there and they had very little idea of the geography. They had dreadful maps and sort of pre-war picture postcards of the attractive areas but nothing much else. So as a briefing it was hopeless. We were issued with our parachutes and things in Monopoli and taken down by truck to Brindisi and given a wonderful meal in a flat there, sort of a last supper, and then taken out to the airfield and into DC3s. These were loaded with a lot of equipment to be dropped to the resistance and to us.

It was about three hours up to the north. There were no fires and no flashing lights and it turned out the Germans had been right by the dropping ground so they didn't light anything up. And so we returned. Two days later there was a second attempt, again just our mission, and when we got up north we were told to stand by the door, which we did. Looking out we were just a little surprised to see an awful lot of lights down below and then orange things started coming up towards us, which we then realised was anti-aircraft fire, and it turned out the plane was circling over Trieste for some reason. I think I said, 'For Heaven's sake, let's go,' and Tilman wrote afterwards that he thought I meant we ought to jump out. I certainly didn't. I thought it was really quite bizarre that we were circling Trieste. So we again returned down to Monopoli. The third time we went we were put with another mission: Paul Brietsche, John Orr-Ewing and their wireless operator and interpreter.

Captain John Orr-Ewing
SOE liaison officer
There were six of us and no dispatcher. Paul said, 'I'm going first. John, you bring up the rear.' So I jumped out of a completely empty plane with nobody to dispatch me, which is a bit crazy, really. We all missed the landing ground. One was stuck in a tree, Tilman hurt his back but recovered, I went right through a tree but I wasn't hurt and the cloud came down and they never dropped any of our goods at all. I never got my stuff until 7 February and this was 31 August.

Major Thomas Macpherson
SOE liaison officer
We went with a Polish aircraft that dropped us at a very great height. We were accustomed to being dropped at about seven hundred feet in hilly country and this must have been nearer seven thousand. We came down extremely slowly but mercifully there was absolutely no wind and we landed not very far adrift from the little lights winking up at us.

Sergeant Harry Hargreaves
SOE wireless operator
Macpherson came in with a kilt on. You can imagine the look on an Eyetie's face – this bloke in a woman's dress! They couldn't understand it.

Lieutenant Stephen Dale
German Jewish SOE liaison officer
The aim was to help partisans in that part of the world to delay the expected German retreat back into Germany. We were to instruct partisans and supply them with arms and ammunition and explosives, provided we had them, and guide back Allied prisoners of war who were liable to be in that area trying to escape. That was the object, but unfortunately for me it never arose.

Just before we left Brindisi, Jimmy Bennett, our conducting officer, said to me, 'You know, you've got nothing to worry about. These pilots have done great work over Warsaw' – they were Polish pilots. Well, after they decanted us from a great height I changed my mind about the efficiency of the Polish pilots. I had the feeling that they just wanted to get shot of us as quickly as possible so they could turn round and go back. There had been a lot of flak on the way up over Venice.

As I got out of the plane, I was the first one, I could see the other parachutes open above me but then I lost sight of them. Not surprising if you consider the time it took us to float down. As I landed, in what appeared to be the only patch of grass in a dried-up riverbed, I saw a light south and I made my way towards it, then heard German and Italian voices and I knew I'd been dropped in the wrong place.

I used all my field-craft, at which we'd all become experts more or less, to get out of there. I made my way up the side of a hill, spent the night there, and in the morning I could see Germans spread out across the valley moving northwards and firing into any sort of cover or anything that looked suspicious to them. They also had dogs. After a while I saw Germans moving south, towards me, on the hillside and I had no option but to go further up the hill in an easterly direction and I spent another night on the side of the hill. Next morning, after I woke up, I could hear voices moving along a path and I climbed up a bank in order to look along the path, and when I saw two Germans approaching I ducked back into cover. In doing so I lost my footing and I fell down perhaps ten feet and by the time I clambered back on to my feet I could see two other Germans on the path moving towards me. So I really had no option. I put up my hands and that was the disappointing, frustrating end of my active life on behalf of SOE.

I was taken prisoner by what turned out to be the Waffen SS. Funnily enough there were lots of Cossacks among them. I realised they were Cossacks not only because I did not understand their language but also because of their Cossack hats and their Cossack sabres, which looked absolutely ludicrous. Almost on the spur of the moment they lined me up against a little mound in the field, they were standing around me in a semicircle, cocking their rifles, and I thought this was the end. Then there was a voice shouting an order in German and a Waffen SS *Sturmführer* approached and gave orders and they took me to their HQ. There they decided to take me to Udine, where I spent the night in a civilian prison.

We went on to Trieste and in Trieste they took me to the Coroneo, which is a civilian prison, staffed by the Italians but run by the Germans. In the cells on my floor were heavy political cases. Many of them disappeared overnight sometimes. You asked the warder in the morning, 'What's happened to so-and-so in the cell over there?' and he'd simply say, 'Shot.' None of it was very encouraging. Nor was the fact that, on a scrap of Italian newspaper I found on the landing, I saw a report that some British officers had been shot in the Milan region as a reprisal for some partisan activities.

Captain John Orr-Ewing
SOE liaison officer
We were not insensitive to our position but were not appreciative always of the danger. But then perhaps that's how you are when you are young. We really didn't appreciate how dangerous our life was.

Captain John Ross
SOE liaison officer
It was an incredible experience and feeling to be like that, five hundred miles from one's base and behind the lines.

Captain Patrick Martin-Smith
SOE liaison officer
When I sat down sometimes and looked at my map I could see that in a dead straight line north of where I was, only eighty or ninety miles away, was Hitler's sort of holiday home. It was near enough to make you realise that you were quite close to Hitler.

Sergeant Harry Hargreaves
SOE wireless operator

Although I was born in Oswaldtwistle, I'd had running hot water in my house; I'd had electric light. When I went to Italy, people were sat there at the door cooking on little charcoal stoves. No electric light. This was Mussolini's great Empire! Italy was a really backward place. The only great places were Rome and the big cities but once you got out of there, it was horse-driven.

Captain Richard Tolson
SOE liaison officer

There was nothing to eat. That was one of the worst things. We used to look towards Venice from the hills and sort of fantasise on the restaurants.

Captain John Orr-Ewing
SOE liaison officer

We couldn't get much, really. Lots of polenta and quite a lot of cheese. The other thing we had was wine, utterly watered down wine. You would hardly know it was wine. We all lost a lot of weight.

As far as sleeping was concerned, they had these big mangers, full of leaves as much as grass, and they had a space under there, took up the floor and made a hole under it, and you slept there, underground, five or six or seven or eight of you. You were pretty safe there. Unless someone gave you away, a normal patrol would be unlikely to find you unless they moved all the cattle and food and everything off it first of all. Alternatively, when there wasn't so much danger, we slept in the cattle shed. It was warm in the middle of the winter in this grass but an awful smell, as you can imagine, when the cows blew off in the middle of the night.

Sergeant Harry Hargreaves
SOE wireless operator

I took my shirt off once and I looked in my shirt and all down the seams of the shirt, where the seam bent over, underneath, was all white eggs, all the way down. I felt terrible about this, so I got down to the stream and started scrubbing away. Hedley Vincent came along and said, 'Hargreaves, what the hell are you doing?' I said, 'I'm having a good scrub, I've got lice.' He said, 'You dirty bugger, Hargreaves.' I said, 'Look, there's nobody washed as much as what I've washed. I've washed more than you.' Well, Vincent was one of these blokes with hair on his chest and when we looked in it, my God, he was inundated with lice. We'd got it off the hay. Everybody had slept on the hay and we were absolutely thick with lice.

Captain John Ross
SOE liaison officer
The villagers who sheltered us, if they were found out by the Germans, their places would have been burned down and the men hanged absolutely straight away. Yet there they were, putting us up and helping us.

I think the northern people, particularly up in the Dolomites, tough, mountaineering, peasant people, were far tougher and more determined and not so volatile as the southern people. There were endless stories of the partisans really doing damn all down south and then parading and showing off and taking credit and so forth as the Allies came up. I think it was a different matter further north. Right across the north, from the Piedmont area through to the Yugoslav frontier, there were all these different units, mainly so-called *Garibaldini*, communist-inspired. Vast numbers of chaps with them were not really communists, they were just ordinary men, and communism didn't really mean much to them; but the organisers were communists. I think they were hoping, as in Greece, that when the war had finished then somehow or other the communists would take over.

There were other ones with other political affiliations, like the *Partito D'Azione*, the Action Party, which was sort of more middle-class, more conservative-minded people. They were well intentioned but I don't think they were as active as the communist units. And I do think, even compared with resistance one's read about in other countries, the Italian resistance was just as successful in keeping German troops occupied. They had to do an enormous amount of guarding of hydroelectric works, railways, roads and everything else, as well as send out parties to try and round up partisans. I think it was successful. There were differences of opinion in the units but I don't think there was quite as much trouble as there was in, say, the French resistance.

Sergeant Harry Hargreaves
SOE wireless operator
It's always the Left that appears to be the strongest in any of these things. In France it was always the communists that became the leading factor. Well, same in Italy. But there were republicans as well. The difference was that the communists, like true Italians, were always dressed to kill – they're all dandies, the Italians – and wore the red neckerchief. The republicans wore the green, white and red neckerchief. And they never used their own names. They all used a *nom de guerre*, a war name. Being Italian they picked some lovely ones,

like Lightning and Thunderbolt and all that. They have to do it in a big way in Italy.

Captain Richard Tolson
SOE liaison officer
The partisans rejected Field Marshal Alexander's recommendation that they should go back for the winter to their homes. The *Nino Nannetti* partisan division wouldn't have that and I think they were quite right, actually. Why should they be dictated to if they were willing to stay and fight?

Major Alastair Macdonald
SOE liaison officer
Telling partisans to go home – what was this supposed to mean? Where could they go? What would this do to their morale? I have to say that I am one among many who feel that Alexander's recommendation was quite unrealistically and not very expertly drafted.

Captain John Ross
SOE liaison officer
German mountain troops surrounded our area and worked their way up. Bill Tilman and I spent a lot of our time with Bruno, the commander of the partisan unit there, trying to persuade them to get away while the going was good. Guerrilla warfare was not a matter of standing up to people when you hadn't even got arms to begin with. It was much better to melt away and be in action another day. But this was considered a sort of cowardly thing and they decided to stick it out.

Bruno was a very brave chap, a very good fellow. He'd been an artillery officer with the regular Italian Army. He had a dreadful old Italian machine gun and he was manning that, firing towards the moving Germans until that got jammed, and I think when it finally jammed he realised that what we'd been saying was the best policy. The vast majority of them just had rather dreadful Italian rifles, mostly pinched from all over the place, and they'd had no training at all, even in firing, let alone moving about. Also they suddenly realised that the Germans were on higher ground around this little plateau. A lot of bullets and things were coming down among us and quite frankly there was quite a bit of a panic then and the partisans started streaming away. Bruno also agreed to go.

Tilman had gone up to talk to Bruno and had told me to get everything ready to move out. The radio equipment was quite heavy and bulky, the radio set weighed thirty-five pounds or so, and I decided to carry that. I'd given all my own personal kit, which was precious little, mainly some shaving stuff and bits and pieces, to the wireless operator. He couldn't be bothered with it and put it on a mule, which promptly disappeared. We lost really everything.

Tilman said he'd take us up on the north face of this mountain where he'd had a look and he thought there was a way down. So we went off, through snow by then, about sixteen of us, mainly escaped prisoners of war and for some reason the partisan cook: a big, tough chap. We went down a gully, several thousand feet above the valley, dreadful, and we got to a point where, quite obviously, you couldn't go any further. It was an absolute precipice. It was dark by then so we decided all we could do was settle there on a ledge and hope no one would find us, although we'd left footprints in the snow. We were there for several days, which was a bit miserable. People got frostbite. Tilman went up and down several times to look over the top. The Germans were quite near but can't have followed our footprints. We were very, very fortunate really. By the third night we reckoned they must have moved down and we came up and got away.

Captain Richard Tolson
SOE liaison officer
We were very junior captains but Tilman was a very senior major. He'd been in the First World War and had been a great mountaineer and we were all in awe of him, I think. 'The Major' we always called him.

Captain John Ross
SOE liaison officer
Even after I met him, I didn't know for quite a long time that Tilman was the chap who'd climbed the highest mountain up to then: Nanda Devi in '36. He was a remarkable character. He was a man of few words: I've often been asked what we might have talked about in the many long evenings in our six months together, just the two of us, but I can't remember. He had written books and he was very well read and he dropped in with two volumes of Carlyle's *French Revolution* in his pockets and a book by Lord Dufferin, *Letters from High Latitudes*, who'd done sailing in the early nineteenth century. He had very wide interests and if you got him talking he was extremely interesting. He's represented very much by others as intolerant and he could be that; but I suppose, under military conditions, one wasn't so conscious of it. One sort of accepted that from him, really, as the leader and commanding officer, and it didn't worry one so much, although I must say one used to get

rather fed up with him. One never relaxed. I can remember hours of trudging behind him over these wretched mountains without a pause and thinking, 'He might stop sometime.' One found him excessively tough at times.

The Far East

Colin Mackenzie
Head, Force 136, India
They kept on saying from London, 'For God's sake, do something.' We could never see anything we could do. In India we came directly under Mountbatten, he wanted to know exactly what we were doing, when and how and, fairly late on, he said, 'You know, when I came out, I had on my list whether I should shut SOE down or not.' And he was quite right. At that time it was very doubtful whether we had justified our existence. He came out in '43 and we still had done practically nothing. It wasn't until later that year that we really began to do a certain amount of intelligence and so on.

Major Jim Gavin
SOE staff officer, Far East, 1941–43
We'd laid great plans. The whole story of the Far East was laying seeds for things and laying plans and then of course nothing much came of them because the Japanese attack was so successful.

Malaya

Captain Richard Broome
SOE officer, Operation 'Gustavus'
We were totally out of touch with Malaya, no intelligence of any really useful kind was coming out whatsoever, so somebody had to go in first and do a blind landing somewhere. That was arranged and John Davis was the man chosen to do it.

Major John Davis
SOE officer, Operation 'Gustavus'
We couldn't go and walk around Malaya if we got in; we had to have Chinese with us. Seemingly the most profitable source of Chinese at that time would have been Calcutta where five thousand Chinese seamen, the crews of all the

various cargo vessels that plied the Far East, were held up. We went over there and set up an office, nominally under the police, to go through the records to see if we could pick up likely people to join us. This wasn't very successful. We got one or two but the calibre of the type of chap we considered would not have made a frightfully good intelligence agent.

Then we had the great good fortune of falling in with a young Chinese from Singapore called Lim Bo Seng, a very attractive fellow, a complete English speaker, and we became very close friends. Lim Bo Seng's great assistance was that he had close contacts with the Chinese Government and he went up into China and recruited a number of young Malayan and one Borneo Chinese who had gone up to China for further education and been caught out by the war up there. Now these people, who he brought down, were far better calibre than the seamen we had been trying to get before, and so the possibilities of a party of people going into Malaya and be useful became very much more hopeful.

The first thing was to get trained for the job and to train them and this we did at a marvellous hill fort above Kharakvasala, above Poona, for some months, while we tried to discover means of getting back. In those days there was no possibility whatsoever of an aeroplane flying that distance. The only possible answer was a submarine. And it wasn't until May 1943 that we got our submarine.

On the first trip I went with five Chinese. We landed blind on a strip of sandy shore and jungle called Sigari, just north of Lumut. The submarine came to within about five miles of the shore. A submarine operating close to enemy territory has got to have enough water underneath it to dive, so you can't just calculate the amount of water a submarine takes to float in. This was the only beach isolated enough to give us a chance of getting away. We got into the jungle, made some sort of camp, I retained one man as a sort of bodyguard and all the other four went out in various directions to make contact with the outside world. One of them went specifically to try and get a junk so that we could get out to make our submarine rendezvous in a month's time. But the effect of my being there and needing to be looked after was that I was holding back my own men. So after a month in the jungle I decided to go out myself on that rendezvous and leave them to work for themselves and I returned to India on that submarine. I went in again with three other Chinese a month later.

Things moved slowly and on the third rendezvous Richard Broome came in. Very soon after that a youngster called Chen Ping came to our camp. He was a bit suspicious of who we were. He was very young, aged about twenty-three, very impressive, quietly spoken. We very soon realised that Chen Ping was a fellow on who we could rely completely. Our first job was to get to the headquarters of the communists and Chen Ping arranged that. Some weeks later he escorted us up into the main range and into a camp that he had organised, about two thousand feet above a town called Bidor, which became our headquarters.

A lot of us had said, 'Look, the people to use in this battle arc the communists.' They were very much on our side then. They were adventurous youngsters who were extremely anti-Japanese and therefore very good material indeed for anything in the way of intelligence and resistance. Chinese youngsters, idealists, who were prepared to risk imprisonment for the sake of it, they were ideal for behind-the-lines work. They were illegal, they were considered dangerous, a rebellious party, but personally one was quite friendly with them and as soon as they were on our side we were only too happy and off we went together.

Captain Richard Broome
SOE officer, Operation 'Gustavus'

The only thing we could do from the point of view of the Chinese communists was to offer them a bit of training. That couldn't be very much because we hadn't any ammunition for them to do any rifle practice or anything like that and really there was very little that we could teach them. But the main object was of course to plan to carry out the instructions we'd had to further the war effort and eventually we had quite a conference with the 'top brass' of the Communist Party. Over a couple of days, within our camp, we hammered out a sort of agreement to the effect that the Chinese would cooperate with SEAC, the South East Asia Command, during our reoccupation of Malaya and would take orders from SEAC, so far as necessary, operationally. And in reply we would supply them with arms and supplies and training, so far as we could.

We were not totally out of touch with Colombo, as we called our head office, because a series of rendezvous had been laid on with the submarine. But whenever Davis or I set out to try to keep the rendezvous it always transpired, from the communists, that things were extremely dangerous and the Japs were patrolling everywhere and that they couldn't get a European through. It may very well have been true at the time. So the only thing we could do was to send out messages and send one of our Chinese to keep the rendezvous, to the submarine, to keep them informed as well as we could. It was quite interesting how we got these messages out. We used to write them on very smallish bits of paper absolutely in minuscule writing and roll them up and conceal them in various ways. We concealed them in a tube of toothpaste and in a tin of Andrews Liver Salts and the final, best one was in the brain pan of a fried fish. The Japanese were constantly putting up roadblocks and searching people left, right and centre but we got these messages away and they did get through.

Major John Davis
SOE officer, Operation 'Gustavus'
When we first went in and things were easy and we were not harassed or anything like that, we fed well, that's really the key, and living in the jungle was very nice. You've got to avoid diseases if you can but apart from that it's very comfortable. Particularly in hill jungle, it's fairly cool. It has a lot going for it. Then things began to go wrong. Our outside men, men we had brought in, not the communists, were captured and that wiped out our outside organisation. So at one blow all our contacts and our ability to make rendezvous were broken. We had no wireless set and we became completely cut off from the outside world. Still well looked after and still working in cooperation with the communists, but with no hope until either a rendezvous or some other means of contact was made. Then the Japanese, almost certainly on information extracted from the breakdown of our organisation, attacked our camp. We weren't ourselves there, Richard Broome and myself. Sufficient warning was given, the whole lot cleared out in time and there were no casualties whatsoever. But unfortunately we lost all our codes, all our money, all our quinine and we were in pretty poor condition, and then we started a very grim period.

Captain Richard Broome
SOE officer, Operation 'Gustavus'
It wasn't an ideal life exactly. One was slightly under-fed all the time, bored stiff most of the time and very anxious to get back to comparative civilisation and get in touch with one's relatives. We made a dartboard. We cut a board out of the roots of a large tree, buttress roots. We had some difficulty in remembering how the numbers went round the board. Darts we made from nails. I also made a chess set out of bamboo, slats of bamboo stuck together, and carved the pieces. Our Chinese made a chess set but they also made mah jong and that was rather an achievement if you think of the number of tiles in a mah jong set. They had a high old time playing mah jong and we, in reply, made a Monopoly set. It was a bit wild to see these Chinese sitting in the

middle of the Malayan jungle, buying and selling Piccadilly and Leicester Square.

Major John Davis
SOE officer, Operation 'Gustavus'
For a long period we were down to four books: the New Testament, the *Pickwick Papers*, which was the most wonderful of the lot, I read it seven times and we had quizzes on it, a very interesting little school collection of essays and, I think, a book on farriery. It's worth remembering that we were all suffering from malnutrition. Our brain processes were slowed down, so the boredom would have been nothing like so extreme as it would have been if we had been in full health. I found myself able to sit and ruminate for quite a long time without suffering too badly.

Malaria was the greatest snag of all, particularly when one hadn't got quinine. You really lived a few days OK, then down, and you weathered that through, and then up again, a few days OK, and then down again. We were all saturated with malaria. The other problem was food. We were, by then, working with the Sakai, the aborigines of the country, and we were getting most of our food from them. Our staple diet was tapioca, not the nice pearl stuff with sugar that you get at home but the actual root itself which is really very similar to an English potato, eked out with a little rice, which the communists managed to buy from the villages on the plains. And perhaps, with luck, a little dry fish. For vitamin C we managed all right because the leafy tops of the tapioca plants and the sweet potato plants gave us what we needed. But we were on a diet which was just warding off beri-beri, just keeping us going. I don't think we were at any stage on the point of death or anything comparable with the POWs on the Siam railway, but we suffered badly from malnutrition, there's no doubt about it. We had practically no clothing left at all but that didn't matter.

China

Lieutenant Colonel Peter Wilkinson
Staff officer, SOE HQ, London
There were some splendid operations carried out by Walter Fletcher in the Far East, smuggling stuff in or out of China, all of which were extremely well paid.

Colin Mackenzie
Head, Force 136, India

Walter was gloriously fat. It was rumoured that he won the hundred yards at Charterhouse when he was nineteen stone. I didn't believe it, but when I saw him running for a bus when he was still nineteen stone I began to believe it might be true.

He apparently became an absolute nuisance to Baker Street because he kept on asking for jobs and they couldn't, wouldn't, give him a job. Eventually he came forward with a scheme for shipping rubber out of Malaya. Rubber was very short at that time. Then he went up to China and started negotiating in strategic materials, funny ones like tung oil and things like that. Then he went on dealing in diamonds, gold watches, whatever the warlords wanted. He did it very well. We had a very good chief accountant in SOE in London, John Venner, and he helped: even in the early days I had £20,000 of diamonds across my desk in one go. One estimate is that the net profit was worth £77 million.

1945

Any Japanese who were able to break across the road and the big valley eventually came through this tall grass to the riverbank, and our chaps let them build rafts and push out into the water and then they'd open fire on them. I remember the river was just full of bodies; for about three days it was full of bodies. Our five hundred chaps probably dealt with several thousand. It was carnage.

In the final months of the war, as the noose around Nazi Germany tightened, SOE continued to operate in front of the Allied armies pressing in from all sides. In Scandinavia and northern Italy, SOE agents remained active until the end, while other teams went in to the Reich itself. And after 8 May, when Germany surrendered, SOE still had jobs to do. One was to discover the fate of agents who had fallen into enemy hands.

As the fighting in Europe came to end, operations against the Japanese reached a peak and many SOE personnel who had fought in Europe arrived in time to take part. Everywhere SOE teams worked closely with local people and guerrilla groups. Operations in Burma to assist the advance of British regular forces and waylay the retreating Japanese were especially effective, but agents were also active from occupied Malaya to Borneo and the Dutch East Indies. And when the atomic bombs were dropped and Japan surrendered, there were again still jobs to do, from liberating remote POW camps to dealing with Japanese who refused to give in.

Italy

Corporal Bill Pickering
SOE wireless operator
We dropped into thick snow. In fact our leader, Major Salvadori, was virtually buried in snow and I had to dig him out with his parachute on and it was quite

a job because there were partisans nearby shouting, 'Hurry up, hurry up, hurry up! The Germans are coming!' It took quite a while to get him out but get him out we did. By that time the partisans had gathered up all the containers of guns: Sten guns, Bren guns. We stuffed all the stuff away in a church, the priest was helping the partisans, and then we split up. I was taken to a farmhouse and hidden there for the night. The next morning, just before dawn, we got out of the farmhouse and went up into the hills and hid in a little oak hut. The Germans knew that someone had dropped during the night, they'd heard the plane, they'd probably know the fires were on, and they came out looking for us, what they called a *rastrellamento*. That means 'a raking in'. They sent troops up and down all these valleys.

Captain John Wolstenholme
Signals intelligence officer, SOE HQ, Southern Italy
As operations moved north and the Germans were getting compressed into a small space and being more able to harry our chaps instead of the other way round, people were losing equipment, equipment was being damaged. They needed supplies, and I, as signals intelligence officer, was asked to look at all the incoming messages from the field, extract from them anything to do with technical problems and try and organise and get to them spares, new equipment, whatever they needed on the technical front. That was by no means easy, for two reasons. First, the sorts of equipment, replacements, might not be readily available to us. Second, even if they were available, if we could draw it off a shelf in the store the same day, the problem was then to get it to northern Italy because we had very limited access to aircraft. We had to put in an indent to the RAF command for an appropriate aircraft to do drops in such and such an area and even when we did that we still had to share our Italian demands with the Yugoslav demands, the Austrian demands, these demands, those demands. We weren't the only SOE units making these requests.

Lieutenant Robin Richards
SOE Naval Section
To see to what extent supply could be done by sea, we commandeered a couple of twenty-five foot runabouts mouldering on the quayside in Nice. We managed to get them into the water and get them working but they were not very reliable. On one occasion, in January 1945, I had been on a little jaunt up the coast by night to deposit Captain Robert Bentley on the beach together with his personnel and stores in one of these small fast craft, and on our way home the single engine stopped. Dawn was breaking and we could see

ourselves ending up in a POW camp at the very best. But by the mercy of God after ten minutes' tinkering we managed to get the single engine working again and got home.

Corporal Bill Pickering
SOE wireless operator
We did a big drop one night, Major Hope, myself and Millard, and we took the drop in, got all the arms, ammunition, etc, and about midnight I set off back to my billet. It was a stable I was sleeping in that night and I hadn't been there half an hour when there was a knock on the door and some partisans came in. 'Come quickly, Major Hope's been killed.' I couldn't believe this. I wondered what they were on about. I went back to the place we'd had the drop and, sure enough, there was Major Hope, dead on the floor. What had happened was that everybody had congratulated one another on the drop and all the arms and ammunition we'd managed to get, and while they were saying goodnight one of the partisans had dropped his Sten gun and it fired one round and killed him.

Commander Gerry Holdsworth
Head, Italian Section, SOE HQ, Southern Italy
We, of all people in Italy, were really informed of what the situation miles behind the front lines was. My job, by then, had really become a bearer of such tidings as could be of use to Field Marshal Alexander and his chief of staff, John Harding, and I used to visit their headquarters certainly once a week. We would tell them of movements coming through the tunnels in the north of Italy, down from Germany, troop movements, armament movements, in or out. It was of considerable use to them. And occasionally we would be requested to make a fuss up on one side of Italy, thus possibly giving the impression that Alexander was going to do something on that side when, of course, this had only been occasioned so that he could do something on the other side.

Major Thomas Macpherson
SOE liaison officer
The railways north and south on each side of us and, to a degree, electric pylons were really the only target. And diversions by long-range sniping at sentries and vehicles along the north-south road, because there was a continuous stream from Austria into north Italy. Unlike France, it was not car banditry. You were on your feet, so things took much longer to do. You

NA 25369

Parachute containers destined for northern Italy.

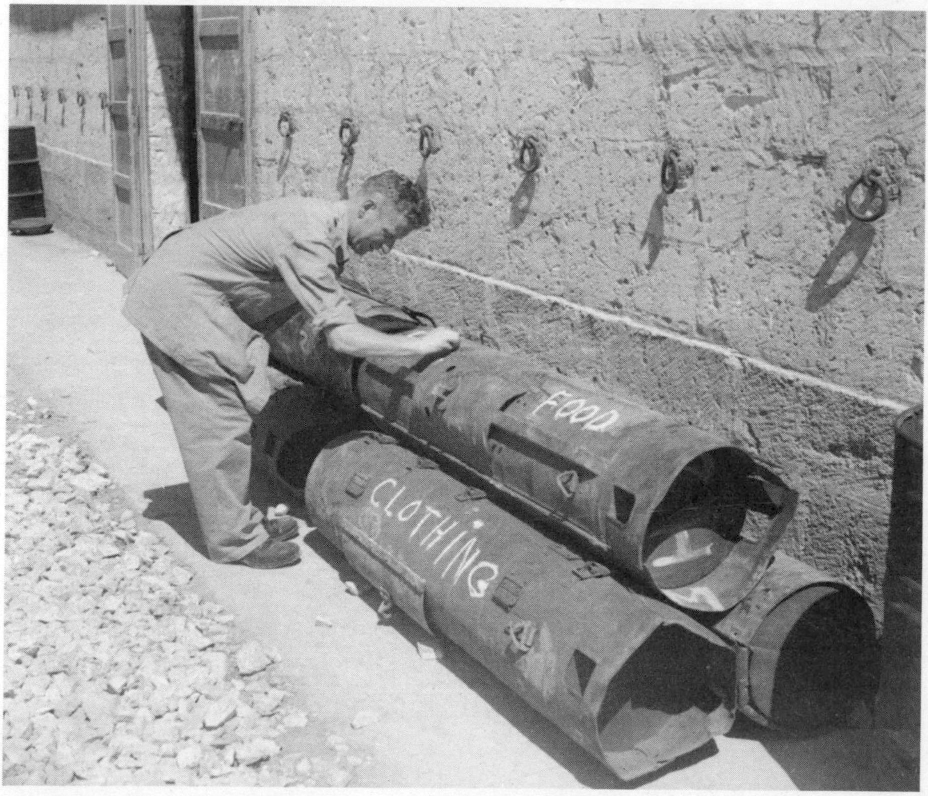

NA 25382

NA 25392

Supply drops into northern Italy.

NA 25393

couldn't say, 'I'll reconnoitre this tonight, and I'll do it tomorrow.' Each task was an expedition. It was also therefore necessary to create little groups in local areas with the sole purpose of railway sabotage. I felt that constant breaking of the line and constant bringing down of electric wires – it was an electric line, although they had some steam locomotives – was more valuable than risking your men and a vast quantity of explosive on bringing down a major bridge. We were able to send weekly signals of interruptions. There was quite an impressive number of line breaks, locomotives derailed and wagons derailed.

Corporal Bill Pickering
SOE wireless operator
We got dressed up as peasants, took a horse and a cart loaded with vegetables and started to walk towards Milan. We crossed the main road from Turin to Milan at a place called Villanova d'Asti. A strange thing happened there. As we were going through the town, Keany and I were walking over a bridge and a train passed underneath us and I said to him, 'If only we'd had some explosive and known this was coming, we could have blown this train up.' I'd no sooner said the words than – boomph! – the damned thing went up. Someone else, the partisans, had done it. So Keany and I had to jump on the cart and thrash the horse and gallop as fast as we could out of the town to the other side.

Sergeant Harry Hargreaves
SOE wireless operator
Taylor and Godwin, they were dead keen on explosives. They did things with explosives that you read about in *Rover* and *Wizard*. I can remember one time they got a damned big cheese, they were scooping out the middle of the cheese, and I said, 'What the hell are you doing there?' They said, 'We're going to put plastic in here, we'll put a time pencil in and we'll get an Italian to take it into the German mess down in Udine.' Things like that. They went down into the valley one night, I remember, and decided to do all the electric pylons going across. We sat on a little hill, sat for about three hours on this hill, and you'd see a flash of light over here and a flash light over there and it was all the pylons going down.

Corporal Bill Pickering
SOE wireless operator
We were in the hills with these partisans and a large group of republican

fascist troops came up, so all the partisans got down and hid on one side of the hill. We watched them all march past in platoons, probably about five or six platoons, there might have been up to sixty, eighty men altogether, and no one fired a shot. Everybody hid behind the hillside. Then they got out of earshot and eyesight and out of the way and Keany just strolled up and down playing hell with the partisans, saying, 'Well, what are you doing this for? Why didn't you shoot all those fascists? You had them in your sights, why didn't you kill them all?' Quite a row went on with the partisan leaders and they said to Keany, 'You can't do this in the hills. There are German garrisons and fascist garrisons all around, all within a very short distance, maybe four miles, and if you get yourself into a big scrap with a load of fascist troops they can call upon reinforcements. We can't, we're stuck. They've only got to radio to get another battalion out.' It didn't seem to sink into Keany, this. His only thought was killing this lot.

Captain John Orr-Ewing
SOE liaison officer
If you got into any sort of open warfare at all, you'd had it. You'd got to be underground.

Corporal Bill Pickering
SOE wireless operator
Keany and I were on the edge of the hill, more or less the ridge, and behind us were these partisans. And for some reason or other I decided to move away from Keany, he was stood next to me, and I hadn't taken more than two or three steps when all hell was let loose – machine guns, sub-machine guns, Schmeissers. Keany immediately fell. He was shot. Turned out he'd got six bullets in him. I got down immediately, got my machine gun out, a Marlin, and started to fire. The Germans had come up below the hill out of our sight. They killed another four partisans, were coming in larger numbers now, we were firing, keeping them down, then we'd move further and further back, then we legged it as fast as we could. Once we realised we were pretty safe, we sat down and the sweat poured out of me. At the time it was happening, you didn't think anything of it. But when you sat down you thought, 'Well, that lot have been killed and here we are.'

Major Thomas Macpherson
SOE liaison officer
We had the odd near miss. After we had moved from our alpine huts, a girl

who had been a courier for us had been sent back to her home, was arrested and tortured and made to reveal where she had been. We woke one day to see on the valley path below us a column of a full company of German Alpine Division soldiers going for those huts, which they found empty and burned, but they didn't find us. We had a curious protector in that there was a pair of ravens nesting in the hill above who became totally used to us but got up and squawked every time there was an alien visitor, which was extremely helpful. It was rather like the Roman geese on the Capitol.

Captain John Ross
SOE liaison officer
We had two drops by the Americans, very skilful drops, and when we finished we wanted to get back to Belluno with all the stuff. All the stuff was transported in trucks, under timber, very successfully. We crossed the mountains as far as we could, then the rest of the way one had to go by road. We'd gone up there walking but there was so much German activity we couldn't do that and it was finally decided we'd go hidden in a truck under a load of wood. So they made a sort of coffin into which we climbed, everything was piled on top, and away we went. We stopped at a number of checkpoints and then at a place called Mas which was known to be a particularly brutal set-up, and we lay there while they had a look at the truck. And I remember looking up, seeing someone poking with a rifle or a bayonet through the wood but not finding us. We were very fortunate.

Sub-Lieutenant Robert Clark
SOE liaison officer
We were warned that they were going to do one of these *rastrellamentos* and the time-honoured custom was to walk out into the open fields and hide either in cowsheds or haystacks. We chose a haystack. The *rastrellamento* passed through us and we were still in the haystack but unfortunately we were given away by some locals with Nazi sympathies and the Germans marched back, straight to our haystack, and found us all there. They took us off to Mondovi. Cauvain and I were separated from Duncan Campbell and the others because we were both in the navy and the rest of them were in the army. We were taken to the local jail in Mondovi and kept there for, I think, about three or four days when we were transferred to Turin.

In Turin they were quite rough but nothing more serious than being beaten about the head. I suppose I was interrogated about eight times on different days. I had an identity card which showed that I belonged to HMS *President*, which was the boat lying on the Thames which was used as a cover-story for naval people in SOE, and I couldn't make them understand why I was attached to a small ship in the Thames and why I was where I was. They thought it was very strange to have naval people with the partisans. But they eventually tired of it and when they discovered they were going to treat their own home guard as regular forces they told me I should go to a prisoner-of-war camp. I stayed in Turin state jail, I suppose, a month. In fact I spent my twenty-first birthday in there, when we were visited by some Catholic nuns, who, on hearing that I was twenty-one, brought me an egg, which was an absolute treasure. Eventually after six weeks I was taken to the *Marlag und Milag* camp outside Bremen.

Major Alastair Macdonald
SOE liaison officer
The partisans attacked a German bus full of NCOs who were going on leave out of Italy, returning to Germany, and they killed the whole lot, which was something the Germans couldn't be expected to take lying down. It was this more than anything else that led to a fairly substantial *rastrellamento* in the Serra in the course of which I unfortunately went perhaps a little too far forward. I found a whole platoon of Waffen SS pouring into the village where I was, leaving me not much chance except to try and get out of the village through fairly deep snow. I found myself being fired on when I was less than a hundred yards from the village, and a radio operator who was with me got hit, fatally. Then they sent a dog after us and there really wasn't anything to be done except surrender.

I was first brought in to their commander and stood in front of him. Then I heard him telephoning his headquarters and saying – this was in German – 'I have here with me a British major, captured with the bands. Shall I have him executed?' This was an awkward moment. Then he went on saying, '*Jawohl, jawohl. Ist gut, ist gut.*' And then, with rather bad grace, he said, 'You'll be treated as a *Kriegsgefangener*' – a prisoner of war. Which wasn't quite what happened, but never mind, I wasn't bumped off.

I had on me when I was captured quite a number of documents that I knew would be of great interest to them. The most vital ones I was able to destroy because at one moment on the way to Verona I was left in a room with a sentry outside and a hot stove. Some of these papers I had managed to keep in my mittens, so that when they gave me a perfunctory search they didn't find them, and I was able to open the stove and drop them in. I burnt myself when

I did this and the stove made a big clang when I shut it again and the sentry came running in, but it was too late, they'd gone.

Captain John Orr-Ewing
SOE liaison officer
The partisans brought to me a German whom they'd captured. He was a young chap, about eighteen or nineteen. He'd been a member of the Hitler Youth. They said, 'We see he did one or two years' training for the Lutheran ministry, perhaps he's different. We thought we'll bring him to you and if you plead on his behalf we might spare his life.' But he was utterly aggressive. There was nothing penitent about him or anything, he was aggressive and absolutely a Nazi. So I'm afraid I said to him, 'They brought you to me to try and save your life, but honestly, the attitude you've taken, what can I do?' And the partisans decided they couldn't keep him and they shot him. We weren't in charge, thank goodness, and I haven't got any guilt about it.

Corporal Bill Pickering
SOE wireless operator
We got a message to say that the Allies were going to advance and under no circumstances were the partisans to occupy the cities – they were to wait for the Allies. Well, of course, this fell on deaf ears. They weren't going to have any of that. They'd done all the fighting. The Allies, they'd done no fighting in the Po Valley at all. So the Germans started to pull out and the partisans immediately decided to occupy the cities. I can remember getting trucks and going into Asti. I felt like Churchill, wandering down the main street, the crowds lined either side, clapping and cheering. We weren't there long and then they said, 'Come on, we're going to occupy Turin.'

We got to the outskirts, at Superga. There was a bit of shooting going on, largely partisans shooting fascists and then burying them in the gardens of a great big mansion there with their arms and legs showing above the ground, just flinging earth over them and letting their arms stick out. As we moved into Turin itself there were all sorts of firing. They have boulevards there and we were behind posts, firing up at these fascists in high buildings who were firing down on us. Every so often there'd be screams, or the partisans would rush a building and get upstairs and grab them and hang them – they'd hang somebody on a lamp post. This went on for twenty-four hours. And I remember the first Allied troops coming into town the next day. The local Italians couldn't get over this because it was a battalion of Japanese Americans that came in.

DENMARK

Wing Commander Thomas Charles Murray
Stirling pilot, 138 (SD) Squadron, RAF, operating over Denmark
We'd found the DZ in a wood, I'd done my circling and I was coming up to drop. But along a roadside, a couple of fields off, was a whole string of lorries, pretty obviously military, and a car bouncing along a track across these fields in full view of the convoy on the road, headlights on, so I immediately aborted. Eventually I got a report back from the doctor with abject apologies for being late. It had been him driving his car to the reception. Brave devil. Headlights full on and everything, dashing there to get there on time.

Reginald Spink
Staff officer, Danish Section, SOE HQ, London
When the Danish resistance movement was fully active, it was very well organised and highly effective. Denmark was a channel for communications between Germany and Norway. It was also, through Denmark, that many troops were sent from east to west and from west to east. Therefore railway sabotage was of great importance in Denmark. There were also certain factories that worked for the Germans in building diesel engines, for instance, which was a Danish speciality, and they were sabotaged. A Freedom Council was set up in Denmark, composed of leading resistance people, and Flemming Muus joined it as our representative. It was a sort of unofficial underground government. Towards the end of 1944 Muus was under increasing pressure, he was being hunted by the Germans, and we had to withdraw him and we sent in our final leader, a man called Ole Lippmann, who had been in the resistance.

Varinka Muus
Wife of Danish SOE agent, Flemming Muus
A hell of a lot of people had been arrested who knew my husband and gave the Gestapo a complete description of him. They had an enormous sum of money on his head and he was very recognisable because he was very near-sighted and had to wear very thick glasses; he couldn't do without them. They had also operated on him in England, they had tried to change his face so that even his family wouldn't recognise him, but they hadn't done a very good job, they'd left some very big scars along his ears. Well, he was the only man in Denmark who had those scars so he was terribly vulnerable to being recognised.

Ole Lippmann
Danish SOE agent

There was the possibility that the Germans would simply surrender and leave Denmark. There was the possibility of an Allied invasion. There was the possibility that Denmark would be cut off, that the Allied troops would go from west to east and seal Denmark off and that we would be left with two hundred thousand German troops. And I had to plan for all these, including a plan to make use of the resistance movement to protect harbours, important installations and so on. My predecessors had in many ways an easier job: organising people to blow them up. I had to protect them.

The whole winter of '44–45 was a very hectic period. The Gestapo had been arresting and killing and torturing a great number of people. They had also managed to arrest a greater part of the Freedom Council. The Royal Air Force had come to our rescue already in October 1944 in bombing the Gestapo headquarters in Jutland. The head of the Gestapo service in Jutland and all the important people at the Gestapo headquarters at Aarhus University were killed in that attack.

Then the Germans, after Aarhus, which was an enormous shock to them, took some of the prominent prisoners to the Shell House building which was the Gestapo headquarters in Copenhagen. The Danish resistance movement asked the Royal Air Force whether they would repeat the attack. The Germans tried to prevent that by putting some of the important prisoners at the top of the building.

One of my briefs was to evaluate the position and find out whether the Danes would accept casualties in connection with this raid on Copenhagen. I couldn't very well go around in Copenhagen and ask, 'Well, will you accept casualties or will you not?' So it was more or less a question I had to decide myself. I knew it was a tough decision because not only was I risking the lives of a number of Royal Air Force pilots but also risking the lives of a lot of Danes and many other things. But then the Gestapo managed to arrest a whole group of leading people in Region Six, which was Copenhagen, most of the leaders of the Copenhagen resistance movement, at the beginning of March. And I felt this was a very bad thing and I knew that these people possessed so much knowledge and that, without the destruction not only of the people but especially the files in the building, this would be a very bad thing for the Danish resistance. So, after taking a long walk and thinking heavily, I sent a signal requesting the attack on the Gestapo headquarters.

Reginald Spink
Staff officer, Danish Section, SOE HQ, London
The RAF said they were prepared to do a low-level precision bombing, hedge-hopping across Denmark so as to avoid the flak as far as possible. A model of the Shell House and its immediate surroundings was made in the SOE unit that used to do this sort of thing in the Natural History Museum, South Kensington. They built a model and the RAF studied this model to get everything right. The object was to hit the building from the side and not from the top. And that duly happened.

Ole Lippmann
Danish SOE agent
Miraculously some of our top people managed to survive and get out. Some Gestapo people were killed and some resistance people were also of course killed. Unfortunately one of the Mosquitoes hit a post at the railway station and tried to land in a park but came down in another part of Copenhagen. The second wave coming in mistook the smoke and bombed the Fredericksberg area where there was a French school and they killed about seventy-six children. It was a very sad thing and you may say unnecessary. The third wave came in and they did all right. Altogether, Second Tactical Air Force lost nine pilots in that operation.

Norway

Birger Rasmussen
Norwegian SOE agent
I was shot on 6 March '45. A friend of mine had just arrived from the UK only a week before, so he was quite green, and we met unexpectedly a patrol of eight, maybe ten, men. We had parked the car to fill up with petrol, because we were going down to help the home forces blow up the railway to slow down the retreating German troops, and we were just strolling in the street when this patrol came along. We went down a cul-de-sac and down into a courtyard in order to try and get into a house, and I was standing there waiting in the courtyard when three men came round the corner. I just stood there and I turned my left side towards them and took up my pistol, a 9-millimetre Beretta, an Italian pistol, we were at a distance of three or four metres, and I shot double shots – bang-bang – in the chest and they naturally went down. Two of them. I should have had all three, which I should easily have managed

CL 3748

The Shell House in Copenhagen burning furiously after a daylight Mosquito raid called in by SOE, March 1945.

because I took them by surprise, but my pistol misfired. And I remember very distinctly, even now, that for a split second I had the feeling that I was so big that I filled up the whole courtyard. And I heard a terrific bang and after a little while I noticed that I was standing up to the wall – fortunately I didn't fall, I managed to stay on my feet – but I looked down and I'd been hit.

There was a fence up to my chest, with some barbed wire on top, and I rolled myself over and down into the courtyard where there was some wood for heating houses. I fell down on top of that heap of wood, and I remember the noise when my back hit the wood, and then I went down to the courtyard and there was a small gateway, a corridor, leading into the street. I was able to walk then but after a short while I was unable to carry on. I think blood was coming out of my nose or mouth or both. Fortunately there was a car and the driver was sitting in the car, so my friend opened the door and I partly crawled and was partly helped by him into it and the man was ordered to drive on and away. And I remember when I was put on the floor in that car wondering whether I was going to die or not, but I didn't feel any special pain. I asked the driver to go to the hospital because I knew that my brother-in-law, who was a doctor, a specialist in children's diseases, was working there. After one month I was well enough to be moved and could be taken to Sweden by boat, across the Oslo Fjord.

Captain Jens-Anton Poulsson
Norwegian SOE agent

Everybody knew that the Germans were going to lose the war sooner or later and in Norway it was very important to protect Norwegian industry against German demolition in case of an Allied invasion or German capitulation. We had plans to attack the guards and so on. Everything was prepared in detail as far as we were able to do it and we had all these weapons delivered by aircraft. We had to collect them, clean them, they were covered in grease, and then get these weapons distributed. The goal was to have the organisation ready in the spring or early summer of '45. What actually happened was that the German commander in Norway, General Böhme, wanted to carry on in Norway after the capitulation but fortunately he was ordered from Germany to capitulate. Then the British and Eisenhower sent over a group to Norway and every order from that group to the German high command was carried out. There were very few incidents. The German discipline was extraordinary, really.

Austria and Germany

Colonel Peter Wilkinson
Staff officer, SOE HQ, London
None of us knew how the war was going to end. We had various theories, that there was going to be a burning, a putting to the sword, of the countries Germany withdrew from, that there was going to be a revolution inside Germany rather similar to the end of the First World War. And it was felt that there might be targets of opportunity SOE could take on, so we held a small reserve of agents and trusties and British officers who would be able to exploit any situation that developed.

Sergeant Paul 'Yogi' Mayer
German Jewish SOE agent
We went in to what we were told was our last exercise in very, very cold winter and we had to parachute in a snowstorm. We didn't know what it was about. There were some steel structures, the police were about and we were caught. And when we came back to Anderson Manor, where we were stationed, the colonel said to me, 'Mayer, this exercise was for you. We have selected three of you Rhinelanders and we want you to be involved in securing the bridgehead across the Rhine. We have contact with the other side, contact with German troops, all we need now is three of you to go over and make contact.' Shortly afterwards we were called in and they said, 'The bridge at Remagen has been captured, there is no need for you to carry out this exercise.' I was delighted, because the chances of success were very small.

Captain Arthur Radley
Staff officer, Austrian Section, SOE HQ, Southern France
As far as Austria was concerned, most of the 'joes' consisted of Jewish refugees who had come over to England in '38, '39, and been recruited. There seemed to be quite a large number of them, about twenty or thirty. One or two were not Jews but were politically opposed to the Nazi regime. One 'joe' as a wireless operator kept up a steady contact from within Vienna itself. That was really something. They were tremendous. They were all very high calibre people themselves; they were intellectuals, they were dons. They were keen young men.

Sergeant Eric Sanders
Austrian Jewish SOE agent
Michael O'Hara and I were very close friends since our training. He was a great bragger, he was tall, he looked like John Wayne and it fitted him, he would twirl his pistol around and grab it, but when you got to know him he was the kindest, most good-hearted fellow you could imagine. He told me that he had a girlfriend in London and didn't know if he would ever see her again. Then one day he disappeared. He was in action. Darton said to me, 'As soon as we get contact with O'Hara, it will be your and Theo's turn.' So at long last I knew what we were waiting for. But O'Hara was caught and killed and we never went into action.

Eric Munter
Danish SOE agent
We should have gone to Germany in December '44 but we were prevented by the Ardennes offensive. We should then have gone in January or February but then the winter was very hard. Then in March we were sent down to Gothenburg, so we should cross over to Denmark, but we were delayed again by various things. Boats couldn't come or boats couldn't leave. We did not get across till early April '45.

We were not permitted to get in touch with Danish Germans who were living there but we did other things. We blew up one of those train turntables and we got in touch with people who had come from Holland and Belgium. We went further south, bicycled, and came to Kiel, which was bombed flat. It looked fantastic. All the way down there were buses and lorries and cars bombed flat. We were stopped by German soldiers on motorcycles, asking us if we'd heard aeroplanes coming over. We said, no, we'd not. The reason why they wanted to ask us this was that when you were on a motorbike you could not hear the aeroplanes.

Major Harvard Gunn
SOE agent, Germany
I joined a unit called Special Allied Airborne Reconnaissance Force. All the people who were in this force were SOE. The purpose of this force was to parachute groups into, believe it or not, German prisoner-of-war camps in order to take over and threaten those who ran the camps that they would be finished if they didn't give up. It was a very strange operation and I think in many ways unrealistic. Only one team was even remotely successful. Otherwise the others didn't come off.

Then various lots of us went by gliders into Germany and eventually I went into part of Schleswig-Holstein. The Germans had come down out of Denmark and gone into two sides of Schleswig-Holstein and nobody knew exactly what they were going to do. The feeling was that they might in fact create some sort of resistance. I went into one part and Paddy Leigh Fermor, who was famous for his capturing of General Kreipe on Crete, went into the other side.

My first effort was to take over a small farmhouse and set up my wireless set. I had only two people with me, a Belgian and a wireless operator. I knew virtually where people were and I went to find the biggest unit near me, a corps headquarters in a huge country house, one of these enormous whitewashed country houses in that part of the world. I had acquired a Mercedes car and I drove up to this farmhouse where, being good German soldiers, there was a guard. I took off an old mac I had with me and put on my Glengarry – I wore a kilt, being in a Highland regiment – got out of the car and shouted at the guard, 'Turn out the Guard!' and they all came tearing out.

They took me to their chief of staff and when I was marched in I recognised immediately this chap as having been up at Oxford with me. I looked at him and went up to him and said, 'Michael, you shit,' and he said, 'Well, you'd have done exactly the same as me' – typical Oxford. I said, 'I want to see the General,' and he said, 'The General's a very nasty man. He's a dangerous man, a horrible man. I can't answer for him. I don't know what he'll do. Anyway, he's having his afternoon snooze.' I said, 'Go wake him up.' We went to the big house and I said, 'Tell him if I'm not out of here within the hour and in contact with my wireless operator this place will be blown to smithereens. I have an aircraft standing by.' Quite untrue. Eventually I saw the General and he agreed to show me everything he was doing. It was an extraordinary situation because the German troops realised that everything was finished, completely finished. I think I'm probably the only person who's patted a German general on the head because he was crying. Not the same general. Another general.

Lieutenant Stephen Dale

Captured German Jewish SOE agent in Brunswick POW camp

On 12 April '45, American tanks rolled into the camp. It was a great moment. They were very depressed because Roosevelt had died that day but they were marvellous to us. As victors, of course, they were on top of the wave and they gave us anything they could do without. It really was a fantastic moment. For me it was also significant in one respect because suddenly this constant fear under which I'd lived from the moment I was taken prisoner didn't exist any more, because I knew now that they wouldn't discover my background. That was a phenomenal relief. It wasn't just a question of identity. The simple fact that, had I been recognised as a German Jew, that would have been enough to spell the end.

Captain Charles Hargreaves
Captured SOE agent in Colditz POW camp
Everybody knew more or less that the Americans were within very, very close range of us and by this time we'd taken over the administration of the castle from the Germans. All that we wanted from them was really for them to look after us, to make certain that the SS didn't come up. But we had complete free range within the castle and we used to clamber outside and get up on the roof and into the bell towers and the cupolas – we had a wonderful view. The weather was extremely nice. It was late spring. And then one day the gates opened and some small American soldier poked his head in and made some sort of ordinary remark, saying, 'Well, we're here. You're free.'

Lieutenant George Abbott
Captured SOE agent in Colditz POW camp
A few minutes later a jeep came in and another jeep and then a jeep with some war correspondents and there was a lot of commotion, people speaking to the Americans and so on. We went to Erfurt and then the whole camp was flown back. Twenty planes took us back and we were landed somewhere I believe in Buckinghamshire and we were taken to a kind of transit camp where we were given new battledress and so on. The next day all the prisoners had to be debriefed and interrogated. There was another chap from SOE there and when our turn came we had to say who we were and the interrogating officer, a captain in the Intelligence Corps, said, 'Ah, yes,' and told us to wait. In the afternoon a fully-fledged colonel came and collected us: Maurice Buckmaster. We were taken back by him to London in a car and we were put up in a nice little flat down in Kensington and then obviously we had to be debriefed, we had to go through the mill. And once we were debriefed we were in fact given one month's leave to go and see our families.

Sub-Lieutenant Robert Clark
Captured SOE agent in Bremen POW camp
Outside Lubeck we were relieved by the British Army, which had advanced right across. As I'd been in SOE they knew I was there and I was taken out the

same day, taken to the RAF headquarters at Luneberg Heath. It was the day that the Germans had agreed to surrender, they were going to sign the next day, so there was a great party at the RAF headquarters. I remember the commanding airman was Johnnie Johnson, the fighter ace, and he was very kind to me, everyone was very kind to me, but they were so kind they gave me two large whiskies and I promptly fell flat on the floor. I don't think I'd had any alcohol for a year. The next day I was flown to Biggin Hill and from there I was given a railway ticket and bus pass to my home in north London. I'd been posted missing when I got caught, my parents thought I was missing presumed killed, and I walked down the avenue where we lived and the first time my father had seen me for two and a half years was when I walked through the front door. He was absolutely astonished, as he thought I wasn't there any more.

The Missing

Lieutenant Robert Sheppard
Captured SOE agent in Dachau concentration camp
The last three or four months at Dachau, it was covered with a typhoid epidemic. Frightful. People dying on the spot. Skeletons. Excrement everywhere. It was absolutely a living cemetery. Imagine a living cemetery with bodies and amongst these bodies some start moving or shouting, or want soup, or even worse, fight for soup. This was the daily life of the camp. I don't think without having lived in this you can realise the horror of four skeletons, practically naked, fighting, really fighting, knocking each other, for a bowl of soup. It is really the lowest grade of the human being and you cannot reproach these people for behaving like this. It needed tremendous force of character to live through that, to try and keep your dignity. We perfectly understood all these people. We managed not to behave like that but it was sometimes very, very hard.

Brian and myself, we managed to disappear in the camp. I was in Block 24 and Brian in Block 22. We had a friend in Block 17, a so-called hospital, a typhus block, and we disappeared in there because no one wanted to enter this block, it was too dangerous. We thought, 'No one will come and fetch us from here.' And we lived the last ten days until the liberation of Dachau in there, in the misery, but in the hope that it would be soon. Suddenly, on the afternoon of 29 April, we heard the guns. All the camp was quiet and Brian and myself, to know what was going on, went right to the corner of the barracks where we could see the entrance, and we saw the Americans at the door. That was the end of a long war.

Lieutenant Brian Stonehouse
Captured SOE agent in Dachau concentration camp
We couldn't believe it: to think that we'd actually survived. A correspondent came in from the Jewish Agency in London and I gave him my name to tell my family that I was alive – that's how they first found out. Bob and I spent that evening with the Americans in the guardroom eating 'K' rations and smoking, which was marvellous.

Odette Sansom
Captured SOE agent in Ravensbrück concentration camp
The commandant at Ravensbrück, with all his authority and his years of dedication to Hitler, a man of great importance who had seen over one hundred thousand women dying, not batting an eyelid, chose to save me by taking me out of my cell and carting me away, travelling all day long. He said to me, 'Do you want to know where we are going?' I said, 'No.' I honestly believed that he would take me to a wood and I would be killed there, therefore not leaving any traces. He said, 'I'm taking you to the Americans.' At about ten o'clock at night we were stopped by some Americans. They took his gun, they broke it and gave it to me, and I was left with this wonderful white Mercedes lined with red leather. They said, 'We are going to find you a room for the night,' and I said, 'No, if you don't mind, I have not seen the sky and the stars for a very long time and I would like to sit in this car till the morning.' The other reason was that I knew he had a lot of documents in the car. I wanted to have a look at those documents and bring them back to this country.

Vera Atkins
Civilian staff, French Section, SOE HQ, London
After 8 May people started streaming back from concentration camps. You'd get their stories and it was from them that you'd hear what had happened to those who'd not returned. When a person was arrested, you did not know what happened to them subsequently – therefore the information brought by the returning agents was more than interesting and more than harrowing.

Patricia Stewart-Bam
FANY staff, French Section, London
I was put to going through the various reports from women agents who'd

survived. I was to read through a report and say 'Pauline had seen Christine somewhere or other' – so at that moment Christine was still alive. Then you'd have to go through the other reports to see whether anyone had seen Pauline later because Pauline was missing. That was the sort of thing. And really some of those reports were appalling reading. It was the most searing experience, really. What some of those people had been through, I don't want to think about it even now.

Major Aonghaìs Fyffe
SOE officer searching for missing agents in Germany
We had a complete card index of all the agents of whom there was no trace and my job was to evaluate what happened to them in concentration camps, *gefangenenlager*, all sorts of detention places. These records were magnificently kept. Everything was noted. Colour of hair, colour of eyes, teeth, distinguishing marks, weight. Everything was down there. And we decided first of all to visit all the concentration camps, whether we knew our agents had been there or not, have a look at their records if there were records available – they weren't always available – and ask questions and find out what was maybe behind the surface. Some folk were quite keen to talk. Some weren't. We'd go down to the American zone and go to Wiesbaden and check what they had done, because they had entered several camps on their side of the border. I'd get damned great sheaves of movement orders and then we'd go through the camps on their side too and search through the records as far as we could.

Vera Atkins
SOE officer searching for missing agents in Germany
It was very difficult to trace people who were moved to camps in what was now the Russian zone. I suppose there are about four untraced finally, which is a pretty good record.

Lieutenant Colonel Ernest van Maurik
SOE officer searching for missing agents in Germany
People like Yeo-Thomas had all been overrun before we got there so we didn't have too many people to find. About a month later I got a message from Baker Street saying Yeo-Thomas would be flying out on an RAF flight and please pick him up, he would explain what he wanted to do. I was delighted. When I picked him up I hardly knew it was him. Before, he was a broad, jolly bloke with a big face and liked his whisky, not in excess, but really a wonderful

character. This gaunt figure got out of the plane and all the sparkle and bonhomie had completely gone. He knew who I was and he was pleased to see me but he was a completely changed man.

We took him back to our mess and he said that on behalf of the War Crimes Commission he wanted to see somebody who had been in Buchenwald with him and who had saved his life. Would I personally drive him to Paderborn and act as interpreter? So I said, 'Yes, of course.' I think he could understand and possibly speak a bit of German but wasn't prepared at any rate to speak a word of that bloody language and that was that. Next morning he didn't tell me much in the car. He was really not feeling much like chatting, it seemed. We got to a small house in a small village on the outskirts of Paderborn and we went in. And as we went on and discussed SS officials and the atrocities committed and what have you, all being noted down by Yeo-Thomas for the War Crimes Commission, I really remember that I began to think that they were both out of their minds. This could not be. It was certainly the most eerie interview I've ever had with anybody and I came away sort of wanting to wash my hands.

The Far East

Major Dick Rubinstein
SOE officer
SOE said to me, 'You've got three options. You can go back to the army, or you can do a job in Germany or you can go to the Far East.' I didn't want to just go back to the army: I didn't know what it meant and I usually liked to have some say in the things that I did. I asked about Germany but they said they couldn't tell me unless I volunteered for it. It was in fact concerned with the operations that were eventually never used, to parachute into POW camps in Germany.

Sergeant Ray Mason
SOE wireless operator
We were called into Rustem Buildings, into one of the offices, to see a colonel, I think, who asked us if we would volunteer for the same sort of operation in the Far East. All seven of us said, 'No thank you very much.' To be mixed up with a German-occupied territory was one thing but to be mixed up with a Japanese-occupied territory was an entirely different kettle of fish. So he said, 'Hang on, we'll give you at least ten days' leave in England before

you go and we'll pay you another ten shillings a day' – which was very unusual. So of course we were dying to get a bit of leave in England and that decided us, really. So we all said yes, we would volunteer. I suppose he thought we were very mercenary, but still.

Major Robert Boiteux
SOE officer
I was an old man then. I should have left the army, I could have found myself a good job in London, but I wanted more adventure.

Sergeant John Ellis
SOE wireless operator
We were going to get enhanced danger money and extra pay as well, but that wasn't really the point. By now we were professional troops for that kind of job, working behind the lines. When I say it held no fears for us, it wasn't a strange experience any more. So we agreed. We shipped out on a trooper to India and then on down to Ceylon, where we had a base. From that base we made up new teams.

Sergeant Jack Grinham
SOE wireless operator
We didn't know exactly where we were going to operate. We knew it would be somewhere in south-east Asia. There was the Burma country section, the Siam country section, the French Indochina country section and the Malaya country section. I went to the Burma country section. It was just the luck of the draw.

Burma

Major Dick Rubinstein
SOE officer, Team 'Chimp'
Burma was just beginning to boil and it was just the right time. The army was really beginning to break out and come down on Mandalay and then on to Rangoon and this was a time when the paramilitaries could really make a contribution.

Sergeant Glyn Loosmore
SOE wireless operator, Special Group 'Mongoose'
They divided us into two main groups: things that they called Jedburgh

operations, which were to recruit the locals, make them into levies and so on, and Special Groups, which were meant to be self-contained fighting units. So I wasn't technically a Jedburgh in Burma, I was a member of a Special Group.

Captain Aubrey Trofimov
SOE officer, Special Group 'Mongoose'
We were to go in and recruit levies from the villagers, send in information back on Jap movements and establish dropping zones and such like. That was reasonable. But at the briefing, 'Peacock Force' started literally quibbling amongst themselves as to who was going to be overall leader. I didn't know the other people, I didn't particularly like them on sight, except for Major Critchley, so whilst this was going on I walked out of the briefing.

I can still see this very clearly. There was a little courtyard and I sat down and thought, 'What am I letting myself in for?' I really felt very confused in my own mind about the whole set up. Suddenly Critchley appeared and he sat down with me. He was a six-foot-four giant and he talked very quietly and he said, 'I know what you're feeling. I saw your face. Forget about the whole set up. We'll go in and you and I will team up and we'll do our own thing.' I took one look at this man and I thought, 'Yes, I can get on with him.' We were duly equipped and were taken out to Dumdum, I think it was, and I'll never forget, as we got into the plane, some wit had put up a placard: 'Is your journey really necessary?'

Captain Oswin Craster
SOE officer, Team 'Zebra'
There was another team going in another aircraft. We looked back and saw it on fire, which wasn't very encouraging. I think they were all burnt.

Sergeant Roger Leney
SOE wireless operator, Special Group 'Mongoose'
There was a mysterious captain with us who I think said his name was Pierce. We only met him boarding the plane. He had two Burmese with him in civilian clothes, local sarongs, shirts and whatnot. Apparently he belonged to some rather mysterious outfit and I think their job was to go down to the Burma–Siam railway and start kidnapping prisoners, virtually living in the shadows, snatching one person at a time and trying to get them away from the railway. After we landed he just took off and we never saw him again.

Major John Smallwood
SOE officer, Team 'Calf'
I dropped into a very good friend of mine, Johnny Shaw, of the Royal Ulster Rifles, who had asked me to go in. He'd been dropped blind with one wireless operator and produced a dropping zone which gave you a very peculiar feeling. It was in a very, very narrow valley and when you looked out of the aircraft you could see the roots of trees at eye level, which is a terrifying thing when you think about it. After we'd landed my sergeant said to me, 'Do you know, sir, I'd never have jumped had it not been for your splendid example.' I said, 'If you'd known how fucking frightened I was, you'd never, ever have followed me.'

Sergeant Norman Smith
SOE wireless operator, Special Group 'Walrus'
The third night we got in and the whole thing was chaos. I heard an enormous crashing and banging. Arthur Denning had landed on one of the burial sites. Out there they put the body on a bamboo table and the scorpions and the buzzards and whatever else nosh up on that, you see. I didn't know where I was. A container nearly killed me.

Sergeant Roger Leney
SOE wireless operator, Special Group 'Mongoose'
I came down and landed with a bit of a bang and I then noticed there were quite a lot of bamboo sticking up in the air from the ground, because the Japanese had stuck these sharpened bamboo spikes up all over the field to stop parachute drops.

Sergeant Donald Gibbs
SOE wireless operator, Special Group 'Walrus'
I landed in a tree. The parachute caught in the upper branches and I was left suspended a few feet above the ground and I couldn't get out. Suddenly it all gave way and I fell on my back and into a ditch and lost my pistol. I also broke my glasses. Villagers led me back to the rest of the party and it turned out that the advance party had had casualties. One of the Burmese had been strangled to death. He'd landed in a tree and had been strangled by his kit coming up round his neck.

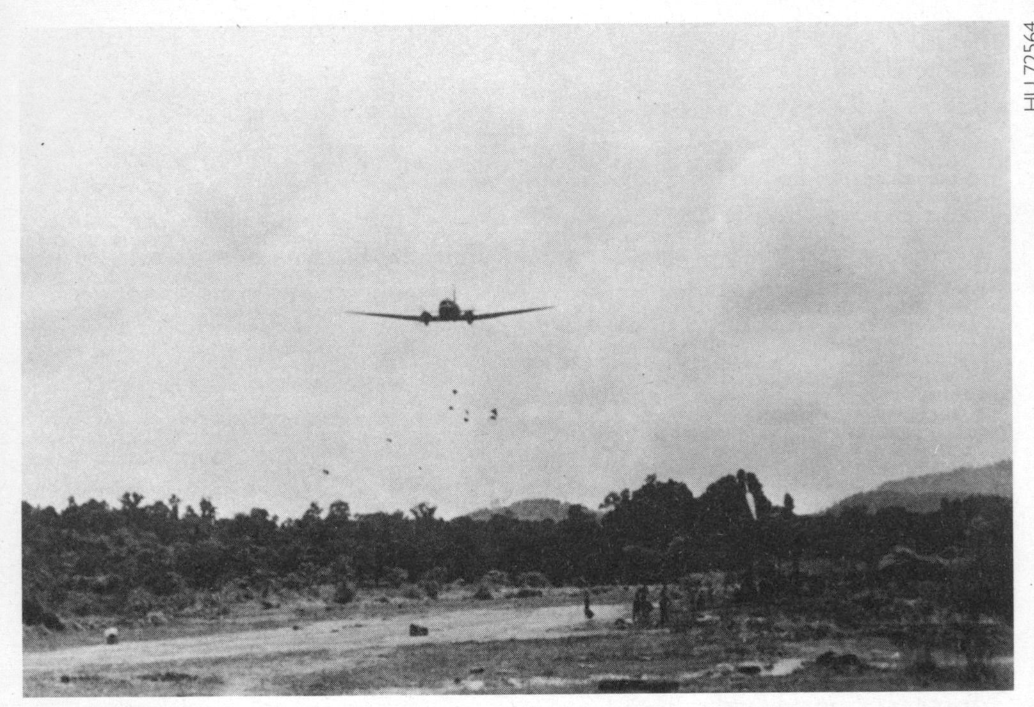

HU 72564

Dakota dropping supplies to an SOE mission in Burma, 1945.

Captain Duncan Guthrie
SOE officer, Special Group 'Walrus'

I was coming down into trees and I remembered somebody saying to me once that if you find yourself falling into trees, you'd be very wise to cross your legs, for obvious reasons. And I thought, 'Yes, I've crossed my legs certainly,' and I sailed down. But they weren't trees. In the moonlight they looked like trees but they were little shrubs, about two foot six high, and, of course, I landed on the ground with my legs crossed and my ankle went just like that. I was in incredible pain and I lay there for a bit and I heard people vaguely shouting for me, and one wondered whether the Japs, who must have heard or seen the parachute operation, were on their way. Then somebody turned up and I gave a shout and said, 'Look, I've broken my leg.'

We all had a little phial of morphine and I found mine and stuck it in my arm, which helped a little bit because the pain was considerable. They made some sort of a stretcher and carried me out of the paddy field into the jungle where I was under cover, so to speak, and I was all rather jolly with the morphine by that time. Then as the morphine wore off and I became a little more rational, I said to myself and to the others, 'You can't carry me, you've got to hide me somewhere. I know you can't carry me. It's quite impossible to lumber yourself with carrying a man flat on his back when the Japs will be up in no time looking for us. You must hide me somewhere and hope for the best.' I was very fortunate that I landed in this part of Burma where the Karens came from and the headman of the village said, 'We will look after him for you.' And for the next three months they looked after me.

Sergeant Glyn Loosmore
SOE wireless operator, Special Group 'Mongoose'

Another group came in a couple of days after us, and we had an accident then. The Japanese weren't far away and we mined the path that they would have come along if they hoped to attack us. When the containers came floating over, one of our helpers, a villager, went charging up this path and of course a mine blew up and blew his leg off. We didn't know quite what to do about this. The poor chap was desperately injured. He wasn't one of ours, he was just a helper, and if the Japanese heard about this they could interrogate him. We just couldn't spend much time looking after him and we had an Indian doctor with us and the officer in charge of the drop wanted the doctor to kill this chap, to put him out of his misery. The doctor was saying, 'No, no, my oath, my oath, I can't do that kind of thing.' The poor chap died while we were arguing about him, so that was the end of that problem.

Sergeant Donald Gibbs
SOE wireless operator, Special Group 'Walrus'
The British Army, the Fourteenth Army, by this time was well into Burma and our operation was to ambush the Japanese with the help of the local people and this is what we did. As soon as we got organised, we got large quantities of arms dropped in and armed the local people. We called them levies. They all got paid small sums and they were very enthusiastic.

Colin Mackenzie
Head, Force 136, India
The Burmese had never made a great success of absorbing or working with their hill tribes. There were the Karens in the middle and south; there were the Kachins, the next important, in the north; the Chins, who were north of Karenni but south of the Kachins; and then there were the Shans, too. All of them in different degrees were against the Burmese. From the very beginning they were actively, or the great bulk of them were, pro-British, because they felt that if they worked with us, they ought to get better conditions.

Captain Robert Barron
SOE officer, Special Group 'Hyena'
The Karens were absolutely excellent. They couldn't do enough for us and they were one hundred per cent for the British. We weren't there to get into main battles with the Japanese initially. Our role was to harass and deny food supplies and so on and ask the Karens in the villages to hide away their stores of food so the Japanese couldn't use them when they were going through the hills and the plains. It was not so easy on the plains of course as it was in the hills. Of course the Karens were in fear of the Japanese, because they were treated very badly, but that didn't stop them from doing whatever they could for the British.

I went down to my particular area on the plains, walking out of the jungle into the foothills with a guide, a Karenni guide, and went to a village. Quite unexpectedly I was ushered into a dimly lit room and there I was met by a room absolutely packed of Karens there to greet me and to question me as to what I was going to do. We had a general talk and I was able to satisfy their enquiries to a certain extent. The next morning I set up my headquarters in the village and started to recruit the people with the help of the headman. Then I arranged an arms drop. It was an excellent drop. He just came over, dropped the containers and went away, not like some occasions when they stooged about a bit. As soon as the containers were on the ground, the bullock carts came out and they put the containers on and away we went, into cover.

Major John Smallwood
SOE officer, Team 'Chimp'
Wherever we went, we were well received. Everyone ran from the village into the mountains, then they would send the oldest woman in, and, if she wasn't killed, they'd send the oldest man in, and then they'd gradually come back. We treated them extremely well. We paid for everything. We were paying in gold and silver and all yellow parachutes went to the Buddhist monks.

Many of the people were very primitive indeed and had never seen a white man in their lives. We began by recruiting Baptist Christians who were Christians theoretically but very steeped in their ancestral backgrounds. We began with that lot and from there we went into the Shans of whom there were several sorts up there: red Shans and yellow Shans and various other ones. After a while we recruited them and we had absolutely no problem politically, as there were no political parties and none of them had any political leanings. There were also some weird people who were animists and they didn't believe in washing – they were washed on birth and washed on death – as water was full of evil spirits, and it was immensely difficult to get them to cross a river. I only had two or three of them.

Sergeant Norman Smith
SOE wireless operator, Special Group 'Walrus'
The Padongs were a hill tribe of people where the brass-necked women every year added another ring so their necks were actually stretched, six inches to a foot. That's why they were known as the giraffe-necked women. They were very anti-Burmese, they hated the Burmese, and the Burmese hated them because they were hill people. I was only twenty-one, then. I had no fear of them at all. They used to sit round and they'd hold your hand and they couldn't believe the whiteness. They were all talking in this funny language, looking at your fingernails, looking at your eyes, because they'd never seen a white bloke before.

The Padongs became the most marvellous fighters. And my fondest memory is that, with me being a radio operator, I was like a god, because I could tell them, 'This afternoon there will be aeroplanes coming.' And sure enough, all being well, aeroplanes would come. The first drop that came, they all got their swords out and they were fighting each other for parachutes, they weren't worried about the containers. 'Out with the swords, lads!' There was only me there, so I fired a few shots in the air and they all quietened down and we got all the stuff back to the place where we were. Then we got them all binoculars, because they liked our binoculars. They'd crawl up the wrong side of a hill, when they were attacking the Japanese or the Japanese were attacking us, get out their big navy binoculars and the chiefs would all stand up on the top of the hill, being shot at, peering away like this. Then we got a doctor dropped in and they'd bring the wounded and they never groaned. They might have been carried four or five days with all their stomach hanging out. Not a word.

Captain Aubrey Trofimov
SOE officer, Special Group 'Mongoose'
We did a lot of toing and froing, looking through the area. Some of the marches were diabolical because all the tracks go to the tops of the mountains and come down again. It goes back to the old days when the Karens were attacked by the Burmese, when they always withdrew back up to the top of the mountains, so all the damned tracks went up to the top and down again. The first month or two, until your stamina level grew, was pretty hellish. The most awful part of it was the insects.

Captain Oswin Craster
SOE officer, Team 'Zebra'
Up and down, up and down, through bamboo woods with the occasional teak tree. It was very, very hard work, though we had these local guides, up and down these paths. Sometimes you had to go up the beds of streams. We'd arrived, of course, with these vast great rucksacks with sixty pounds of stuff inside them, mostly ammunition, very heavy, but of course the Burmese carried them. They didn't put them on their backs. Two of them slung one rucksack on a pole between them.

We were given some benzedrine pills, to keep us awake. I took some, the moon rose, we were all lying around in the open there, and I was the only one awake, which was lucky, really, because I was able to give everybody a jolly good kick and get the show on the road again. People complain about drugs and how it kills them. I reckon they saved our lives. They were very addictive. You could walk along and you'd walk on air. It was absolutely marvellous.

Sergeant Roger Leney
SOE wireless operator, Special Group 'Mongoose'
Malaria was very bad out there. In fact at one time, at the height of the monsoon, when we were out of radio contact and not getting supplies in, we

ran out of mepacrine tablets, and I think we had at least half our strength down at any one time with malaria.

Sergeant Harry Verlander
SOE wireless operator, Special Group 'Walrus'
Major Bowles was taken ill at one time. I think it was only malaria but he was pretty ill and we had to leave him in a cave with a few supplies. In Burma if anybody was injured or ill there wasn't much you could do with them and if we had to move on it was understood that they'd have to be left behind. So we left him, with a few supplies and his gun, but fortunately he did get better and was picked up later and brought back to the group, so he got away with it.

Sergeant Norman Smith
SOE wireless operator, Special Group 'Walrus'
We were lucky. Where we were, we were quite high up and there were no mosquitoes. We weren't in the jungle; it was like tea estate country, you didn't need mozzie nets. They were no snakes, no mozzies. A few of us had amoebic dysentery. That was unpleasant.

Sergeant Gordon Tack
SOE wireless operator, Team 'Pig'
Ants were a problem. You had to watch out for them as they travelled in columns. You could hear the ants coming, because they buzzed, they rustled, and you just got out of there, sharpish. The snakes invariably didn't trouble you. They mainly travelled across the tops of trees. They were more scared of me than I was of them, I think.

Sergeant Neville Wood
SOE wireless operator, Special Group 'Walrus'
They gave us a little phial of salt tablets and said, 'Take these every day,' and I religiously took them. A lot of people didn't take salt regularly and they'd get scratches on their legs that would turn ulcerous. Mine didn't. I kept fairly free. I had a friend who had ulcers and he could dig them out with a spoon.

Sergeant Donald Gibbs
SOE wireless operator, Special Group 'Walrus'
Most of the Karen villages were on the tops of hills or close to the tops of hills. Water was very scarce and had to be fetched up in pots so we didn't wash very often, certainly never had a bath, and we all had beards.

Sergeant Harry Verlander
SOE wireless operator, Special Group 'Walrus'
We had our jungle-green wear. That was torn and worn. It didn't last very long in the jungle. Boots didn't last long either so most of the time we were barefoot and wearing very little clothes. We became as wild as the country we were living in.

Sergeant Fred Bailey
SOE wireless operator, Team 'Cow'
Food-wise the diet was rice mixed with some tree roots; chicken, if you happened to pass through a village; and we shot one or two monkeys and ate those. Once we shot a barking deer and ate that, plus bully beef and bits and pieces we got from the supply drops.

Sergeant Neville Wood
SOE wireless operator, Special Group 'Walrus'
The Japanese would come into a village and they'd take what they wanted. They'd pinch the women; they'd pinch the cattle, chickens, rice. They'd pinch a cow in one village and drive it along and next time they wanted a meal they'd cut a steak off its rump and drive it along to the next village. The beast would be howling in agony by then. After about two or three days of cutting steaks off they'd kill it and eat it. They'd do all sorts of horrible things, the Japs.

Major Tom Carew
SOE officer, Team 'Weasel'
People of my height are two a penny now but going back a lot of years they were not. And when I walked through the paddy fields my footprint was enormous and that wasn't very clever. So I used to have somebody walking behind me treading it in, so that there was nothing left there. But my real trick was – when I told the people when I came back, they were furious with me – I got teams of small boys, I think three teams of small boys, and they formed a screen which went in front of me. And I said, 'When you see a Japanese, get a piece of mud out and sling it at him and show your arse at him and then run back and tell me where they are.' So this screen went out and I was able to progress through Burma with this screen of boys. I used to have one lot back, put another screen out and of course if was marvellous. I didn't believe, you see, in carrying a rifle and things. I had a pistol. That was all I carried because I thought that if I got to that stage I was finished anyway. The thing was not to get caught.

Major John Smallwood
SOE officer, Team 'Chimp'
The SOE motto should have been, and I always taught people this, 'He who fights and runs away, lives to fight another day.' In my view we were too valuable to be slaughtered unnecessarily. I hope we weren't frightened and did our duty but the object was to annoy people, to the maximum, and stay alive. It was very expensive getting you here, they had trained you and bothered with you, and it was a great mistake to go and get yourself killed.

Sergeant Gordon Tack
SOE wireless operator, Team 'Pig'
We were going across country when we were betrayed by the driver of a bullock cart that we were travelling in and we were ambushed by the INA, the Indian National Army, a section of the Japanese Army composed entirely of Indians. They surrounded us and ordered us to surrender. Captain Brown went in to try and negotiate with them and left us still surrounded. When it was obvious that he wasn't going to be able to negotiate any sort of freedom, Major Cox, Captain Read and myself got shoulder-to-shoulder with our guns and shot a hole in the Indians. We then ran through the hole. They stayed together and I went off on my own for about six days and five nights. I didn't eat anything at all and drank paddy field water. I stayed undercover all day and travelled only at night. I kept clear of all the villages. You could always tell when you were coming near a village because the dogs barked.

Sergeant David Cottingham
SOE wireless operator, Special Group 'Otter'
Our job was a killing mission. We used to put grenade traps along the main tracks when they knew any Japs were coming, lay these grenade traps a hundred yards long, and the Japs used to walk in and pull the string and away the grenades went, grenades strung together on cortex: an instantaneous explosion. We concentrated on laying grenade traps in the fireplaces in the empty villages, so that when the Japs cooked their rice, bang! And we got quite a few casualties there. We didn't bother to go down to see but we could hear the grenades banging. And we knocked the road traffic off, Japanese moving up to the front line. We'd throw grenades into the back of the trucks.

Sergeant Neville Wood
SOE wireless operator, Special Group 'Walrus'
We used to get a drop of explosives in, about a mile or two from the main

road, and we'd mine the road with about a ton of explosives. And then, when the Japanese columns came down, we'd let it go. Then we'd run up and open fire with everything we'd got for about two minutes and then run away. After two minutes it was no longer a surprise.

Sergeant Harry Verlander
SOE wireless operator, Special Group 'Walrus'
Hit and run raids, all the time. It went pretty well.

Sergeant Roger Leney
SOE wireless operator, Special Group 'Mongoose'
If you knew there was a Japanese group coming and you knew virtually how many there were, you could set up an ambush on the track by finding a suitable spot where you could get the Japs concentrated in your line of fire. The orders were that everybody fired one magazine of ammunition and then ran like hell. Very often you could stop a Jap patrol by sticking something like a cigarette tin in the middle of the track. The Japs would arrive and would see this object sitting in the middle of the track and they would then stop and virtually have a conference over it, get in a group. They would start looking all ways and you could hit them.

Sergeant Glyn Loosmore
SOE wireless operator, Special Group 'Mongoose'
I remember going down on one ambush and we had white phosphorus and we'd thrown this and it lit up a whole platoon of them, tramping along the road. A Japanese NCO had stood up in the middle of all this, quite clearly in all the phosphorous light, getting the men down, getting them firing, without any concern at all for his own safety. Very impressive soldiering. But of course we didn't have much sympathy for them because they were abominable to the Karens.

Major Dick Rubinstein
SOE officer, Team 'Chimp'
If the parties were big we had to let them go but we could bring an air strike down on them. If the parties were small we could deal with them ourselves. We were quite successful. We had fantastic luck in picking up what seemed to be a headquarters party. We dealt with them, it was just a party of about seventeen Japs, but when we went to see what we'd done we found a chap wearing major generals' tabs and a number of other senior officers.

Sergeant Ron Brierley
SOE wireless operator, Team 'Reindeer'
We made that our base in Kywebwe, a small village on the edge of the jungle about 150 miles north of Rangoon, about thirty miles south of Toungoo. We knew it was an area where there was loyal, local support from the Burmans, who'd had quite enough of the Japanese by that time and were willing to co-operate and work with us. We had a group of about 250 men based on Kywebwe, loyal as they come, and a tremendous intelligence network in the Sittang valley. By the time we'd been there three or four weeks, every time a Japanese soldier went to the toilet we knew. It really was quite incredible. We were so successful in our setting of ambushes and the like that we forced the Jap in the Sittang valley to move entirely at night. Not only were we able to organise ambushes but we were also able, after the RAF had established themselves in the Mandalay area, to call on literally cab ranks of RAF fighter planes and direct them on to the targets.

Sergeant Neville Wood
SOE wireless operator, Special Group 'Walrus'
The Japs used to send wounded people back to the hospitals, back through the hills, maybe half a dozen men with a corporal and one rifle. We used to call them 'weary willies'. The natives would say 'There's a party of x number' and we'd go along and kill them. The Japs only gave them a rifle and about ten rounds of ammo, so, by the time they'd exhausted that, they were fairly easy meat. We did that dozens of times.

Sergeant Roger Leney
SOE wireless operator, Special Group 'Mongoose'
It was not only our patrols that were dealing with Jap parties but the local villagers were beginning to pick them off, knocking them off with crossbows. They used crossbows with poisoned arrows, which they normally used for hunting, so they were silent. Sometimes they were shooting them with shotguns but mostly it was crossbows. We used to get quite a procession of villagers who would come in with this woven bag slung over their shoulder and start fishing out things like a Japanese army pay book, badges off Japanese uniforms, Japanese bayonets. Or they would come in with a Japanese rifle and bits of equipment.

Major Dick Rubinstein
SOE officer, Team 'Chimp'
The Burmese were claiming so many casualties amongst the Japanese that I began to question their veracity. Whereupon, for a short period, I was presented with little parcels of green leaves, wrapped up with bamboo string. When I opened these I found they were ears and it was pointed out to me that these were all 'right' ears. I stood this for a few days and then said I'd accept their figures.

Sergeant Maurice Roe
SOE wireless operator, Special Group 'Hyena'
The locals, as far as they were concerned, would kill any Japanese they caught. But once or twice we would be delivered a Japanese and, as soon as you wirelessed you'd got a Japanese prisoner, a Lysander was in to pick him up. The valleys were very tight. I think the Lysander wanted four hundred yards, so you put bamboo markers out every fifty yards, but we hadn't got four hundred yards so we put the bamboo markers out at forty yards but didn't let on: let the pilot suppose they were the same fifty yards that he expected. But what could you do? These were tight valleys.

Sergeant Ronald Eric Chatten
SOE wireless operator, Special Group 'Ferret'
There was one came near us and I thought he was drunk when they got him. He was wandering about on his own. In civilian life he was a chef in a hotel in Tokyo. They brought him back and they didn't know what to do with him and one of these gurkhas, the sergeant, came to me one night and said, 'Japanese says he doesn't want to leave, he'll stop here with us and do our cooking.' And when we left the camp – they'd dropped replacements in for us – we left him there and he was actually crying when we left. He wanted to come away with us. He was as happy as a cuckoo with us. There was only one trouble with him. If you was in the camp, trying to read a book or something, nothing to do, he'd create all afternoon, every ten minutes, 'Cuppa tea? Cuppa tea?'

Sergeant Harry Verlander
SOE wireless operator, Special Group 'Walrus'
We had no facilities for keeping captives, so none were taken.

Sergeant Donald Gibbs
SOE wireless operator, Special Group 'Walrus'
The operation as a whole was remarkably successful. Thousands of Japanese were killed by the various levies; they were demoralised and short of ammunition and weapons; a lot of them were sick. You could call it murder.

Sergeant Harry Verlander
SOE wireless operator, Special Group 'Walrus'
The Japanese started hunting us after a while. One particular group not far from us were surrounded and attacked. We could hear the shooting across the hills and the valleys and there was one officer who arrived almost naked in our camp one morning: he'd escaped from being attacked. It wasn't long after when the Japs arrived at our small camp and we got chased out.

Sergeant Norman Smith
SOE wireless operator, Special Group 'Walrus'
The Japs used to sling sixty men at you, and they were bloody good. If you could get a couple of hours' notice you could be long gone, as long as the natives were with you and didn't sell you out, which our lot wouldn't do.

Sergeant Harry Verlander
SOE wireless operator, Special Group 'Walrus'
The Japanese surrounded us on a hill. There was a valley most of the way round it and high ground at the far side and they made a determined effort to finish us off. They dropped mountain artillery and quite a few mortars and they started bombarding us on this hillock. It went on for several days. We asked for supplies – we were getting very low on ammunition – and something new was tried: they sent over small planes with just one container slung underneath. And small planes like Lysanders came over and just dropped the box of ammunition out without any parachute on it. This worked quite well on the small ammunition, like 9-millimetre, but anything larger, like rifle bullets for the Lee Enfield rifles, were damaged. And for well over a week, as soon as the stuff hit the ground, we were breaking open the boxes and firing them back continuously. The ammunition was being used as fast as it arrived. Then one morning the Japanese had withdrawn. Whether we'd hit back hard enough or whether they'd given up and had other things to do, I don't know, but one morning it was all over. They'd gone. None of the Europeans had got touched at all; although mortars and rifle fire had been firing at us for a week quite continuously, nobody had got hit. It was rather surprising, as there was

HU 72565

Westland Lysander on the ground behind Japanese lines in Burma, 1945.

quite a lot of stuff flying about. We lost a few of the Padongs, but it was their ferociousness in fighting back that saved us.

Sergeant Norman Smith
SOE wireless operator, Special Group 'Walrus'
We were only supplied with a limited amount of bullets by airdrop: obviously there was plenty of people around having drops, besides us. The only local bloke that spoke much English was a chap who had been at the missionary school so, somewhere along the line, Denning said to him, 'We can only give you fifty rounds a head, because you're shooting off too much ammunition.' One day, Denning was away and I was on the landing zone waiting to get a drop and all these lads came up. They were Nagas, who used to do some work for us, and they had their baskets on their backs, held by a band on their heads. I saw this lot coming up and I thought, 'Yeah, this is great.' I thought it was presents, you see, that they'd unearthed loads of silver or loot for the white gods. Then I noticed all the flies. They all came down and they all bowed and put their baskets down and they all lifted the lids off and in each basket was Japanese heads. And they said, 'You said fifty rounds a head. Here's some heads. Where's the bullets?'

Major John Smallwood
SOE officer, Team 'Calf'
The Royal Air Force was absolutely miraculous from the point of view of supplies. They were super. We'd been warned that we wouldn't get supplies during the monsoon and we thought we'd live on the country, which we did, but they did go on flying right through the monsoon. They took endless trouble coming in, made several circuits and very low drops. They were absolutely great and I have the highest possible respect for them. Of course they lost a lot of aircraft doing it.

Sergeant Norman Smith
SOE wireless operator, Special Group 'Walrus'
You couldn't praise the pilots enough. The Dakotas and the others were unarmed. Sometimes we had to switch off the radar and put the fires out. They were flying round the mountains in these big bombers, in bad weather, low visibility, and we switched them off even though we needed the stuff. We couldn't risk it.

Sergeant Neville Wood
SOE wireless operator, Special Group 'Walrus'
A plane crashed. It had 28,000 Indian rupees on board. The colonel said, 'Go down there and collect up what you can.' So I went down there and the villagers were a bit naughty. I told them if they didn't give up what they'd got I'd burn the village down. As war goes on, you get more into it and you do things that you'd never, ever contemplate doing in a civilian environment.

Sergeant Maurice Roe
SOE wireless operator, Special Group 'Hyena'
We received two officers and we were sitting around the campsite chatting, probably having a drink, and they said something about Truman. I said, 'Who's Truman?' 'Oh, Roosevelt's dead. Truman's the new President.' And we went on chatting and suddenly it came out that the war had been over for two weeks in Europe. Nobody had told us. I suppose the people in Calcutta who were sending the operational messages never thought of putting at the end of one of them, 'The war in Europe's over.'

Sergeant Ron Brierley
SOE wireless operator, Team 'Reindeer'
Burma is a country divided by three major rivers: the Irrawaddy, the Sittang and the Salween. They run virtually north to south, there's very little lateral communication in Burma, and the Sittang is the river at whose most southernmost point is Rangoon. And one anticipated, if the pressure from Fourteenth Army was going to come from the north, as one was expecting, then eventually the Japanese would have to withdraw up the Sittang river from Rangoon and move east, to a place called Mawchi, and on into Indochina. That was the way back to China and Japan. By this time the 17th Indian Division and the 19th Indian Division had come down the valley, they'd taken Toungoo, and really the Jap now ceased to exist in recognisable unit form so far as troops coming out of Rangoon were concerned. But what was now happening was that the Japanese divisions that had been fighting in the Arakan were now filtering through the jungle, coming down the Sittang valley, and then working their way back to Toungoo and across to Mawchi. And so, from fighting and all the guerrilla activity that we'd had in the Sittang valley, we suddenly had to turn our attention to these Japanese units that were coming across from the Arakan.

Major Dick Rubinstein
SOE officer, Team 'Chimp'
Towards the end of May '45, the Japs were massing and were going to break out east. 'Reindeer' had a big mileage to try to patrol and wanted help. 'Reindeer' had been a team of Major Dave Britton, Captain Jock Waller and Sergeant Ron Brierley, all of whom had been in France in their different operations. The day we arrived at 'Reindeer' headquarters, Dave Britton, who had gone on a patrol in tall grass, was killed. Dave was a very brave bloke, he had gone out on a patrol towards the river and he was probably the only head standing up above this grass and he was shot in the neck. So the upshot was that I took over 'Reindeer'.

Three of us were covering a length of about thirty miles, north to south. We'd each got forces, we'd each got perhaps 150 people, and they were patrolling, keeping in touch with the Japanese who were building up for their break-out. And eventually they broke out, July-time. We had been able to tell the army almost exactly what was happening and they told us to look after the river lines, so we put our lads out on to the river. Any Japanese who were able to break across the road and the big valley eventually came through this tall grass to the riverbank, and our chaps let them build rafts and push out into the water and then they'd open fire on them. I remember the river was just full of bodies; for about three days it was full of bodies. Our 500 chaps probably dealt with several thousand. It was carnage.

Sergeant Roger Leney
SOE wireless operator, Special Group 'Mongoose'
We set up base in a village on the side of a hill overlooking the Shwegyin River. Freddie Milner then deployed the troops right up and down the river, so we had people in little foxholes dug in along the riverbank. The Japs were then massing on the other side of the river, which was, I suppose, a hundred yards wide and coming down in full flood, a really torrential river. Trofimov came up with his group of levies from further south and joined us for support. Over something like a fifteen- to twenty-mile stretch of river, we were just dotted along, all within range of each other, holding this river with the Japs massing on the other side.

Captain Aubrey Trofimov
SOE officer, Special Group 'Mongoose'
It was really quite shattering. The Japs would come at dawn, or sometimes just before dark, and they would come over in masses and they would fire at us of

course. They would have so many people firing at us while the others were building rafts with bundles of bamboo canes, putting one hand over them and sort of drifting down the river. Well, we blew those things out of the water.

Sergeant Roger Leney
SOE wireless operator, Special Group 'Mongoose'
Every time they tried to cross, the Karens just knocked them off. They always tried to cross at night and it was a question of shooting at anything that you saw coming down the river, because they would try hanging on to bamboo or branches or anything. Anything you saw moving in the river, branches or debris, anything got shot at. Down at Shwegyin they were more or less counting the bodies as they were floating down. I think, in total, there were about three thousand Japanese killed on the Shwegyin River.

This went on night after night after night. All night long there was firing with the Karens trying to stop them. I was giving weather reports daily to the RAF, weather reports on the hour, but conditions were extremely bad, it was raining, it was very, very low cloud, and we were getting short of ammunition. The situation got so bad that one night we were down to one magazine per man, I think. Freddie Milner came up from the river and he said, 'Well, if we don't get any ammunition today, this is it. If you hear firing tonight, if we haven't had in any ammunition today, pack everything up. Take your boys and go back to the old camp and stay there, keep in radio contact, and hopefully we'll try and join you.' We virtually said goodbye to each other.

That afternoon there was a bit of a break in the clouds and I suddenly heard a Lysander coming. I shouted, 'Quick, make smoke, light the fires!' We had these fires laid ready, we ran down there like hell and this Lysander appeared out of the clouds, flying about twenty feet above ground, and he came down and saw the paddy field. The hood was open at the back and the chap in the back cockpit was throwing sacks of ammunition out. I then got every villager I could lay my hands on and got people with baskets and sand bags full of ammunition and shot it all down to the river. That was enough ammunition to keep them going that night, to hold them off.

When the weather improved, Dakotas came in virtually every day. Sometimes we had two or three drops a day if it was a good day. The Japs were trying to shoot at them with small arms and rifles as they did their circuit over the river; in fact, they tried lobbing small mortar bombs up at them. This was getting worrying and we thought one of these Dakotas was sooner or later going to get hit. Then a Dakota came in one morning, he came straight in and dropped a lot of stuff out of the door, turned and went over the river and there was a whole series of explosions and we were very worried. In fact, the dispatchers on the plane, who were bunging the stuff out, had taken on board a crate of hand grenades. As they went over the river they were busy pulling the pins out of the hand grenades and lobbing them out of the door to keep the Japs' heads down.

Sergeant Ron Brierley
SOE wireless operator, Team 'Reindeer'
The extent of the damage and mayhem that we created amongst the occupying forces in Burma was really quite something. Maybe the lessons one had learned in Europe were more readily translatable into a country that certainly does lend itself to guerrilla warfare. I mean, these three great rivers with three great plains and the rest of the country being ideal bandit country for want of a better name, where you can just hide out with very little chance of being caught. There was very little chance of aerial reconnaissance picking you out in that incredibly concentrated and deep jungle of Burma. And it was a classic area where the weaponry that you had at your disposal was quite adequate. You weren't taking on a Panzer division. You weren't taking on a highly modernised, mechanised, mobile army. You were dealing mainly with lightly armed soldiers. Guerrillas and resistance people become unstuck badly when they do try to take on these major targets which are far beyond their capability. It's easy enough to shoot a sentry but to take a Tiger tank on is not a recipe for success.

Sergeant Glyn Loosmore
SOE wireless operator, Special Group 'Mongoose'
Force 136 achieved, I think, far more in Burma than the Jedburghs achieved in France, although I suppose people will dispute it. Force 136 impeded the Japanese in the race to get to Toungoo. After that, when the Japanese were reassembling in the Pegu Yomas, there was a line of regular British troops down in the valley and Force 136 up in the hills, to the east, and the breakout was a massacre. Force 136 kept a game-book, talked about killing Japanese as if you were bagging animals, claimed thirty thousand Japanese casualties.

Sergeant Roger Leney
SOE wireless operator, Special Group 'Mongoose'
The Karens did not want us to leave. By the end of the war you had a Labour government who were giving Burma back to the Burmese. The Karens were terrified about being left under the thumb of the Burmese. All the ethnic hill

HU 72571

Japanese train derailed by SOE saboteurs in Burma, 1945.

tribes in Burma were in general quite hostile to the Burmese because the Burmese did not treat them properly. The Karens were quite desperate that they wanted to eventually become an independent nation, as part of the British Commonwealth. They wanted the British officials to stay and govern them until such time they could run their own affairs. Of course this didn't happen. I think a lot of us who were Jeds in Force 136 in Burma felt the Karens were betrayed at the end of the war.

Captain Oswin Craster
SOE officer, Team 'Zebra'
I think we looked after all the hill tribes quite well. And I think it's quite disgraceful how we abandoned them all.

Siam and Indochina

Major David Smiley
SOE officer, Siam
The Japanese had occupied Siam and Siam was at war with us; they were forced by the Japanese to declare war on us. There were various groups of guerrillas; I was the first British officer to be parachuted in and my job was to try and get supply drops for them, then train them. There was quite a lot of Japanese about in the area but the Siamese were completely double-crossing the Japanese. On most occasions, for instance, I used to get a message from the Siamese Army saying, 'We've got to lead the Japanese to one of your camps. Will you please go away?' We'd go away and the Siamese would lead the Japanese to an empty camp.

I really had rather a good time until I had a most ghastly accident. Someone came dashing into the camp, saying the Japanese were about half a mile away and we must scram. I had with me a briefcase, which was made by the special effects people in SOE. It had six pounds of thermite in the bottom and could be used either as a booby trap – you could leave it and whoever opened it would blow themselves up – or, if you wanted to destroy secret documents and things, you could put the documents in the brief case, press a button and after about five seconds it would explode. And I was packing my code-books and various signals I'd received into this briefcase when it exploded in my hands. Must have short-circuited somewhere. Six pounds of thermite blew up and I was extremely badly burnt. My hands and knees were burnt; my face was burnt; my eyes were closed: I'd shut my eyes when the thing went off and I couldn't open them again. I was nearly three weeks in Siam before they got me out. My wireless operator and Kong, this medical student, looked after me. There were no medical supplies. They told me to keep the burns wrapped up which I did with parachute stuff. It was all very painful. Then I got maggots in my wounds.

Sergeant Ed Lawson
SOE wireless operator, Siam
I hadn't been in Calcutta very long when one day I was told to report to SOE's Siamese country section building. I went into the office and there was a man in a green and gold dress hat with a large walrus moustache. 'Sergeant,' he said. 'We drop in Siam tomorrow.'

We went out to the airstrip at about 11am. There stood a specially converted long-range Liberator. Some of these aircraft could stay in the air for almost twenty-four hours. On the nose of the aircraft there was a cartoon-like figure of a gentleman with a tall black opera hat, a black red-lined cloak and he was clutching a round anarchistic smoking bomb behind his back. The plane was named, very aptly I thought, 'Vernon the Villain': a very suitable aircraft for cloak-and-dagger operations.

At the back of the plane was a small wooden chute. Winn was jumping number one and I was to jump number two and we had to sit in this chute so that we would speed down clearing the tail with our parachutes. I asked Kemp to check that I was fully secured and pinned up but he was very vague. I noticed that Winn, as he waited for action stations to come, was intoning, as we thought, a prayer. Later we discovered he wasn't in fact praying but intoning from Noël Coward, very appropriately, 'Mad dogs and Englishmen go out in the midday sun.' The lights went on, Winn shot out, I pulled my legs into the wooden chute and I too shot out under the tail and almost immediately my parachute opened.

Major Peter Kemp
SOE officer, Siam
We had had to fly a long way over Burma and a lot of Siam because we were being dropped right in the north-east, almost by the Mekong river, which was the frontier with what was then French Indochina. Up till March the French in Indochina had been treated rather like those in Vichy France. Then the Japanese suddenly struck and killed all the men they could find and imprisoned the women and children, and a lot of them were in a very bad way. There were a few French officers with some Laotian irregulars holding out in

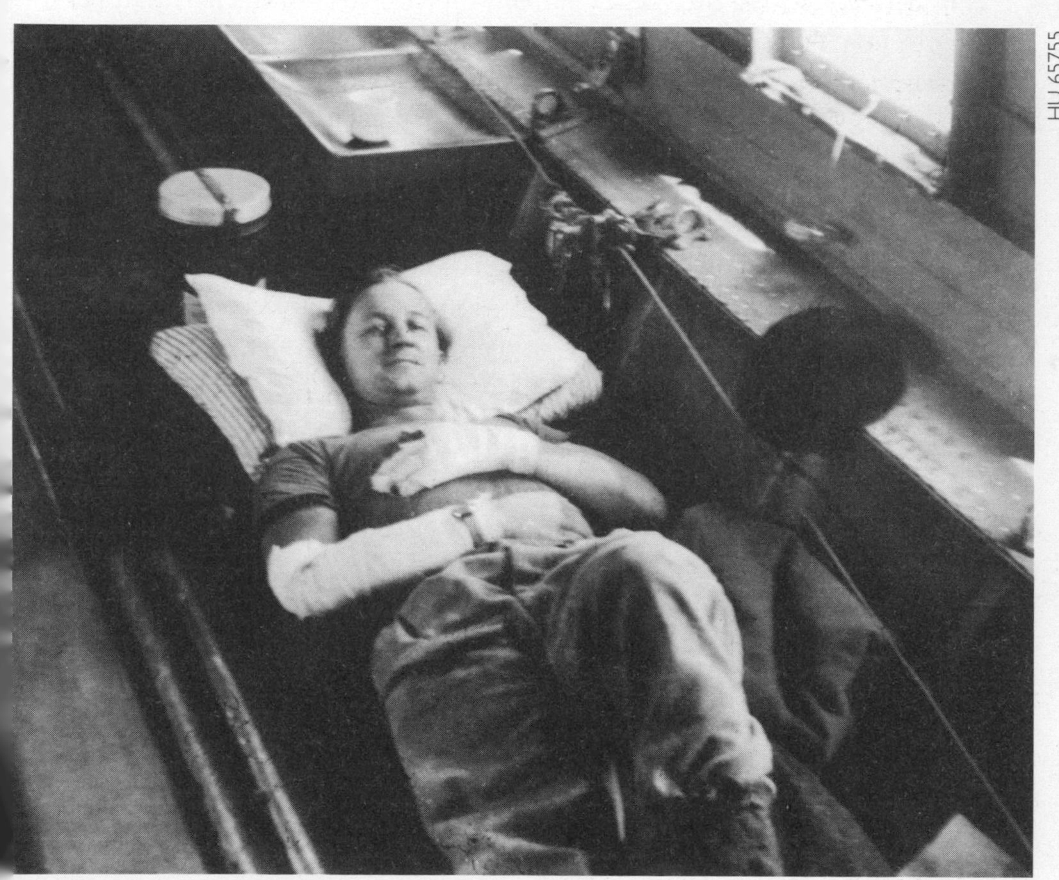
HU 65755

David Smiley being airlifted out of Siam after an accident with his incendiary briefcase, June 1945.

the jungle against the Vietminh, the communist Vietnamese, and our job was to help them and the refugees. That involved night journeys across the river with arms, food and medicines.

Colin Mackenzie
Head, Force 136, India
OSS was pouring money into the Vietminh – Ho Chi Minh – because they considered they were good democrats and they would fight the Japanese, but they had no intention of fighting the Japanese. They knew the Japanese were beaten by that time and were leaving and they were merely collecting stuff to use it against anybody, which turned out eventually to be the Americans themselves, who got in the way of them establishing what they meant to be a real communist state.

Captain Neville Hogan
SOE officer, Burma–Siam border
We got our orders and I flew and was dropped in the Ye area of the Tenasserim with a view to covering the Three Pagodas Pass. We were overlooking, or near, prisoner of war camps but had to await a signal to move in to give medical supplies to the doctors to treat the poor, starving prisoners of war. On two, possibly three, occasions, however, I went into the camps at one, two in the morning, taking with me M&B 693, mepacrine, quinine, but no bandages or gentian violet because that would show up and the Japs would know that medical supplies were being smuggled in. I was reprimanded for it, in case the medicines were found and reprisals were taken against the doctors.

The Dutch East Indies and Borneo

Sergeant Jim Chambers
SOE wireless operator, SOE HQ, Morotai Island, Dutch East Indies
One operation they were carrying out from Morotai was in a Catalina flying boat. They would go to nearby islands that were occupied by Japanese troops and they'd land on the sea. Invariably some of the locals would come out in their canoes and on a few occasions a luckless person would be dragged into the Catalina and flown off back to base, where he'd be interrogated about all the Japanese on the island. On one occasion the Catalina went out and the team actually went on to the island and they got involved in a gunfight with the Japanese and one of the Australian officers was killed. He did the

unforgivable: he went up to a Japanese body that was laying down and that he thought was dead but the man wasn't dead and he picked his gun up and shot the officer.

Major Bob Martin
SOE officer, Borneo

The natives themselves, what natives there were around, built their houses on huge rafts, there were no houses on land, and they used to move with long poles from A to B. We got a tremendous amount of intelligence from these villages, because they were moving the whole time, going around to various other raft villages, finding out movements of the Japanese and so on. They had been treated very badly by the Japanese. I suggested to Dave, 'Why shouldn't we recruit some of these men from the raft villages to reinforce our outposts?' He thought it was a good idea. I said, 'Let's get some rifles and we can train them to fire them and pay them' – which would give the villages an income. We spoke to the villagers about this and we said that we would probably need up to forty. They thought it was great. So off went the signal and in came another aircraft loaded with four boxes of .303 Lee Enfields. Instead of dropping these darned rifles with parachutes, they free-dropped them, they just pushed them out, with the result that only one of the four boxes dropped within reach. So I got a party together of locals and I said, 'If we can only find one more box in the swamp, it would help.' Well, we went out into the swamps, up to our armpits, feeling with our feet for a box, when the leader of their party said, 'No further.' They were scared of crocodiles. I had no hesitation in getting myself back, too.

Lieutenant Stanley Eadie
SOE officer, Borneo

The Japs had withdrawn a lot of their troops to be together to combat the Allied invasion of Borneo, which had started on Labuan Island and then moved on to the mainland. We finished up at the only town in the area; there were some Japs there but when they heard we were coming they cleared out. Then the Japs decided that they didn't like us being there and they came back in force to deal with us.

We got word of them going to do this, so we thought we'd ambush them on the way upriver but we hadn't enough people to do very much. Usually they travelled with a small scout craft, then the main big craft and then a small one at the back, and of course on this occasion, unusually, the two small ones were first. So we killed them all but the big one started opening fire on us, too, so we decided it wasn't very healthy and came away. We had canoes planted at the other end of the town and we had left two British NCOs just to cover us and to drop back as soon as we were well away. The Japs started coming up the pathway, so they opened fire and killed a whole lot of them and then came back.

Toby Carter was standing next to his canoe and I was standing next to mine when these two NCOs came running and got in. And just as we were going to get in there was a yell from further up. A group came towards us, two Indian Sikhs who had managed to escape from a prison camp but were so weak they couldn't walk, and four locals who were more or less carrying these two. Toby Carter took one in his canoe and I took one in my canoe. They were just absolutely exhausted.

We went upriver. We weren't followed or anything. The chap in my canoe never moved for ages and then I could see there was a slight movement, so he was still alive. Eventually he did come to and saw me. I don't think he could believe his eyes – a British officer in uniform. And then he must have put his hand down and felt the Bren gun. He looked down at it and he looked at me and I just nodded to show him that it was a Bren gun and I've never seen such a wonderful smile. He spent the rest of the journey just stroking this Bren gun. He couldn't have lifted it. He couldn't have done anything with it. We just lifted the two of them out of the canoes when we got to where we were going. Then we made contact with headquarters and they sent in a Catalina the next day and picked them up.

Malaya

Colonel John Davis
SOE officer
By about February, our radio was working so that with tremendous effort, by pedalling the dynamo, we could get a certain amount out of the battery. And our wireless operator, one of the Chinese, managed to get picked up in Ceylon.

Major Richard Broome
SOE officer
By that time, the office at Colombo had come to the conclusion that we were to be written off either as having been captured by the Japanese or dead, because it had been many, many months since we had been in any touch at all. Fortunately they had been keeping a listening watch for us and we sent off

this signal and it was actually heard and reported. But they did suspect that it was probably not genuine, that we were either in the hands of the Japanese or they were using our equipment, so they started sending us security checks, questions and things. It was rather stupid of us – we didn't recognise that they were security checks. We didn't give the right answers and they had got to the point where they had decided that we were off and they were going to hand over the whole operation to D branch, the deception branch.

Fortunately, a Malayan policeman who was over there, a man called Tremlett, said, 'Well, give them one more chance. Let me send a signal which will settle the issue.' And he concocted a signal whose contained details could only be known to him and to one or two of us. He sent a signal referring to Davis' nickname, which was Titus, and referring to my wife's name, which is Tamsin. So when these things came over the penny at last dropped and we realised that they were suspicious of us. The problem then was to concoct a signal which would make it obvious to them that it was not the Japs running the set but us, so we concocted a fairly ribald reply which ended up, 'Are you satisfied now, you bastards? If not, come and pedal the bloody machine yourselves.' And when this arrived in Colombo it was obvious to them that we were still alive.

Well, the next thing that was to happen was physical contact with Colombo. That meant arranging an airdrop. We set up the triangular system of flares for this aeroplane. That was a tremendously exciting time, where we were so worried that we shouldn't be seen that we lit colossal bonfires, which I'm told nearly frightened the aeroplane off when they saw them. Well, they came over and the belly of the thing opened and parachutes came whistling down. The head of the reinforcements was a chap called Jim Hannah and he came up on this moonlit clearing, dressed in his full regalia as a parachutist with his wings on and so on, and he came up to me. We were looking terribly shabby by then, almost dressed in rags. He saluted smartly and brought out his cigarette case and said, 'Have a cigarette, you've been waiting a year for them.' That was a wonderful moment.

Colonel John Davis
SOE officer

Now we were in contact, India undertook to supply arms by aeroplane to the guerrillas, provided they accepted British liaison officers, not actually to command them, but as advisers. And over the next few months, at tremendous speed really, we would indicate where a guerrilla patrol was, an RV would be arranged or sometimes they dropped in blind, and they dropped in these parties. Usually a liaison officer with a wireless set and a large number of arms to fit out the patrol and for training purposes. In this way we rapidly built up a force, arming in the end about 4,500 to 5,000 men, up and down the country. The guerrillas were not intending at that time to do anything of military value. The whole point was that the British invasion was coming in the middle of the country and, as soon as the invasion started, they would come out and attack and disrupt. They were to be a guerrilla attempt to completely disrupt the Japanese communications.

Sergeant Ray Mason
SOE wireless operator
As we reached the coast of Malaya, the Liberator came down to just above sea level, I suppose to avoid the Japanese radar, and then zoomed up over the trees into the higher ground where we were due to drop. The pilot then said to me, 'You'd better get back and get your parachute on. Good luck and safe landing.' So I went back into the rear of the compartment where the dispatcher had put up a slide, like a child's slide, that led to the square opening in the bottom of the Liberator.

The three of us, who by then had got our parachutes on, sat on this slide, looking backwards, just seeing the trees pass below us, and I remember saying to the officer in front of me, 'Can you see the DZ?' He said, 'No, I can't see a thing.' I said, 'You should, because back at Colombo, the conducting officer, when I asked him what sort of DZ it was, he said, "Oh, quite big, as big as Wembley football stadium."' By this time the pilot was dropping our containers, my radio set and various other bits of equipment, and then this chap in front of me said, 'Well, I can see something which looks about the size of No.1 Court at Wimbledon,' which sounded pretty small to me.

Our turn came, the green light came on and out we shot. There was no question of jumping, we just put our feet together and slid down the slide. Very low altitude, actually, not more than about five hundred feet. Our parachutes opened and of course we parted from each other in the air and within seconds I crashed through the trees and the parachute caught in the trees and slowed me down. Then on landing I hit a log across a stream and shot up to my waist in water, feeling quite happy really to be on the ground at all. Then I heard various shouts in the distance and could almost feel people approach me and two Chinese dressed in uniform with the three-star badge, the communist badge, on their caps – they looked like Japanese to me – jumped in the water to release me from my harness and lifted me out.

HU49049

Liberator dropping supplies over Serendah, Malaya, 1945.

Sergeant Gordon Tack
SOE wireless operator
We were dropping into a group that was already there and what we took with us was what they wanted. They wanted a war dog, so we took a war dog, Cleo, an Alsatian bitch. She was killed on the drop. They dropped her by basket, with a parachute on the basket, and the parachute didn't open properly and the basket hit the ground and smashed.

Major George Brownie
SOE officer
We made a blind jump into a spot near Ipoh in Perak. It wasn't exactly our dropping zone but having flown 1,400 miles one could hardly blame the RAF for being just a little bit out of alignment. We all got down safely, we buried our parachutes and having landed in the blukar, the secondary jungle, we headed inland for the better cover of the jungle. After three days our food began to run out and we thought, 'Look, we simply must get into touch with somebody here.'

We barged into a village and I spoke to the headman and said, in Malay of course, 'Are there any Japanese around here? Who are you? And how can we get in touch with the alleged Anti-Japanese Army?' They were very friendly. They fed us, they obviously knew we were in the area and they very soon produced a Chinese gentleman who came into the village, studied us and said, 'Look here, I think you had better come with me and we will hole you up for a bit.' After some days a very senior-looking Chinese came along, questioned us, and then we got down to business and we put ourselves then in the hands of the Malayan People's Anti-Japanese Army, which was completely Chinese of course. We arranged for supply drops of arms and ammunition for them and of course food for ourselves and signalled out such intelligence as we could get.

Sergeant Ray Mason
SOE wireless operator
The idea of the missions in the jungle was not so much sabotage but obtaining intelligence on Japanese movements, troop movements, the state of the defences on the beaches. We had native agents who discovered that sort of information and would come back and tell us, 'South of Penang, a mile from the beach, is a battery of 105-millimetre guns,' and so on and so forth. And all that intelligence would be sent back to Colombo.

Sergeant John Ellis
SOE wireless operator
The Japanese were on occasions actively trying to hunt us out. In Baling there were five thousand troops stationed. They didn't wander into the jungle very often. They certainly never came anywhere where we were as far as I could make out. The only Jap I heard of in the jungle was a sergeant out of their intelligence section. He was captured by the guerrillas and he suffered a very horrendous fate at their hands. They gave him the death of a thousand knife cuts. They found the British Army knife very good for that. They finished him off by tying a hand grenade to him and pulling the pin out with a piece of string. I didn't see it but I heard his screams from up the jungle.

Lloyd Chinfen
SOE wireless operator
I was very frightened at times. In the jungle, because of the thickness of the jungle, you could only see a few feet in front of you and if you were attacked you had very little warning. And there were times when I really enjoyed it. I like open countryside. I'd always had a fancy of being in the jungle. I like walking in the hills. At times it was very pleasant. It rained an awful lot, quite often we had to sleep on the ground just covered with a wet blanket, but mainly our camps were on higher ground and when it was dry it could be quite pleasant.

Sergeant Ray Mason
SOE wireless operator
We reached this jungle camp. There was quite a good set-up there, with palm leaf huts and a cooking area and a radio shack covered in palm leaves. By this time it was dusk and someone had prepared a sort of bed. I put my sleeping bag on to that and the doctor came to have a look at my leg and said, 'Well, it's too dark for me to do anything tonight. I'll have a look in the morning.' I slept quite well and early next morning he came to where I was lying. I was in an American-type sleeping bag, green outside with a whitish nylon interior, and when I zipped it open the doctor was horrified to find about eight or nine things that looked like large sausages were in bed with me. They were actually leeches that had been feeding on me all night.

Sergeant John Ellis
SOE wireless operator
Major Latham, who was rather elderly for the job, somehow got a wound in

HU 66113

Chinese communist guerrillas training with Bren guns in Malaya, 1945.

HU 49057

Chinese communist guerrillas of an SOE patrol in Malaya, 1945.

his leg, in the jungle. One of my extraneous duties was to do the first aid. He didn't want me fiddling about with him so he treated himself but he became very ill so Hislop eventually had to step in and asked me to go and look at his leg. I did so and I didn't like it one little bit. Sergeant Holden was also called over and he was the only one of us who had seen or had anything to do with gangrene. He looked and sniffed and said that it was going or had gone gangrenous. Hell.

I got on the radio to Ceylon and explained the situation to them. They came back to me and told me what treatment to do with the M&B and what have you, to change the tablets to something else and step up various other things. I spent all night on the radio with all the details there, seeing whether or not I would have to take his leg off. I'm no surgeon and we had very little instruments; it would have been death either way I am quite sure. The last message I had was about six o'clock in the morning, asking could we accept a doctor and an orderly at four o'clock in the afternoon? I didn't even ask permission. I said, 'Yes.' A Dr Dumoulin dropped in at four o'clock. I don't know what treatment he gave Latham but it cleared it up and he didn't lose his leg.

Major Richard Broome
SOE officer

After we'd arranged for the supply of liaison officers and of arms and ammunition, the next step was to get somebody out of the jungle to go back and report affairs. The lot fell upon me and on Freddy Spencer Chapman. I must say that when I first went in on this operation, I had expected to come out again in two or three months; I had now spent about twenty months there so I was delighted to be going out. Chapman had been in the jungle from the beginning of the war and it was high time he was sent out, too. John Davis stayed on. He was the chief officer in the field and orders from SEAC came to him. He had several skirmishes with the Japanese and I think he said he enjoyed it because it made a change from sitting about in the jungle.

Colonel John Davis
SOE officer

I walked into one of our camps and immediately expounded to the British patrol leader what we hoped to do when the invasion came. He seemed a little uncomfortable but he let me run on a bit. Then he said, 'Have you been on the wireless for the last twenty-four hours?' I said, 'No, we've been off, we've been walking.' He said, 'Well, the war has ended.'

The End

Major Ken Scott
SOE officer, India
The intention was that we should be dropped to keep the railway line closed between Siam and Singapore. At that time the Japanese were using it quite extensively for supporting their operations and would be withdrawing, hopefully, on the invasion of Malaya. Our task was to keep the railway line cut. We were about to be given our operation order but the first atomic bomb was dropped in the middle of August and there was utter confusion at headquarters. My first concern was whether or not we were going ahead with the operation. We'd been trained for it, I was anxious to go and do it. I had two chaps with me, we all knew each other and we were all keen to go.

Captain Richard Tolson
SOE officer, India
We were quite confident that we'd be dropped in somewhere. Then luckily – I've always said luckily – the atom bomb was dropped. We were actually on the airfield waiting to be emplaned. I was going to the Celebes and I'd had the darkest forebodings: jungle right down to the sea and horrible Japanese lurking around.

Captain John Wolstenholme
Signals officer, SOE HQ, Ceylon
We were spending our time almost entirely trying to communicate the fact that the war was over. That communication was beamed as much at the forward Japanese troops as it was at anybody else. We started sending out signals in clear English so that as many people as possible got the message.

Major John Smallwood
SOE officer, Burma
The day the atomic bomb was dropped we'd been promised reinforcements of ten British officers and were going to take the war to the Japanese in a big way. Before that we'd driven in all their outposts, we'd done a lot of patrol work and shooting up people and so on, I'd been blowing up lorries on the road, a strategic road, that ran through there. We were very upset the war was over because we were just getting into our stride.

Sergeant Ron Brierley
SOE wireless operator, Burma
I heard on the radio of course when the bomb had been dropped in Japan and one thought, 'Well, that's it, pack up and go home,' but far from it. Our troubles were only just starting then because the Jap would not believe it, and convincing the retreating Japanese soldier that he should give himself up was really a very difficult task. They would rather commit suicide, blow themselves up, and, if they could, blow you up with them.

Sergeant Harry Verlander
SOE wireless operator, Burma
We were crossing some paddy fields, Major Bowles, Captain Coomber and myself, and there was a small hut in the middle of a field and we got into this and were resting, I was listening to the radio, and it was there that I heard the war had finished. While we were lying there we saw some Japanese walk alongside the paddy field. There were only three or four of them and we were going to shoot at them from the hut, it would have been quite easy to take them out, but because we heard the war was over we decided to let them go. We just let them walk on past. Whether that was a good idea or not, I don't know, because it was only a couple of days later that we walked into another small ambush. We were walking along and they just jumped out of the side of the jungle path. A Jap came straight at me with his double-handed sword raised, shouting. I had just enough time to pull out my .45 and shot him as the blade dropped. In fact I stepped back at the same time as I fired. I was pretty lucky. The blade was close enough to scratch me.

Sergeant Maurice Roe
SOE wireless operator, Burma
We killed our last two Japanese something like 9 or 10 September. There were two of them in a hut and they wouldn't surrender so finally we just blew the hut up. What do you do?

Sergeant Roger Leney
SOE wireless operator, Burma
This signal came in and I decoded it and it was a personal message from my parents. It said something to the effect of, 'Thank God the war is over and you are now safe.' Down on the river there was all hell being let loose, there was firing in all directions! These Japanese certainly were in no way going to give in. They were out of touch, they hadn't got any radio communication

and all they were intent on doing was getting back to Japan or at least getting out of Burma. It was about 20 September when the shooting actually stopped.

Sergeant Ron Brierley
SOE wireless operator, Burma

We were still having considerable problems with them and some pretty nasty fighting right through to November. They had no heavy equipment, having trailed through the jungle for hundreds of miles. They were short of food; they lived off the land as they went. They were suffering from typical tropical illnesses; they were short of medicines, they were short of drugs. But they still had this fanatical zeal to die for the Emperor. They'd ceased to be operational units in the sense of an organised brigade or even at regimental or battalion level but they were small groups of perhaps fifty to a hundred people who were still determined that they would not surrender. We used to have these surrender leaflets in Japanese, the RAF dropped them along jungle trails and we used to nail them on to trees, but they just wouldn't believe it.

Captain Robert Barron
SOE officer, Burma

They sent up Japanese officers and non-commissioned officers to us so that we could use them to liaise with odd Japanese pockets if necessary. They would go and tell them that the war was over and that they should surrender. We had one officer with us, he was quite correct and all that sort of thing and when he went he thanked me for the hospitality. I didn't fraternise with him. I made him eat by himself. I thought at the time that we treated him much better than he would have treated us.

Major John Smallwood
SOE officer, Burma

I re-established the frontier post at Tarkilek, which was in the golden triangle for opium, rebuilt a house, cut down the largest palm tree I could find and flew a very large Union flag, and we watched the Siamese and the Japanese pull out. We had been told they were going to concentrate in northern Siam and surrender there, so my seventy Lahu and myself lined the ditches and watched them go out under a white flag. The Japanese were covering us with machine guns all the way. They were very windy indeed. They were going out on elephants – a most amazing sight.

Major Ken Scott
SOE officer, Siam

A Dakota was allocated to us and dropped us and our stores on a tin mine about a hundred miles north of the Malaya border, on the east coast, on a clear evening in a wooded valley. It was well into the post-surrender period but there was no information of the Japanese reactions in that particular area. No knowledge at all of what they might do. In the absence of any instructions from Ceylon we decided that we had to do something so we went down to Songkla and established ourselves in a very nice house, an old British mission, on the seafront. The Japanese in the area were most co-operative. We were very well received, very well met, and I took the surrender of the local Japanese division.

Sergeant Geoff Bence
SOE wireless operator, Siam

A Japanese sergeant major came to escort me to a Japanese camp down in the forest. They only had oil lamps and it was all rather dim and foreboding with wood smoke in the air. I went into the camp and a box was placed in front of me and I stood with my arms crossed trying to look important and they all trooped up. First the Japanese officer came up and bowed and placed his sword in the box and then they trooped up in order of seniority, bowed and placed their rifles in the box and when the ceremony was completed I closed the box and took it all back. They were put on a train and packed off home.

Sergeant Ray Mason
SOE wireless operator, Malaya

One of the officers, about a week or so after the atomic bomb had dropped, went down through the jungle to Baling, which was the regimental headquarters of quite a large Japanese group, to ask for their surrender. They just sent him away, told him to clear off. Nothing was done to him. They just said, 'Go back into the jungle, we're not surrendering to you.' I think he was awfully brave to go down there, really.

Later, the Supreme Commander made his famous broadcast calling on all Japanese to lay down their arms and, in the name of the Emperor, to surrender unconditionally, so we decided to move down again. We left our heavy gear in the charge of the Chinese and after a day's march, slithering and sliding through the jungle, we got down to a place at the end of the metalled road that led to Baling. After negotiations with the Japanese a lorry was provided and we were driven into Baling, where we were accommodated in the village school but were told not to wander around. They still hadn't decided locally whether to continue the fight. Finally the Japanese general in command in Northern Kedah decided that this was enough and he officially surrendered.

Colonel John Davis
SOE officer, Malaya

Of course, the great desire of the guerrillas was to dash down, come out into the open and beat up anybody who they felt needed beating up and show what good chaps they were. Our problem was to keep them in the jungle. Some did tend to come down and create trouble. The usual trouble that takes place of hunting collaborators and that sort of thing, with all the injustices of a chap coming in and telling the guerrillas that a chap he doesn't like had been a collaborator, and who was then executed on the spot. All these horrible things, and they did happen. But by and large not where British liaison officers had penetrated; by and large the discipline of the guerrillas we had armed was very good.

Major Roger Landes
SOE officer, Malaya

We had to wait until the army came to relieve us. We waited for about six weeks for the army and in that time we had to use the Japanese against the communists and the communists against the Japanese, to try and survive, really, until the army took over. The Japanese were still armed and we had to tell the Chinese that if they didn't behave nicely we would be using the Japanese to fight them. When the Japanese used to do the same thing, we said, well, we're going to use our communist army. We had to play cat and mouse for about six weeks.

Jane Buckland
FANY wireless operator, SOE HQ, Colombo

After VJ Day I suddenly started getting messages in clear – *en clair*. In other words, I'd be working a schedule and suddenly, instead of taking down coded letters, an agent would come up and it would be so exciting because for the first time you'd get a clear message, in clear language. If I remember rightly they were gradually discovering the POW camps. Force 136 people were in some cases the first people to arrive, because they were behind the lines already.

Colonel John Davis
SOE officer, Malaya

I managed to get down to Singapore, a wonderful moment, because I managed to get into the internment camp and meet all my old friends. There were very, very few of us that had got out of Malaya. The rest were almost entirely interned, which meant that ninety-five per cent of my friends were in internment, and the dramatic thing was to go in there expecting that half of them at least were dead and find that most of them by and large had survived. There's never been a moment like it in my life. And through our wireless sets, because communications back to England in the chaos were very slow indeed, I was able to wireless through that I'd seen a number of people and get on to their parents or wives.

Sergeant Gordon Tack
SOE wireless operator, Malaya

We moved to a civilian internee camp and were able to help a lot there. We were able to organise food drops. We organised a medical team that came in and that sort of thing. The medical team was particularly good and very useful, because there were about two thousand, fifteen hundred, there and they'd been there some while, living off rice, and were not very fit. They were all civilians, of all nationalities. There were about six hundred Chinese and the rest were all sorts, Russians and Irish, every other nationality you can think of, except British.

Major Robert Boiteux
SOE officer, Sumatra

I was parachuted into Sumatra to organise the evacuation of five thousand Allied POWs; I jumped with a doctor, two medical orderlies and a second-in-command and a wireless operator.

The POWs were dying twelve a day. They were in a terrible condition: beri-beri; jungle ulcers that went right through one side of the leg to the other; and they'd had very bad treatment by the Japs. They were beaten a great deal, starved. But of course, having a doctor with me, he gave a few injections and after about two weeks they stopped dying. Twelve a day, then ten a day, eight a day and so on. And after a couple of weeks, no more dying.

Captain James White
SOE officer, Siam
We were flown in the bomb bay of a Liberator to an area on the Mekong River near a town called Ubon. There was a prisoner-of-war camp some ten miles to the north with fifteen hundred Dutch, fifteen hundred British and one hundred Australians. The appreciation was that after the first atomic bomb was dropped things would go round like wildfire right through the Far East, but it was not known whether the Japanese would react by killing the prisoners of war, because of the shame that was descending on their country, or whether they would give themselves up.

When we dropped, and it was darkness, I made my way to the camp with my four and I decided that rather than creeping up stealthily, which might frighten the Japanese into reacting, I would break from the jungle some two hundred yards away from the compound. I would openly get up, I would let them see me throw my rifle to the ground, and then I would walk with one other towards the camp main gate. And it worked. The Japanese came out, they laid down all their arms and ammunition and they said, 'We'll now take you to the British camp commandant. He is the boss here.' The camp commandant was a man called Lieutenant Colonel Toosey. He had been marvellous. The discipline in the camp was terrific, absolutely terrific.

Major David Smiley
SOE officer, Siam
Toosey was a gunner from Liverpool and he had all these chaps on parade. They sang '*God save the King*' and the Dutch national anthem. It was all terribly emotional. They were all absolutely stark naked except for a ball bag. Most of them had bellies, what they call rice bellies, from starvation.

Major Peter Kemp
SOE officer, Siam
After the Japanese surrendered in Indochina they quite wrongly handed over their arms to the communists who said that they were going to guard these French refugees. Well, naturally, the refugees were terrified and it was our job to persuade the Japanese who still had arms to help us get these people out and we were in fact able to do so. It was interesting and quite exciting, these night trips in small dugout canoes across the Mekong.

Major David Smiley
SOE officer, Siam

I rearmed a company of Japanese and took them into Indochina. We fought a pitched battle with the communists, we called them Annamite communists, they eventually became Vietminh, and we won, we killed quite a few. They withdrew. We got all these women and children and nuns, quite a lot of nuns, back over the Mekong to Siam.

Aftermath

I said to the mayor of Annecy how sorry I was I'd made such a hash of it – this was some years later – and he said, 'No, no, you were the chiquenaude.*' And I had to find a dictionary. '*Chiquenaude*: the fillip, the match that lights the fire.'*

Major Dick Rubinstein
SOE officer in France and Burma

We came out on 26 August. We went through Calcutta and back to Ceylon. There was the possibility of dropping in on British POW camps with a doctor and two or three chaps and try to help these people initially before real help could get to them. I'd thought that would be a wonderful way to have finished it all but people pointed out that I'd had four operations and there were other chaps who needed to justify themselves too.

I'd always been very critical of the way we operational people were treated when we went through Calcutta: we always seemed to be interfering with the staff officers' social life. This is very much a young man's view. When you go in, you're tense, you're taut. When you come out, you're stinking like a stoat probably and you reckon the world owes you a living for a little while. And you'd arrive at the headquarters in Calcutta and, as often as not, you'd find you weren't expected and that really to arrive on a Friday at 8.15pm was a bit thoughtless and one should realise that other people had got a life to lead.

But the lad who had been supposed to act as the liaison officer for the operational chaps as they went through the headquarters, he caught polio, so I was asked if I'd go up and do it. So, for three months really, September till the end of the year, they gave me a wonderful house – we only had the bottom floor – and here I made it a rule to meet everybody when they came in, I'd meet them at the airfield if I could, and for twenty-four hours I'd let them feel that the world did owe them a living. Then I would gradually try to bring them down to earth for their debriefing and, eventually, their onward transmission to wherever they were due to go. We made contact with our cipher girls, who generally we'd never met before, and used to have a super party at the house every Sunday lunch and end up with a bonfire round the lake in the evening. It was a good way to end up. We had people coming back from Borneo, from far into Burma, where the surrender didn't reach for a long time.

Major Brian Dillon
SOE liaison officer in Greece
SOE was wound up as an organisation in Greece. Gone. Finished. Everybody was withdrawn. We had nothing to do and were told, 'It's time to go, old boy. You're wanted back in Cairo.' And we went and sat there writing up reports. We even had to be psychoanalysed. One chap, who sadly got killed later on, he took it all as a bit of a joke and pretended he'd got a dog on a lead. It was a lady trick cyclist and he took the piss out of her. I said, 'You're very naughty, she's only trying to help.' They were genuinely concerned that we'd been under considerable pressure for some time. I said, 'I'm all right, I'm just about to get married, I'm very happy.'

Captain Robert Wade
SOE liaison officer in Yugoslavia
If I'd known how cheap medals are today, I'd have recommended all my party for medals. There we were, jumping in, no Red Cross, nothing. If you were caught you were in the hands of the Gestapo. If you were wounded you were a damned nuisance to everybody, a liability.

Major John Smallwood
SOE officer in France and Burma
We reckoned that anyone who did three missions went round the twist. It's not the time when you are in, it's when you come out and the pressure's off. You can cope with it while it's there, all round you.

Sergeant Donald Gibbs
SOE wireless operator in Burma
I was quite relieved when we left, I must admit. We were under great strain. We were miles from anywhere, right in the middle of nowhere. We depended on stuff being dropped to us. We had no contact with the outside world except by radio. I would say that everyone towards the end was getting rather nervous and jittery. That's my impression. But I regard it as the most exciting period of my life, quite honestly. Although I got a bit scared towards the end, it was very enjoyable and very interesting. A unique experience.

Lieutenant Stephen Dale
German Jewish SOE officer captured in Italy
There was no counselling. In fact I would have approved the idea of counselling. The immediate post-war period was for me one of depression.

Major Brian Dillon
SOE liaison officer in Greece
'Post-traumatic shock' is the new word they've invented since. Then you were just told to get on. 'Report to the sergeant major. He'll tell you what to do.'

Major Dick Rubinstein
SOE officer in France and Burma
There was a house in Knightsbridge called the White Eagle Club, taken over by the Poles, a little bit of Poland in London for the chaps who were on leave. Nothing to do with SOE at all. However, at the end of the war, Sir Colin Gubbins was anxious that there should be a regimental association for SOE and also a benevolent fund. Now the Poles must have found they had this fairly expensive lease on this house in Knightsbridge, and what were they going to do with it now that peace had come? And I suppose the Polish community was beginning to find it didn't want a military club any more.

So there was a coming together and SOE was able to form a club and it took over the lease of this house in Knightsbridge. Particularly for young lads like me, coming back from the Far East knowing that we'd got to go and be students in a little while, it was a great place to let one's hair down gradually. When we came back we had quite a lot of rank on our shoulders, we were quite well paid and we'd probably spend the equivalent of fifty pounds a night in there. But we all knew we'd got to be students on a further education and training grant and come September we'd be in there spending five pounds a night.

Major Harvard Gunn
SOE officer in France and Germany
I was very fortunate. I was married and had a base to go back to in 1945. Many people didn't. They'd been in situations which would never occur again and they found the thought of a normal life very, very difficult to digest. It was very difficult for some people. They melted back, some of them. A few stayed in the army. A few went back to jobs. Many found it very, very difficult to settle down. I think single women who had led this extraordinary life found it more difficult than the men to come back to normal life. For women who'd

been in that kind of situation, often in positions of command and certainly in positions of terror, it's difficult to be told, 'Well, you come back and you become a secretary.'

Captain Brian Stonehouse
***SOE** wireless operator captured in France*

I must have been very tough, actually, in my own way. I've never had a nervous breakdown – something to look forward to! But I couldn't go through that again. For instance, from Christmas '42 until October '43, after I was told that I'd be executed as an enemy agent, every week or twice a week at four or five in the morning the guards would come round and get out of the cells whoever was going to be executed that day. I could hear the footsteps, steeling myself for them to stop at my door, which they never did. I'd go out of my mind if I had to go through that again.

Lieutenant George Abbott
***SOE** circuit organiser captured in France*

I don't think that I am in any way mentally deranged but I think an experience of this kind is bound to have had an effect on the way you look at things. I think I'm in many ways far more tolerant than I used to be. I think that it's very difficult to condemn people and so on. I think it has also taught me in a way to be more patient, although – this is another consequence – I'm patient for so long that at the end if I lose my patience I have a tendency of exploding.

Captain Charles Hargreaves
***SOE** liaison officer captured in Yugoslavia*

Certainly for quite a long time after the war it took a tremendous amount of readjustment. There were a lot of very, very unpleasant memories. I found that I was very intolerant, very bad tempered, very, very hard to live with. You become unreasonable, you know you're being unreasonable and you know you're being impossible, but it just seems to be that you can't control it. It's very, very difficult indeed.

During one of the interrogations one of the Germans was smoking a large cigar and he thought it was a very amusing thing to come across and stub it out on my penis. You know it was not particularly brutal but it was sickening and it made me feel ill and I created like mad. When I got back downstairs to the jail I said I was in pain and I wanted a doctor. A doctor was produced and I heard a lot of giggling. They were laughing like mad. This chap merely looked at me and produced a large syringe. He said, 'Ah, I've just got the thing for that, I'll give you an injection.' What he did was to put the tip of the syringe into my penis and inject corrosive acids into my bladder. It was agony, as you can imagine, but at the same time one couldn't help, well, almost feeling amused, because they were absolutely paralytic with laughter, crying with laughter. They thought it was so funny. But this is something that has of course affected me for the rest of my life.

Odette Sansom
SOE agent captured in France
I had no toenails for three years so I was walking very badly because I had one septic toe and I learnt to walk on my heels to save my toes. In fact when I came back to England I could only wear a pair of men's shoes. And I had a bad spine because on coming down from a mountain in France three days before we were captured I had hurt my back on the edge of a rock. Of course it was never attended to. To this day it is not what it should be.

Major Dick Barry
Staff officer, Operations Section, SOE HQ, London
As far as the value of SOE as a whole is concerned, it's a question I've very often been asked and it's an extremely difficult one to come to any conclusion about, I think. There are a number of factors. In the first place the effort expended by us in SOE, in comparison to the war effort as a whole, was really very small. Not very, very many people nor very, very enormous resources, so we were putting not an enormous amount into it. Now, what did we get out of it? I think you've got to put one thing, probably only one, in a category entirely by itself, which was the Norway heavy water operation. Now that could have had a really major effect on the whole thing. The rest of it? The military value? Well, there are certain things where SOE did do something which was of considerable military value. The delay factor on the German reinforcements to the bridgehead in Normandy, now that, I think, was quite a significant factor. The main thing that I think you can't quarrel with is the maintenance of the morale of the occupied populations. And what value was that? Supposing it had never happened, wouldn't we have won the war just the same? But I think the net result is to say that SOE must come out on the plus side of the balance sheet. Because although the military successes were perhaps not enormous, the morale factor was big and the effort we put in, compared to the whole Allied war effort, was small.

Major Jim Davies
SOE liaison officer in Greece and Italy
I think the war would have been won anyway but I'm quite sure that SOE facilitated the smoother winning of objectives and also greatly aided the cooperation of peoples who were occupied by the enemy. By working with the resistance in those countries it aided the rehabilitation of their feelings and made them take pride in having shared, in however small a way, in the Allied victory.

Captain Harry Rée
SOE circuit organiser in France
I think the morale effect was enormous. I think the fact that we were there, a sort of living presence, and we were known to be there, was a kind of earnest of our intentions to support the French and support the war.

Major Jim Davies
SOE liaison officer in Greece and Italy
One felt that one was a presence in Greece that the Greeks rather leant on. It was a reassurance to them that they weren't just being, or would be, thrown to the wolves.

Lieutenant Colonel Hardy Amies
Head, Belgian Section, SOE HQ, London
The impression that we got when we went over there – I spent about six months in Brussels after the liberation – was that we had done quite a good role in maintaining morale. Even if you've parachuted somebody into the outskirts of a village and he fell straight into the hands of the Germans, which is a terrible thing to have done but obviously one of those things that happen in war, the rumour went around the village like lightning that we had done something and that we were trying to do something for them.

Squadron Leader Frank Griffiths
Halifax pilot, 138 (SD) Squadron, RAF, crashed in France, 1943
Everybody knew the aircraft had crashed. They even knew my name, because they'd got my helmet, and they knew what was in the load. And suddenly, the resistance, everybody in the area, was pro-Ally. Indeed afterwards I said to the mayor of Annecy how sorry I was I'd made such a hash of it – this was some years later – and he said, 'No, no, you were the *chiquenaude*.' And I had to find a dictionary. '*Chiquenaude*: the fillip, the match that lights the fire.' I said I wish I'd landed in the lake. He said, 'No, no. It was far better to kill

those people and land there and get your load because the whole area of Haute Savoie realised that somebody was bringing them help.'

Captain Harry Despaigne
SOE wireless operator in France
Even today, in France, when you go and visit the museums of the wartime Maquis and what have you, SOE is never mentioned. It's the French that have done it all. I know jolly well that if we hadn't been in Cannes in '42 there would have been no resistance in that part of France, whatsoever. Even the French Maquis run by de Gaulle got their money, their ammunition, from London. But France has forgotten that.

Marjorie Hindley
Technician at The Thatched Barn, Hertfordshire
What I've minded almost more than anything is the fact that after all this time I've had to share my secret with everybody, because for me it's been a secret part of my life, a closed book, starting very young and going right through to now. I'm not sure it's a good idea even now that this has happened, that we've been given this freedom. I think we might have been better left alone because the secrets could have gone with us.

Elisabeth Small
Civilian secretary, French Section, SOE HQ, London
I remember my mother saying once, 'Oh, you used to be so open, so easy and open, and now you're so closed about certain things.' I think I've never stopped, in a way. My first husband was an agent, a Belgian. I didn't marry him till a long time afterwards but we never talked about it.

Captain Oswin Craster
SOE officer in France and Burma
We'd have thought we'd have been shot if we'd mentioned the word 'SOE'. I never thought of saying that for twenty-five years.

Captain Selwyn Jepson
SOE recruiting officer, French Section, SOE HQ, London
All these years I have absolutely refused to talk about it because it brought back that life and death responsibility which I had so abhorred. My casualties were less than in the frontline infantry or any other frontline unit. They were still casualties.

Odette Sansom
SOE agent captured in France

People used to say to me when I came back, 'You must have such a terrible idea of human beings. You must be frightened almost of human beings.' I used to say, 'No, why? Nothing has changed. There were always bad people. I've seen a lot of bad people but because of those evil ones I've also seen the most noble people and I've been very greatly inspired.' This is what I wish to remember of it. I consider it has been an extraordinary experience. I'm a thousand years old and I love people. I do, definitely do. Bitterness is a waste of everything. What you have to do is to remember, because it is a duty one has to the people who did great things, to one's comrades, to all the good and brave people. You have to remember them. But there's no point in being bitter and wanting to create the same kind of feelings of hatred. It's pointless and harmful.

Captain Brian Stonehouse
SOE wireless operator captured in France

After the war, I was stationed in Germany with the British Army of the Rhine. Then I was demobbed in June '46 and I had some American friends in the American Army and they got me a job as an interrogator at Darmstadt, at the main American enclosure for automatic arrests of all the people who had been Nazis, Gestapo, whatever. I had my little office in the camp there in one of the buildings. There were several offices for other American interrogators, and my job was to interrogate so many people every day and put down the info, scribble it on a piece of paper. Then it was sent to a typing pool across the corridor staffed by German prisoners who spoke English. They had to speak English because the interrogation was done in German but it all had to be typed down in English. The following morning the previous day's interrogation would come to me for signing.

I had my name on the door and on my desk and this man used to come in from the typing pool, this German prisoner. And I remember the first time he came in, he was standing there, his head was bent and all I saw was the bald top of his head. I thought, 'The top of that head looks vaguely familiar,' but I had no idea who he was, and this went on for several days. 'Well, why doesn't he ever look up? Is there something wrong with his neck?' And then he looked up and I recognised him. It was my interrogator in Paris. He was absolutely petrified because he'd recognised my name on the door. I told the Americans and said, 'God, would you believe it? There's this Arnold Schneider, etc, etc.' And they said, 'Well, what we'll do, Captain Stonehouse,

HE 49810

Reburial, near Stavanger, Norway, in July 1945, of British commandos executed by the Germans in 1942 after Operation 'Freshman', the failed attempt to destroy the Vemork heavy water plant.

we'll close the camp for the day. You can beat him, you can do what you like with him, and here's a machine gun and you can kill him and no one will ever know.' And I said, 'No, I can't do that. If I did that I'd be no better than the Germans. In any case, I'm free and he isn't.'

Lieutenant Joachim Rønneberg
Norwegian SOE agent, commander of Operation 'Gunnerside'
I was once visiting the neighbourhood of Egersund, that's outside Stavanger, twenty-five years after the war and a friend of mine took me up one of the side valleys just inside Egersund and he showed me a bronze plaque on the rock. It was the story of the fourteen British commandos shot on 20 November 1942, and I remember standing there thinking they'd met with bad luck. These young chaps, who were my age, the last things they realised in life were cold rocks in Norway and a German firing squad.

And that is one of the reasons why you go round and tell your story to other people, to try to share with them the experience you had during the war. Because during the war, when you were in rather tight situations, you would probably say, 'If I ever get out of this corner, as the lucky one, I will promise to do as much as I can to prevent it happening again.' And the only way to answer that promise is to tell your story to future generations and hope that it goes in. You must be willing to defend peace and serenity every day, always. You have the possibility of shaping a good future for the people, the inhabitants, of your nation.

Glossary

AK Army – Armia Krajowa (Polish Home Army)

ATS – Auxiliary Territorial Service (women's branch of the British Army)

Bren gun – light machine gun (British)

CIGS – Chief of the Imperial General Staff (senior British Army Commander)

Cortex – detonating fuse for connecting explosives

DC3 – Dakota transport aircraft

DF – direction-finding, a radio receiver system for searching for and locating the source of enemy radio signals

DSO – Distinguished Service Order (British award for acts of gallantry and distinguished leadership)

Dumdum bullet – one designed to expand on impact

DZ – dropping zone

EAM – Ethnikón Apeleftherotikón Métopon (National Liberation Front), the communist-sponsored resistance movement in Greece (see also ELAS)

E-Boat – small, fast, German torpedo boat

EDES – Ethnikós Dimokratikós Ellinikós Syndesmos (Greek National Democratic League), the main non-communist resistance movement in Greece, led by General Napoleon Zervas

ELAS – Ethnikós Laïkós Apeleftherotikós Stratós (National Popular Liberation Army), the military wing of the Greek resistance movement, EAM

FFI – Forces Française de l'Intérieur (French Forces of the Interior), the united French resistance force organised under General Charles de Gaulle and General Marie-Pierre Koenig

FTP – Francs-Tireurs et Partisans, a communist-organised French resistance group

G1 – British Army staff officer responsible for personnel matters

Gammon grenade – a powerful hand grenade that could be primed to explode on impact (British)

GSO II and GSO III – General Staff Officer, Grades II and III (British Army)

HMG – His Majesty's Government

'K' Rations – US Army rations for use by combat troops

Lee Enfield – standard British Army rifle

M&B 693 – sulphonamide anti-bacterial powder

Marlin – the Marlin-Hyde M2 sub-machine gun (American)

Maquis – armed fighters of the French Resistance

MC – Military Cross (British gallantry award)

Mills bomb – hand grenade (British)

MTB – Motor Torpedo Boat

NKVD – Narodnyi Komissariat Vnutrennikh Del, the Soviet secret police, responsible for state security and counter-intelligence

OSS – Office of Strategic Services, an American organisation broadly similar, in many of its activities, to SOE

RV – rendezvous

Schmeisser – sub-machine gun (German)

SEAC – South East Asia Command, the Allied command in overall charge of operations in South-East Asia

Sked – wireless transmission (short for 'schedule')

Sten gun – sub-machine gun (British)

Thompson / tommy gun – sub-machine gun (American)

VC – Victoria Cross (highest British award for gallantry in the face of the enemy)

Very light – a coloured flare fired from a pistol

Vichy – name given to the collaborationist government of France, headed by Marshal Philippe Petain, which had its administrative centre in the town of Vichy

Index of Contributors

Number in brackets denotes IWM Sound Archive catalogue number.
Page numbers in **bold** refer to photographs.

PM denotes Private Material supplied by the author

General Index

Page numbers in **bold** refer to photographs.

Contact details for the Imperial War Museum Collecting Departments:

Sound Archive
Imperial War Museum
All Saints Annexe, Austral Street
London SE11 4SL
United Kingdom

Email sound@iwm.org.uk
Telephone +44 (0) 20 7416 5344

Photograph Archive
Imperial War Museum
All Saints Annexe, Austral Street
London SE11 4SL
United Kingdom

Email photos@iwm.org.uk
Telephone +44 (0) 20 7416 5333

Department of Documents
Imperial War Museum
Lambeth Road
London SE1 6HZ
United Kingdom

Email docs@iwm.org.uk
Telephone +44 (0)20 7416 5222